NEUROPHYSIOLOGICAL CONCEPTS IN HUMAN BEHAVIOR

The tree of learning

NEUROPHYSIOLOGICAL CONCEPTS IN HUMAN BEHAVIOR
The tree of learning

MARGOT C. HEINIGER

SHIRLEY L. RANDOLPH

With **156** illustrations

Drawings by **Sandra Orton;** photographs by **Janet Stilwell**

The C. V. Mosby Company

ST. LOUIS · TORONTO · LONDON   1981

The C. V. Mosby Company
11830 Westline Industrial Drive, St. Louis, Missouri 63141

Library of Congress Cataloging in Publication Data

Heiniger, Margot C
  Neurophysiological concepts in human behavior.

  Bibliography: p.
  Includes index.
  1. Neuropsychology. 2. Human behavior.
I. Randolph, Shirley L., joint author.
II. Title. [DNLM: 1. Neurophysiology. 2. Handi-
capped. 3. Rehabilitation—In infancy and childhood.
WS 368 H468n]
QP360.H44   152   80-25454
ISBN 0-8016-2203-4

GC/CB/B 9 8 7 6 5 4 3 2   01/C/063

To the individuals in the past
who have contributed to our understanding and inspiration,

to those in the present
who have sustained and affirmed our efforts, and

to those in the future
who will continue our concern for the quality of life
for all people.

Preface

The aim of this book is to provide a neurophysiological structure into which pieces of information may be positioned, to develop a strategy for evaluating problems, and to give direction to early intervention techniques. The structure, evaluation, and intervention should be helpful not only to medical professionals, educators, and students but also to parents.

The time has come, we suggest, when we can no longer afford to be dependent on isolated approaches of training, teaching, or treatment. If we are to be truly effective in combating disease, injury, and deficits, we must develop an interdisciplinary, neurophysiologically integrated approach to management. We must stop separating mind, body, and spirit.

Some readers may be startled to find so much reference to God, to love, to priorities, and to the meaning of life in a neurophysiologically oriented book. We are purposely not approaching this presentation from narrow technical or medical objectives but rather from a broader humanistic focus. When are we going to deal with total individuals with human needs instead of diseased parts? When are we going to provide creative alternatives instead of standard procedures? When are we going to dissolve the many barriers to self-actualization instead of isolating the handicapped and their families?

Because of our continued frustration with the fragmented management of children, we have developed nine concepts or areas of emphasis. These concepts are arranged in a developmental hierarchy. Each concept is presented from a neuroanatomical and neurophysiological standpoint, which is followed by the practical application of the concept to intervention. Our major concern is to present an initial block of information for the reader. With this block of information we hope to assist the reader to place specific techniques from different intervention approaches into the appropriate concept. By doing this, professionals should develop a strategy for combining specific techniques into the proper sequence for a particular client instead of being restricted to one interventional approach for all patients. No one approach has the answer for all patients. It is our conviction that only by appropriate combination of elements of all the approaches can the epitome of management be conceived for every client. The emphasis on children is merely a reflection of our experience and not indicative of the lack of application to adults. So often the function that the adult has lost as a result of disease or injury is essentially the same as what the child has failed to develop.

Concept 1 deals with the autonomic nervous system, how it influences our interpretation of the environment and regulates our stress reactions. Concepts 2 through 6 deal with different aspects of sensory input. Focusing attention through synaptic activity, Concept 7, and the orientation of the body to the force of gravity, Concept 8, are essential components of the integrative process. In Concept 9 sensory integration is demonstrated by the presence of basic motor skills of prekindergarten readiness.

An internal visualization process is at the core of acquiring new information, integrating it with past knowledge and experience, and using it effectively in problem solving. We have attempted to assist this visualization process by developing three diagrams on which to locate the nine concepts.

The **tree** is the first diagram and is a model of the individual. The ground depicts the autonomic nervous system, which influences how all information is interpreted. Each root of the tree represents a different source of sensory information. The sensory information must travel up to higher levels of the nervous system, depicted by the branches of the tree, to be integrated and available for motor expression.

The second diagram is the **cross-section,** which is a model of the temporal growth of the individual. The center represents the prenatal period in which so much growth occurs and so many functional patterns are initiated and practiced. Birth is merely a change in environment and heralds the continuing journey through experiences. A wide ring symbolizes the tremendous growth and development necessary in the first 3 years. A narrower band represents the ages from 3 through 5 years. The 5- to 7-year ring is very thin. The terminology of four approaches, Kephart, Ayres, Rood, and Piaget, have been placed in relationship to each other on the temporal sequence. We have purposely stopped at 7 years because it is our firm conviction that with early identification and appropriate intervention the majority of developmental problems may be alleviated by that time.

The third diagram is the **pyramid;** it is a model of the developmental sequence of education. We marvel at our failure to realize what is so obvious—that learning is a total mind, body, and spirit experience. Learning in any area, physical, emotional, intellectual, or spiritual, involves the whole person. Anyone in a helping profession must be cognizant of the interdependence of all areas and all professions. Motor ability is related to academic achievement. The autonomic nervous system is the foundation for reception of information from the environment. The dimensions of space and time have their origin in the most basic biological functions and are integral components of every aspect of learning. Each step of the pyramid is built on the previous steps. In evaluating learning problems one may start at the top of the pyramid and move down to find the source of the problem or start at the bottom and predict potential difficulties in higher steps.

It is not our intent to present an exhaustive review of the literature or research in any specific area. Nor is it our intent to cover in a comprehensive manner any of the approaches that have previously been or are currently being published. We have chosen to use a few selected books and articles that we have found helpful in our endeavor to amalgamate many ideas, theories, and techniques. Many of the references have extensive bibliographies that readers may find helpful in their quest for understanding.

This book is not meant to be the answer to all questions about intervention. It is meant to be a beginning—a challenge to all of us dealing with persons in difficulty to join our knowledge, understanding, and techniques for the benefit of the whole person. Perhaps at no other time have we had so much potential at our disposal to upgrade the quality of life for the recipient but also for the provider.

We would like to acknowledge the very real motivation created by stress and frustration. Rarely are changes instituted, ideas conceived, and concepts developed without this experience.

Our acknowledgment of individuals is arranged chronologically as related to the development of this book.

Dr. Ann Craig and Frances Corley provided initial acceptance and enthusiastic support. How prophetic was the admonition "only time will tell whether you have a tiger by the tail or if the tiger has you by the tail."

Dr. A. Jean Ayres' receptive analysis of the illustration of the tree afforded impetus to the organization of the first workshop. Her continued support and suggestions have been deeply appreciated.

Erma Myer's tireless attempt to transcribe the tapes from an early workshop proved the necessity for presenting the material in written form.

Clara Chaney's expressed need and desire for our kind of information to explain her results with children nurtured our determination to bridge the communication gap with teachers and parents.

We owe a very large debt of gratitude to Bernice Krumhansl for her gentle, loving, time-consuming dissection of the original manuscript and her enthusiastic approval of each ensuing revision.

Without the sustaining friendship and professional support of Lillian Parent, Carolyn Crutchfield, and Mary Lou Barnes, the manuscript might well have been discarded.

We are also indebted to the following individuals for their critical reviews of the manuscript: Charlotte Brim, Dr. Gerald Arnold, George Soper, Joan Gentile, Nancy Patton, Paul Fogle, Sue Lewis, Robert Abbott, Jean L. Pyfer, and Diane Shapiro.

We extend a very special thank you to Betty Rubbert for rescuing our tree and providing the very necessary three-dimensional effect.

A special acknowledgment is needed to all the workshop participants for their expressed desire for the book and for their many stimulating questions and contributions over the years.

All of the children and adults with disabilities and their families have contributed immeasurably to the search for answers and solutions. They have greatly enhanced our understanding and appreciation of the potential and unique value of each human being.

Finally, we are indebted to our families for their patience, acceptance, and forbearance through the years of teaching and writing.

Margot C. Heiniger
Shirley L. Randolph

Contents

Ergotropic-trophotropic continuum

stress reactions

Concept
Background
  Ergotropic system
  Trophotropic system
  Ergotropic-trophotropic
continuum

Psychophysiology of stress
  Autonomic nervous system
  Endocrine system
  Immune system
  Brain function

Practical application
  Primary care
  Therapeutic intervention
  Normal control of stressors
  Nutrition

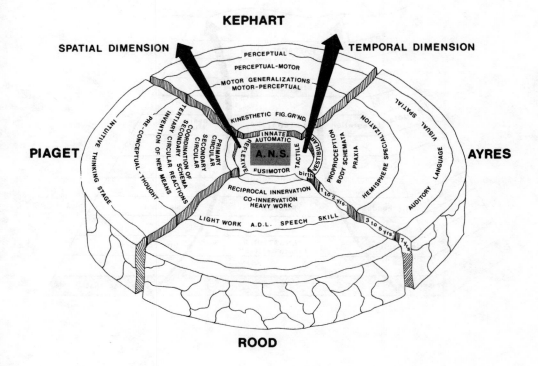

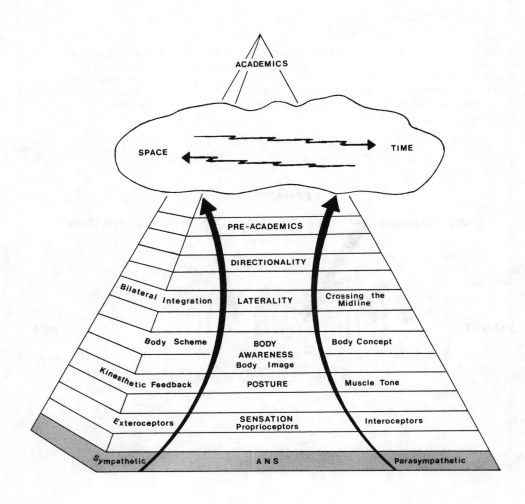

Concept   The body's adaptive processes to external or internal stressors may be altered by manipulation of the ergotropic-trophotropic elements.

The three ergotropic-trophotropic elements include autonomic nervous system, somatic muscle, and cortical activity. The autonomic nervous system appears to be the dominant element and is used as the pivot for the concept. The **tree,** as the model of the individual, illustrates the relationship of the ground or soil to the roots of the tree. Just as the soil affects the roots of a tree, the dominance of either the sympathetic or parasympathetic divisions of the autonomic system determines how sensory stimuli will be interpreted by the individual.

The autonomic nervous system (ANS) is placed in the center of the **cross-section.** This placement is to emphasize the importance of sympathetic-parasympathetic interactions during the prenatal period.

The autonomic nervous system (ANS) is again given primary consideration as it forms the broad base of the **pyramid.** Throughout the book we will attempt to relate inappropriate responses at this autonomic system level with interferences with higher educational functions.

Background

The terms ergotropic and trophotropic were coined by Hess in the 1930s (Gellhorn, 1967). All of the stress reactions that initiate a fight-or-flight reaction can be considered ergotropic (Greek *ergos*—work). The opposite reactions toward deep relaxation and vegetative functions can be considered trophotropic (Greek *trophos*—nutrition).

ERGOTROPIC SYSTEM

The term ergotropic combines the triad of
1. Increased sympathetic activity
2. Increased somatic action
3. Cortical desynchronization or alpha rhythm (an alert or aroused cortex)

This triad is an integrated whole. Any increase or decrease in discharge of one element is paralleled in the other two elements.

The anatomical integrative "hub" for the ergotropic system (Fig. 1-1) includes the posterior hypothalamus (sympathetic), the cingulate gyrus, and the reticular facilitory area of the pons to thalamus. There are other brain structures that contribute to the arousal associated with the ergotropic syn-

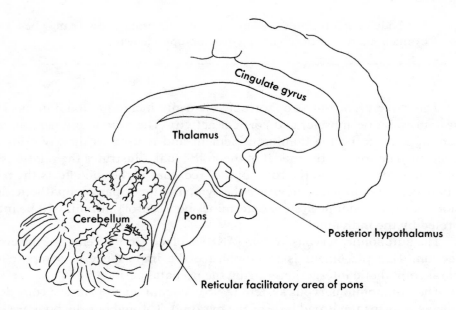

Fig. 1-1. The anatomical integrative "hub" for the ergotropic system includes the posterior hypothalamus (sympathetic), cingulate gyrus, and reticular facilitory area of the pons.

drome such as parts of the neocortex (sensorimotor, temporal, and occipital) as well as association areas. Stimulation of the anterior lobe of the cerebellum also elicits an ergotropic response (Gellhorn, 1967).

TROPHOTROPIC SYSTEM

The term trophotropic combines the triad of
1. Increased parasympathetic activity
2. Somatic muscle relaxation
3. Cortical synchronization or beta rhythm (sleep)

Just like the ergotropic triad, this triad is an integrated whole. Any shift in discharge of one element is paralleled in the other two elements.

The anatomical integrative "hub" for the trophotropic system (Fig. 1-2) consists of the anterior hypothalamus (parasympathetic), the hippocampus, and the reticular inhibitory area of the medulla oblongata and the caudal pons. Stimulation of the posterior lobe of the cerebellum elicits the trophotropic response. The intensity and frequency of cutaneous stimuli are the critical factors in determining which system will respond. If the stimuli are of low intensity and frequency, the trophotropic system will respond. The same stimuli, however, applied at a *high* frequency or intensity may produce an ergotropic response.

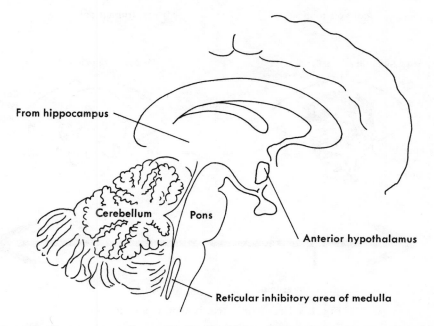

From hippocampus

Cerebellum   **Pons**

Anterior hypothalamus

Reticular inhibitory area of medulla

Fig. 1-2. The anatomical integrative "hub" for the trophotropic system includes the anterior hypothalamus (parasympathetic), the hippocampus, and the reticular inhibitory area of the medulla oblongata.

ERGOTROPIC-TROPHOTROPIC CONTINUUM

In order to provide some practical direction, it may be helpful to place these two systems at each end of a continuum as seen in Fig. 1-3. Each person functions at some point on that continuum. Depending on what happens in a given situation, the person may move toward the ergotropic end or in the opposite direction toward the trophotropic end.

There is a very important reciprocal relationship between the two systems. Any change in one element of the triad is paralleled by a change in the other two elements; therefore any change in the ergotropic system is paralleled by a change in the trophotropic system. There is constant shifting in discharges from individual elements, which affects the balance of the entire system.

According to Gellhorn (1967), tonic activity of the nervous system constantly controls these two systems in a balance. Phasic activity modifies the tonic state in a specific organ or function. The combination of phasic and tonic activity provides an enormous variety of ergotropic-trophotropic patterns to deal with different local demands at any given state of central autonomic balance. The combination of phasic and tonic activity ensures smooth

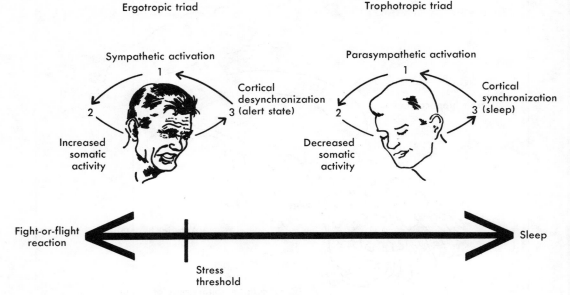

Fig. 1-3. Ergotropic-trophotropic continuum.

transition from ergotropic to trophotropic responses. The reciprocal balancing also ensures minute gradations of each system's responses at every level of excitation.

The critical point on this continuum is the stress threshold. This is the point at which stressors are interpreted as potentially dangerous, and a protective fight-or-flight response is triggered. Messages are sent throughout the neuroendocrine system, causing significant changes in the individual's biochemistry. Once the neurophysiological stress response subsides, the body should rebound into a deep relaxation or trophotropic state and ultimately seek its homeostasis. When a stress response is prolonged and unabated, the biochemical changes may become detrimental to the individual's health (Pelletier, 1977).

PSYCHOPHYSIOLOGY OF STRESS

We must assume that every individual operates at a level of tolerable nonpathogenic stress. This stress actually heightens awareness, function, and performance. This healthy equilibrium can be upset by a wide variety of psychological, physical, and environmental stressors.

According to Selye "stress is the common denominator of all adaptive reactions in the body." Since he believed this to be simple and true but too vague for scientific analysis, he developed an "operational definition":

"Stress is the state manifested by a specific syndrome which consists of all the nonspecifically induced changes within a biological system." Stress has its very own form and composition but no particular cause. There are definite visible changes that are characteristic of its form regardless of the cause.

Since the term "stress" has been used so loosely, Selye states what stress is not.*

1. "Stress is not simply nervous tension."
2. "Stress is not an emergency discharge of hormones from the adrenal medulla. Adrenaline discharge is frequently seen in the sympathetic fight or flight response of the whole body."
3. "Stress is not everything that causes a secretion by the adrenal cortex of its hormones, the corticoids." The corticoids can be discharged without producing any evidence of stress.
4. "Stress is not always the nonspecific result of damage." Many normal activities, especially sports, can produce considerable stress without actual damage.
5. "Stress is not the same as a deviation from homeostasis." Any specific biological function can cause marked deviations from the normal resting state of the body.
6. "Stress is not anything that causes an alarm reaction." A stressor causes the alarm reaction, not stress itself.
7. "Stress is not identical with the alarm reaction or the G.A.S. (general adaptive syndrome)." Both of these reactions embody certain measurable changes in organs, which are *caused* by stress, so they could not *be* stress.
8. "Stress is not a nonspecific reaction." Stress has a very specific pattern, affecting certain organs in a selective manner.
9. "Stress is not a specific reaction." By definition, stress cannot be a specific reaction because it can be produced by practically any agent.
10. "Stress is not necessarily something bad." The stress of creative, successful work is beneficial. It is not the stress but how one takes it that makes the difference.
11. "Stress cannot and should not be avoided." Without stress life would be very dull and unrewarding.

After defining stress, Selye found it necessary to coin a name for his syndrome—the general adaptation syndrome (GAS). The syndrome evolves in time through three stages. The alarm reaction, the first stage, affects the body as a whole. In his early work he found the following triad produced*:

1. Considerable enlargement of the adrenal cortex.

---

* Selye, H.: The stress of life, revised edition, New York, 1976, McGraw-Hill Book Co.

2. An intense shrinking or atrophy of the thymus, spleen, lymph nodes, and all other lymphatic structures.
3. Deep bleeding ulcers in the stomach and duodenum.

No living organism can survive a continuous alarm reaction.

The second stage of the GAS is the stage of resistance. During this time many of the alarm reaction elements are reversed, seemingly in an attempt to adapt to the situation and increase resistance.

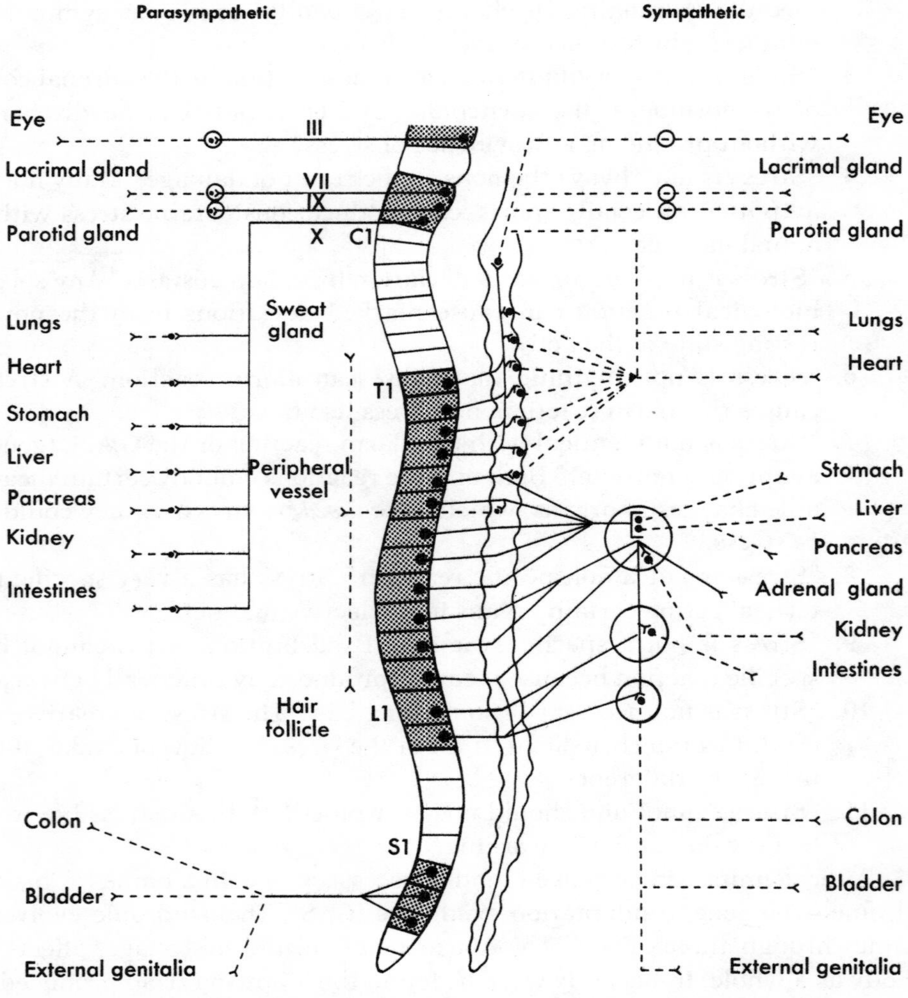

Fig. 1-4. Autonomic nervous system innervation. The left side of the illustration represents those organs supplied by the parasympathetic nervous system. The sympathetic nervous system innervation is represented on the right hand side.

The third stage is one of exhaustion. During this time the adaptation energy appears to be used up. The alarm reaction reappears, and the individual dies.

The helping professionals must become increasingly aware of their role in maintaining healthy equilibrium or assisting in its restoration. How many times we are oblivious to the stress that our intervention techniques may produce in the client and family. How unfortunate it is when the very person who should be the source of assistance, education, and support becomes an additional stress producer.

In order for us to fully appreciate stress reactions it is necessary to consider the interactions of the autonomic nervous system, endocrine system, immune system, and brain function.

Autonomic nervous system

The autonomic nervous system is divided into two separate but interdependent systems—sympathetic and parasympathetic. The sympathetic system may act selectively; however, it usually acts as a total unit, exciting neural and glandular function. The fight-or-flight reaction is the body's most comprehensive reaction to extreme stress. The parasympathetic system is relatively specific and selective in its activation of organs. The parasympathetic system is primarily concerned with the vegetative functions of the body. (See Fig. 1-4.)

The opposing functions of the two systems may be illustrated by placing their specific actions in two columns. Each of the actions may serve as a clue to the individual that he or she is under stress or has recovered from stress.

Sympathetic	Parasympathetic
Dilates pupil	Constricts pupil
Increases heart rate	Decreases heart rate
Increases blood pressure	Decreases blood pressure
Activates somatic muscle	Relaxes somatic muscle
Vasoconstriction	Vasodilation
Cold perspiration	Warm perspiration
Thick viscous saliva	Thin serous saliva
Decreases digestive enzymes	Increases digestive enzymes
Slows peristalsis	Increases peristalsis
Shunts blood away from gastrointestinal tract	Increases blood to gastrointestinal tract
Activates endocrine system	

The fight-or-flight response consists of three parts. The first is a physical or verbal attack. The second is a physical flight in which the person removes himself from the situation. The third part is frequently overlooked because it is an emotional or psychological flight or withdrawal.

We believe that frequently the child who daydreams in the classroom, the elderly senile person in the nursing home, and certain psychiatric patients are using the third part of the fight-or-flight response. When the physical characteristics of the sympathetic nervous system are evaluated, they may be found to prevail in all three individuals. This would indicate that the individual has passed his stress threshold on the ergotropic-trophotropic continuum.

The anatomical origin and neuronal distribution of the two systems are illustrated in Fig. 1-4. The parasympathetic system originates in the cranial and sacral areas of the central nervous system. This system has long preganglionic neurons extending from cranial nerve nuclei to ganglia in the specific areas of innervation. The postganglionic neurons are short and produce a discrete function in the local area.

The cranial portion of the parasympathetic system is included in the oculomotor nerve, which controls the ciliary muscles and the sphincter muscles of the iris. The facial nerve supplies the lacrimal gland for tear secretion. The facial nerve and glossopharyngeal nerve supply the submaxillary, sublingual, and parotid salivary glands. The largest portion of this system is the vagus nerve, supplying the fibers of the heart, lungs, bronchi, blood vessels in the lungs, esophagus, stomach, small intestine, upper colon, pancreas, and liver.

The sacral portion of the parasympathetic system originates from sacral levels two, three, and four. These segments supply the uterus, lower colon, rectum, bladder, and blood vessels within the erectile tissues of the genitals.

The sympathetic system originates in the thoracolumbar areas of the spinal cord. This system has short preganglionic neurons originating in the lateral gray horn of the first thoracic to third lumbar segments of the spinal cord. These neurons synapse in the sympathetic trunk or chain ganglia. Some fibers bypass the chain ganglia and extend to collateral ganglia such as the celiac, the superior mesenteric, or the inferior mesenteric. In contrast to the parasympathetic division, the sympathetic postganglionic neurons are much longer and initiate a more generalized response in a much larger area.

The sympathetic outflow to the head is from thoracic levels through preganglionic neurons ascending in the chain ganglia. Postganglionic neurons leave the chain ganglia and are carried to their ultimate termination primarily on blood vessels and the trigeminal nerve. The trigeminal nerve is responsible for general sensation in the head and is considered the protective nerve for the face. We will expand this idea as it relates to sucking in Concept 5.

It is important to remember that the eyes, heart, salivary glands, digestive system, and pelvic viscera receive innervations from both parasympathetic and sympathetic systems. This functional importance should become evident as Concept 1 is developed.

Before leaving the functional organization of the autonomic nervous system, consider the possibility of a developmental sequence of function. Prenatally there is a shifting from one autonomic system to the other as demonstrated by avoidance and approaching reactions. Hooker (1952) demonstrated that tactile stimulus in the perioral area of an 8-week-old embryo will produce a flexion, adduction, internal rotation avoidance pattern of arms and legs with lateral flexion of the trunk. He also demonstrated that a 27-week-old fetus has sufficient muscle strength of the grasp reflex when elicited to support most of the body weight.

Perhaps some of the difficulties encountered by the premature infant may be explained by a dominance of the sympathetic nervous system. The rocking isolette provides a slow, rhythmical, repetitive stimulus that deactivates the sympathetic system domination and allows a more vegetative state to flourish. The premature infant's feeding, digesting, and eliminating processes would be enhanced by parasympathetic dominance. Certainly any early intervention program must concern itself with the fundamental question of providing appropriate autonomic nervous system stimulation.

There is little doubt that for many infants the birth process is a very stressful, unpleasant, sympathetically dominated experience. It would certainly seem advantageous to deactivate this sympathetic reaction as quickly as possible after birth.

During the neontal period there seems to be a return to parasympathetic dominance as the infant becomes acclimated to his new environment. There are certainly periods of strong sympathetic stress such as prior to feeding times and during diaper changes.

We strongly urge anyone dealing with infants to read Ribble's *The Rights of Infants* (1943). Although this book was written in 1943, the material presented is still pertinent to high-risk infants and early infant care. She makes repeated reference to the importance of "mothering," the human handling and close body contact that is necessary for survival and cannot be replaced by advanced technology.

As the individual matures, there are stages of development at which the sympathetic system is activated by the physical stress of gravity. Three examples are (1) the face-lying infant working against gravity, (2) folded up on hands and knees preparatory to the all fours position, and (3) trying to attain the erect posture. When muscles are used against physical stress, the sympathetic activation will be exhausted quickly and the body will return to a homeostatic base. As we observe an infant he appears to learn to enjoy physical stress and muscle activity, and thus he prevents the sympathetic system from dominating.

As the individual develops socially, there are periods when the sympathetic system is fired by emotional stress. Perhaps adolescence is the best example of this. The emotional, social, parental, and peer pressures constantly produce stress, which activates sympathetic fight-or-flight reactions. The sympathetic somatic muscle activation from emotional stress is demonstrated by "the first date" or "the big dance" clumsiness and incoordination. Emotional sympathetic activation is easily recognized in the job interview, in-service training, the demonstration before the Garden Club, or the critical speech before the zoning board. It is important for everyone to be aware of some tension-releasing mechanisms useful during these situations. Perhaps the best examples are slow, deep, rhythmical breathing and contact or firm pressure on the palms of the hands. Everyone should appreciate the role of physical activity (big muscle work) after an emotionally stressful situation to assist the body in returning to homeostasis. Are you providing opportunities for your patients to use their muscles as a means of releasing some of their emotional stress? Do your paraplegics have punching bags? Teachers, are you providing some physical activity (relay race) after that stressful math session? How much body movement do you provide during extended periods of bad weather?

Koizumi and Brooks (1972) discuss the association of autonomic and somatic reactions. No one denies that somatic and autonomic responses are part of all behavioral reactions. Most research studies, however, focus on just one system, not both. Consequently, the usual implication is that there are two, separate, independent systems. The most logical concept, which has been presented many times, is to consider the somatic and autonomic systems as two motor outflows from a common central nervous system. The sensory system must be considered an activator of common centers, which integrate responses of the two motor outflows.

Endocrine system

According to Pelletier (1977), when the sympathetic system is activated by stress, it works in close coordination with the endocrine system (Fig. 1-5). Knowledge of this interaction is extremely important in understanding how a psychological event is translated into physiological reactions. The glands of the endocrine system include the pituitary, thyroid, parathyroids, islets of Langerhans, adrenals, and gonads.

The hypothalamus exercises a vital control over the pituitary, which controls the rest of the endocrine system. The hypothalamus is connected to the pituitary by a neuronal as well as a secretory pathway. The hypothalamic secretion goes directly to the anterior lobe of the pituitary. The hypothalamic nerve endings go to the posterior lobe of the pituitary. As a part of the integrative hub of the ergotropic system, the posterior hypothalamus stimulates sympathetic system reactions. We now see the same posterior hypothalamus stimulating the release of pituitary stress hormones. This system comprises an important link between the neurological and biochemical systems of the body.

The anterior lobe of the pituitary releases two stress hormones, adrenocorticotropic (ACTH) and thyrotropic (TTH). The ACTH acts on the adrenal

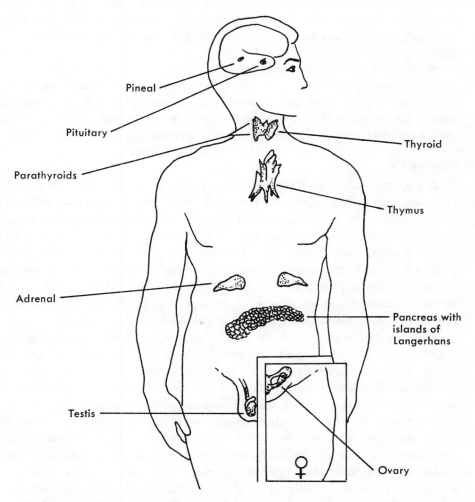

Fig. 1-5. The endocrine system includes the pituitary, thyroid, parathyroid and adrenal glands, the islets of Langerhans, and the gonads.

medulla producing adrenalin (epinephrine) and noradrenalin (norepineph-rine). Why adrenalin is released in one instance and noradrenalin in another is not clearly understood. Some researchers regard noradrenalin as the "anger hormone" and adrenalin as the "fear hormone" (Pelletier, 1977). It is amazing that a psychological factor seems to be the determining element in how the adrenal medulla responds.

The TTH acts on the thyroid gland to produce thyroxine, which intensely stimulates tissue metabolism. These two hormones, adrenalin and thyroxine, work together and produce many of the same subjective symptoms. Adrenalin seems to play a larger part in short-term stress. Thyroxine seems to be present in more prolonged stress. The state of hyperactivation caused by high levels of thyroxine causes the individual to sweat easily, feel nervous and shaky, have rapid heart rate and respiration, and frequently have chronic fatigue and insomnia.

ACTH also stimulates the adrenal cortex to produce two groups of hormones. One group acts to inhibit inflammation (anti-inflammatory corticoids), and the other group promotes inflammation (proinflammatory corticoids). These hormones are associated with long-term stress and play a major role in the body's immune responses (Pelletier, 1977).

Immune system

It appears that one of the most negative results of excessive stress is the effect on the body's immune responses. The immune responses are man's major defense against microorganisms. The idea that disease is caused by germs that infect a certain system is a theory, not a proved fact (Pelletier, 1977). Germs undoubtedly play a major role in a disease process. When a person is faced with a stressful situation, a response mobilizes him to action. If the individual is unable to cope, the body breaks down at the weakest point, which is determined by a combination of psychophysiological factors, past experience, and the interaction of genetics (Pelletier, 1977).

Pelletier believes that there is a connection between the hypothalamus and the thymus, which plays a central role in the immune response. Since the thymus is stress responsive through the hypothalamus, it is involved in a feedback loop regulating endocrine function. The thymus affects the production of thyroxine, which was discussed earlier. Another effect of stress is the increase in the proinflammatory and anti-inflammatory corticoids, which may seriously interfere with the immune responses. Proinflammatory hormones increase the inflammatory barricade and fluid formation, which walls off the irritant and prevents damage to adjacent tissue. Anti-inflammatory hormones actually prevent the formation of the inflammatory barricade and promote peaceful coexistence with potentially harmless pathogens and such things as transplants. It is hypothesized that extreme emotional reactivity, as a result of stressful life changes, is sufficient to disrupt the basic immunological balance (Pelletier, 1977).

Brain function

The hypothalamus, a portion of the diencephalon, has been linked repeatedly to the psychophysiology of stress. This structure controls body temperature and hunger and is a strong pleasure center. We have seen how it activates the autonomic nervous system and the endocrine system. The most important function is the regulation of the pituitary gland.

Above the diencephalon in the brain hierachy is the limbic system. The limbic system is frequently called the visceral brain since it is evolutionarily very old and is involved with basic biological functions.

At the top of the brain hierarchy is the cerebral cortex. The cortex is responsible for the high-level, abstract activities of language, memory, and judgment. The cortex initiates voluntary muscle movements but is not responsible for the gradation or coordination of muscular activity (Evarts, 1973).

Perhaps one of the most crucial brain structures in stress responses is the reticular-activating system. According to French (1957), it awakens the brain to consciousness and keeps it alert; it monitors all the stimuli beating on our senses, accepting what is needed and rejecting the irrelevant; and it refines our muscular activity. It also contributes to the highest mental processes—focusing attention, introspection, and probably all forms of reasoning.

The reticular formation is a sort of two-way street, relaying all forms of sensory information up to the cortex as well as relaying messages from the cortex down to the muscles and organs. Because of this structure, a physical stressor can influence higher centers and a mentally perceived stressor can create neurophysiological responses. The reticular formation is one of the best pieces of neurophysiological evidence for profound interconnections between mind and body (Pelletier, 1977).

Furthermore, the reticular system seems to be totally responsible for screening all stimuli from the autonomic nervous system and selecting what is to be registered at the conscious level of the brain. With this critical integrative role it demonstrates a continuum of mind and body interactions as presented with the ergotropic-trophotropic continuum. It will be important to keep this integrative role and impact on conscious awareness in mind as we deal with the specific and nonspecific sensory input of Concept 2.

Practical application

Any practical application of this concept is directly related to the ergotropic-trophotropic continuum, manipulation of the elements of the triads, and structuring the environment to capitalize on the desired responses. The application will be divided into the areas of primary care, therapeutic intervention, normal control of stressors, and nutrition.

PRIMARY CARE

Undoubtedly, the birth process for many infants is a very stressful, unpleasant, ergotropic response primarily because of the efficient technological hospital procedures. In *Birth Without Violence* (1975) Leboyer has encompassed many aspects of the trophotropic response in his method of delivery. How much more humanistic is the decreased light and noise, the maintenance of the flexed position, and the immersion in warm water where the infant is gently massaged. The proof of reduction of stress by this method is the beautiful smiles on the faces of infants so treated as compared to the crying contortions of the less fortunate ones.

How many similar situations exist in our current hospital practice? When one scrutinizes the overall management of patient care one is appalled at the dehumanization that exists for the sake of schedules and procedures. How much more productive our medical care could be if our attention was focused on the whole person and on supportive and educational aspects, as well as technological services. The patient must be made a vital, integral, contributing member of the team instead of a passive recipient of procedures.

THERAPEUTIC INTERVENTION

This section is primarily directed toward occupational therapists, physical therapists, and speech pathologists. It does, however, have implications for all of the helping professionals involved with any form of intervention, such as classroom teachers, teachers of adaptive physical education, volunteers in athletic programs, and parents.

We are primarily concerned with the manipulation of the triad of elements of the ergotropic-trophotropic continuum. As we manipulate one element we can alter the other two elements in the triad and regulate the balance between the two systems.

When working with individuals, our first consideration is to determine as accurately as possible where on the continuum they are functioning. Is the individual at his usual, normal, resting minimal stress point? Has the hospitalization produced sufficient stress that he is operating closer to the ergotropic end? Has some family problem or environmental situation prior to entering the treatment sessions produced an ergotropic response? Is the individual's feeling of inadequacy in dealing with specific subject matter in the classroom producing enough stress to move him toward the stress threshold? Being able to determine this resting point is dependent on our sensitivity to the whole person and to total reactions. It demands that we be involved in the other person's life.

Once we determine where the client is functioning on the continuum, it is then possible to predict whether he needs to be moved toward the trophotropic end or more toward the ergotropic end.

As rapport is established and communications achieved, the ultimate value of intervention is determined by how skillfully the client is maintained at his optimal functioning point for whatever activity is being performed. Unfortunately many patients are "set-up" for failure by inappropriate positioning on the ergotropic-trophotropic continuum. For example, if the physical therapist has been emphasizing somatic muscle activity, the individual is going to be closer to the ergotropic end. If the activity is abruptly stopped because the client is scheduled for speech therapy to work on articulation, there will be a conflict of continuum placement. Either the physical therapist must assume the responsibility for moving the individual to a more trophotropic position or the speech pathologist must recognize the situation and use appropriate stimuli before beginning the treatment session. A similar situation exists between the classroom teacher and the physical education teacher. This entire area seems obvious and a matter of common sense to those individuals accustomed to viewing individual behavior as related to the continuum.

The final consideration related to this continuum is where the therapists, teacher, or parent is on his or her own continuum. If the adult is operating close to the stress threshold, then even the most innocent behavior may trigger an ergotropic fight-or-flight reaction. Problems with rapport may relate more to one's own position on the continuum than to the position of those one is treating. The quality of interpersonal relationships may be directly related to the interaction of the individuals' continua.

We may now turn our attention to specific manipulation of the triad elements. We indicated that the autonomic nervous system was the first element of the triad. Rood (1957, 1958, 1960, 1970, 1974, 1975) has from the beginning of her approach emphasized the importance of altering the autonomic nervous system resting point. She has taught us to manipulate the sympathetic or parasympathetic dominance by using sensory stimulation. Any stimulus applied in a slow, rhythmical repetitive fashion may inhibit the sympathetic domination and allow parasympathetic function. Examples of these stimuli are slow rocking, rolling, shaking, stroking of the skin down the back, and soft low voice. Other examples include neutral warmth and contact on the palms of the hands, on soles of the feet, and on the abdomen. Decreased light, soft music, and pleasant odors may also be classified as parasympathetic stimuli. Gellhorn (1967) indicates that stimuli of low intensity and frequency will produce a trophotropic response, while stimuli of high intensity and frequency will produce an ergotropic response.

Certain stimuli are routinely interpreted as potentially dangerous and may trigger a sympathetic reaction. Examples of these stimuli are ice and pain from the external environment. Gellhorn (1967) emphasizes that visceral pain, instead of producing an ergotropic response, does in fact produce a trophotropic response since it is futile to fight or flee an internal pain.

The second element of the triad is somatic muscle activity. An ergotropic response activates somatic muscle and a trophotropic response relaxes somatic muscle. Somatic muscles include all of the voluntary muscles of the body as opposed to the smooth muscles of the autonomic nervous system.

Gellhorn (1967) insists that the fusimotor system is the key to maintaining the reciprocal relationship between the ergotropic and trophotropic systems. The fusimotor supply is the motor innervation to the muscle spindle and will be discussed in detail in Concept 5. Gellhorn indicates that the fusimotor system is the key because of the intimate relationship between fusimotor activity and ergotropic excitation. Since we have available excellent ways of influencing muscle tone, we can manipulate the balance between the two systems. As we relax tense muscles, the individual becomes less aggressive and moves toward the trophotropic end of the continuum.

E. Jacobson (1978) first wrote of progressive relaxation in 1929. His methods of promoting relaxation have long been accepted and used to help people learn to control their level of muscular tension.

The manipulation of muscle tone by positioning will be presented in Concept 4 as it relates to the carotid sinus and the vestibular system.

The third element of the triad is cortical activity. An ergotropic response produces an alert desynchronized cortical pattern, while a trophotropic response produces a synchronized cortical pattern. We would like to relate this aspect to the problem of mental retardation. Since the mind and body operate as a unit, is there not a direct relationship between the amount of muscle tone and the alertness of the cortex? Is it not possible to alter the muscle tone of retarded individuals and affect their mental abilities? There are undoubtedly many areas for application of this third element to intellectual and emotional function. This relationship will again be important as we deal with Concept 2 and the role of the nonspecific sensory input to the reticular formation.

NORMAL CONTROL OF STRESSORS

Knowledge is the first concern of the scientist because he is looking for facts, but *wisdom* is everybody's ultimate intellectual goal. Wisdom involves the ability to judge logically and deal shrewdly with facts, especially as they are related to one's life or conduct. It is our strong conviction that amassing facts and techniques of implementation relative to this concept is of very little value. The real value lies in the wisdom of application to interpersonal relationships and thus one's philosophy of life. Hans Selye took a huge risk as a medical scientist when he ventured into the philosophical implications of stress. He has given us courage to make evident from the beginning of this book our concern for the humanistic application of neurophysiological facts to the loving concern for the quality of life of all people. Selye (1976) states that "the more man learns about ways to combat external causes of death (germs, cold, hunger) the more likely is he to die from his own voluntary, 'suicidal behavior.'"* In Selye's *Stress Without Distress* (1974) he uses his many years of laboratory research on stress as a basis for a rewarding life style in harmony with the laws of nature. This life style is built on the following three principles.

1. He emphasizes the real value in satisfying work, which for the individual is play, as a means of self-expression and achievement. Man's need for work is as basic as his need for sleep, food, or air. Stress is associated with every kind of work, but distress does not have to be. By the enjoyment of work, one of the greatest negative stressors of modern life is eliminated.

2. Selye presents altruistic egoism as the most humane way of assuring our security in society. Egoism or selfishness is life's most ancient characteristic feature. It is the very instinct of self-preservation. Selfishness does not have to conflict with our wish to help others. Altruism is a sort of collective selfishness that helps the community in that it engenders gratitude. Individuals use their abilities to create trust and gratitude in others and hence induce them to share their own natural wish for well-being. This altruistic egoism is the basis of his creed.

> To earn goodwill and appreciation of our actions is the only scientific foundation for a natural code that gives us guidelines of conduct, satisfactory both to ourselves and society. . . . It supplies a purpose of unquestionable value, and I would consider it the major accomplishment of my life if I could present the case for altruistic egoism so clearly and convincingly as to make it the motto for human ethics in general.†

When man fully understands this philosophy he is no longer ashamed of being self-centered and acting for his own good. He sets out greedily to amass his fortune of goodwill, respect, gratitude, and love and becomes indispensable to his neighbors.

---

*From Selye, H.: The stress of life, revised edition, New York, 1976, McGraw-Hill Book Co.
†From Selye, H.: Stress without distress, Philadelphia, 1974, J. B. Lippincott Co.

3. Closely aligned with the above philosophy is the command to "earn thy neighbors' love." The only treasure that is yours forever is your ability to earn the love of your neighbors. As you work to perfect yourself you ensure your usefulness no matter what fate does to you. Since man is a social being he must avoid being alone. He must reach out and trust people, despite their apparent untrustworthiness. If you earn your neighbors' love, you will never be alone or have reason to doubt your worth.

These three principles are derived from the basic mechanisms that maintain homeostasis in cells, people, and entire societies. They help us face the stressors encountered in our constant fight for survival, security, and well-being.

There are many techniques for improving our quality of life such as exercise, saunas, running, yoga, or transcendental meditation. There are excellent books written on all of these techniques. There are also many books written on the management of stress. Now there are books being written on holistic medicine.

It is our opinion that Pelletier's *Mind as Healer, Mind as Slayer* (1977) offers much in both managing stress and in initiating our thinking into holistic medicine. It is our belief that as physical and occupational therapists become more involved in preventive health care and move away from in-hospital service, they will need to depend more and more on the criteria of holistic medicine.

The first criterion of Pelletier is that all states of health and disorder are considered to be psychosomatic. The patient is not just a disease, and healing involves more than removing the overt manifestations of the disease process. Treatment requires attention to the whole person and his *volition* in the course of health and disease.

The second criterion states that each individual is unique and represents a complex interaction of body, mind, and spirit.

The third criterion states that the patient and health practitioners share the responsibility for the healing process.

The fourth criterion is that health care is not the exclusive responsibility of orthodox medicine.

The fifth criterion is seeing illness as a creative opportunity for the patient to learn more about himself and his values. Illness must be viewed within the entire life span.

The final criterion is that the provider of service must come to know himself as a human being.

As the remaining eight concepts are presented we intend to implement these six criteria. It is our firm conviction that they are essential components to the optimal realization of physical, emotional, intellectual, and spiritual development of every person.

NUTRITION

A final consideration in this concept is that of nutrition. In 1954 Dr. W. D. Currier, national secretary of the American Academy of Nutrition, wrote the following in his foreword to Adelle Davis' *Let's Eat Right To Keep Fit*: "If the principles set forth in this book were followed by most people, I believe a greater advancement in health would result than from any other occurrence in the history of mankind. It surely represents the basis of preventive medicine."[*]

If, as Davis says, our nutrition can determine our zest for life, the good we put into it, and the fulfillment we get from it, we certainly need to spend some time and effort obtaining the most accurate information possible.

There is probably no area of health that is more confusing or controversial than that of nutrition, with the high fiber diet (Reuben, 1975), the fructose diet (Cooper, 1979), Atkins' diet revolution (Atkins, 1973), and many others. Many people are poorly educated as to what constitutes a proper diet, one that will actually make them and keep them healthy. We are constantly bombarded by food processing companies' advertisements, health food advocates' rebuttals, and either medical apathy or hostility. Our plea is for all people to become responsible for obtaining sufficient information to make their own decisions as to what they will or will not eat. Fredericks (1976b) has emphasized that our individual biochemical differences are greater than our similarities, and thus our nutritional needs vary considerably. He also points out that laboratory tests cannot evaluate the *potential* that may be made available to the body by altering the nutritional intake to meet the requirements of *your* body and *your* metabolism. There is a tremendous need for all people to be open-minded, willing to learn, and committed to improving their own diets. Perhaps in no other area is there such a pressing need for people to be receptive to common sense. There is no consensus on human nutritional needs. Hofmann's book, *The Great American Nutrition Hassle* (1978), explores conflicting ideas on nutrition. In the "Prevention and Therapy Through Nutrition" section, Atkins and Linde present a very convincing case for the use of vitamins and mineral supplements, and Passwater argues for the use of megavitamins for treatment of mental and emotional disorders. An article by Deutsch argues conversely that there could not possibly be a vitamin deficiency in our diets and that the United States Recommended Dietary Allowances (USRDA) are certainly adequate. Other writers believe that since our individual quantitative and qualitative needs are so different, the RDA should stand for "ridiculous, dangerous, and arbitrary." Even Senator William Proxmire of Wisconsin has stated that the Food and Nutrition Board of the National Research Council which sets the RDA stan-

---

[*]From Davis, A.: Let's eat right to keep fit, New York, 1970, Harcourt Brace Jovanovich, Inc.

dards "is both the creature of the food industry and heavily financed by the food industry." Thousands of research projects have been financed by the food industry to credit or discredit issues.

It seems to us that there is a sequence of assumptions that needs to be examined.

1. Just as every other area of our lives has changed dramatically in the last 100 years, so has our food supply, and not necessarily for the better (M. Jacobson, 1978). For many people the days are gone forever when they could provide their own eggs, meat, milk, raw vegetables, and fruit. Instead we depend on fruits and vegetables from Florida, California, or elsewhere that have to be picked before they ripen to withstand transporting over long distances. We are dependent on the food industry to package nearly everything we eat.

2. Good nutrition is no longer guaranteed by eating from the "basic four" because so much "basic" is removed in the processing. For instance, over 90 % of the 11,000 items stocked by the average supermarket have had nearly every scrap of roughage (fiber) removed in the manufacturing or refining process (Reuben, 1975).

3. Food processors seem determined to remove as much food value from a substance as possible to lengthen the packaged shelf life of the product. They then commit a further crime by adding chemical fortifiers, softeners, agers, whiteners, fresheners, preservers, and coloring. Some 3800 to 4000 chemicals are entering the American diet at a rate of a billion pounds per year (Hofmann, 1978).

As if what manufacturers have done to food is not enough, they have also spent billions of dollars in advertising to convince the public that their products are better than nature's original or superior to their competitors' equally nutritionally empty products. Still worse, they develop and market complete substitute chemical "foods."

4. It is almost impossible to avoid the consumption of sugar. Nearly all canned or packaged products, including fruits, vegetables, juices, meats, soups, and mixes of all kinds, contain some form of sugar. Our individual consumption of sugar and other sweeteners is now about 130 lb per year (Hofmann, 1978). Studies show that three fourths of the sugar we consume is hidden in processed foods.

5. We must question seriously the steadily rising cost of food in light of the high cost of processing a product to render it nutritionally empty and the cost of adding to this nutritionally empty product synthetic vitamins to restore the natural food value destroyed in the processing. Is the public being duped again?

6. We must assume that the closer we can get to the source of food, the

less processing will be needed and the greater will be the nutritional value. This is especially true if the food is eaten raw.

7. Returning to the source of food presents another huge set of problems because of the widespread use of chemical fertilizers, pesticides, and herbicides.

8. The advent of agribusinesses has almost eliminated the closed cycle of farming. In the "good ole days" a farmer had a complete farm. He raised animals to work on the farm and to provide food for his family. He raised crops to feed the animals and the family. The waste from the animals was returned to the land to constantly replenish the minerals and humus in the soil.

9. The United States is probably one of the most overfed and undernourished countries in the world, as evidenced by the incidence of degenerative diseases, allergies, and mental and emotional diseases. Investigators believe that causes for many of these diseases may stem from poor diets (Atkins, 1973; Reuben, 1975; Fredericks, 1976b).

10. It must be assumed that even in metropolitan areas thousands of people could be involved in raising some of their own food. They could enrich their soil with grass clippings and mulched leaves.

11. Even apartment dwellers could grow a constant supply of sprouts. These sprouts would supply a concentrated source of vitamins and minerals.

Good nutrition may involve a simple change in eating habits or food preparation. However, a major alteration in food selection and preparation, as well as specific vitamin or mineral supplements may be required.

Any time evidence exists that indicates that more than minor alterations in diet are necessary, it is advisable to obtain a nutritional evaluation. The minimal testing that should be done is blood, urine, and hair analyses. The results of these tests must be interpreted by a nutritional management expert. There are many well-informed and reliable people involved in nutritional education.

We would like to direct the reader's attention to a general nutritional program. One of the first things to determine is the individual's response to the removal from the diet of refined flour and sugar (in the form of bread, cake, rolls, and pastry). It is constantly amazing to us how many people cannot tolerate refined flour and sugar. Some of the behavioral changes in an individual after this removal are spectacular.

There are many sources of information about vitamins and minerals. The following information has been compiled from the writings of Reuben (1975, 1979), Frederick (1976a,b), Hofmann (1978), Davis (1970), and Donsback (1977a,b) as well as numerous articles.

The correlation between the level of stress and the supply of B complex vitamins must become one of our primary concerns. The B complex vitamins are essential for the normal functioning of the nervous system. They may be the single most important factor for health of nerves. This is a critical issue when working with physically handicapped, emotionally disturbed, and learning disabled children. The addition of brewer's yeast to the diet is a relatively easy way to supplement the B vitamins as well as the amino acids and minerals. Consumption of yogurt or acidophilus milk makes possible the return of the necessary bacteria to the digestive system to aid the body in the production of vitamin B.

Because of the importance of vitamin C in healing, fighting infection, and iron absorption, this supplement should be high on the list of priorities. The need of growing children may be as much as 40 times more than the official recommendation. Under stress the need may be even higher. With small children it is much easier to use vitamin C powder or crystals for supplementation. With any supplement, we are recommending the natural source over the synthetic.

The fat soluble vitamins are A, D, E, and K. Fortunately these vitamins are not as easily destroyed by heat and oxygen as vitamins C and B complex. Therefore these vitamins are not as easily destroyed by cooking and food processing. For this reason they may not have to be supplemented as frequently as the water soluble ones.

Probably under no circumstance should a vitamin supplement be given without a mineral complement. Minerals have been referred to as the "unsung heroes of life" because vitamins have received all of the attention since their discovery. The body's need for minerals is as critical as its need for oxygen. The body can tolerate a deficiency in vitamins for a much longer period than it can a deficiency in minerals. Neither nerves nor muscles can function normally unless the correct amounts of minerals are present in the tissue fluids. The balance of minerals is determined chiefly by hormones. If stress is excessive and the endocrine system is overworked, producing excesses of certain hormones, the mineral balance is going to be adversely affected. Also the hormones have to rely on certain vitamins, amino acids, and fatty acids for their production. Therefore there is a multiple linkage between nutrients.

Minerals are very important in regulation of the acid-base balance of the body. Cells function best in a slightly alkaline medium. There are elaborate mechanisms that keep the blood and tissue fluids within a pH range of 7.35 and 7.45. Most of the body waste is in the form of some acid. The body frequently unites base minerals with acids for elimination.

A very large portion of the mineral calcium is deposited in bones and teeth and a small portion in soft tissue. For the body to function properly, calcium must be accompanied by phosphorus, magnesium, and A, C, and D vitamins. Calcium is intimately involved with muscle tone, irritability, and normal nerve transmission. Calcium is poorly absorbed and that absorption is influenced by acid mediums in the stomach. Because absorption takes place in the duodenum, time plays a very important role.

Phosphorus has more functions in the body than any other mineral. About 80% of phosphorus is in bones and teeth; the other 20% is in soft tissue. A delicate calcium-phosphorus balance must exist for normal function of the body. This balance can be seriously affected by excessive consumption of sugar. Phosphorus content is high in protein foods such as meat, fish, poultry, and cereals. Phosphorus is more efficiently absorbed than is calcium; so calcium intake should be supplemented to be at least twice as much as phosphorus in order to be balanced.

Potassium is found mostly inside the cells. Since it is widely distributed in many common foods such as brewer's yeast, wheat germ, prunes, and bananas, there is usually a lack of emphasis on this mineral. However, the necessary intake is approximately 2500 mg, which is more than twice that of calcium or phosphorus. There are numerous factors that can lead to a negative balance in the body, such as excessive salt intake, renal disease, vomiting, diarrhea, and the use of diuretics and cortisones.

Sodium is almost completely limited to extracellular fluid. It is a major element in nerve impulse conduction and in regulation of the pH body fluids. Dehydration results from a deficiency of sodium, while edema and hypertension are associated with excessive sodium intake. People who have water softeners on their water supply should be informed that two parts of sodium are added for every part of calcium or magnesium removed. Therefore it is strongly suggested that softened water not be consumed. It is also recommended that salt for seasoning be a combination of sodium and potassium chloride. An adrenal cortex insufficiency may create a strong craving for salt because the sodium retention hormone is deficient.

Magnesium is another mineral that is poorly absorbed, with less than 35% of the amount eaten being absorbed. Deficiencies of this mineral produce nerve and muscle irritability, convulsions, seizures, and tics or twitches. Since calcium and magnesium share many functions, there should always be a ratio of approximately two parts calcium to one part magnesium.

Iron may be the most poorly absorbed mineral, since only about 10% is usually absorbed. This small absorption is dependent on adequate hydrochloric acid in the stomach as well as vitamins C and E and a protein called gastroferrin. Small amounts of iron are found in every tissue cell and every component of the cell. The iron-containing substances are responsible for oxygen uptake of the cell.

Manganese is found in greatest concentration in the pancreas, liver, pituitary, and kidneys. It is a very important catalyst and a component of many enzymes. Few minerals have as many metabolic functions, although many of its mechanisms are still not completely understood.

Iodine was the first nutrient to be identified as being essential for man. It is a vital part of the thyroid hormones that help to regulate many metabolic functions.

Copper is an essential trace mineral. The requirement for copper is frequently not considered because the amount needed is so small. It is essential in iron absorption; however, an excess may interfere with appropriate iron absorption. It is also essential in the oxidation of vitamin C. A source of excessive copper in the diet is copper tubing in household water supplies.

Chromium may soon become one of the most important supplements since it is lost through so many of the food-refining processes. It is essential in glucose metabolism and increases the effectiveness of insulin. There is increasing scientific evidence that the addition of chromium to the diet helps to reverse atherosclerosis (Donsback, 1977a).

Zinc is the second most important trace mineral in the body and is one of the most essential minerals for good health. It is a component of insulin as well as being part of the composition of over 25 enzymes involved in digestion and metabolism. Zinc is necessary for proper absorption and activity of vitamins, especially the B complex.

This is a very superficial presentation of the role of vitamins and minerals in nutrition. Perhaps the greatest lesson to be learned about both vitamins and minerals is their integration with and interdependence on one another. The safest and most rational approach is to support total nutrition with both food and food supplements. All the nutrients should be included so that, if a specific deficiency exists, it can be readily identified from symptoms occurring in an individual. Many unrelated conditions may improve when an individual's diet is changed.

We wholeheartedly agree with Pfeiffer (1978) that there is a tremendous need for preventive nutrition, in which the emphasis is placed on a preventive approach to disease rather than on the role of diet in treating problems after they develop. Nutritional education should start early in school to equip children with the knowledge to develop and practice the intelligent nutritional habits and correct food choices essential for physical, mental, and emotional health. Also, wherever possible in medicine, nutrients should be used as the first choice of treatment since they are safer and cheaper and cause far fewer side effects than drugs. Certainly any time surgery is required the patient should be prepared nutritionally for the additional stress. We as health professionals must face the fact that the well-nourished American is a myth.

KEY WORDS

activating
adduction
afferent
antagonistic
anterior hypothalamus
anterior lobe of cerebellum
autonomic nervous system
bronchi
celiac ganglion
central awareness
ciliary muscles
cingulate gyrus
collateral ganglia
cranial
cutaneous stimuli
deactivating
dilates pupil
ergotropic syndrome
esophagus
excitation
flexion
fusimotor activity
ganglia
gestational age
hippocampus
homeostatic vegetative system
inferior mesenteric ganglia

inner life
innervation
intensity of stimuli
internal rotation
joint receptors
lacrimal gland
lateral flexion
lateral gray horn
lumbar segments
medial lemniscus
medulla oblongata
neocortex
neonatal period
nuclei
outer life
pancreas
paradox
parasympathetic nervous
  system
parotid salivary gland
perioral area
peristalsis
posterior
posterior hypothalamus
postganglionic neurons
preganglionic neurons
premature

protective reaction
psychiatric patients
rebound reaction
reciprocal relationship
reticular facilitory area
reticular facilitory area of
  pons
sacral
senile patients
sinoaortic chemoreceptors
somatic (voluntary) muscles
sphincter muscles of the iris
stress threshold
sublingual gland
submaxillary gland
superior mesenteric
  ganglion
sympathetic nervous system
sympathetic trunk of chain
  ganglia
tactile
temporal growth
thalamus
thoracic segments
trophotropic syndrome
vasodilation
viscera

Exteroceptor sensory input

tactile or skin information

Concept	Types of receptors	Special senses
Background	Exteroceptors	*Practical application*
Theories of sensation	Specific receptors	Therapeutic use
Receptors as transducers	Nonspecific receptors	Tactile defensiveness

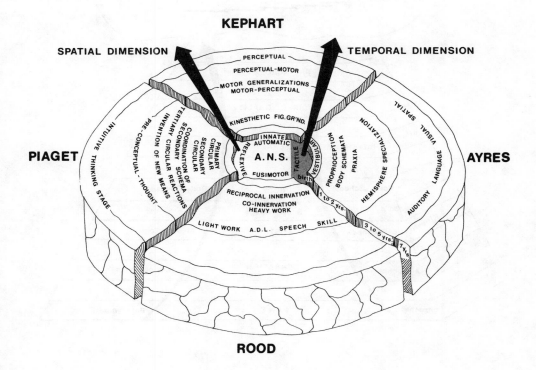

KEPHART

SPATIAL DIMENSION   TEMPORAL DIMENSION

PIAGET   AYRES

ROOD

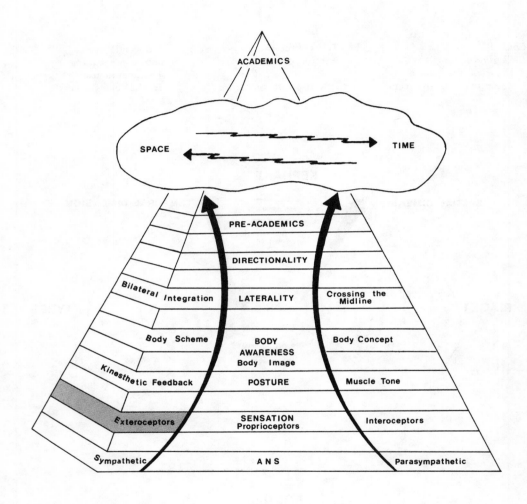

Concept   Normal sensation is dependent on parasympathetic nervous system domination and the appropriate combination of specific and nonspecific sensory input.

Exteroceptor sensory input is either specific, vital, and critical or nonspecific, generalized, and noncritical. If the specific sensory input is interpreted
as potentially dangerous, a protective fight-or-flight response will be initiated by the sympathetic system. On the **tree** the protective portion of the
specific category is placed directly under the autonomic nervous system to
illustrate the close relationship. A brief discussion of the special senses is
included to complete the picture of information received from the individual's external environment.

The exteroceptor input is represented by the word tactile in the central
core of the **cross-section.** This sensory input is responsible for initiating the
innate reflexes dealing with the external environment.

On the **pyramid,** sensation is the first step above the autonomic nervous
system (ANS). Here again the autonomic system determines the nature of
the sensory input. Concept 2 is made up of two parts. One part represents
the sympathetic system, which must be deactivated below the stress threshold so that the individual is operating more parasympathetically. The second
part is the nonspecific sensory input foundation, which is essential for discrimination to develop. Unless both systems are dealt with appropriately,
the preferred response will not be obtained.

Background

THEORIES OF SENSATION

Before launching into the specific neurophysiology of this concept, it may
be helpful to review some of the theories of somesthetic sensation. Melzack
and Wall (1962) examined the controversial issues of these theories and attempted to resolve some of them. Our purpose is to use their article as a
source for a brief presentation of the theories in order for the reader to appreciate that our understanding in any area is a constant, ongoing process.
The application of Melzack and Wall's "gate theory" will be incorporated into
Ayres' explanation of tactile defensiveness at the end of this concept.

Muller made a monumental contribution to our understanding of the sensory process. In 1842 he recognized that the brain could only receive information about external objects through the sensory nerves. He dealt with

only the sensations of light, sound, taste, smell, and feeling or touch. It was von Frey who tried to account for the qualities of somesthetic sensation by proposing four separate modalities. These modalities consisted of touch served by Meissner corpuscles and hair cells, warmth by Ruffini end-organs, cold by Krause end-bulbs, and pain by free nerve endings. Research has proved that receptors are specialized physiologically, and out of this has developed the concept of the "adequate stimulus." The very valid part of von Frey's theory is that skin receptors have specialized physiological properties.

After Erlanger, Gasser, and Bishop (Rush and colleagues, 1965) discovered that the conduction velocity of an impulse varied with the diameter of the nerve, an attempt was made to associate each fiber-diameter group with a particular sensory modality. This remains one of the most widely accepted theories of somesthesis in contemporary physiology.

In the 1950s Weddell and Sinclair proposed their pattern theory as a replacement for von Frey's theory. The simplest modality coding would be the firing of sense organs at different impulse frequencies in response to different energies. Recent research has shown that receptors will fire at different frequencies as a result of different intensities of stimuli as well as different energies.

Melzack and Wall (1962) did not believe these theories were mutually exclusive but rather that they contained valuable concepts that supplement each other. As we view each new advance in research it is important for us to constantly seek to integrate that which is relevant and to lovingly lay aside that which may at the time seem irrelevant. Selye expresses this beautifully.

> All the ingredients of my code have been known before, and many of them have been expressed more forcefully elsewhere. However, this lack of originality does not disturb me; it only reinforces my conviction that they are basic facts. The greatest truths which the structure of the human brain allows the mind to perceive and formulate have been expressed by wise men for thousands of years. All that the thinkers of any one period can do is to rediscover them under the thick layer of irrelevant trivialities in which they are constantly reburied by the dust of time, and then translate them into contemporary language.*

RECEPTORS AS TRANSDUCERS

The receptor acts as a transducer by taking whatever stimulus is presented and changing that stimulus into an electrical current. This electrical current is called a generator potential and has five characteristics.

Characteristic 1: Any receptor serves only a small area; consequently the

---

*From Selye, H.: Stress without distress, Philadelphia, 1974, J. B. Lippincott Co.

generator potential will be moving only within this prescribed area. Thus the generator potential is said to be stationary, nonpropagated, and confined to the terminal.

Characteristic 2: As the generator potential moves within the receptor area it rapidly diminishes in strength, which is designated conduction with decrement.

Characteristic 3: The generator potential has no absolute or relative refractory period. Refractory periods are found in the neuron not the receptor and will be discussed under action potential.

Characteristic 4: Stimuli of the same or different intensities may be added together or summated to produce a generator potential.

Characteristic 5: The amplitude or size of the generator potential is variable through a wide range. This amplitude is directly related to the intensity of the stimulus.

Once the generator potential reaches the threshold of the initial segment, which in a sensory neuron is the first node of Ranvier, an action potential of a fixed frequency is fired on the neuron. As the generator potential increases above the threshold level it increases the frequency of the action potential. Consequently, the stronger the stimulus, the larger the amplitude of the generator potential and the higher the frequency of the action potential. This is a basic tenet of the pattern theory of sensation.

It may be helpful to compare the receptor mechanism and generator potential to an empty container with a hole in one side (Fig. 2-1).

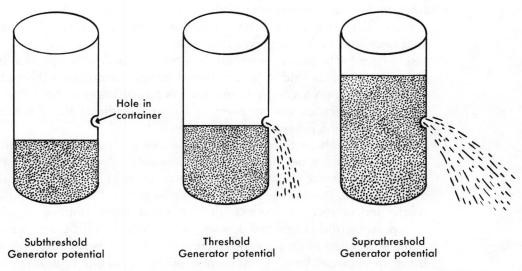

Hole in
container

Subthreshold
Generator potential

Threshold
Generator potential

Suprathreshold
Generator potential

Fig. 2-1. The stages of a generator potential compared to the fluid level in a container.

1. The container has a specific area or size as does the receptor.

2. Water has to be placed in the container, filling it to the level of the hole, before any water can run out, just as the stimuli have to be increased in intensity or summated until they reach the threshold of the neuron.

3. When the water reaches the level of the hole it will begin to dribble out, just as the action potential will have a set frequency at threshold value.

4. As the water level is increased above the level of the hole the water will run out in a stronger and stronger stream, projecting farther from the side of the container. The frequency of the action potential increases as the intensity of the stimulus increases and the amplitude of the generator potential is increased.

When one understands this sequence, in which the physical stimulus produces a generator potential that initiates the action potential, or the sensory impulse, the transducer function of sensory receptors is clarified. This sequence should help remove some of the awesome mystery of sensory stimulation as a form of treatment. Only the most relevant portions of the anatomical and physiological aspects of sensory receptor stimulation have been discussed. The psychological interpretation of sensation is not included in this concept. The elements of sensation such as temperature, touch, or pressure may be manipulated individually but should never be isolated from the total anatomical, physiological, and psychological interrelationships.

Before leaving the concept of receptors as transducers, it is important to consider the characteristics of the action potential. These characteristics are exactly the opposite of those of the generator potential.

Characteristic 1: The action potential is not confined to a specific area but travels along the neuron. It is in fact self-propagated, which means that once it is started it moves itself.

Characteristic 2: The action potential does not diminish as it travels along the neuron so it is said to be conducted without decrement. This also means that regardless of how much a neuron diverges or branches in the central nervous system every individual terminal has the same amount of action potential.

Characteristic 3: The action potential possesses both an absolute and a relative refractory period. During the absolute refractory period, the neuron is in a state of depolarization; regardless of the strength of the stimulus, it is impossible for the neuron to conduct another impulse. As the neuron recovers from conducting the previous impulse, a point of repolarization is reached, known as the relative refractory period. During this period an impulse of greater intensity is capable of initiating an impulse. An explanation of depolarization and repolarization is made by Mountcastle (1979).

Characteristic 4: The action potential is an all-or-none response; so it cannot be added to or summated.

Characteristic 5: The amplitude of the action potential is fixed for each neuron; so it cannot be altered.

As explained earlier, it is the frequency of the action potential that is variable. There is a direct relationship among the intensity of the stimulus, the amplitude of the generator potential, and the frequency of the action potential. As stated earlier, this relationship forms the foundation of the "pattern theory" of sensation. According to this theory the individual obtains certain information about the intensity of the stimulus from the frequency or pattern of impulses arriving in the central nervous system.

A relatively simple way to illustrate this relationship is to place a fingernail on the back of the opposite hand. If the nail is lightly touching the skin, a definite sensation is experienced. When the pressure is gradually increased, the sensation will be altered from light touch to a firm contact, to deep pressure, and ultimately to pain.

● ● ●

In the discussion of synaptic activity in Concept 7, the characteristics of the generator and action potentials with a similar sequence of events will be presented. We believe that relating neurophysiological information to the clinical application of techniques is paramount in establishing a neurophysiological philosophy of patient management. Each time a professional applies a sensory stimulus he should be consciously aware of the sequence of events set in motion. The professional must have his own explanation and justification for the techniques used.

TYPES OF RECEPTORS

Sensory receptors are classified as being either phasic or tonic in nature. Phasic receptors are also described as being fast adapting. When stimulated they fire an on response or spike. Adaptation begins, and no matter how long the stimulus is maintained, no more activity is recorded until the stimulus is removed. This produces an off response or spike. Consequently these receptors are concerned with change, and the related motor activity is movement.

The tonic receptors may also be called slow-adapting receptors. Some may be essentially nonadapting because they may fire for hours. When stimulated these receptors fire an on response or spike. They then drop to a plateau and continue to fire at a steady rate as long as the stimulus intensity is maintained. When the stimulus is finally removed, these receptors will fire an off response or spike just as did the phasic receptors.

The unique characteristic of the tonic receptors is plateau firing, which shows an intensity-frequency relationship. If the intensity is increased during the plateau, the frequency increases, and if the intensity decreases, the frequency will decrease. The tonic receptors provide a maintained sensory input, and the related motor activity is a maintained contraction. Since the motor activity is determined by the type of sensory receptor stimulated, care must be exercised in the method of stimulation. If stability or posture is desired, tonic, not phasic, receptors must be used because of their maintained sensory input.

EXTEROCEPTORS
Specific receptors

Exteroceptors are responsible for providing information about the external environment. This information may be of a specific, vital, critical nature. The information may be interpreted as being potentially dangerous to the individual and would therefore elicit a protective or sympathetic nervous system response. These receptors may be categorized as protective receptors. As illustrated in Fig. 2-2, the three protective roots labeled extremes of temperature, hair cells, and pain, are diagrammed directly below the soil to show the direct relationship of protective receptors to the autonomic nervous system.

The protective receptors can function without a blood supply. This condition exists during sympathetic nervous system vasoconstriction of the blood vessels in the skin. Stepping into a shower or tub only to jump out immediately and not know whether the water was too hot or too cold illustrates a protective response to extremes of temperature. The alerting hair cell response results when the hair cells are turned the wrong way or against the growth pattern. This response explains the extremely annoying, irritating, and disturbing feelings we experience when an insect crawls on the skin and turns many hair cells the wrong direction. Any degree of pain can trigger an avoidance response relative to the individual's tolerance or stress threshold. All of these receptors can trigger the sympathetic system as a unit and produce a fight-or-flight reaction aimed at saving the organism from a potentially dangerous situation.

The discriminatory receptors must be allowed to operate if the individual is going to interact in a meaningful way with his environment. Interaction with the environment is the basis of all learning. As illustrated in Fig. 2-2, the discriminative receptor roots are labeled pressure, touch, temperature, and pain. These receptors must have a blood supply in order to function, which means that the sympathetic nervous system with its vasoconstriction must not be allowed to dominate.

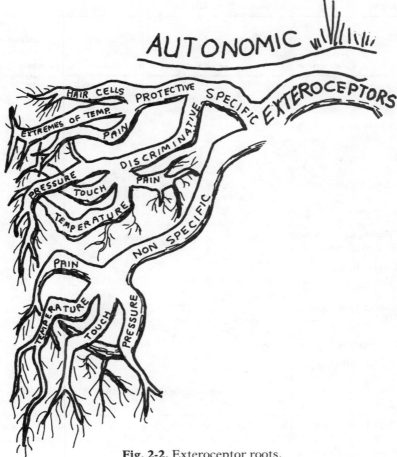

Fig. 2-2. Exteroceptor roots.

The size of the sensory neuron and the speed of conduction are functionally important. The velocity of conduction depends on the diameter of the fiber. As the diameter of the fiber increases, the amount of resistance to the passage of the current decreases (Schmidt, 1975).

Myelination also increases the velocity of conduction. Neurons were originally classified according to conduction velocity by Erlanger and associates (1924). They used the alphabetical system with division into A alpha, beta, gamma, and delta, B, and C fibers. All of the A fibers and the B fibers are myelinated; the C fibers are unmyelinated. Lloyd reclassified the fibers according to fiber diameter and used Roman numerals (Ruch and colleagues, 1965). There has been considerable confusion between the two systems. It is beneficial to have a comparison of the systems (Table 1) if one is reviewing the literature. The muscle afferents from the muscle spindle (Ia)

Table 1. Classification of nerve fibers*

Fiber group	Examples of function	Mean fiber diameter (μm)	Mean conduction velocity (m/sec)
Muscle afferents			
Ia	Primary muscle spindle ending	13	75
Ib	Golgi tendon organ		
Equivalent to A alpha fibers			
Muscle afferent			
II	Secondary muscle spindle ending	9	55
Cutaneous afferents			
II	Low-threshold myelinated afferent		
	Mechanoreceptor of skin		
Equivalent to A beta and gamma fibers			
Muscle afferent			
III	High-threshold myelinated afferent	3	11
Cutaneous afferent			
III	High-threshold myelinated afferent		
Equivalent to A delta fibers			
Muscle and cutaneous afferent			
IV	C fiber, unmyelinated afferent	1	1
Equivalent to C fibers			

*Data from Schmidt, R. F.: Presynaptic inhibition in the vertebrate central nervous system, Ergeb. Physiol. **63**:20-101, 1971; and Schmidt, R. F., editor: Fundamentals of neurophysiology, New York, 1975, Springer-Verlag New York, Inc.

and from the Golgi tendon organs (Ib) have diameters ranging from 12 to 20 μm and conduction velocities of 70 to 120 m/sec. These two fibers are equivalent to the A alpha fibers (Ganong, 1969).

The muscle afferents from the muscle spindle (II) and the cutaneous afferents from the low-threshold mechanoreceptors in the skin (II) have diameters of 5 to 12 μm and velocities of 30 to 70 m/sec. They are equivalent to the A beta and gamma fibers.

The muscle afferents from joint receptors, pressure, and high-threshold receptors (III) and the high-threshold cutaneous afferents (III) have diameters of 2 to 5 μm and velocities of 12 to 30 m/sec. They are equivalent to the A delta fibers.

Unmyelinated muscle and cutaneous afferents (IV) have diameters of 0.4 to 1.2 μm and velocities of 0.5 to 2 m/sec. They are equivalent to the C fibers. The cutaneous fibers in some articles are designated drC because cell bodies are found in the dorsal root ganglion. The sC fibers are not afferent but are sympathetic postganglionic fibers.

The B fibers of Erlanger and associates are preganglionic neurons. The B fibers do not have a roman numeral equivalent.

The large-diameter myelinated A fibers (I to III) are found in the sensory pathways ascending the lemniscal tracts. They terminate in the postero-lateral ventral nucleus of the thalamus for sensation from the body and the posteromedial ventral nucleus for sensation from the face. The final termination of sensation is the neocortex, sensory areas 3, 1, and 2.

Nonspecific receptors

There are twice as many of the small C fibers as there are large A fibers. They are not divided into protective and discriminative groups as are the A fibers. As illustrated in Fig. 2-2, the nonspecific receptor roots are labeled pressure, touch, temperature, and pain to correspond to the similar specific discriminative roots. Analysis of single C fibers shows that these fibers carry all types of sensation and not just pain (Iggo, 1959). These C fibers have a much higher threshold than corresponding A fibers. After a C fiber is stimulated it goes into a long positive after-potential state. This means that functionally it is less sensitive and requires an even stronger stimulus than the original one in order to fire. Ruch, and colleagues (1965) state that this long positive after-potential state is changed into a long negative after-potential state by a fast repetitive stimulus. The long negative after-potential state means that the fiber is more sensitive and requires a less intense stimulus than the original one. They also state that when the skin temperature is rapidly dropped by 10° C, three fourths of all the C fibers in the skin area are activated. Theoretically, the use of cold and fast repetitive stimuli can afford two ways of providing C fiber nonspecific stimulation. Ice, however, must not be used to the point that a sympathetic protective response is triggered.

These small unmyelinated C fibers (IV) ascend to the reticular formation. From the reticular formation connections are made into the intralaminar nuclei of the thalamus. The cortical projection from the thalamus is to the cingulate gyrus, which in turn can provide widespread inhibition or facilitation to the entire brain.

A variety of experiences can be provided to emphasize the sensory input from either specific or nonspecific exteroceptors (Fig. 2-3). In a similar manner many games can be devised to emphasize one or the other type of sensory input as well as a combination of the two (Fig. 2-4).

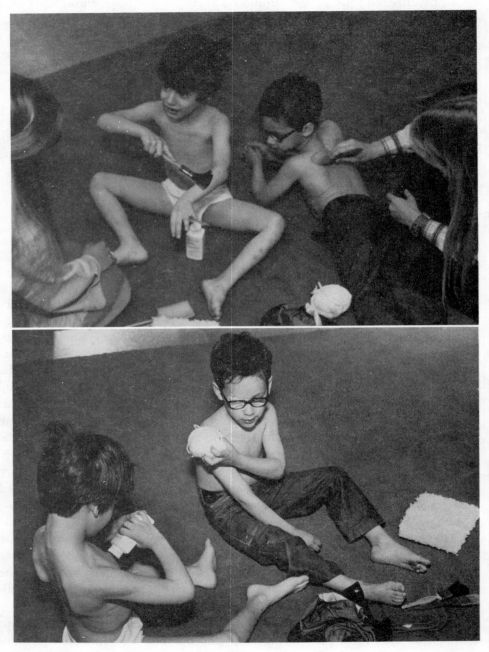

Fig. 2-3. A variety of media may be used to provide generalized tactile stimulation.

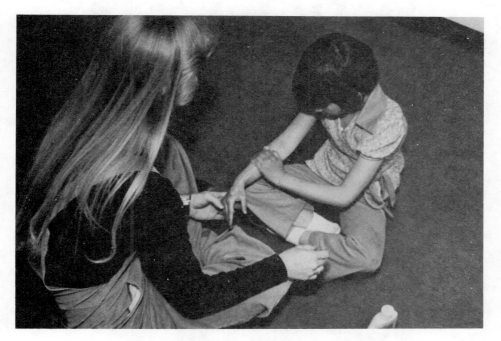

Fig. 2-3, cont'd. For legend see opposite page.

Continued.

Fig. 2-4. Many games can be devised that use tactile stimulation.

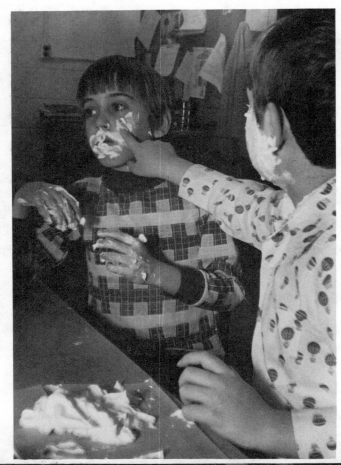

Fig. 2-4, cont'd. Many games can be devised that use tactile stimulation.

Special senses

This brief presentation of the special senses is included to complete the picture of information received from the individual's external environment. The special senses are not, however, incorporated into this concept. The special senses include smell, sight, sound, and taste.

The sense of smell is carried in the olfactory nerve (I). Functionally, the sense of smell is very elaborate and intricate in its connections with the limbic system and resultant affective behavior. There is a critical need for clinical investigation and application of the use of smell and its excitatory and inhibitory effects. This is especially true in the case of traumatic head injury and early intervention programs.

Farber (1978) provides an excellent introduction into the use of olfaction as a therapeutic modality. She presents a foundation of neuroanatomy and neurophysiology, pertinent research, and some therapeutic implications. She lists from Schneider (1974) four main functions of the olfactory system: protection of the individual, contribution to his emotional life, assistance in digestion, and facilitation of recollections.

Farber discusses smell as it relates to human infant responses. She cites Cheal's (1974) belief that infants form associations based on early olfactory experience. This would certainly indicate the importance of early and frequent exposure of high-risk infants to their parents. It would seem to us also extremely important to provide these familiar odors to the individual with traumatic head injury early in the recovery period. There have been numerous reports in our workshops of combative patients with traumatic head injury becoming quiet and more responsive when presented with familiar family odors such as perfume, after-shave lotion, or cooking aromas.

Of prime importance in any feeding program is the use of odors that promote parasympathetic responses and sucking-swallowing motions. Steiner (1974) found that 15- to 16-hour-old infants would relax their facial muscles, producing a smilelike expression, and perform sucking and licking movements when presented with banana and vanilla extract (sweet smells) or good nutrient tastes. Aversive, disgustlike responses were seen in the presence of rotten egg odor and unpleasant tastes. He concluded that these are instinctive responses mediated through the limbic system to assist the individual in determining the ingestibility of substances. There is little doubt that olfaction can guide and direct behavior before either vision or hearing are developed.

The therapeutic implications of smell are directly related to whether a discriminative reaction or a protective response is desired. As with any medium, there may be an inhibitory or facilitory effect to each odor. How an individual responds to a given odor seems to be influenced by age, sex, culture, and previous experience. Consequently, any treatment using odors should be closely coordinated with the family. Extreme care should be exercised to avoid any odor that could be overtly threatening to the individual. Since the therapeutic use of odors is such an undocumented area, accurate records should be kept of procedures and responses. Farber (1978) suggests evaluating such areas as: facial responses, reflex patterns, muscle tone, spontaneous behavior, and verbal responses.

Closely aligned with the sense of smell is the sense of taste. Haagen-Smit (1952) has explained very clearly the chemical aspects of these two sensations. The sense of taste is mediated over one of three cranial nerves, depending on the area of the tongue involved. The anterior two thirds of the tongue is innervated by the facial nerve (VII), the posterior one third of the tongue by the glossopharyngeal nerve (IX), and the area around the epiglottis by the vagus nerve (X). The sensation of taste includes only those things that are sweet, sour, bitter, or salty. Consequently, that delicious piece of hot apple pie is an intricate combination of sensation involving smell, taste, sight, temperature, touch, and memory.

The optic nerve (II) carries the special sense of vision or sight. This channel of sensory input is an excellent source of facilitory or inhibitory sensory input when one is working on physical activities.

The auditory or cochlear portion of the vestibulocochlear nerve (VIII) carries the special sense of hearing. Hearing is another sense that is an excellent source of facilitory and inhibitory sensory input. Concepts 3 and 4 will present the vestibular part of the VIII cranial nerve.

Practical application

The practical application of this concept will be rather arbitrarily divided into a section on touching and a section on the therapeutic use of exteroceptor sensory input.

TOUCHING

Leboyer has expressed the importance of touching very poetically.

> Life begins at birth. . . .Within the womb is the fetus dead? . . . What begins at the moment we are born? . . . Fear and the child are born together. . . . The baby is terrified of . . . the thousand and one new sensations of the world. . . . Life was rich in the womb . . . rich in noises and sounds . . . movements. . . . All alone . . . not a sound. . . . Not a whisper. . . . And worst of all . . . there is no movement. . . . What is this "thing" inside my belly. . . . Hunger. . . . Inside, the terrible "gnawing thing", and the remedy . . . outside. . . . Inside and outside. . . . Space is born. Oneness is lost. . . . Inside and outside and, in between, waiting. Waiting which is pain. . . . agony . . . time. . . . and so it is that time and space are born with appetite. A baby's belly is hungry. . . . But its skin is just as hungry. . . . Its skin is craving, and so is its back, and so is its spine, craving for touch, craving for sensations. . . . The terrible nothingness is simply no touching, nothing along my back!. . . . Feeding babies with touches, giving food to their skins and their backs, is just as important as filling their stomachs.*

Let us not forget that each of us have powerful, though vague, memories that come long before words. Memories of being held, stroked, and caressed that told us we were secure and loved. Davis (1978) speaks of "skin hunger"— an American disease. How very true it is. How many thousands of people yearn for a human touch. Davis indicates that most adult Americans are touch-poor. Our culture, she says, is to blame, since any but the most formal contacts are suspected of having sexual overtones. Why have we given up our right to be touched and held in nonsexual ways? Why is Buscaliga (1972) so sure that we have forgotten how to love each other? Are the one million pregnancies a year in 12- to 17-year-old girls (Elkind, 1979) a result of preoccupation with sex or the result of teenagers' crying need to touch and be touched? Maybe our young people would "feel more secure" if they were touched and held more freely.

---

* From Leboyer, F.: Loving hands, New York, 1976, Alfred A. Knopf, Inc.

We may approach this problem from yet a different angle. Lynch (1977) in his book *The Broken Heart: The Medical Consequences of Loneliness* made some rather startling discoveries. The book was written to document the fact that loneliness is not only pushing our culture to the breaking point but also pushing our physical health to the breaking point. It has in many cases already pushed the human heart beyond the breaking point. Those individuals who lack the comfort of another human being may lack one of nature's most powerful antidotes to stress.

One of the most basic needs is to communicate. Lynch found the final hospital goodbye was most often touching—a hand, arm, body, and even foot. He indicated that the most simple and direct type of human communication does not need words. In his study he found that the heart of a comatose patient responded to the simple quiet comforting of a nurse holding the patient's hand. His statistics showed the death rate from heart disease to be as much as two to ten times higher for single individuals than married ones of comparable ages. The central assumption of the book is that a person's life may be shortened by the lack of human companionship. Even a simple form of human contact such as holding hands does have dramatic effects on the body, especially the heart.

Montagu (1971) treats the skin as a sense organ and indicates that the human significance of touching is even more profound than supposed. Touch is fundamental in the development of human behavior. He postulates that the need for tactile stimulation should be added to the basic needs for oxygen, food, rest, sleep, elimination, avoidance of pain, and escape from danger. His evidence indicates that adequate tactile experience during infancy and childhood is vitally important for the healthy behavioral development of the individual. Tactile stimulation should begin with the newborn in as natural a setting as possible—the mother's arms, at the breast, or remaining beside her.

> Fondling of an infant can scarcely be overdone—a reasonably sensible human being is not likely to over stimulate an infant—hence if one is to err in any direction it were better in the direction of too much rather than too little fondling.*

At this point something needs to be said about mother-child bonding. Kennell and associates (1975) have suggested that there is a sensitive period for this bonding immediately after birth. They found that mothers who were allowed 1 hour of contact with their nude baby in the first 2 hours after birth plus 15 extra hours of contact in the first 3 days after birth showed signifi-

---

* From Montagu, A.: Touching: the human significance of the skin, New York, 1971, Harper & Row, Publishers, Inc.

cant differences in their behavior. This behavior was demonstrated as more soothing during the physical examination at 1 month, more eye-to-eye contact, and more fondling during feeding. At 1 year the mothers spent more time assisting the physician and soothing the infant. At 2 years these mothers used twice as many questions, more words per proposition, fewer content words, more adjectives, and fewer commands than the control group mothers when talking to their children.

Klaus and colleagues (1975) showed a definite sequence of touching in the first few minutes of contact. The nude infant was placed beside the mother at shoulder level. The mother immediately started touching the infant's extremities with her fingertips. Within 4 to 8 minutes she then proceeded to massage the trunk with the palm of her hand. There was considerable eye-to-eye contact. Whenever this sensitive period is passed without the contact, several visits with the infant are needed for the sequence to develop.

We would like to make a strong point of the difference between touching or fondling an infant and the sensory stimulation that may be done in high-risk infant nurseries. There is grave danger in overstimulating an infant especially if that infant is under considerable stress and operating at the ergotropic end of the continuum. There is also grave danger in turning on an infant's visual mechanism before he really learns internally about his own body. Postnatal development is dependent on prenatal patterns. Care must be taken to assure development of those primitive patterns before advancing to higher nervous system functions (Snapp, 1979). We need to feed the skin with a loving concerned touch but be careful of too much touch or the wrong kind of touch. Huss (1977) believes that if occupational therapists would begin to use touch in a caring manner, in time they could make a difference in our culture. It is absolutely essential that those who use exteroceptor input to determine motor performance be constantly alert to the behavioral implications of our stimulation. There is a busy two-way street between touching the skin and physical or behavioral responses.

We have found that adults are just as hungry for touch—perhaps more so than infants. The first day of our workshops we indicate that we are "touching" people, and unless the participants indicate their desire not to be touched we will be touching them. It is amazing how much freedom and a feeling of closeness can develop among 30 people in 8 days when they are free to reach out and contact each other. How very nice it is to be free to encircle the waist or shoulders of either sex and feel that comforting little hug returned. How much easier it is to discuss a conflicting viewpoint with a touch to the arm or shoulder. How much less threatening is a question if it is asked in combination with some type of contact. Our plea throughout this book will be to put love and caring back into the implementation of our technology before our behavior kills us!

THERAPEUTIC USE

As we turn to the therapeutic use of exteroceptor input it is important to realize that a sensory stimulus is rarely just facilitory or inhibitory. Rather, the function will vary according to a combination of a least four parameters.

Parameter 1: What is the stimulus? Ice is a potentially dangerous stimulus. Neutral warmth or body temperature is soothing and nondangerous.

Parameter 2: Where is the stimulus applied? Pressure applied manually into a muscle belly facilitates contraction. Pressure applied across the tendon inhibits a spastic contraction.

Parameter 3: How is the stimulus applied? This relates to the speed and also the duration.

Parameter 4: What pattern of function is being used? Is the pattern a reciprocal one, a cocontraction one, or one of heavy work movement? These patterns will be expanded in Concept 5.

Rood (1970) presented four rules of sensory input and motor output as a convenient way to organize parameter 3.

Rule 1. *"A fast brief stimulus produces a large synchronous motor output."*

This type of stimulation will verify intact reflex arcs. It will indicate that there are (1) receptors to receive the stimuli, (2) functioning sensory neurons that make connection with functioning alpha motor neurons, and (3) motor neurons connected to contractile muscle fibers that can produce a movement. The first disadvantage of this type of stimulation is the frequent production of a rebound movement in the opposite direction. Clinically, this rebound can be seen as a maintained positioning. A possible example is the child with cerebral palsy who is extremely sensitive to light touch in the lower extremities and who exhibits strong total flexion withdrawal patterns whenever touched. Following this withdrawal pattern, the legs will return to the exact opposite position of extension, adduction, internal rotation, and plantar flexion. This typical scissor position is actively maintained. In a normal child following a withdrawal pattern the legs relax and are free for isolated joint motion.

According to Rood any sensory stimulus will affect the mind as well as the body. This type of stimulus appears to produce a brief arousal of the cortex with a similar rebound of prolonged inhibition, which is a second disadvantage.

A third disadvantage of this type of sensory stimulus is the metabolic cost to the body. Any large synchronous motor response will require a burst of energy and the production of an oxygen debt and will necessitate a recovery period. Rood believes this type of stimulus uses a high-energy system. This system will be further discussed in Concept 5.

Rule 2. *"A fast repetitive sensory input produces a maintained response."*

In the presentation of nonspecific receptors and C fibers, the importance of using a fast, repetitive stimulus was discussed. This rule has a direct implication to the stimulation of C fibers. The C fibers are believed to have a widespread impact on fusimotor activity supplying the muscle spindle, indirectly by way of the reticular formation and directly at spinal cord levels. Since a maintained response is produced there is no problem of rebound as in rule 1. With the maintained response, tonic receptors will provide constant information to support the contraction and provide kinesthetic feedback. Since this contraction operates at a low nervous system level of receptor directly to effector, it is metabolically inexpensive. This is the low–energy system counterpart to rule 1, which will be discussed as a unit in Concept 5.

Rule 3. *"A maintained sensory input produces a maintained response."*

The best example of this maintained sensory input is the force of gravity. Kephart (1971) emphasizes that gravity is the only constant force in our environment. Ayres (1976) states that dealing with the force of gravity is even more basic than the mother-child relationship.

Contact in the form of touch or pressure is another excellent maintained sensory input. The contact of the body surface against a supporting surface may well have more impact on muscle tone than has been recognized.

Rule 4. *"Slow, rhythmical, repetitive sensory input deactivates body and mind."*

The application of this rule was discussed in Concept 1, when the ergotropic and trophotropic triads were delineated. Low-intensity and low-frequency cutaneous stimuli activate the trophotropic system. There is danger of a rebound associated with this phenomenon. If too many types of parasympathetic stimuli or too prolonged a use of stimuli are employed, a sympathetic protective reaction may be triggered.

Some examples of parasympathetic stimuli are slow rocking, rolling, shaking of the body, a slow-moving light, and low, soft music. Slow stroking down the midline of the back in the area of the posterior primary rami is very relaxing. Another parasympathetic-type stimulus is constant touch or contact on the palms of the hands, soles of the feet, abdomen, and upper lip. The maintenance of body temperature, which is a neutral warmth, is also deactivating.

Many of these parasympathetic stimuli may be observed in exclusive retail shops, where lovely music, soft light, deep carpet, beautiful color, and appealing displays make it almost a physical impossibility to continue at the original hurried pace or to resist the desire to stop and caress the "delectable treasures." This use of parasympathetic type stimuli is also becoming increasingly evident in doctors' and dentists' offices with the use of furniture, colors, and music to help minimize the stress and tension associated with anticipating discomfort.

Since such excellent ways of manipulating the parasympathetic nervous system are available, they should provide a means of regulating the intensity of the trophotropic discharge and the balance between the inhibitory and facilitory systems.

TACTILE DEFENSIVENESS

The most obvious clinical application of Concept 2 is in the individual who demonstrates tactile defensiveness. The reader is referred to Ayres' *Sensory Integration and Learning Disorders* (1972), Chapter 13, for the excellent presentation "Tactile Defensiveness and Related Behavioral Disorders."

Tactile defensiveness is an adversive response to tactile stimuli. The primitive protective survival responses are elicited instead of the integrative discriminative responses. The behaviors of distractibility and hyperactivity may be more evident than the defensiveness. All hyperactive children are not tactilely defensive. Because of the disorder of the tactile system there may be an associated developmental apraxia (Ayres, 1976).

If the child's nervous system is biased toward the ergotropic end of the continuum, he will interpret stimuli as potentially dangerous. He will therefore demonstrate an abnormal degree of defensive or aggressive behavior. Since he frequently responds to stimuli in his environment that seem irrelevent to others, he is considered distractible. The activity of the sympathetic nervous system activates somatic muscles and results in activity; therefore the child is considered hyperactive. Since many elements in his environment are threatening to him, he is undoubtedly anxious and hence is considered emotionally labile. He is ill prepared to cope with our complicated civilization.

We appreciate Ayres' (1972) combination of concepts from Head, Mountcastle, and Melzack and Wall in her neurobiological considerations of the problem. Head's (1920) theory of tactile function was related to a dual system of protopathic and epicritic sensation. The protopathic system was primitive in character and designed to protect the individual from possible harm. The epicritic system was superimposed on the older system and concerned with higher discriminatory function. Head conceptualized the epicritic system as exercising control over or checking the lower protopathic system.

Poggio and Mountcastle (1960) divided somatic sensation into dual tracts and projections. Neurons in the spinothalamic system responded to potentially dangerous stimuli as well as light touch and hair displacement. Strong, emotional, escapelike behaviors are elicited on stimulation. The lemniscal system serves in the highly discriminative interpretation of spatial and temporal parameters of touch-pressure and kinesthetic stimuli. Melzack and Wall (1965) believed that the lemniscal system could mediate Head's epicritic system, and the spinothalamic system could mediate his protopathic system.

Ayres (1972) described Melzack and Wall's "gate control" theory of sensation as follows: As the sensory impulses enter the dorsal horn they project to a group of cells that operate the gate (gelatinous substance) before they connect with the second neuron or T cell in the sensory pathway. Large-fiber impulses facilitate the cells of the gelatinous substance to increase their inhibition on the synapse with the T cell, and so the gate is closed. Small-fiber impulses inhibit the cells of the gelatinous substance which decreases their inhibition on the T cells and so open the gate. These small, slow-adapting neurons tend to hold the gate open. When large fibers adapt to continuous stimulation, the closed gate tends to open again. The opening and closing of the gate is influenced by the balance of small-fiber activity versus large-fiber activity, the nature of the stimulus, and the neural activity prior to the stimulation.

We believe the key factor in the gate theory is the balance between large- and small-fiber input. The correct balance is necessary for normal sensation. It has been our experience that the adverse responses of the sympathetic nervous system must be decreased by shifting the individual toward the trophotropic end of his continuum. Once this shift has been accomplished, appropriate kinds and amounts of C fiber stimulation can be tolerated, and more normal discriminative behaviors are exhibited.

Rood's four rules of sensory input may be applied to the treatment of individuals exhibiting tactile defensive behavior. Rule 4 states that slow rhythmical repetitive stimuli deactivate mind and body. The use of these kinds of stimuli will be seen to shift the individual from the ergotropic end of his continiuum toward the trophotropic end.

Rule 2 encompassed the use of fast repetitive stimuli as a source of nonspecific sensory input. Ayres (1972) discusses C fibers in her presentation of developmental apraxia. The C fibers are the oldest somatosensory neurons and carry diffuse touch as well as pain and temperature sensations. Many of these fibers end in the brain stem to meet a low-level adaptive function.

Because they have such a high threshold, they probably require rapid and prolonged stimulation. If the discriminative system is superimposed on the primitive one, then the activation of the small tactile fibers is important to the development of discriminative touch.

Rule 3 states that a maintained stimulus produces a maintained cocontraction. The most constantly maintained stimulus is the force of gravity, which stimulates proprioceptors. Ayres (1972) indicates that proprioception that activates the posterior column–medial lemniscal system also seems to "close the gate," thereby reducing hyperactivity and distractibility. Kephart (1969) initiated the use of proprioceptors in his "behavior control through movement control" approach to hyperactive children. This approach will be presented in detail in Concept 7.

It has been our experience that many children have been labeled tactile defensive inappropriately. We believe that this term should be reserved for the individual who shows an avoidance response to tactile stimuli. At the beginning of tactile stimulation, the avoidance response may be minimal, but as the stimuli continue, the avoidance becomes more marked and intense. Light touch appears to be the critical stimulus. Many hyperactive and distractible children appear to be tactilely defensive, when in fact their problems are lack of attention and their brief contact with elements in their environment. When their freedom is restricted and they are required to attend to tactile stimulation, they are not defensive.

Truly tactilely defensive individuals will exhibit the negative or avoidance response to being touched even to the extent of wearing long sleeves and long pants to protect the skin from continuous exposure to light touch (Ayres, 1976). They may exhibit similar supersensitivity to high-intensity stimuli of light, sound, and odor. Remember that high-intensity stimuli tend to activate the ergotrophic system. When we are dealing with these tactilely defensive individuals, we must be aware that the balance between the ergotropic and trophotropic systems is just as critical as providing the nonspecific generalized tactile stimulation. For instance, a child may not be able to tolerate having his skin rubbed with a washcloth unless he is provided with some slow rocking before, during, and after the rubbing.

Rarely is this problem of tactile defensiveness seen in isolation. It may mask problems of apraxia and vestibular bilateral integration. Tactile defensiveness is not restricted to a developmental problem in children but may also appear in adults because of disease or injury.

It is not unusual to find adults who have managed to compensate for this disorder and are unaware of the problem. When these adults become parents, a new and unsuspected problem may arise. They may inadvertently withhold tactile stimulation from their infant. The literature is full of evi-

dence indicating that infants who lack normal mothering and tactile stimulation in early infancy demonstrate an inability to handle stress. The complexity of this problem and the ramifications for the family behoove us to be
on the alert for those parents who may be unaware that they are using a
minimal amount of touching in their child care.

• • •

In summary, it should be evident that a constant symphony between A
and C fiber activity and sympathetic-parasympathetic activity is being
played. At the moment that A fiber information is interpreted as harmful,
the sympathetic nervous system will discharge as a total unit, producing a
fight-or-flight reaction. We must be able to anticipate this and immediately
provide adequate parasympathetic stimuli to reestablish the balance. Addi-
tionally we must be constantly aware of the need for generalized, nonspecific
C fiber stimulation as a foundation for discrimination.

All of the exteroceptor roots have been described. All of the information
from the external environment has been presented. However, Concept 1 and
Concept 2 will be incorporated repeatedly into future concepts.

KEY WORDS

A fiber activity
adaptive function
after potential
   negative
   positive
auditory
aversive
beaded network or hediform
   plexuses
brain stem
brief arousal of the cortex
cochlear
cocontraction pattern
combative traumatic head
   injury patients
conducted with decrement
depolarization
developmental dyspraxia
diameter of the fibers
distractability
divergence
emotionally labile
epicritic
exteroceptors
facilitate
fast repetitive stimulus
fast-adapting receptors

frequency of the action
   potential
gelatinous substance
   (substantia gelatinosa)
generator potential
gravity
hair cells
high-risk infants
hyperactivity
inhibition
innate reflexes
ionic changes
kinesthetic feedback
kinesthetic stimuli
lemniscal tracts
limbic system
low-energy system
maintained contraction
medullated
myelination
nervous system is biased
neuron
neutral warmth
nonadapting receptors
nonpropagated
nonspecific
phasic receptors

plantar flexion
posterior medial ventral
   nucleus of the thalamus
proprioceptors
protopathic
rebound
receptor mechanism
receptors
reciprocal pattern
repolarization
self-propagated
slow-adapting receptors
somatic sensation
special senses
specific
synchronous motor output
tactile defensiveness
tendons
terminal
threshold
tonic receptors
transducers
unmedullated
velocity of conduction
vestibular bilateral
   integration
vestibulocochlear

Vestibular mechanism—motion

movement of the body

Concept
Background
  Anatomical organization
    Semicircular canals
    Saccule and utricle
    Sensory neuron
    Central termination
  Physiological organization

Vestibular nuclei
  Lateral nucleus
  Medial nucleus
  Superior nucleus
  Descending nucleus
Practical application
  Screening vestibular function
    Infants
      Lawrence and Feind

Eviatar and colleagues
  de Quiros
Children
  de Quiros
  Ayres
  Heiniger
Adults
  Heiniger and Randolph

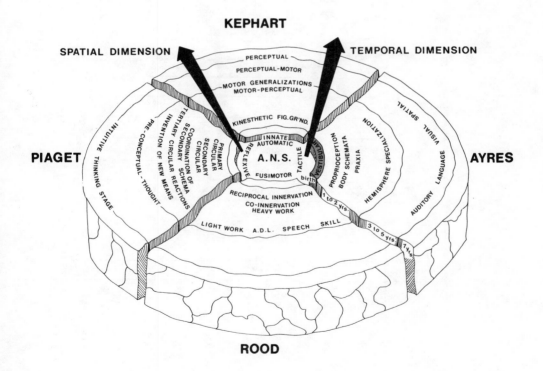

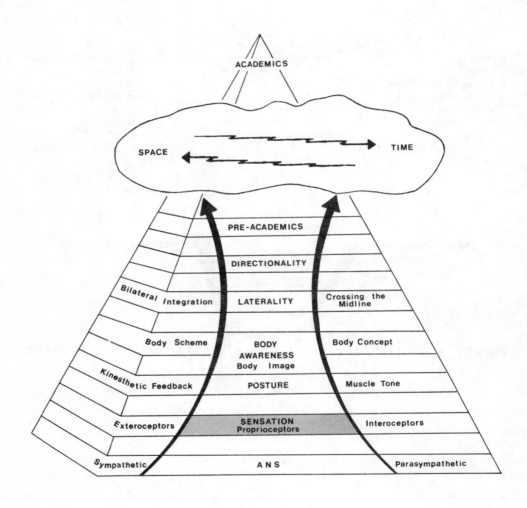

Concept   Vestibular sensory input is related either to motion or position of the head in relationship to the force of gravity. The integration of the motion portion of the vestibular mechanism may be demonstrated by dizziness or nystagmus or both after stimulation.

The position portion of the vestibular mechanism will be considered in Concept 4. The **tree** shows vestibular input as a large division of the proprioceptor roots. One portion is labeled movement. The four smaller roots are labeled for the four planes of motion: forward-backward, side-to-side, rotational, and up-down. The motion portion of the vestibular mechanism is concerned with angular and linear acceleration and deceleration.

On the **cross-section** the vestibular system is in the area of birth to denote the new gravitational environment. At birth the infant should have a vestibular system that is capable of functioning because the peripheral organs are mature and there is a myelinated tract, the medial longitudinal fasciculus, available for functional integration. The lowest level of the nervous system, where integration of vestibular input with eyes, neck, and trunk motions occurs, is at the brain stem level.

On the **pyramid** vestibular input is part of the proprioceptor portion of sensation. Concepts 4, 5, and 6 will also deal with portions of proprioceptive sensation. All of this proprioception must be integrated if the individual is to make an adaptive behavioral response to a change in either his external or internal environment.

Since there is so much information available concerning the vestibular system, we will suggest a few references with special emphasis. Sage's *Introduction to Motor Behavior: A Neuropsychological Approach* (1971), is concise and elementary. The book by Schilder, *Mind: Perception and Thought in Their Constructive Aspects* (1942), although written over 30 years ago, is interesting in its application to perception and emotions. Ayres' book, *Sensory Integration and Learning Disorders* (1972), has a short section on the vestibular system and numerous references for treatment. *Myotatic, Kinesthetic, and Vestibular Mechanisms*, edited by de Reuck and Knight (1967), is quite elaborate and detailed. It is superb for occupational therapists and physical therapists. *The Vestibular System*, edited by Naunton (1975), the proceedings of a 1973 symposium, has excellent articles on anatomy and physiology as well as vestibular examination and diseases of the peripheral and central nervous systems. Mountcastle's *Medical Physiology* (1979) is one of many physiology texts that are quite complex and include considerable detailed material.

Background

ANATOMICAL ORGANIZATION
Semicircular canals

Anatomically the vestibular apparatus or membranous labyrinth, is made up of five components: the three semicircular canals, the saccule, and the utricle. The anatomical relationship of the external, middle, and inner ears is illustrated in Fig. 3-1. The three semicircular canals are in planes at right angles to each other. The canals primarily register movement of the head or the body in any plane or combination of planes. An easy way to visualize these three canals is by using the hands as a model (Fig. 3-2). Hold one hand open with palm up. Place the other hand, with fingers held at a 90-degree angle to the palm, on top of the first hand. The flat hand represents the horizontal or lateral, which reacts to rotation around the central body axis. The fingers represent the anterior or inferior canal, which reacts to ro-

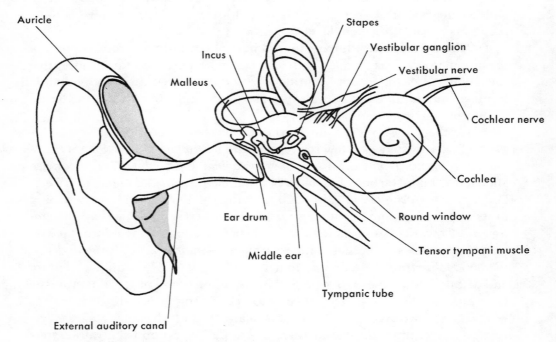

Fig. 3-1. The anatomical relationships of the external, middle, and inner ears.

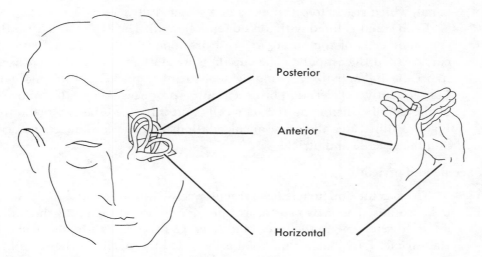

Fig. 3-2. The hands can be placed in a specific way to illustrate the positions of the semicircular canals.

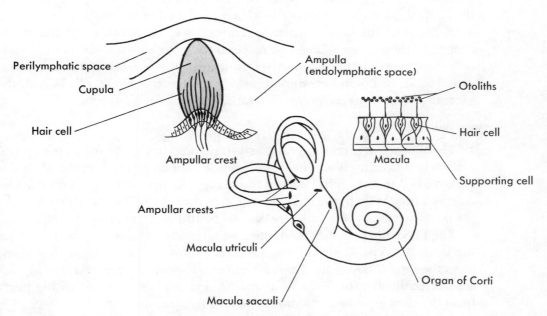

Fig. 3-3. The ampullar crest is the receptor mechanism of the semicircular canals. The macula is the receptor mechanism of the saccule and utricle. The organ of Corti is the auditory receptor.

tation as in rolling. The palm of the hand represents the vertical or posterior canal, which reacts to rotation, as in a somersault.

Each canal is filled with a fluid (endolymph). The Type I and Type II sensory hair cells of the ampullar crest are found in the enlarged end of the canal called the ampulla. The cupula is a gelatinous mass that encases the hair cells and acts like a swinging door to any movement of the endolymph. Consequently, acceleration or deceleration produces the greatest movement of the cupula, distorting the hair cells and initiating the sensory impulse. Fig. 3-3 illustrates the anatomical relationships of the semicircular canals and the saccule and utricle.

Saccule and utricle

The saccule and utricle have receptor cells similar to those in the semicircular canals. These two structures provide information about the body position in reference to the force of gravity. The saccule is smaller in size than the utricle. Each has a thickened area called the macula. The macula contains the sensory hair cells, which project up through a gelatinous mass in which are embedded calcium carbonate crystals called otoconia. When the head position is suddenly changed, the otoconia bend the hair cells, which initiate the nerve impulse. Since gravity constantly pulls on the otoconia, the central nervous system is constantly informed about spatial orientation of the head or tilt in any direction. Hair cells in the saccule are mostly arranged in the vertical plane and respond to linear side-to-side motion. Hair cells in the utricle are primarily arranged in the horizontal plane and respond to linear up-and-down motion. A combination of hair cells in both the saccule and utricle responds to forward and backward motion.

Sensory neuron

The sensory neuron is bipolar, and the cell bodies are found in the vestibular (Scarpa's) ganglion. The fibers from the superior and horizontal canals are grouped in the rostral part of the nerve. The neurons from both the saccule and utricle lie in the caudal portion of the nerve. The contribution from the posterior canal is found between the rostral and caudal portions.

The nerve fibers are divided into a small group of large-size neurons coming from the type I hair cells and a large group of small-size fibers coming from the type II hair cells. These fibers from the canals are separated in their central pathway. The large and small fibers are also present in the nerve from the utricle and saccule but appear to be intermingled.

Central termination

The neurons from the canals bifurcate into ascending and descending branches as they enter the area of the lateral vestibular nucleus. The ascending branch extends to the superior vestibular nucleus and on to the cerebellum. The descending branch gives off collaterals to the medial vestibular nucleus and to the ventral part of the lateral nucleus.

The termination of the neurons arising from the superior and horizontal canals is different from that of the neurons arising from the posterior canal. The superior and horizontal canal neurons end in the rostral and ventral area of the superior nucleus. The posterior canal neurons end in the caudal and central part of the superior nucleus.

There is also a different termination of neurons in the medial vestibular nucleus. The posterior canal neurons end more dorsally than those of the other two canals. One explanation for the similar terminations of the superior and horizontal canals is that the horizontal canal is a more recent phylogenic development and is derived from the older superior canal.

The ascending branch of the utricular neurons ends in the ventral part of the lateral nucleus and the rostral part of the medial nucleus. The descending branch ends predominately in the medial nucleus.

The saccular neurons terminate in the ventral portion of the lateral nucleus and in the medial nucleus. Some of these fibers may connect backward to the dorsal cochlear nucleus.

The fibers that extend on to the cerebellum are believed to end in the flocculus, nodulus, and the fastigial nuclei. There is increasing evidence that fibers may also end in the ventral paraflocculus and the ventral part of the uvula (Walberg, 1975).

PHYSIOLOGICAL ORGANIZATION

It seems more advantageous to discuss the vestibular nuclei (Fig. 3-4) and their input and projections from a functional standpoint. Knowledge of the function of the vestibular nuclei is more important to the practitioner than knowledge of the anatomy.

Vestibular nuclei

Lateral nucleus. The lateral nucleus (Deiters') is generally divided into a ventral part, which receives input from the utricle, saccule, and the semicircular canals, and a dorsal part, which receives only minor input from these structures. The major input to the dorsal part is from the somatosensory receptors directly or from relays through the cerebellum.

The somatosensory input comes from both high- and low-threshold cutaneous neurons and group II and III fibers in muscle nerve. Apparently, there is little input from either Golgi tendon organs or muscle spindles. These two receptors will be discussed in detail in Concept 5. Lastly, the input from joint receptors seems quite effective in influencing activity in this nucleus (Wilson, 1975).

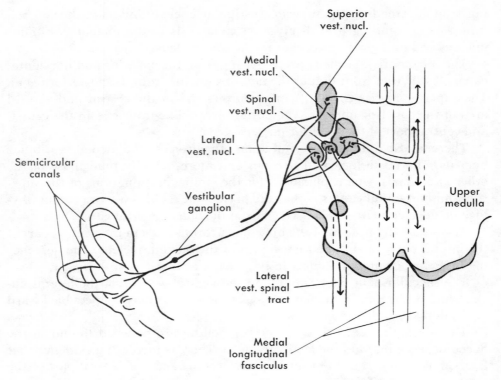

Fig. 3-4. The vestibular nuclei and their projections.

There does not seem to be a somatotopic organization of the direct somatosensory input to this nucleus. However, the somatosensory input by way of the cerebellum does introduce a somatotopic organization to this nucleus.

Pompeiano and Brodal's (1975) initial anatomical study in the cat showed a definite somatotopic organization of the lateral nucleus. Briefly the cells arising in the dorsocaudal region project to lumbosacral levels and are identified as L cells. Those cells in the ventral half of the lateral nucleus are C cells, which project to cervicothoracic levels and outnumber the L cells. Recent investigations indicate that there are a large number of CL cells. These CL cells seem to innervate both cervical and lumbar levels and may afford a degree of coordination between the limbs (Wilson, 1975).

The descending outflow from the lateral nucleus is by way of the lateral vestibulospinal tract. The influence of this tract is on motoneurons from cervical to sacral levels of the cord. The termination of these fibers is in the ventral horn of gray matter in the entire lamina VIII and adjoining medial and central parts of lamina VII. A few fibers are seen in lamina IX and the ventral part of lamina VI. In the thoracic cord a few fibers terminate around motoneurons of the ventromedial group.

There is a lack of evidence to indicate that the lateral vestibulospinal neurons actually end on the cell bodies of motoneurons in lamina IX. However, it has been well established that dendrites of these motoneurons extend into both laminae VII and VIII, which would afford monosynaptic connections. It seems that the majority of the tract neurons terminate on interneurons in the two laminae, which then synapse with lamina IX motoneurons. This organization allows extensive interplay of vestibular input onto spinal reflex pathways.

Generally, stimulation of the lateral vestibular nucleus produces monosynaptic excitation in extensor motoneurons of the upper cervical, thoracic, and to a slight degree, lumbosacral cord. This effect is strongest to motoneurons supplying neck muscles, emphasizing the important relationship between the membranous labyrinth, the vestibular nuclei, and the neck muscles.

The impulses in these tracts exert a tonic excitatory effect on postural tonus through the spinal extensor mechanisms. Both alpha and fusimotor (gamma) motoneurons are affected. The effect on the fusimotor motoneurons is more conspicuous on the static fibers than on the dynamic ones. Since the static fibers appear to maintain muscle spindle firing during muscle contraction there seems to be a coactivation linkage of alpha and fusimotor motoneurons (P. B. C. Matthews, 1972). The full importance of this nucleus and tract should be appreciated as Concepts 4 and 5 are presented.

Medial nucleus. The medial vestibular nucleus is less specifically organized than the lateral nucleus. The neurons are influenced by input from the semicircular canals as well as from the otolith receptors. The cells are also influenced by input from the cerebellum, primarily the fastigial nucleus and the nodulus and flocculus. The somatosensory input is predominately from the joint receptors affected by movement of the neck, from the vertebral column, and from the proximal joints of the limbs. The primary endings from the muscle spindle appear to have no effect, while the Golgi tendon organs can influence the activity of the nucleus slightly.

The descending outflow of the medial vestibular nucleus is the medial vestibulospinal tract. The fibers of this tract descend within the medial longitudinal fasciculus. The pathway is bilateral to midthoracic levels. The ipsilateral fibers in this tract far outnumber the contralateral fibers (there are many more fibers descending on the same side of the cord than on the opposite side). The fibers themselves are smaller, and the tract as a whole is much smaller than the lateral vestibulospinal tract.

The fibers in the medial tract terminate in the dorsal half of lamina VIII and the medial part of lamina VII. No fibers end on the soma of motoneurons in lamina IX. The monosynaptic effect therefore is probably by way of synapses with the dendrites of the motoneurons. The area of termination is much less than for the lateral vestibulospinal tract.

Since those fibers are restricted to the upper cord, it may be assumed that functionally they are concerned with the tone in neck muscles and head position. Many of these neurons bifurcate, sending ascending branches up to eye muscle motor nuclei and descending branches down to cervical levels. This provides an anatomical structure for coordination of vestibular input, conjugate eye movements, and suitable head positioning.

Functionally it appears that stimulation of the medial vestibular nucleus produces monosynaptic inhibition of neck extensor motoneurons. This tract is involved with axial musculature and not forelimb or hindlimb motoneurons. There does appear to be a balance of excitation by the lateral vestibulospinal tract and inhibition by the medial vestibulospinal tract. It seems important to emphasize here that a balance between excitation and inhibition is the critical element in function. Frequently clinicians seem to overemphasize excitation at the expense of inhibition. It has been our clinical experience that when emphasis is placed on inhibiting the unwanted action, the desired action is allowed to operate.

The rostral medial nucleus is also an important relay nucleus in vestibulo-ocular reflex arcs. There are three nuclei that control the movements of the eye. The rostral medial vestibular nucleus projects to the contralateral (opposite) abducens nucleus, to the contralateral trochlear nucleus, and to both the ipsilateral (same) and contralateral oculomotor nuclei. All these connections appear to be excitatory monosynaptic ones.

The following may help to clarify the motor innervation of the extraocular muscles of the eye:

1. The abducens nucleus supplies the lateral rectus muscle.
2. The trochlear nucleus supplies the superior oblique muscle.
3. The oculomotor nucleus supplies the medial rectus, superior rectus, inferior rectus, inferior oblique, and levator of the eyelids.

The motoneurons for each of the muscles supplied by the oculomotor nucleus are arranged in groups and in a specific organization.

There is an ipsilateral inhibitory connection between the rostral medial nucleus and the abducens nucleus. This connection tends to confuse somewhat the function of the medial nucleus. It is important to be aware that the information presented concerning this nucleus was obtained from study of cats and rabbits. One can only speculate that a similar condition exists for man. However, it is difficult to find substantiating research or data.

The medial nucleus appears to have a large projection to the viscera. This connection would be responsible for the autonomic reactions of nausea, vomiting, and pallor associated with motion sickness.

Superior nucleus. The superior nucleus, along with the rostral medial nucleus, is responsible for all projections to extraocular neurons. The superior nucleus gives rise to commissural and reticular fibers, but very little is known of their function.

The labyrinthine input to this nucleus comes primarily from the semicircular canals; however, physiological studies indicate there is input from cells that respond to horizontal or vertical acceleration and deceleration. The vestibulocerebellar circuits (nodulus, uvula, and flocculus) send many fibers into this nucleus as a means of modulating its activity.

The fibers from this nucleus pass into the ipsilateral medial longitudinal fasciculus to ascend to nuclei supplying the extraocular muscles. The termination of the fibers is extensive, bilateral, and overlaps with that from the rostral medial nucleus. Functionally, these two pathways provide excitation from the medial nucleus and inhibition from the superior nucleus to the oculomotor nuclei. A similar arrangement may exist for the abducens and trochlear nuclei. This is extremely important since any movement of the eyes is going to require an extensive coordination of facilitation and inhibition of all muscles controlling the eye.

Descending nucleus. The descending nucleus has not been studied as extensively as the other nuclei. It does receive input from the semicircular canals and the utricle. In fact, the strongest response to lateral tilt is observed in the rostral part of this nucleus.

There is physiological evidence that this nucleus sends fibers into the medial vestibulospinal tract, which affords an influence at spinal cord levels. There is a projection also to the cerebellum. It is not known whether these fibers are excitatory or inhibitory.

Finally, all of the vestibular nuclei project fibers into the reticular formation from which arises the reticulospinal tract. Functionally it seems that the reticulospinal tract is opposite to the lateral vestibulospinal tract, providing another reciprocal mechanism to control motoneurons. Table 2 summarizes the vestibular nuclei according to input, output, termination, and function.

Practical application

SCREENING VESTIBULAR FUNCTION

The practical application of this concept is encountered when screening vestibular function in infants, children, and adults.

Table 2. Vestibular nuclei function

Nucleus	Input	Output	Termination	Function
Lateral				
Ventral	Semicircular canals	Lateral vestibulo-spinal tract	Cervical (monosynaptic) to lumbar segments (trisynaptic) Lamina VII and VIII Dendritic to IX	Excitatory influence on extensor alpha and fusimotor neurons (coactivation)
Dorsal	Somatosensory—direct (spinovestibular) High and low threshold II and III muscle nerve Somatosensory—cerebellum	Ascending	Higher levels	
		Horizontal	Opposite vestibular nerve	
Medial				
Rostral	Semicircular canals Utricle	Opposite medial longitudinal fasciculus	Opposite abducens and trochlear Bilateral oculomotor Ipsilateral abducens	Excitation of extraocular motor neurons Inhibition ipsilateral lateral rectus muscle
Caudal part	Semicircular canals Utricle Saccule Cerebellum Somatosensory—joint receptors, neck, vertebral column, proximal limb	Medial vestibulo-spinal tract	Bilaterally to midthoracic Lamina VII and VIII Dendritic connect to lamina IX	Inhibition to extensor muscle in neck and thorax (Reciprocal between lateral and medial tracts)

	Input	Efferent Tract	Projection	Effect
Superior	Semicircular canals Utricle and saccule (physiological study evidence) Cerebellum	Ascending: Medial longitudinal fasciculus (ipsilateral)	Ipsilateral abducens Bilateral oculomotor Bilateral trochlear (overlaps with rostral medial nucleus)	Inhibition of extraocular muscles (Reciprocal pattern with rostral medial nucleus)
		Descending: Pontine reticulospinal tract Medullary reticulo-spinal tract	Cervical to lumbar segments Cervical to lumbar segments	Excitation to flexor alpha and fusimotor neurons Inhibition to flexor and extensor motoneurons
Descending	Semicircular canals Utricle Saccule Cerebellum	Contributes to medial vestibulospinal tract	Cervical to midthoracic segments Lamina VII and VIII Dendritic to lamina IX	Simultaneous activation of alpha and fusimotor neurons Excitation of flexor Inhibition of extension
	Somatosensory Reticular formation	Pontine and medul-lary reticulospinal tract	Cervical to lumbar segments	Same as superior nucleus

Infants

It is known from embryological studies that the peripheral organ of equilibrium is anatomically fully differentiated and mature in the embryo at mid term, that is, 9 to 21 weeks. It is also known that the medial longitudinal fasciculus is myelinated and functional at full term, which is 38 to 42 weeks.

Reviewing the literature on vestibular stimulation becomes an enjoyable but overwhelming experience. We have chosen only a few articles to substantiate what we think are important ideas. The most basic idea is that at the time of birth infants have the structure and functional ability to demonstrate nystagmus when rotated or when given a caloric test. The second idea is that the absence of the normal response of nystagmus is indicative of an immature nervous system, as is seen in prematurity, or of a deficit in either structure or function.

Lawrence and Feind. Lawrence and Feind (1953) tested 64 newborn infants. They were all healthy and were considered normal. Their ages were from 3 hours to 10 days. Sex and cultural background were not considered. Caloric tests were found to be unsatisfactory because of the small external canal and apparent discomfort demonstrated by crying and tightly closed eyes, which made observation impossible.

The infants were placed supine with the head extended 60 degrees from the frontal plane of the body in order to place the lateral semicircular canal in the plane of rotation. The electrically driven turntable was rotated ten times in 20 seconds and braked to a stop. After a 3- to 5-minute rest period the rotation was repeated in the opposite direction.

Nystagmus to acceleration and deceleration was observed in 100% of the 64 cases. It was variable in rate and intensity, but its direction was always parallel to the plane of rotation. The duration of postrotational nystagmus varied from 3 to 35 seconds. In any individual infant the duration was equal or within a few seconds in either direction. Skin flushing, eructation, and voiding were frequent during the rotation.

Eight infants were rotated when asleep as well as awake. None of the infants showed postrotational nystagmus while asleep.

Lawrence and Feind also reviewed the literature on adults and found no study comparable to theirs. The impression at that time, however, was that the infant's amplitude of nystagmus is greater, frequency slower, and duration shorter than the nystagmus of adults.

The caloric test may be done by using cold water, warm water, or both. The procedure is to place the subject supine with the head tilted 60 degrees from the upright in order to stimulate the horizontal canal. Cold water at 30° C is placed in the external auditory meatus. The convection currents create a flow of endolymph that distorts the cupula. Cold bends the cupula toward the ear being stimulated (ampulofugal), which inhibits the horizontal canal. Warm water at 44° C bends the cupula away from the ear being stimulated (ampulopetal) and facilitates the horizontal canal.

Eviatar and colleagues. Eviatar and colleagues (1974) studied 121 infants to determine the appearance of their vestibular response as demonstrated by nystagmus following torsion swing stimulation and ice-cold caloric stimulation. Thirty-two infants were designated as being small for gestational age (SGA); seven were preterm (34- to 37-weeks gestation), and 25 were full term (38- to 42-weeks gestation). Eighty-one infants were of weight appropriate for gestational age (AGA); four were preterm, and 77 were full term. Eight infants were full term and large for gestational age (LGA).

Eighty-three percent of the AGA infants responded with nystagmus to the torsion swing stimulation. Only 24% of the SGA infants responded. Sixty-nine percent of the AGA infants responded with nystagmus to cold caloric stimulation. Only 26% of the SGA infants responded. All of the LGA infants responded with strong nystagmus to both kinds of stimulation. None of the preterm infants showed nystagmus to either type of stimulation within 10 to 75 days after birth. Eviatar and associates concluded that "Neurophysiological studies indicate that the vestibular system is intimately connected with the proprioceptive, visual, and motor systems in the acquisition of developmental reflexes and postural control." They believed that vestibular responses (nystagmus) may be a sensitive indicator of central nervous system maturity.

de Quiros. de Quiros (1976) states that vestibular disorders and related postural disturbances can produce learning disabilities. He also states that vestibular disorders can be diagnosed within the first few hours or months of life, while learning disabilities frequently are not identified until the child starts to school. At that time a diagnosis of "minimal brain dysfunction" may be made on the basis of "soft signs."

de Quiros conducted his first study from 1958 to 1961 on 68 newborns. This study led him to conclude that, just as some children are born deaf, others are born with vestibular deficits and proprioceptive disturbances.

In a second study by de Quiros in 1962 to 1965, the development of 77 vestibularly disabled infants and 83 vestibularly normal infants was followed for 3 years. The vestibular diagnosis of all 160 children was done between 93 minutes and 7 hours after birth. The data indicated a syndrome of vestibular disability in the 77 infants with the four major characteristics of:

1. Vestibular areflexia to the caloric test
2. Delay of motor development
3. Walking instability
4. Speech delay

The interaction of adequate information from the body and the immediate environment is a fundamental requirement for the later development of learning, especially that kind of learning connected with human communication (de Quiros, 1976).

Children

de Quiros. Between the years 1958 and 1967 de Quiros studied 1902 children. His first two studies were presented in the previous section on infants. During his third study he found 52 out of 63 identified learning disabled children to have abnormal vestibular responses to caloric stimulation. However, in this study of normal, deaf, mentally retarded, and slow-learning primary school–age children, the caloric test did not differentiate the different groups. These data would seem to indicate the necessity of including both the caloric and a turning test when evaluating the vestibular proprioceptive mechanisms. de Quiros presents nine assumptions that may be used as a basis for the significance of his neurolabyrinthine examination:

Significance—"Learning how to learn," a phrase frequently used by educators in the field of learning disabilities, as a psychophysiological basis which is important also in the field of medicine. Physicians have a responsibility to appraise, at an early age, the mechanisms which might disrupt the learning process and to advise parents when therapeutic intervention could be useful. The significance of the neurolabyrinthine examination can be explained on the basis of the following assumptions;

1. The reflex activity of the body in relation to space provides the infant with information which enables him to maintain posture, to develop useful equilibrium, and in time to perform purposeful motor acts.
2. The nature of the mechanisms involved in maintaining posture, equilibrium, and purposeful motor acts can be assessed with greater accuracy when a neurolabyrinthine examination of vestibular-proprioceptive function includes caloric and turning tests.
3. On the basis of tests performed during the first hours of life, it is possible to predict whether or not neurological development will progress at a normal rate.
4. When vestibular, proprioceptive, cerebellar and visual disorders persist, learning disabilities may occur.
5. Young children have not yet developed cerebral dominance. In time, however, as body information is integrated and spatial relationships are established, automatic purposeful motor acts are in most cases relegated to the control of one hemisphere while the other hemisphere develops dominance in the control of communication skills.
6. If, however, normal development does not occur, dominance is late in being established. To the extent that voluntary control is needed to maintain posture, equilibrium, and purposeful motor acts, there will be a corresponding delay in the development of symbolic skills controlled by the dominant hemisphere. When body-spatial information predominates against symbolic work, progress

in symbolic learning at higher cortical levels is seriously disturbed. When the circuits available to handle corporal-spatial information are inadequate, circuits which should be used for higher problems are called into action. Higher level circuits then become overloaded with body information while correcting for lower circuit inadequacies. Thus higher level circuits are not free to fulfill their appropriate functions.

7. Language development, language internalization, speech, reading, writing, and other symbolic processes progress as the child is able to exclude from the conscious or awareness level a great amount of body information or external information transmitted through body perceptors.

8. Restlessness, poor posture, difficulty in sustained equilibrium, poor coordination of sequential movements, problems in selective attention, difficulty with spatial relations, and slow progress in the development of dominance and in learning to read and write are characteristics of many students with learning disabilities.

9. Identification of vestibular-proprioceptive disorders during early infancy could alert physicians and parents to the need for therapeutic intervention with these children at an early age.*

We think these nine assumptions have strong indications for everyone involved with early intervention programs. First, it is critical that vestibular-proprioceptive function be a key part in any evaluation. When vestibular-proprioceptive function is inadequate, normal development of dominance and symbolic skills is delayed. Higher circuits must be free from body information if they are to participate in language development as well as the symbolic processes of reading and writing. Attention to vestibular-proprioceptive disorders is the first step in early prevention of school failure. This relationship between body and mind will be expanded in Concept 9.

Ayres. As Ayres evaluated children with learning disorders, it became very evident that many of them possessed some problem in their vestibular function. In 1975 she began a study which resulted in the standardization of the Ayres Postrotary Nystagmus Test (Ayres, 1975). This test was standardized on 111 boys and 115 girls from 5 to 9 years of age living in Los Angeles County, California. All the normal children showed postrotary nystagmus, the longest duration lasting 24 seconds. All the learning disabled children showed a decreased duration of nystagmus, with 80% having nystagmus lasting only 6 to 15 seconds.

From the standardization data it appeared that the changes in nystagmus from one age group to another were caused by a sampling error. The data did indicate that a more precise evaluation can be made by using separate

*From de Quiros, J. B.: Diagnosis of vestibular disorder in the learning disabled, J. Learning Disabilities 9(1):39-47, 1976. Reprinted by special permission of Professional Press Inc., the copyright holder.

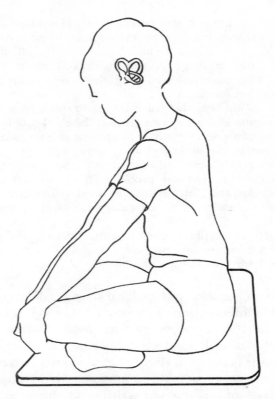

Fig. 3-5. The appropriate sitting position on the nystagmus board to place the horizontal canal in the optimal stimulation plane.

norms for girls and boys. The average maximal excursion of the eyeball in the normative group was a little more than 1 mm. The subjects with longer duration tended to have greater excursions. The evaluation of excursion offers less diagnostic value than evaluations of duration (Ayres, 1975).

In Ayres' test the child is positioned in a cross-legged sitting posture, with the head inclined 30 degrees. This places the lateral semicircular canal in the optimum position for stimulation (Figs. 3-5 to 3-6). The child is rotated ten times in 20 seconds at a constant velocity and stopped abruptly. The child must be instructed to keep the head inclined 30 degrees until the rotation stops. He is then instructed to lift the head and look off into the distance. Care must be taken that there is nothing for the child to focus on that would inhibit the nystagmus. The eyes should be kept open during rotation. It is wise to avoid doing the test on a patterned floor because of the distraction and the desire to focus.

The rotation must be smooth, at a constant velocity, and without jerks.

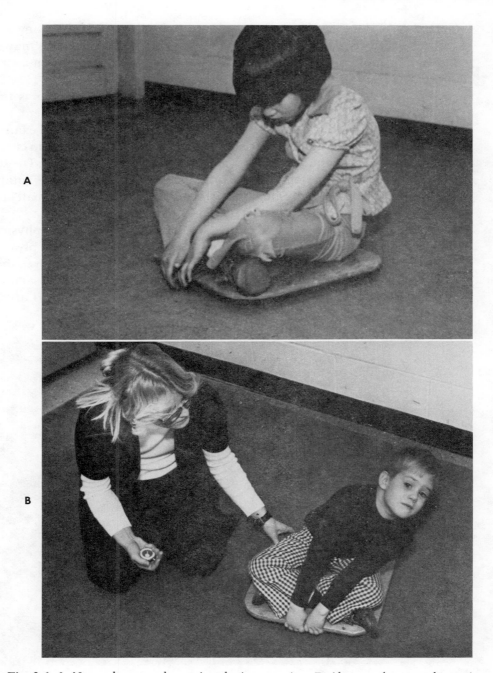

Fig. 3-6. A, Normal postural reaction during rotation. **B**, Abnormal postural reaction during rotation.

This may be done easiest by pushing on the child's knees or by using a motorized board (Fig. 3-7). If an adult is being rotated the pressure may also have to be applied behind the individual on the board to maintain a steady speed.

After the rotations are stopped, the duration of the nystagmus is timed with a stopwatch. The horizontal back-and-forth reflex movement is the postrotary nystagmus. When the nystagmus has stopped, the examiner should continue to watch the edge of the iris for at least 2 seconds in case the movement starts again. The duration of the nystagmus is recorded. The score is the sum of the durations after counterclockwise and clockwise rotation. Maximal excursion is estimated by observing the sweep of the eyeball and is recorded in approximate millimeters.

There are no norms for this test for the emotionally disturbed, physically handicapped, or mentally retarded child. However, this test does provide a valuable source of information concerning the integration of the vestibular system. Care in interpreting the results and implications is necessary since there are many structures and conditions that can contribute to atypical nystagmus responses.

Fig. 3-7. A, Motorized nystagmus board. **B,** Motorized nystagmus board with attachments to maintain correct body position during rotation.

According to Ayres (1976) there are three abnormal responses to the rotation. The first response is a depressed nystagmus, or hyposensitivity. Any duration less than 9 seconds for girls and 10 seconds for boys is significant.

The second abnormal response is a prolonged nystagmus, or hypersensitivity. A duration greater than 27 seconds for girls and 30 seconds for boys is significant.

The third abnormal response is an unusual pattern of nystagmus. It has been our experience that the unusual patterns come in myriad forms. The most prevalent pattern is a rotary rather than horizontal back-and-forth motion. We have found this most frequently with instability in the sitting position, loss of balance during rotation, and varying degrees of head tilt during rotation.

The second most frequent unusual pattern we have observed is motion that starts, then slows dramatically, but continues for several seconds. We have never observed a motion that stopped completely and then started again.

The third unusual pattern is a vertical motion instead of a horizontal one. It seems that the pattern drifts in an upward direction.

Some of the other responses that may be observed are

1. Nystagmus only to clockwise rotation or to counterclockwise rotation
2. Nystagmus in only one eye
3. Nystagmus of different speeds or excursions in the two eyes
4. Nystagmus in only one direction to both rotations

There are numerous physical manifestations of the rotation that should be observed. Because of the severity of some of these physical responses, we recommend stabilizing the individual with one hand around the back of the neck immediately on stopping the rotation. This prevents many individuals from falling off the board. It also makes it easier to observe the eye movement. The hand is able to evaluate the pulse in the side of the neck and the amount of swallowing, as well as the muscle tension. In this position the examiner can appraise many postural responses, such as the startle reflex, equilibrium reactions, and fluctuating muscle tone without being diverted from visual observation of the nystagmus. When these physical responses are intense, it is advisable to alert responsible adults to possible aftereffects for a period of several hours. Some of the typical aftereffects include nausea, sweating, dizziness, lack of attention or confusion, restlessness, or nightmares.

Heiniger. In 1976 Heiniger used Ayres' Postrotary Nystagmus Test as a part of a prekindergarten screening. All of the children were white. Most of the children were from middle income families. Their ages were from 4½ to 6 years.

Two-hundred and one children were available for evaluation. There were 106 boys and 95 girls. Eighteen of the 201 children refused to participate in the testing; 11 were boys, and seven were girls.

According to Ayres (1975), a score of 10 to 30 seconds for boys and 8 to 27 seconds for girls is within normal limits. These scores are approximately 1.5 standard deviations below and above the mean of the normative sample. Ayres indicates that the scores are significant only if below or above this 1.5 standard deviation.

Of the 106 boys tested by Heiniger, 22 scored below 10 seconds and were identified as being hyposensitive to rotation. Twenty-nine of the 95 girls tested scored below 8 seconds and were identified as being hyposensitive. In the prolonged range of scores, ten boys scored 30 seconds or above and were identified as hypersensitive to rotation. Sixteen girls scored above 27 seconds and were identified as being hypersensitive. Sixty-three boys and 43 girls scored within normal limits. From our experience, we would anticipate that the 18 children who refused to participate would probably demonstrate an abnormal response since they all evidenced lack of muscle tone, poor posture, or hypermobility in the screening observations.

A summary of the screening data provided these results.

1. There were 25 children, 15 boys and ten girls, who showed no nystagmus on the screening.
2. These same 25 children showed vestibular-proprioceptive disturbances in the form of hypotonicity of trunk extensor muscles, influence of symmetrical and asymmetrical tonic neck reflexes, or lack of stability in the all fours position.
3. On the *Santa Clara Inventory of Developmental Tasks* (Gainer, 1974) these children showed scores of 6 months to 1 year below their chronological age in the motor coordination area.
4. These children were all identified by either a special education teacher or speech pathologist as functioning 6 months to 1 year below their chronological age in visual, auditory, or language areas.
5. At the end of first grade all 25 children were available for a follow-up study. One boy was repeating kindergarten. There were two boys and one girl in the special needs classrooms. Two boys and one girl were in remedial reading classes. The largest number of children were receiving speech therapy—seven boys and five girls. There were two boys receiving help in two areas, and they were both in special needs classrooms. One boy was also receiving speech therapy, and the other one was in remedial reading class. A total of 17 of the 25 children required some kind of supportive service.

The results of this study appear to support de Quiros' assertion that vestibular-proprioceptive deficits herald human communication problems and learning disabilities.

● ● ●

We have developed some strong convictions as a result of observation of children in kindergarten.
1. Prekindergarten screening must include evaluation of vestibular-proprioceptive function.
2. Where vestibular-proprioceptive deficits are identified, an intervention program should be initiated immediately.
3. When speech and language problems are identified, the child should be referred for evaluation of vestibular-proprioceptive function.
4. When a child is identified as learning disabled, there should be as much emphasis and time spent on correcting the vestibular-proprioceptive deficits as is spent on the academic remediation program.
5. The individuals responsible for the vestibular-proprioceptive remedial program must have a thorough understanding and education in evaluation and treatment of these problems.

Adults

Heiniger and Randolph. It has been a frustrating experience to find so many abnormal nystagmus responses in normal prekindergarten screening. Seeing a large number of rotary patterns was especially disconcerting. The final frustration to the examiner was the children's inability to communicate precisely their reactions and sensations. For these reasons we felt obligated to investigate the responses of adults to Ayres' Postrotary Nystagmus Test.

Students attending our Tree of Learning courses were asked to participate in the testing. The participants included either practicing physical therapists, occupational therapists, speech pathologists, special education teachers, guidance counselors or undergraduate students of these professions. We thought it was important for the students to experience the test if they were going to administer it to clients. It also gave the students the opportunity to observe the reactions of normal adult professionals to the test.

As the normal adults were tested, it was evident that more information was necessary than was obtained with the Ayres record sheet. Thus began the development of a record sheet that included all of the aspects presented by the testing situation. Ultimately, the Nystagmus Survey Sheet (Fig. 3-8) was designed. The sheet is divided into six areas covering general information, the condition of the subject prior to testing, during testing, and immediately following testing, the aftereffects, and any significant learning problems.

```
                          NYSTAGMUS SURVEY

General information

Name_____    Dominant hand____  Dominant eye_____
Age _____ Birth date_____
Date of Test _____
Wears glasses_____ Type of correction_____  Degree_____
State of arousal (time of day tested)_____
Significant early developmental history_____
(Premature birth, diseases, ear disorders)
Feelings concerning motion
     Childhood _____
     Adult _____

Prior to rotation
     Sympathetic reactions
          Size of pupils_____
          Respiration rate_____
          Hesitation (anxiety)_____
          Sitting posture (head tilt, body tilt)_____
     Additional comments:

During rotation
     Body responses
          Head tilt_____ None_____ Slight_____ Pronounced_____
          Body tilt (Stable_____ unstable _____ )_____
     Additional comments:

                                        (Lt)                (Rt)
Following rotation                      CCW                 CW
     Duration of nystagmus              _____
     Excursion patterns
          (Constant, change, or rate irregular)_____
     Body Reactions
          Slight tension of neck and face   _____
          Head tilt                         _____
          Head/body tilt                    _____
          Extreme responses of head,
               body, and extremities        _____

     Sympathetic reactions
          Size of pupils                    _____
          Respiration rate                  _____
          Excessive swallowing              _____
          Sweat                             _____
          Pale face                         _____
          Nausea                            _____
          Pulse                             _____

After effects
     Type of After effects_____
     Duration of After effects_____

Significant learning problems (motor, language, educational  reading and/or math):


                                        Heiniger/Randolph
                                          Revised, 1977
```

Fig. 3-8. Individual nystagmus survey record sheet.

Review of the survey sheets showed a large number of participants with significant early histories, including breech delivery, prematurity, prolonged labor, repeated ear infections and high temperature, and allergies. Some of the early school problems included severe tension, difficulty in taking notes, poor eye-hand coordination, mathematics and reading difficulties, gross incoordination, and poor depth perception.

Prior to rotation the adult's sitting posture was much better than that of a child. During rotation the adults seldom showed head or body tilt, whereas many children showed pronounced head and body tilt with trunk instability. Following the rotation, adults showed a wide range of body reactions, from slight neck tension and twitching of eye, lip, or chin to severe startle reactions. The adults' sympathetic responses also showed a wide range, from minor pupillary changes to excessive swallowing, sweating, blanching of the skin, and nausea. The aftereffects ranged from a temporary loss of attention to prolonged nausea for as much as 4 to 6 hours.

There were a total of 131 adults tested, 115 were women and 16 were men. The age range of the women was 20 to 58 years and of the men, 20 to 36 years. The scores for the women ranged from 4 to 75 seconds. There were 32 women who fell within Ayres' normal limits of 8 to 27 seconds. There

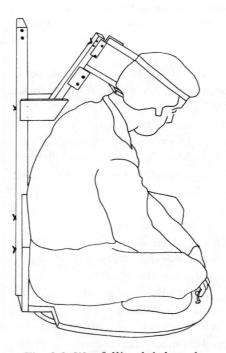

Fig. 3-9. Westfall's adult board.

were 81 women who scored above 27 seconds. The highest scores of 72 and 75 seconds were received by a 21-year-old woman and a 56-year-old woman, respectively. The score of 75 seconds was found in a 21-year-old woman, and the lowest score of 4 seconds was found in a 34-year-old woman.

The scores for men ranged from 18 to 50 seconds. There were five men who fell within Ayres' normal limits of 10 to 30 seconds. There were 11 men who scored above 30 seconds. The highest score of 50 seconds was received by a 33-year-old man. The lowest score of 18 seconds was received by a 22-year-old man.

This study seemed to confirm the connection between head tilt or unstable sitting posture and rotary eye patterns. Only a few adults demonstrated rotary eye patterns and corresponding head tilt or unstable posture. These adults expressed the fear that they were going to fall off the board. Neurophysiologically, the rotary pattern might be explained by the stimulation of a combination of canals instead of the isolated lateral canals that produce the horizontal nystagmus.

This study also helped to explain the second unusual pattern seen in children, in which there was a dramatic slowing but continued nystagmus. There appeared to be a direct connection between the change in frequency of the nystagmus and the point at which the adult felt reoriented in space.

A question of the normal duration of nystagmus for adults was raised by this study. It appears that there is a normal lengthening of duration as one ages.

An interest in investigating the relationship between age and duration of nystagmus was expressed by physical therapy students at West Virginia University. Westfall (1977) designed and constructed a manually operated turntable that maintained correct body alignment for the Ayres Postrotary Nystagmus Test. She tested 14 men and 20 women ages 20 to 30 years. The entire range was 14.0 to 51.5 seconds. According to the frequency distribution, the greatest number of subjects fell in the 19.5- to 29.5-second bracket. The mean duration for men was 32 seconds; for boys aged 7 to 9 years, 15 seconds. The mean duration of postrotary nystagmus for women was 32.8 seconds; for girls aged 7 to 9 years, 13.5 seconds.

Matthews (1978), using the same equipment and research design, tested 11 men and nine women aged 50 to 60 years. She found the mean duration of postrotary nystagmus for the men to be 51.0 seconds. The entire range was from 26.7 to 74.8 seconds. The greatest number of subjects were found in the 49.9- to 59.9-second bracket.

She found the entire range of postrotary nystagmus in women to be from 31.0 to 61.3 seconds. The mean duration for women aged 50 to 60 years was

48.3 seconds; for women aged 20 to 30 years, 32.8 seconds; and for girls aged 7 to 9 years, 13.5 seconds.

We are acutely aware of the small sampling in both of these studies. We would like therefore to encourage professional students to become involved in research on normal subjects during their academic education. If research problems, design, and equipment were compared between professional schools, a tremendous amount of necessary information could be obtained. In the process of gathering data, students could be taught good research methods and interpretation. It would certainly seem logical to expect that students who have participated in research on normal subjects would be more interested and more adept in research on abnormal subjects when they begin to function in a clinical setting.

This discussion of the Postrotary Nystagmus Test should not be construed as replacing the Ayres manual. Anyone involved in any way with nystagmus testing or vestibular stimulation should thoroughly understand the material presented in the manual.

KEY WORDS

abducens
AGA infants
ampulla
ampullar crest (crista
  ampullaris)
angular acceleration
bifurcate
  ascending
  descending
calcium carbonate crystals
caloric test
caudal
cerebellum
cupula
excitation
extraocular muscles

fluctuating muscle tone
habituates
inferior oblique
inferior rectus
inhibition
interneurons
laminae
learning disorders
LGA infants
linear motion
  acceleration
  deceleration
medial longitudinal fasciculus
medial rectus
monosynaptic
neurolabyrinthine examination

nystagmus
peripheral organs
phylogenetic development
rostral
saccule
SGA infants
somatosensory
startle reflex
superior rectus
trochlear
utricle
vestibular apparatus
vestibular mechanism
vestibular-proprioceptive
  deficits
viscera

Vestibular mechanism–position

position of the body

Concept	Practical application	Children
Background	Adults	Blood pressure problems
Interoceptors	Blood pressure problems	Physical handicaps
Parasympathetic response	Generalized relaxation	Learning disabilities
Tonic labyrinthine inverted response	Increased extensor muscle tone	Vestibular stimulation program

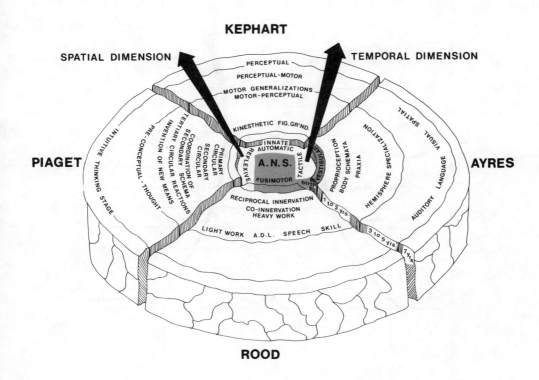

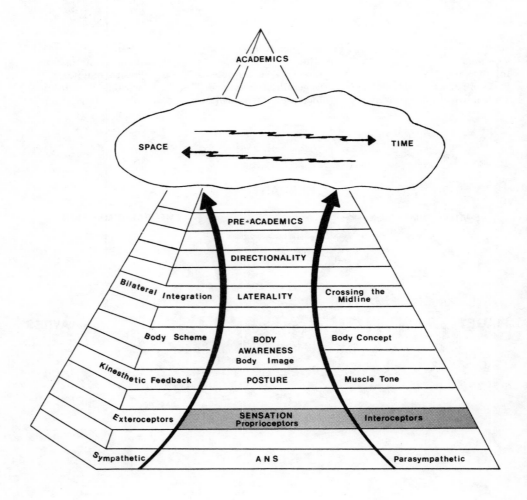

Concept   The position portion of the vestibular mechanism may be used in treatment by placing the individual in the inverted position. This position produces three sequential responses: (1) decreased blood pressure from carotid sinus stimulation, (2) decreased generalized muscle tone from fusimotor inhibition, and (3) increased fusimotor activity to key extensor muscles from the vestibular system. The third response lays the foundation for co-contraction.

On the **tree** the roots involved in this concept are the tonic labyrinthine inverted of the proprioceptors and the stretch root of the interoceptors. This treatment concept from Rood combines information from Gellhorn's (1967) ergotropic and trophotropic syndromes with Tokizane and colleagues' (1951) research on the reflex effects of the tonic labyrinthine reflex in the inverted (head-down) position.

On the **cross-section** this concept deals with the central core of the autonomic nervous system (ANS) and the effect of sensation on fusimotor activity to the muscle spindles of key extensor muscles. For many people this Concept and Concept 5 may present a completely new way of looking at problems of muscle imbalance. These concepts direct our attention to strong one-joint extensor muscles being used to achieve cocontraction. Other terms that are synonymous with cocontraction are stability, posture, and balanced muscle strength.

In the diagram of the **pyramid,** this concept includes the autonomic nervous system (ANS) step and the sensation step and extends into the posture step. The two components of posture are kinesthetic feedback and muscle tone. Without appropriate feedback from the proprioceptors, muscle tone is abnormal, and posture will be abnormal or inadequate.

Background

This is a relatively short concept. However, its shortness in length should in no way be construed as decreasing its value. It is a small unit of material but is very significant in the application of the Rood approach to patient management. It has been our experience that when the desired result is not obtained in the inverted position, there will not be a normal response to Ayres' Postrotary Nystagmus Test. Since the parts of the vestibular mechanism are so intimately interrelated, a deficit or malfunction in one part will undoubtedly influence the other parts. We have therefore made Ayres' Postrotary Nystagmus Test an integral part of any evaluation.

A second point to be made in reference to this concept is the introduction of interoceptors. At the present time these receptors are infrequently used in treatment. Unfortunately, many people are unaware of the tremendous influence of head position on autonomic nervous system activities, especially blood pressure. This concept was purposely written in the three step sequence to illustrate this dramatic effect.

INTEROCEPTORS

Interoceptors provide information about the internal environment of the individual. They are associated with the parasympathetic system in its function of maintaining homeostasis. These receptors are divided functionally into the categories of pain, chemical, pressure, and stretch.

As clinicians we must constantly be aware of the problem of pain and the response produced. According to Gellhorn (1967), pain generated by an interoceptor produces a trophotropic effect of inactivity, since a fight-or-flight reaction would be useless against an assault from inside the body. Pain generated by an exteroceptor produces an ergotropic response of fight or flight, which limits the integrative action of sensation.

The chemical interoceptors have considerable overlap with the special senses of taste and smell as they relate to the gastrointestinal tract. The chemical receptors involved with the composition of blood are undoubtedly useful in treatment procedures. For example, the technique of having a cerebral palsied child breathe into a bag for specified periods of time is believed to decrease the amount of athetosis by increasing the carbon dioxide level in the blood.

Pacinian corpuscles are found in the gastrointestinal tract and provide information about pressure. They undoubtedly play an important role in the total ingestive, digestive, and elimination process.

Two interoceptors that respond to stretch have received considerable attention from Rood (1970). The stretch of the bladder or detrusor muscle is involved in the micturition reflex; it will not be discussed here. The carotid sinus is presented in detail as it relates to the inverted position.

At least a rudimentary understanding of the carotid sinus as a stretch receptor (baroreceptor) is necessary. The receptor is found in the walls of the internal carotid artery. Structurally it resembles a Golgi tendon organ. Its afferent fibers are carried in the glossopharyngeal nerve (IX) to the bulbar vasomotor and cardioinhibitory centers. Efferent fibers from these centers establish a reflex feedback system to stabilize blood pressure and heart rate. Normally these fibers discharge at a tonic, slow rate. However, when pressure is increased in the sinus, the discharge rate increases, and a fall in blood pressure is produced. This fall in blood pressure results because activity in the afferent fibers inhibits the tonic discharge in the vasoconstrictor nerves, producing dilation of arterioles and decreasing cardiac output. It is important to understand that in cases of chronic hypertension the baroreceptor reflex mechanism is "reset" to maintain the elevated blood pressure.

PARASYMPATHETIC RESPONSE

According to Gellhorn (1967), in the head down position blood pressure declines. In cases of denervation of the carotid sinus the effect is absent; therefore it may be assumed that stimulation of the carotid sinus increases the activity in the trophotropic system. In Concept 1 it was stated that if the activity in any part of the triad (cortical, autonomic, or somatic) is altered, the balance of excitation and inhibition between the two systems shifts. When the activity of a single fusimotor neuron was recorded during and following a rise in pressure in the carotid sinus, there was a complete inhibition of fusimotor activity that outlasted the stimulation by several minutes. This decreased fusimotor activity must be responsible for the generalized decrease in muscle tone seen in the inverted position. The alpha fibers seem to be insignificantly involved in this reaction.

TONIC LABYRINTHINE INVERTED RESPONSE

The primary aim of the inverted position is facilitation of key muscles. The three responses, however, will occur in sequence; so their effect and relative merit must be constantly appraised.

The extensive physiological connection of the vestibular system to the neck and trunk was presented in Concept 3. Tokizane (1967) established a specific pattern of muscle facilitation from the vestibular mechanism in both the upright and inverted positions (Fig. 4-1 and Table 3).

Rood (1970) capitalizes on this inverted position for vestibular facilitation to neck and midline trunk extensor muscles, elbow and wrist extension for a protective parachute arm position, and hip and knee extension with strong plantar flexion by the soleus muscle in the lower extremity.

Practical application

ADULTS
Blood pressure problems

Providing the carotid sinus is functioning properly, even the slightest inclination of the head may produce a change in blood pressure. However, if the carotid sinus is malfunctioning, the normal regulation of blood pressure is absent when the head is inclined. This can be extremely dangerous for

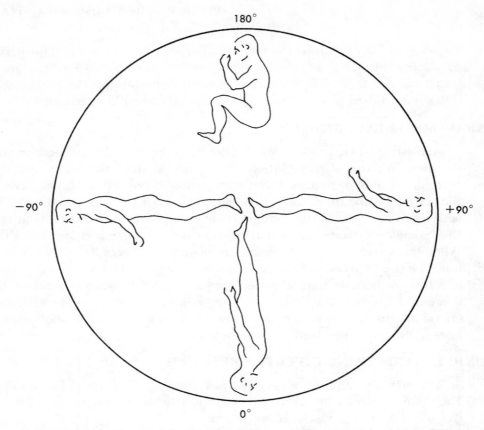

Fig. 4-1. Minimal extensor tone of labyrinthine origin in human beings is seen at an angle of 180 degrees, which corresponds to the upright posture, with the mouth cleft parallel to the horizontal plane. Maximal extensor tone of labyrinthine origin is seen at 0 degrees, which corresponds to the head down posture.

Table 3. Reflex effects in the tonic labyrinthine reflex*

Muscles	Position of the head	
	180 degrees	0 degrees
M. deltoideus	−	+
M. triceps brachii	− −	+ +
M. biceps brachii	+ +	− −
M. extensor carpi radialis et ulnaris	− − −	+ + +
M. flexor carpi radialis et ulnaris	+ + +	− − −
M. gluteus maximus	−	+
M. rectus femoris	− −	+ +
M. vastus tibilis	− −	+ +
M. vastus fibialis	− −	+ +
M. biceps femoris caput longum	− −	+ +
M. gastrocnemius	− −	+ +
M. soleus	− − −	+ + +
M. tibialis anterior	+ + +	− − −

*From Tokizane and others: Jpn. J. Physiol. **2**:130, 1951.

certain patients. For these patients it is important to keep explicit records of resting blood pressure, amount of inversion, length of time inverted, blood pressure while inverted, blood pressure when returned to resting position, and length of time until blood pressure returns to the original resting level. One should be aware of other signs that may indicate that the patient is suffering from stress. These signs may include flushed face, engorged (red or purple) nose or ears, ringing in the ears, difficult breathing, sweating, nausea, or increased pulse rate. When any of these signs are present, the person should be returned slowly to either the horizontal or sitting position. In subsequent inversions the degree or length of time may need to be decreased.

Patients who have had cerebral vascular accidents consistently show elevated blood pressure. This may result from the degeneration of the carotid sinus frequently associated with chronic hypertension.

How much of this degeneration of the carotid sinus is a result of lack of normal stimulation? The typical reaction of the individual who experiences dizziness, disorientation, or momentary blackout when bending over is to

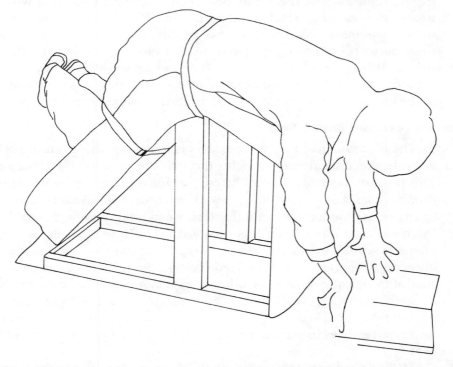

Fig. 4-2. Adult on inverted frame. Relaxation of arms is evident. Relaxation at knees may not occur unless lower legs are supported. Additional strap around thighs may be necessary only for additional safety.

avoid putting themselves in a head-down position. This may be the exact opposite approach to what is needed. When the carotid sinus begins to malfunction it might be beneficial to provide a regular schedule of inverted positioning. When are we going to appreciate and use natural stimuli as an approach to preventive medicine? An interesting speculation is do consistent practitioners of hatha yoga exhibit the normal ratio of strokes per age? If the ratio is lower, why is it? Would the inverted position (such as yoga's head stands and shoulder stands) be a possible early intervention treatment in certain types of hypertension?

Generalized relaxation

Sequentially, the second effect to occur in the inverted position is the generalized decrease in muscle tone through the fusimotor system. This is an excellent method for decreasing severe spasticity. Relaxation is especially evident in the spastic upper extremities (Fig. 4-2).

Because the carotid sinus is a parasympathetic receptor and activates the trophotropic system, there may be a visible calming associated with relaxation of muscle tone, which can be immensely advantageous for the patient with a traumatic head injury who exhibits combative behavior. Many of these patients become interested in and are physically able to perform activities in this inverted position that they cannot in the sitting position. One disadvantage of this second effect is the domination of relaxation and failure of the patient to pass on to the final excitation of extensor muscles.

Increased extensor muscle tone

The ultimate goal for most patients is the use of the inverted position to activate specific extensor muscles through the tonic labyrinthine reaction. This position is ideal for trunk strengthening for stroke patients. How often do we recognize the imbalance in back extensors? Do we stop to realize that spastic extensors on the hemiplegic side can, and many times will, inhibit the back extensors on the less involved side? How often do we recognize unstable scapulas demonstrated by winging on the less involved side? If one observes the patient in the inverted position carefully, the decrease in muscle tone of the spastic muscles is followed by a more balanced contraction when bilateral extension is called for in an activity. This same decrease in spasticity followed by a more balanced tone can be seen in both the upper and lower extremities in similar patterns. This will be further expanded in Concept 5.

The inverted position can be modified for any type of patient if the therapist exercises ingenuity. Such a modification might be hanging the head over the edge of the bed for the very elderly patient. Also it is very easy to reverse the patient's position on the tilt table. One of the most ingenious ways to invert a tall person is by putting a mat across parallel bars, placing the patient across the bars and then raising the bars until the patient is inverted to the desirable degree.

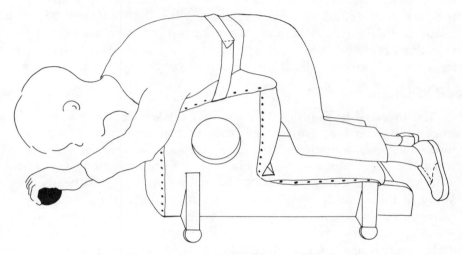

Fig. 4-3. Child at rest on tonic labyrinthine inverted board.

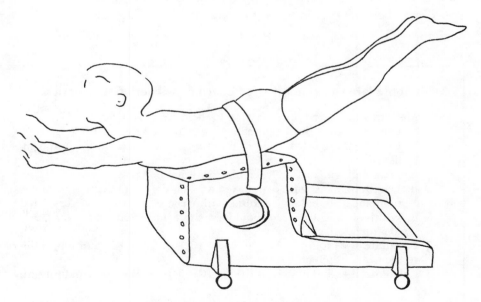

Fig. 4-4. Child in complete extension on tonic labyrinthine board.

CHILDREN
Blood pressure problems

In applying this concept to children we must also be cognizant of their blood pressure problems. Occasionally, there will be a child who does not tolerate the inverted position as evidenced by a flushed face and ringing in the ears. Some children may develop nose bleeds. We should be especially aware of the increased number of young children who are having cerebral vascular accidents. The traumatic head injury patient of any age must be treated with extreme care if there is any possibility of further bleeding.

Physical handicaps

The inverted position may be used for physically handicapped children to capitalize on the resultant decrease in hypertonicity or increase in the tone of extensor muscles where there is hypotonicity (Figs. 4-3 and 4-4). A word of caution: if these children lack equilibrium reactions, care should be used when changing positions because they may be posturally insecure. Many of these children will exhibit a strong Moro reflex, which is a light work, phasic extension movement of superficial back extensor muscles not the deep extensor muscles necessary for trunk stability. Contrary to immediate impressions, these children do need the inverted position to develop strong tonic contractions of the deep midline back extensor muscles. This idea will be further developed in Concept 5. A tonic labyrinthine inverted board may be constructed from the following instructions:

Tonic labyrinthine inverted board construction instructions

1. Measure and record the following to the nearest ¼ inch:
   a. Length of lower leg from malleolus to top of patella with leg straight
   b. Length of thigh from top of patella to flexed hip with hip and knee flexed
   c. Length of trunk from flexed hip to sternal notch
   d. Length of arms, with arm flexed at shoulder to 90 degrees from chest to metacarpophalangeal joints with wrist straight and fingers fisted
   e. Width of chest between shoulders with arms extended forward (add 4 to 6 inches to each side)
2. Calculate E as follows: $E = (0.866) \times (C) + A$. Round remaining fraction to the nearest ⅛ inch.
3. Calculate F as follows: $F = ([0.5] \times [C] + D) - B$. Round remaining fraction to the nearest ⅛ inch.

Corley, Randolph, and Wetherill, 1976

4. If ½-inch plywood is used, follow directions as stated. If ¼-inch plywood is used, substitute ½ inch for each − 1 inch as it appears in the directions.
5. Layout and cut two bottom boards from ½-inch plywood. They are G − 1 inch long and 2 inches wide.
6. Layout and cut one parallel knee board from ½-inch plywood. It is A + 1 inch long by G − 1 inch wide.
7. Layout and cut one perpendicular knee board from ½-inch plywood. It is B − ½ inch long by G − 1 inch wide.
8. Layout and cut one slanted body board from ½-inch plywood. It is C − 1 inch long by G − 1 inch wide.
9. Assemble with all boards fastened between the sides as indicated.
10. Cut off sharp edges of sides even with top of perpendicular knee board.
11. Cut balance boards from ½-inch plywood 2 inches wide by G + 4 inches long. Round top edges if desired.
12. Fasten a ½-inch thick pad G wide to both knee and body boards. The ends should wrap around to cover the ends of the boards.
13. Attach necessary restraining straps to hold child to board. Perhaps two to hold trunk to slanted body board and one to hold thighs to perpendicular knee board.

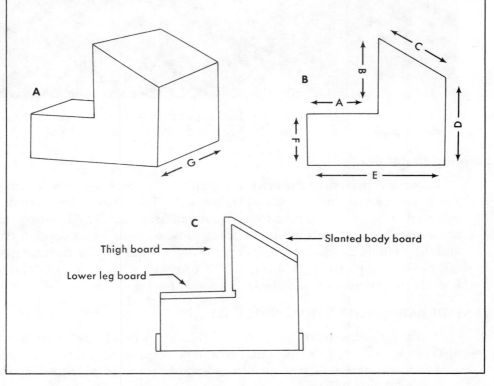

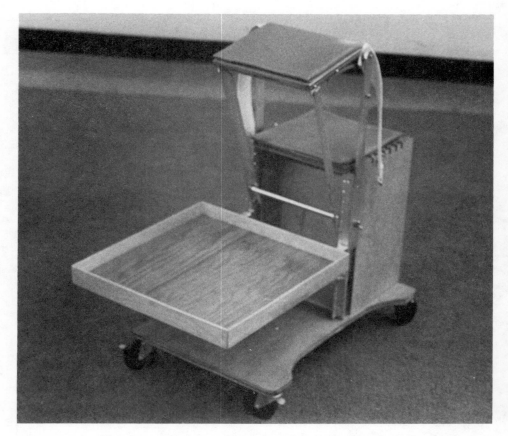

Fig. 4-5. Stilwell's adjustable inverted board can be easily altered to change the angle of inversion and the appropriate length required for arms, legs, and trunk.

Learning disabilities

Concept 3 presented the critical significance of an integrated vestibular mechanism for learning disabled children. As the system is integrated, the inverted position can be used to facilitate extensor muscles. The importance of having these strong midline extensor muscles in order to develop trunk stability will be developed in Concept 5. Figs. 4-5 and 4-6 illustrate an ingenuous table designed by Stilwell (1977) to position four to eight children quickly for therapeutic, academic, or recreational group activity.

VESTIBULAR STIMULATION PROGRAM

A vestibular treatment program should incorporate both Concepts 3 and 4. There are several principles that should be considered in any program.

1. Linear motion may be used in a forward-backward, side-to-side, or up-and-down direction.

Fig. 4-6. Stilwell's board may be used individually or combined for group activities for four to eight children.

Fig. 4-7. Children participating in body awareness activity on inverted boards.

Fig. 4-8. A variety of directions and equipment may be used to provide vestibular stimulation.

Fig. 4-8, cont'd. For legend see opposite page.

2. Angular motion may be employed in a forward direction as in somersaulting, sideward direction as in rolling, or around the body axis as in spinning.
3. Any motion must be interrupted frequently since the receptors respond to acceleration and deceleration.
4. Rotation around the body axis should be both clockwise and counterclockwise and be balanced.
5. The blood pressure and amount of relaxation must be monitored closely when using the inverted position.
6. Short periods of stimulation many times a day are better than one or two extended periods.
7. Stimulation that is initiated by the individual is more desirable than stimulation imposed on the passive individual.

Some equipment for vestibular stimulation is listed below.

Inside equipment
Linear (forward and backward, side to side, and up and down)
    Baby swing
    Johnny Jump-up (with appropriate shoes)
    Rocking or spring horse
    Molded animals on wheels
    Rocking chair
    Gymnastic or beach ball
    Hoppity balls
    Inner tube bouncer
    Hammock (single-point suspension)
    Scooterboard
    Trampoline
    Water bed
Angular (forward and backward, sideward, and around body axis)
    Sit-and-Spin
    Snow saucer
    Barrels or tubes
    Three or four inner tubes tied together
    Inflatables, all kinds and shapes
    Tilt board
Outside equipment
Linear
    Swing set, double or single suspension, tire, ladder, circle board, rope, Ayres platform, bolster
    Gliders
    Bench animal, two-seater
    Slippery slides
    Teeter-totters
    Rope
    Spring platform

Outside equipment—cont'd
Angular
    Merry-go-round
    Witch's hat
    Barrels, tires, inner tubes
    Monkey bars
    Jungle gyms
Positioning
    Tilt-table
    Beanbag
    Wedges
    Bolsters
    Inflatables
    Slant or prone board
    Tonic labyrinthine inverted board
    Hammock
    Footstools

A specific program is not outlined because of the tremendous variation of responses to stimulation. Specific records of the stimulation provided and the responses exhibited should be kept. Any adverse reactions should be analysed carefully to determine the cause-effect relationship. Frequently an adverse reaction will occur only once or at very irregular intervals. The presence of seizure activity or controlling medication does not preclude the use of vestibular stimulation. Stimulation of the severe hypotonic individual should be gradually increased to prevent overloading the nervous system.

In our experience, short periods of stimulation throughout the day appear to be more beneficial than one or two lengthy periods. Because of the potency of vestibular stimulation, the individual should be free to determine the intensity and duration. Stimulation should not be forcefully imposed on an individual. The apprehensive child may need to be held by an adult for beginning experiences. Extreme care must be exercised to prevent any injury to the child.

KEY WORDS

afferent fibers
baroreceptor reflex
  mechanism
bulbar vasomotor area

cardioinhibitory center
carotid sinus
detrusor muscle
efferent fibers

interoceptors
micturition reflex
pacinian corpuscles

CONCEPT 5

Muscle spindle and Golgi tendon organ

stability against gravity

Concept
Background
- Muscle spindle
  - History
  - Anatomy
  - Sensory neurons
  - Range
  - Comparison of function
- Golgi tendon organ
- Muscle spindle motor innervation

Practical application
- Definition
- Developmental sequence
  - Muscles into two groups
  - Body into two parts
  - Work into two limits
  - Function into four stages
- Evaluation

Media
- General principles
  - Area
  - Rate
  - Duration of stimulation
  - Type of stimulus
- Specific media

Treatment
- Treatment progression
- Everted foot pattern
- Sucking
- Dynamic sling
- Management

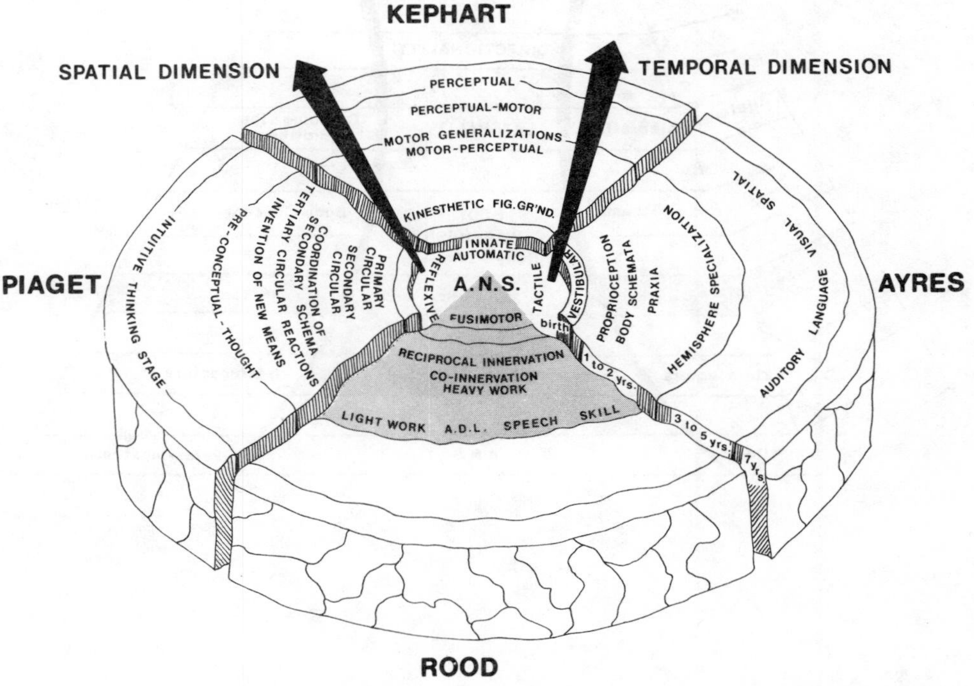

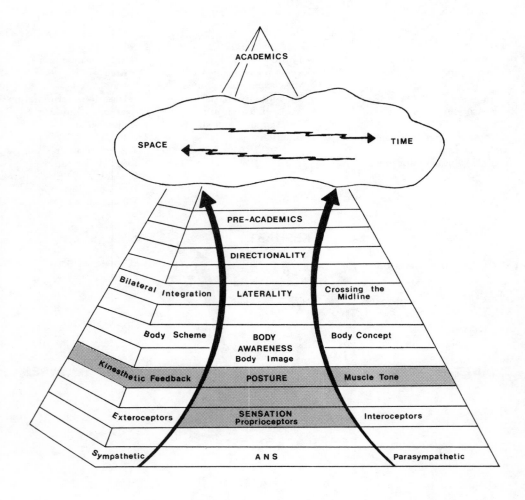

Concept   Strong one-joint extensor muscles can be developed in the inverted position. These extensor muscles are placed on stretch in their physiological maximally lengthened range to use their muscle spindles' second classical function, which facilitates the flexor muscles in a cocontraction pattern. The cocontraction should override the inhibition from the low-threshold Golgi tendon organs and provide the foundation for kinesthetic figure-ground.

On the **tree** the concept includes the muscle spindle root with its two components of nuclear bag and nuclear chain. The concept also includes the Golgi tendon organ (GTO) root but only the low-threshold component of contraction. The Golgi tendon organ component of stretch is a high-threshold protective receptor and is not involved in normal physiological motion.

This concept begins at the level of fusimotor activity on the **cross-section.** It extends outward to the level of skill with practical application of the Rood approach.

On the **pyramid** the concept includes the sensation and posture steps. On the sensation step the proprioceptors provide the muscle tone and kinesthetic feedback associated with posture. The muscle spindle and Golgi tendon organ are intimately interrelated in the maintenance of posture.

Background

MUSCLE SPINDLE
History

The muscle spindle is not a newly discovered neurophysiological phenomenon! To fully appreciate this, one must refer to a review of the literature.

Matthews (1964) wrote an excellent review in which Hassall is credited with first describing the small muscle fibers in 1851. In 1863 Kuhne called them muscle spindles by virtue of their shape. In 1888 Kerschner concluded that these spindles were sensory organs under motor control. After Sherrington's experiments and Ruffini's illustrated observations in 1894, the idea that muscle spindles are elaborately organized sense organs became generally accepted. As laboratory technology has advanced, more and more has been learned about the minute structure of the spindles. As we review the literature, we find evidence of a continuous shifting of hypothesis as to what structures are responsible for the two classical functions; however, these two functions have remained the same:

1. Stimulation of the muscle spindle produces facilitation of the homologous muscle and inhibition of the antagonist muscle.
2. Stimulation of the muscle spindle produces facilitation of flexor and inhibition of extensor regardless of which muscle is subjected to stimulation.

It is of interest to note that Matthew's review (1972) of the muscle spindle literature from 1964 to 1972 consists of a 630-page book. This book is very complete and well organized with a resumé at the end of each chapter. If the reader is serious about obtaining a good working knowledge of muscle spindle structure and function, the programmed text by Crutchfield and Barnes (1973) is an excellent learning tool.

Anatomy

We are presenting only the basic material on anatomy needed to understand this concept. The muscle spindle is a sensory receptor. This receptor is intimately involved in elaborate mechanisms regulating muscle length. As seen in Fig. 5-1, the typical muscle spindle consists of nuclear bag fibers named for their structural arrangement of nuclei in a bag in the center. The

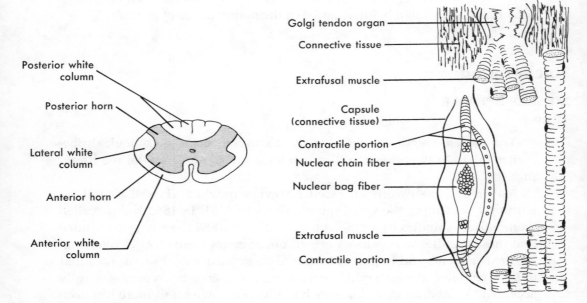

Fig. 5-1. Anatomical components of the muscle spindle, Golgi tendon organ, and cross-section of the spinal cord.

second component is called a nuclear chain fiber because the nuclei are arranged in a single chain. Usually the two contractile ends of the nuclear chain fibers are attached to the contractile ends of the nuclear bag fibers. The nuclear bag fibers extend outside the capsule and are attached to the extrafusal muscle fibers in a parallel arrangement. It is the extrafusal fibers that are responsible for doing the work of the muscle. The muscle spindle in no way contributes any force to this work.

Sensory neurons

Two sensory neurons carry information from the muscle spindle to the central nervous system (Fig. 5-2). The first neural ending is called a Ia phasic and originates in a spiral fashion from around the nuclear bag area of the nuclear bag fiber. It responds to a quick stretch anywhere in the range of the muscle and results in a quick contraction. The Ia phasic action, called the phasic stretch or myotatic reflex, is facilitory to its own muscle and inhibitory to its antagonist muscle.

The Ia tonic ending is a branch of the previous neuron. This ending originates in a spiral fashion around the nuclear area of the nuclear chain fiber. It responds to a maintained stretch in the submaximal or middle range of the muscle. Its action, the tonic stretch reflex, is facilitory to its own muscle

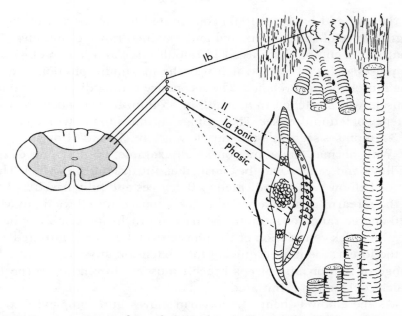

Fig. 5-2. Sensory neurons from the muscle spindle and the Golgi tendon organ.

and inhibitory to its antagonist muscle. Anyone unfamiliar with the difference between phasic and tonic stretch reflexes and mechanisms can find additional information in articles by DeGail and associates (1966) and Lance and colleagues (1966) and in the book by Lance (1970).

The II, or secondary sensory, ending originates in a spray fashion at the two juxtaequatorial areas of the nuclear chain fiber. This area is at the transition between the equatorial region and the contractile fiber. The secondary ending responds to a maintained stretch in the maximal or lengthened range of the muscle. For several years the II ending was believed to be responsible for the second classical function of the muscle spindle, facilitation of flexor muscles and inhibition of extensor muscles, regardless of which muscle was being stretched. Matthews (1969) postulated that the secondary ending was not responsible for this function. Undue alarm concerning this new development is pointless because, through the years, research has supported the original two functions. If future research disproves the function of the secondary ending, surely it will determine what structure is responsible for the second classical function. For our purpose the second classical function will be the result of a maintained stretch to the extensor in its maximal range, facilitating the flexor and inhibiting the extensor.

Range

Bessou and Laporte (1962) contributed to our concept of the functional significance of the submaximal and maximal range of muscles. They found that the Ia ending discharged 18 impulses/sec at a length of 47 mm and 37 impulses/sec at 61 mm, which was the maximum physiological length for the muscle being stretched. The secondary ending did not respond until the muscle was stretched to a length of 55 mm. It responded then with a frequency of 9 impulses/sec. The ending continued to fire with a peak frequency of 34 impulses/sec while the muscle was stretched to 61 mm.

With normal elbow motion as an example, the function of the sensory endings and ranges may be clarified as illustrated in Fig. 5-3. The fully extended elbow will be indicated as 0 degrees and fully flexed as 130 degrees. If the forearm is passively and quickly moved into flexion anywhere in the 130-degree range of motion, the triceps brachii muscle's Ia phasic neuron fires. A quick contraction or the phasic stretch reflex is initiated. Conversely, if the forearm is moved quickly into extension anywhere in the 130-degree range of motion, the biceps brachii muscle's Ia phasic neuron fires and a quick contraction is initiated.

As the elbow is bent, the forearm moves into complete flexion and the triceps brachii (extensor) muscle will be required to "play out" its longest, or maximum physiological, length. In normal range of motion this maximum range is believed to be approximately the last 20 degrees. Likewise, as the forearm is moved into complete extension, the last 20 degrees of motion will require the maximum physiological length of the biceps brachii muscle (flexor).

If a static or maintained stretch is applied to the flexor in its maximal range, facilitation of the flexor and inhibition of the extensor can be seen or felt. However, if a maintained stretch is applied to the extensor in its maximal range, a strange phenomenon occurs. In this situation the flexor is again facilitated and the extensor inhibited—the second classical function of the muscle spindle! If the extensor is sufficiently active to continue to contract despite the strong inhibition assailing it, we can produce a state of contraction or stability in which both agonist and antagonist are contracting equally. Clinically a strong active extensor muscle may be used to facilitate or drive a flexor muscle to contract with the extensor. This second classical function of the muscle spindle constitutes one of the primary theses of the Rood approach. Anyone intending to practice this approach must accept the hypothesis that *stability* is a result of a superiorly functioning extensor driving the flexor in a balanced cocontraction.

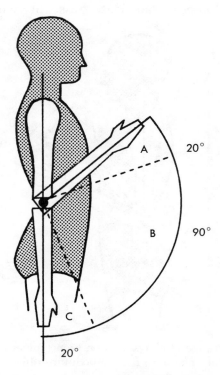

Fig. 5-3. Ranges of normal elbow motion. *A,* Maximum range for extensors; *B,* submaximum range; *C,* maximum range for flexors.

The submaximal range lies between the maximal range for flexor and the maximal range for extensor muscles. In the example of the elbow this range amounts to 90 degrees (130 degrees of total range minus 20 degrees for flexor and 20 degrees for extensor muscles equal 90 degrees of submaximal range). If a static or maintained stretch is applied anywhere in this 90 degrees to a flexor muscle, it will be facilitated and the extensor muscle inhibited. If a similar static or maintained stretch is applied to the extensor anywhere in the 90-degree submaximal range, the extensor muscle will be facilitated and the flexor muscle inhibited. This reaction is the tonic stretch reflex. It is through the tonic stretch reflex that excellent extensor muscles can be developed in the inverted position.

These three ranges exist also in the joint limited by spasticity. For example, the severely spastic individual (Fig. 5-4) with motion from only 100 to 130 degrees has the 30 degrees of motion divided into maximal range for flexor and maximal range for extensor with common submaximal range in the middle. There does not seem to be any arbitrary way of dividing the 30 degrees into the three ranges. The therapist can only experiment with the reactions to determine how the individual is functioning. Many times in treatment it will appear that there is essentially no submaximal range for

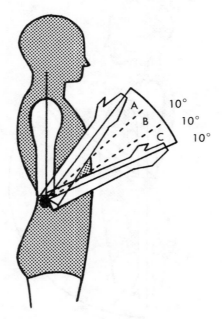

Fig. 5-4. Limited range of elbow motion seen typically in cases with spasticity. *A*, Maximum range for extensors; *B*, submaximum range; *C*, maximum range for flexors.

the extensor muscles. Regardless of how and where one moves the extremity, the flexor seems always to be facilitated.

Comparison of function

How do the individual sensory endings faciliate and inhibit muscle action? Consider first the activity related to the flexor muscle:

1. Quick stretch anywhere in the range fires the Ia phasic ending, facilitating the flexor and inhibiting the extensor.
2. Maintained stretch in the submaximal range fires the Ia tonic ending, facilitating the flexor and inhibiting the extensor.
3. Maintained stretch in the maximal range of the flexor fires the II ending, facilitating the flexor and inhibiting the extensor.
4. Maintained stretch in the maximal range of the *extensor* fires the extensor's II ending, facilitating the flexor and inhibiting the extensor.

Four different kinds of sensory endings were stimulated, and four different ranges were used for stretching. All four endings resulted in facilitation of flexors and inhibition of extensors (Table 4). If this is true, how can we justify neurophysiologically all of the stretching, passive range of motion, splinting, bracing, and positioning directed toward spastic or contractured flexor muscles?

Hooker (1952) grouped flexors, adductors, and internal rotators together into functioning units prenatally. What is true of the muscle spindles of flexors can be true clinically of adductors, internal rotators, and specific multiarthrodial extensors. These extensors include the gastrocnemius, rectus femoris, long head of the triceps brachii muscle, and superficial lateral back extensors.

Consider the pattern of activity produced by the muscle spindle of the extensor muscles when we stretch the extensor.

1. Quick stretch anywhere in the range fires the Ia phasic ending, facilitating the extensor and inhibiting the flexor.
2. Maintained stretch in the submaximal range fires the Ia tonic ending, facilitating the extensor and inhibiting the flexor. This is the range in

Table 4. Pattern of activity when flexors are stretched*

Receptor (in flexor)	Flexor	Extensor
Ia phasic	+	−
Ia tonic	+	−
II	+	−
II (in extensor)	+	−

*+, Facilitation; −, inhibition.

Table 5. Pattern of activity when extensors are stretched*

Receptor (in extensor)	Extensor	Flexor
Ia phasic	+	−
Ia tonic	+	−
II	−	+
II (in flexor)	−	+

*+, Facilitation; −, inhibition.

which extensor muscles must be exercised to make them superstrong by using their muscles' spindle facilitation.

3. Maintained stretch in the maximal range of the extensor fires the II ending, *inhibiting* the extensor and facilitating the flexor.
4. Maintained stretch in the maximal range of the *flexor* fires the flexor's II ending, facilitating the flexor and inhibiting the extensor.

Four different kinds of sensory endings and four different ranges are used for stretching; two facilitate extensors, and two facilitate flexors (Table 5). Extensor muscles must be very strong in their submaximal range in order for them to continue to contract in the maximal range in which their II endings are inhibiting them and driving or facilitating the flexors to cocontract with them.

In the Rood approach cocontraction means a balance of contraction between agonist and antagonist that produces a stable joint or stable posture. This stability must develop from the strong extensor muscles and not from a strengthening of the flexor muscles.

GOLGI TENDON ORGAN

The function of the Golgi tendon organ must be included in any discussion of muscle spindle activity (Fig. 5-2). The *low-threshold* Golgi tendon organ that responds to the tension of muscle contraction (Moore, 1974) presents an important and perhaps new dimension to our clinical observations. As soon as a muscle begins to contract, even one motor unit, certain Golgi tendon organs are fired, resulting in inhibition to that muscle and facilitation to the antagonist. Clinically, if an appropriate maintained resistance is applied in the submaximal range, then a maintained contraction can be produced and the inhibition from the Golgi tendon organ is overridden or prevented from dominating. This may explain why some patients can initiate skilled movements but cannot maintain the contraction because of the immediate inhibition from the Golgi tendon organ. Before we are trapped by oversimplification of muscle spindle and Golgi tendon organ activity, let us remember that whether or not a motoneuron fires is determined by the algebraic sum of all the facilitation and inhibition occurring at any given time.

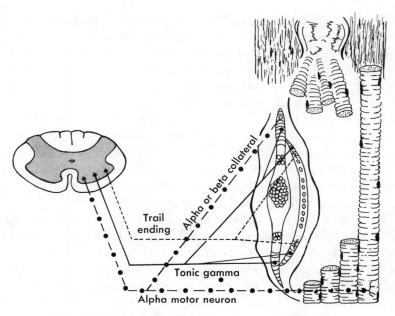

Fig. 5-5. Motor innervation to the muscle spindle.

This algebraic sum of 500 to 1000 converging signals occurs in fractions of a millisecond. We professionals must analyze the infinite possibilities available for manipulation of muscle spindle and Golgi tendon organ activity in our patients. The reader is referred to Houk (1974) for an excellent presentation of the complexity of feedback and peripheral mechanisms involved in the control of muscle and movement. Moore (1974) includes the various terms used to designate structures and nerve endings in recent years.

MUSCLE SPINDLE MOTOR INNERVATION

Three fusimotor neurons supply the muscle spindle. The fusimotor system was previously called the gamma motor system.

The first fusimotor neuron, according to Barker (1967), is called the tonic gamma and goes equally to nuclear bag and nuclear chain fibers. It branches in order to supply both contractile ends of both types of fibers (Fig. 5-5). Tonic gamma neurons have a platelike structure and may also be labeled P_2 endings.

The second fusimotor neuron is called the trail ending because it does not have a specialized motor end-plate but rather spreads out in a diffuse manner. This ending predominately supplies nuclear chain fibers. There is undoubtedly a functional significance associated with the fact that trail endings are supplying the same juxtaequatorial region from which secondary endings are originating. Could they be protecting the secondary endings from distortion until the maximum physiological range is reached?

The third fusimotor ending may be a beta collateral branch from the alpha motor neuron to the extrafusal fibers and may be labeled a P_1 ending. Some writers indicate that this ending is a beta-size motor neuron. The beta ending supplies mostly nuclear bag fibers.

There is a tendency to label the fusimotor neurons as either static or dynamic fibers, but the anatomical focus of these functions has not been determined. Impulses in gamma static fibers produce a marked increase in firing frequency of both primary and secondary sensory neurons from the spindle. Impulses in gamma dynamics produce no effect on secondary endings and a small increase in firing of primary endings (Moore, 1974).

The importance of fusimotor activity falls into three major areas. The first area of consideration is original sensitivity of the spindle and therefore of the muscle to stretch. Without tonic fusimotor activity, the muscle spindle will not be in a ready state capable of translating information about the length of the extrafusal muscle fibers into appropriate feedback signals. The muscles with insufficient fusimotor activity do not have stretch reflexes or they have hypoactive stretch reflexes.

The second area of consideration is in the realm of facilitation of alpha motoneuron or alpha "driving." By increased fusimotor activity the muscle spindle can be stimulated to set up the mechanism for alpha motor activity through the stretch reflex arc.

The third area of consideration is referred to as bias. During activity there must be appropriate adjustment of muscle spindle length and extrafusal muscle fiber length in both agonist and antagonist. As a muscle shortens, its muscle spindles must adjust, or bias, to the new length of the extrafusal fiber. Conversely, the antagonist extrafusal fibers must lengthen and their muscle spindles adjust, or bias, to the new longer length.

Let us consider the problem of spasticity in light of these three areas of fusimotor activity. A high percentage of spasticity is designated as fusimotor, or gamma, in origin. The excessive fusimotor input is "driving" the muscle spindle, keeping it hypersensitive, and through the stretch reflex arc, keeping the extrafusal fibers in a constant state of facilitation or contraction. As a result of the constant contraction of the spastic muscle, reciprocal innervation is providing constant inhibition to the antagonist motor activity. This inhibition interferes with the appropriate fusimotor activity and produces an antagonist muscle with hypoactive or zero stretch reflexes. As sensory input is manipulated to decrease fusimotor activity to the hypersensitive muscle spindles and to increase fusimotor activity to the hyposensitive muscle spindles, the contraction of extrafusal fibers can be altered and the bias altered.

At this point it is important to refer back to Concept 4 and the importance of the inverted position. One effect of that position was a generalized decrease in muscle tone through the parasympathetic receptor and the dominance of the trophotropic response on fusimotor neurons. This is an excellent means of decreasing the fusimotor activity to the hypersensitive muscle spindles in the spastic muscles. As indicated, the tonic labyrinthine input was from the vestibular system directly to the fusimotor neurons of the neck and midline trunk extensor muscles. As these muscles maintain their contraction against the maintained stimulus of gravity, the inhibition from the low-threshold Golgi tendon organ to contraction is overridden and the muscles become "super strong" in the submaximal range. This super strong label involves the dual concept of muscle spindle sensitivity and extrafusal fiber hypertrophy. The extensor muscles may be placed in their maximal range and the second classical function of the muscle spindle used to facilitate the flexor in cocontraction. Cocontraction provides the kinesthetic feedback that makes differentiation and the development of kinesthetic figure-ground possible.

Practical application

The value of any historical review is to identify changes in philosophy or technique or both. If such a review of Rood's approach were available, it would be very valuable. Stockmeyer's (1967) presentation is representative of the approach as it was practiced in the 1960s. The following material will include the dramatic changes in the approach in the early 1970s. The primary change was a shift from using exteroceptor sensory input to using proprioceptor sensory input, specifically the use of the inverted position and vibration.

The following information has been combined from courses and workshops presented by Rood in 1957, 1958, 1960, 1970, 1974, and 1975. To facilitate the organization of voluminous information, four developmental cornerstones have been identified. These cornerstones are dividing muscles into two groups, dividing the body into two parts, dividing work into two limits, and dividing function into four stages. These four elements must constantly agree and be implemented on the combined foundation of Concepts 1, 2, and 4.

DEFINITION

The Rood approach may be defined as the activation, facilitation, and inhibition of muscle action, voluntary (or somatic) and involuntary (or autonomic), through the anatomically intact reflex arc. Where there is insufficient fusimotor activity to the muscle spindle for a stretch reflex to be initi-

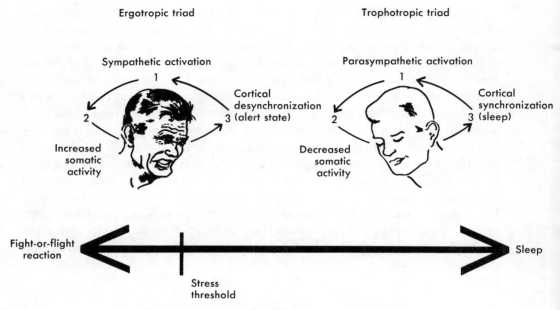

Fig. 5-6. Ergotropic-trophotropic continuum.

ated, activation techniques must be used. Facilitation techniques are employed whenever stretch reflexes are present but stronger contractions are desired. Of the three techniques, the inhibition techniques are definitely the most valuable. Clinically, it can be demonstrated that if appropriate inhibition is provided in the correct place, at the correct time, considerably less activation or facilitation is needed.

Manipulation of the autonomic nervous system was discussed in Concept 1. Techniques are used to inhibit sympathetic activity or to allow parasympathetic activity to dominate. The balance within the components of the triads (Fig. 5-6) are altered as well as the balance between the ergotropic and trophotropic reactions.

The anatomically intact reflex arc identifies the necessity of a sensory neuron carrying information into the central nervous system and a motor neuron carrying the impulse to the effector. Once inside the central nervous system the potential connections and pathways are limitless.

DEVELOPMENTAL SEQUENCE
Muscles into two groups

The principle of directional developmental sequence includes such components as proximal to distal, head to tail, gross to fine, and bilateral to unilateral to contralateral. During analysis of an infant's movements the sequence of flexion then extension, adduction then abduction, and internal rotation then external rotation also becomes evident. Combining this with Hooker's (1952) grouping of muscles prenatally, it follows that one group of muscles includes flexors, adductors, and internal rotators, while the second group includes extensors, abductors, and external rotators. As explained earlier in this chapter, the major functional difference between these two muscle groups is their responses to maintained stretch. The flexor, adductor, internal rotator group (group 1) muscles are facilitated by maintained stretch and their antagonist muscles inhibited. When the extensor, abductor, external rotator group (group II) muscles are provided with a maintained stretch in their maximal physiological length, spindle input will facilitate their antagonists or group I muscles. It was also explained in the background section that clinically the gastrocnemius, rectus femoris, and superficial lateral back extensors must be placed in the flexor group since they function in a similar manner.

A second functional difference between the groups is their responses to isotonic and isometric exercise. According to the study done by Ward and Fisk (1964), flexors require exercise both isotonically and isometrically if they are to function in movement and stability. However, the extensors require only isometric exercise to function in either activity.

The third functional difference is related to the muscles' efficiency. This idea will be elaborated in the section on dividing work into two limits. Here it is necessary only to understand that because of the muscle spindle function, the flexors operate more efficiently in a rhythmical and repetitive fashion using reciprocal facilitation and inhibition. The extensors function most efficiently when they can maintain a shortened contraction against a maintained stimulus such as gravity.

The fourth functional difference relates only to the extensors. According to McMinn and Vrbová (1967), the extensors must have stretch or resistance or both when they contract or the muscle will rapidly atrophy or degenerate. Such is the case with the soleus but not with the gastrocnemius.

The final functional difference relates to fusimotor activity. As one understands the function of the muscle spindle, it becomes evident that the extensor muscle spindles must receive their fusimotor activity first. This enables them to work against gravity with a maintained contraction in the submaximal range in order to develop the strength and sensitivity necessary for co-contraction.

Body into two parts

When the infant begins postnatal development, it becomes clear that the neck and midline trunk develop differently from the extremities. The sequential development of the neck and midline trunk will be discussed first. It is true that a newborn is in a position of flexion. However, initial volitional activity involves picking up the head or extending the neck while in the prone position. The extension of neck and trunk against gravity progresses in a cephalocaudal direction over a period of approximately 6 months to culminate in the Landau reflex, which is a tonic maintained midline extension of deep back extensor muscles. The Landau reflex inhibits the Moro reflex, which is a phasic movement of the more superficial and lateral back extensor muscles. Bobath and Bobath (1965) directed our attention to the fact that the Moro reflex disappears as the Landau reflex becomes dominant. The importance of this sequence is the development of the physiological cervical curve, thoracic extension, the physiological lumbar curve, and hip hyperextension.

As the cervical curve is perfected, the infant will be seen to shift into cocontraction (Fig. 5-7). This cocontraction involves changing the head position by "tucking" his chin in and looking directly down. This activity provides maintained stretch of the neck extensors in the maximal range, using their second classical function to drive the prevertebral neck flexor in cocontraction, and establishes neck cocontraction or stability.

As thoracic extension and the physiological lumbar curve are perfected, the infant will use the extended arms to push his body back over folded up legs. Thus the term "folded up all fours" is coined (Fig. 5-8). This position provides the maintained stretch of back extensors in the maximal range using their second classical function to drive the abdominal muscles in cocontraction and establish trunk cocontraction or stability.

As the lumbar curve is perfected it stabilizes the pelvis, providing a fixed origin for the hip extensor muscles. The legs are brought into hyperextension and held, developing very strong hip extension. In the preceding folded up all fours position the strong hip extensor muscles are placed on stretch in the maximal range using the second classical function to drive the hip flexors in cocontraction. Thus the folded up all fours position provides not only cocontraction of the trunk but also cocontraction of the hip joints. At this point stability in the neck, trunk, and hip has been accomplished.

The neck and midline trunk development now progresses from the horizontal cocontraction pattern into the upright or erect posture. In this position the proprioceptive input for cocontraction is lost because body weight (the force of gravity) is inhibitory to all muscles not put on stretch by gravity. The erect position involves a mechanical stacking of body segments. The muscles are stretched reciprocally as the center of gravity shifts from the midline. Because the erect posture inhibits cocontraction, many adults have developed poor sitting and standing postures. This is also the reason why it is absurd to place the patient that does not possess good neck, trunk, and hip

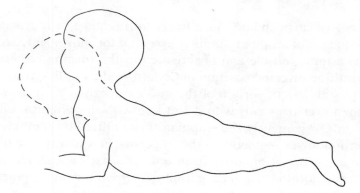

Fig. 5-7. Child prone with neck in extension followed by chin "tucked," which produces neck cocontraction. Both activities can be accomplished in the same body position.

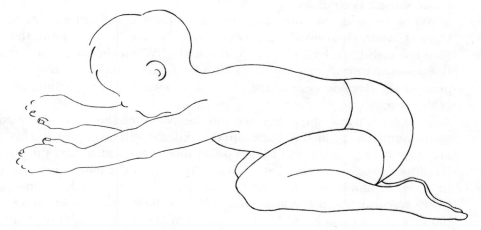

Fig. 5-8. Folded up all fours position stretches the back extensors, which drive the abdominals for trunk cocontraction at the same time they stretch the hip extensors, which drive the hip flexors for hip cocontraction.

cocontraction in a sitting or standing position. Because weight greater than body weight is facilitory to cocontraction, it is easy to understand why in countries in which it is the practice to carry heavy loads on the head the inhabitants demonstrate such enviable posture and carriage.

The extremities develop first in movement with the distal ends free. They move in a windmill fashion from the shoulder. Therefore it is very important that an infant who is not moving all four extremities freely and in the same patterns be provided with such experiences. The importance of the joint receptors in conscious awareness of position and movement will be discussed in Concept 6.

Since the arm should move freely in this stage, it is crucial to recognize the sequence of scapular stability essential for movement. The upper trapezius is a tonic muscle and is activated in the sucking pattern. In the tonic labyrinthine inverted position of Concept 4 the midline trunk muscles were seen to stabilize the origin of the lower trapezius. With the arm beside the ear, the lower trapezius is in direct line with the extended elbow and wrist position. Consequently, the scapulae are stabilized by combined action of the upper and lower segments of the trapezius. Frequently, one will observe the lower trapezius originating from only the sixth and seventh thoracic segments and nothing originating from the remaining four segments. This is not an anatomical anomaly but a lack of stabilization by the midline trunk extensor muscles. As the trunk muscles are activated to stabilize the origin of the lower trapezius, thin strips of muscle will appear until eventually the entire muscle is contracting.

When the arms are brought back along the trunk, with elbows bent so there is hyperextension and external rotation at the shoulder joint, the scapulae are stabilized by the rhomboid muscles. When the rhomboids are active, as in an unintegrated Moro reflex, they tend to inhibit the trapezius and prevent the development of the protective extension or parachute reaction of the arms.

As soon as trunk and arm extension is established the infant will push up on his hands. As he pushes back into the folded up all fours position his arms are supporting weight and the scapulae must be stabilized by the anterior serratus and smaller pectoral muscles. As soon as the hands and knees are involved in supporting the body weight, kinesthetic feedback becomes critical in learning about the body, and this lays the foundation for perceptual-motor skills. As trunk and hip cocontraction are achieved, the weight is automatically shifted forward in preparation for locomotion.

After the extremities have supported the body in the all fours position, the infant will progress to the upright stance. In Concept 4 the strongest effect of the tonic labyrinthine inverted position in the lower extremity was facilitation of the soleus, which undoubtedly contributes to the strong plantar flexion seen in the Landau reflex. Strong plantar flexion is used in the squat by putting the soleus on stretch in the maximal range and using its second classical function to drive the dorsiflexors in cocontraction at the ankle. When the erect position is attained and the dorsiflexion maintained, the individual will walk with a normal heel-toe gait. This erect posture frees the arms for movement and skilled activity.

Work into two limits

The idea of division of work into two limits combines two separate but intimately involved ideas. The idea of two types of muscle fibers with different functions has existed for many years. There has been much discussion and dispute through the years over the acceptance of white and red muscle, phasic and tonic muscle, and various other nomenclature related to fiber types in man. The critical concept here is not the dichotomy of muscles but the continuum of fiber types from the white, phasic, light work at one end to the red, tonic, heavy work at the other end. Any given human muscle contains fibers from all parts of the continuum.

To illustrate this point, consider the patient recovering from knee surgery who has received therapy consisting of progressive resistive exercise in various ways, including the DeLorme boot, sandbags, or the N-K table, but continues to have pain and difficulty in walking up or down stairs or on rough ground. The problem is that the light work muscle fibers have been exercised with the foot free from weight bearing, but the heavy work muscle fibers that must work when the bodyweight is supported on the foot have not been exercised.

The criteria that may be used in determining light work activity are:
1. The distal segment is free and the muscle is working from its insertion.
2. The superficial, two-joint muscles, which are more effective in performing movement, are predominantly light work fibers.
3. The activity of light work fibers will be more skilled, requiring more cortical control of the anterior muscles in a reciprocal innervation arrhythmical pattern with erect trunk.

The criteria for heavy work activity are:
1. The distal segment is fixed, and therefore the muscle is working from its origin.
2. The deep, one-joint muscles, which are more efficient as stabilizers, are predominantly heavy work fibers.
3. The activity of heavy work fibers is less skilled, using more reflexly controlled posterior muscles in a rhythmical pattern with the trunk horizontal to gravity.

These muscle fibers, arranged in motor units governed by anterior horn cells of varying sizes, function in fairly clear-cut, delineated patterns of activity. If the object of exercise is to hypertrophy muscle fibers, it is essential to engage the individual in the type or pattern of activity that uses the motor units of the appropriate fibers.

These criteria represent the extreme ends of light work and heavy work activity. It is important to remember that there are multitudinous combinations existing between the two extremes. The most useful criterion to use when making a decision is whether the distal segment of hand or elbow and foot or knee is free or fixed in the pattern. To further illustrate this concept, the light work motor units of the anterior tibialis work from the insertion when the distal segment is free in the pickup phase of gait. When the individual is standing and sways backward, the heavy work motor units of the anterior tibialis work from their origin to pull the body forward over the foot, the fixed distal segment.

The second idea embodied in this developmental sequence is related to the efficiency of muscle function. It is either efficient and inexpensive for the body to do the activity or it is inefficient and expensive. For instance, it is inefficient to use a two-joint–moving muscle to stabilize a joint. Evarts (1973) indicates that the cerebellum and basal ganglions are the *highest levels* of organization of muscle activity or motor coordination and **not** the cortex. The human cortex exists for abstract, loftier thought processes, not the coordination of muscles. Consequently, cortically controlled, voluntary light work, phasic, reciprocal innervation patterns of white muscle fiber motor units will tend to be very inefficient. On the other hand subcortically controlled, automatic, heavy work, tonic, cocontraction patterns of red muscle fiber motor units will be efficient.

In consideration of efficiency of patterns, the reciprocal innervation patterns are typically more expensive. There is, however, a cocontraction pattern that is inefficient—the light work, two-joint gastrocnemius, hamstrings, and rectus femoris cocontract to produce a rigid pillar of the legs. This pattern is seen in the positive supporting reaction or typical scissor position of the cerebral palsied patient. Typically cocontraction patterns are less expensive. However, the reciprocal innervation pattern of the tonic labyrinthine inverted reflex is efficient because of the direct stimulation of the extensor muscles by the vestibular system.

Function into four stages

Division of function into four stages is related to the developmental sequence of the nervous system and the skeletal and vital activities that are related to each state as seen in Fig. 5-9. The first motor manifestation of the nervous system is a reciprocal innervation pattern with facilitation of one set of muscles and inhibition of the antagonistic set of muscles. The second stage of development is coinnervation in the nervous system, which sends impulses simultaneously to agonist and antagonist to produce cocontraction in the muscles. The third stage in development is the combination of the first two stages; thus reciprocal innervation movement is superimposed on cocontraction. Heavy work movement is the name usually given to this stage because it immediately brings to mind the fact that the distal segment is fixed and the body is moving over that segment. The final stage of development is designated skill because it is the combination of the first three stages as they are needed in the activity. As an example, in gait the pickup is light-work reciprocal innervation. When weight is placed on the foot, there must

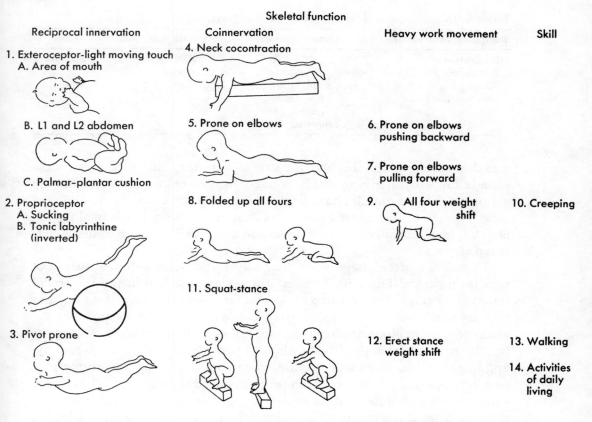

Fig. 5-9. The 14 developmental steps of skeletal function are arranged in the columns of reciprocal innervation, coinnervation, heavy work movement, and skill.

be cocontraction at the ankle for stability. When the weight is shifted forward over the fixed foot, the movement is heavy work. If each component appears in sequence the individual has a normal gait. Skill may be defined as the ability of the muscles to function automatically at a subcortical level with cortical interference only to initiate, adjust, or change from one pattern to another.

There are eight steps in the developmental sequence of vital activities as seen in Table 6. Under reciprocal innervation are step 1, inspiration, and step 2, expiration. Step 3, sucking, is reciprocal in nature since the individual sucks and breathes, sucks and breathes. Sucking is also cocontraction since it involves simultaneous contraction of certain muscles. It is of no value to be able to suck unless one can swallow fluids, which moves the sequence to heavy work movement in step 4. Phonation, step 5, is skill because it uses the

Table 6. Developmental sequence of vital activities

Reciprocal innervation	Coinnervation	Heavy work movement	Skill
1. Inspiration		4. Swallowing fluids	5. Phonation
2. Expiration		6. Chewing	
3. Sucking in pattern of suck-swallow and breathe	3. Sucking in muscle action as lips, cheeks, and jaw closure all work together	7. Swallowing solids	8. Speech

muscles developed in the first three stages as they are needed to make sounds. Chewing, step 6, moves back under heavy work movement in muscle action since some muscles have to move and some have to hold. Swallowing solids, step 7, is also under heavy work movement. Speech, the final step 8, is a skill involving all of the muscle actions and patterns acquired in the first seven steps.

There are fourteen steps in the four stages of developmental sequence of skeletal function (Fig. 5-9). The first three steps are within the reciprocal innervation stage. The first step of skeletal function is the response to a light moving touch, which stimulates exteroceptors. This is the most recent development of the Rood approach. We are presently in the process of integrating the neurophysiological basis, the components of the patterns, and the application of the treatment to children and adults. As our integration process develops, the present interpretation may need to be revised. The critical value of this technique to us is to determine if touch produces a "parasympathetic toward" response, which allows the individual to interact with his environment. The opposite reaction to touch produces a "sympathetic away from" response, which is a protective avoidance reaction because the stimulus has been interpreted as potentially dangerous. The key areas for the light touch stimuli are midline on the upper lip, the corner of the mouth, the iliohypogastric nerve on the abdomen below the umbilicus, the palmar cushion, and the plantar cushion.

Patients who demonstrate sympathetic responses will require additional parasympathetic stimuli to move them toward the trophotropic end of the continuum as explained in Concept 1. As the sympathetic nervous system domination is decreased the touch response should produce the desirable "parasympathetic toward" muscle pattern.

The second step of function includes two activities that use proprioceptor stimulation. Sucking was placed first since it is a vital activity but must be intimately involved here as it relates to and interacts with the skeletal function of midline stability. The sequence of sucking begins with the contraction of the orbicularis oris, protruding the lips to contact the nipple. This puts a stretch on the buccinator, initiating its contraction, which in turn stretches the superior pharyngeal constrictor, initiating its contraction to lift the larynx up out of the way for swallowing.

There is a continuous process of suck-swallow, suck-swallow. The better the sucking pattern, the better the respiratory pattern and the better the midline stability.

There are three primary sources of interference with the sucking pattern.

1. Hypersensitive skin around the mouth may inhibit the contraction of the orbicularis oris and block the activity at the initial stage.
2. Hypersensitive skin over the masseter inhibits its contraction and prevents the mouth from being closed.
3. Hypersensitive tongue may demonstrate an overactive gag reflex or a withdrawal of the tongue into the extreme posterior oral cavity.

Four secondary sources of interference include:

1. The resting state of the autonomic nervous system, which must be parasympathetic as discussed in Concept 1
2. The amount of extensor tone, which may inhibit the flexion pattern
3. Malocclusion resulting from a retracted mandible associated with bilateral inactivity of the lateral pterygoid muscles
4. Breathing through the mouth because of nasal obstruction.

Any or all of these interferences may be demonstrated in patients exhibiting difficulty in sucking.

The second activity in this proprioceptive step is the tonic labyrinthine inverted position. As discussed earlier in Concept 4, this position involves three effects that must be considered in sequence. The carotid sinus must operate normally to regulate blood pressure; otherwise, the individual will experience difficulty maintaining the position. The parasympathetic relaxation will decrease muscle tone throughout the body. The third effect is the primary goal of this position, which is the use of vestibular stimulation to facilitate specific extensor muscles.

The third step of reciprocal innervation function is the pivot prone position. The only difference between this position and the tonic labyrinthine inverted position occurs in the arms. After the scapulae have been stabilized by the upper and lower trapezius, with arms reaching over the head, the individual activates the rhomboids. As soon as the rhomboids contract, they stabilize the scapulae for hyperextension and external rotation at the shoulder joint, and the arms automatically assume this pivot prone position. Normal function of the lower trapezius must be present before the child activates the rhomboids. If the rhomboids dominate, as in the Moro reflex, the function of the lower trapezius is blocked, and the development of protective extension of the arms is prevented.

The fourth step is neck cocontraction in the prone position, which is the first coinnervation pattern. All of the cocontraction patterns will be seen to progress in a cephalocaudal direction. To allow achievement of this position of cocontraction of the neck, the strong extensors from the cervical curve are placed on stretch in the maximal range using their second classical function to drive the preverteberal flexors in cocontraction. The head should be directly in line with a straight spine and maintained for a reasonable period of time without dropping, lifting, or showing asymmetrical turning or shifting. The procedure for cocontraction has been discussed previously in the section on dividing the body into two parts. The importance of Rood's theory and treatment, however, cannot be overstressed. If there is one single principle existing throughout the approach, it is that of using the strong extensors from the inverted position to drive the flexors in cocontraction to provide stability for all subsequent activity.

The fifth step in function, prone on elbows, is also under coinnervation. In this position the elbows are close to the sides of the body, not propped out in front under the shoulder joint. This position should develop shoulder joint stability. It does not, however, follow the typical sequence of putting the stretch on extensors to drive flexors in cocontraction. In analyzing the gravitational stretch of muscles, the flexor, adductor, and internal rotator muscle groups are being stimulated at the shoulder joint, inhibiting the antagonist muscles. Scapular instability is frequently encountered in this position and must be corrected immediately. Additional facilitation to scapular stabilizers can be provided by placing an elastic band around the arms above the elbows, which pulls the arms toward each other and stimulates the scapular muscles to stabilize. Any elastic material may be used, such as dental dam, Thera-band rubber or surgical tubing, inner tube, or regular elastic. If the hands or forearms tend to cross because of the internal rotation of the arms, this position should not be allowed. Anyone using floor activities with children must be aware of scapular stabilization and arm positions and use the activities appropriately.

Steps six and seven are heavy work movement in the prone on elbows position. The elbows are the fixed distal segments and the body moves over them. Step six is pushing backward; this is a flexion motion at the shoulder joint and precedes the pulling forward that is the extension motion of step seven. Scapular stability must be watched very closely. If instability persists, the child should have more treatment in the inverted position. The legs should remain in a relaxed, straight position.

Step eight in the sequence returns to the coinnervation column and presents a specific progression. The head is lifted and weight is borne on the hands with elbows extended. The trunk is pushed back over relaxed legs into the folded up all fours position, as described in the section on dividing the body into two parts. The critical consideration is again putting the strong back and hip extensors on stretch in maximal range and using their second classical function to drive the abdominals and hip flexors into cocontraction. Without these super strong extensors, the folded up all fours position will not be able to provide the necessary trunk and hip stability. It is very important to realize that trunk stability comes from the back extensors driving the abdominals. In the patient with poor trunk stability, strengthening the abdominals will not solve the problem.

The treatment progression consists of inverted, to a cocontraction pattern, to inverted, again to a concontraction pattern. The individual may return as often as necessary to the inverted position to provide the necessary stimulation of fusimotor activity into those key midline neck and trunk extensor muscles.

Many times a child is unable to lift his head and extend the arms to push backward. Consequently he leaves the head down and merely pulls his knees up under his chest. Invariably when he reaches this point, the trunk is brought erect and he sits with the buttocks between the legs. As a result he loses the advantage of the stretch, which provides trunk and hip stability.

Three sequential activities progress from this folded up all fours cocontraction. As midline stability is developed:

1. The primitive postural reflexes are integrated into voluntary motor patterns.
2. The kinesthetic feedback from this cocontraction provides the necessary information for development of kinesthetic figure-ground. The midline stability provides the basis for recognition of movement and nonmovement. The nonmovement is the basis for orientation of the trunk to the force of gravity. On this trunk stability the extremities are free to move. The kinesthetic figure-ground is knowing internally the difference between the muscle tone of a stable trunk, which is the ground, and the muscle tone of moving extremities, which comprises the figure.
3. This cocontraction pattern is the beginning of bilateral integration and body awareness. Is it any wonder that children who lack folded up all fours stability demonstrate widespread problems?

For example, we believe that the developmentally apraxic child can be viewed in the following manner: He does not have adequate motor planning to initiate motor activity or to maintain that motor activity because he lacks body schema. He lacks body schema because he has inadequate kinesthetic figure-ground. He is deficient in kinesthetic figure-ground because he has inadequate kinesthetic feedback. His kinesthetic feedback is incomplete because he has not developed cocontraction. His lack of cocontraction is directly related to his lack of extensor muscle tone. The subnormal extensor muscle tone may be the result of inadequate integration of the vestibular mechanism.

The emotional lability of these children may be related to the domination of the sympathetic nervous system producing protective avoidance reactions. These protective reactions prevent discriminative interactions with the environment.

As soon as the child establishes trunk and hip stability he will begin to shift weight forward onto his hands. This is, of course, heavy work movement because the hands and knees are fixed and the body is moving over them. The hands and knees position becomes step nine in skeletal function. The infant will very soon begin to rock rapidly forward and backward, stimulating the semicircular canals of the vestibular mechanism. This is perhaps the very best facilitation of all muscle action throughout the entire body. However, in this position the infant has body weight on the patellar tendons, which inhibits the strong vestibular facilitation of the extensor pattern of the legs. This extensor pattern of the legs of cerebral palsied children must be prevented if triggered by vestibular stimulation.

Fast repetitive stimulation of semicircular canals is an excellent stimulus for maintained arousal of the cortex. Many parents have been awakened at two or three o'clock in the morning by the rocking baby who is ready to play. On the other hand, the next time you think you cannot stay awake to meet tomorrow's deadline, experiment with this technique. Although some adults may have difficulty in developing sufficient speed rocking on their hands and knees, they will find the cortical arousal dramatic if they persevere.

In the all fours heavy work movement position the weight will be shifted forward and backward in a bilateral pattern, then from side to side in a unilateral pattern, and finally diagonally. The diagonal pattern is a critical one for rotation of the pelvis and is assisted by the tonic lumbar reflex.

Creeping in an alternating pattern, step ten, is possible when the infant has acquired the ability to shift his weight diagonally across the midline of the body. This is the first skill function, and it is made up of reciprocal innervation in pickup, cocontraction when weight is taken on the extremity, and heavy work movement when the weight is shifted forward. When the individual elements of a skill pattern are provided in the developmental sequence, it is unnecessary to spend treatment time teaching the skill.

Step eleven in function is again a cocontraction pattern that provides stability of the ankle. The child pulls up from a squat to stance and returns to a squat. This pattern uses the strong soleus (from the inverted position) on stretch in its maximal range. The squat stance position uses the second classical function relative to the soleus to drive the dorsiflexors (anterior tibialis, extensor digitorum longus, and peroneus tertius) in cocontraction. As seen in Fig. 5-9, it is advantageous to have the individual, child or adult, squatting with weight just on his heels on a block of wood. This prevents both touch and pressure on the ball of the foot, which triggers the positive supporting reaction. The positive supporting reaction is a cocontraction of the gastrocnemius, rectus femoris, and hamstrings, which are light work, two-joint muscles. They should be moving instead of stabilizing as explained in the section on dividing work into two limits. As the individual begins to stand from the squat, the feet will be held in dorsiflexion. He may reach a point where his toes go down in a total extension pattern, indicating that he has gone too far. He must be allowed to extend at hip and knee only to a point at which he can maintain the dorsiflexion and hold, hold, hold that position. With time, full extension is possible while maintaining dorsiflexion.

There is an added advantage of the squatting block since pressure on the calcaneus is inhibitory to the gastrocnemius. The addition of inhibition or prevention of activation is a critical part of all neurophysiological treatment. In this one position the gastrocnemius is controlled by bending the knee, by pressure on the calcaneus, and by preventing touch or pressure to the ball of the foot. In the same position the soleus is being used to drive the dorsiflexors for stability at the ankle. The dorsiflexors will then be more able to counteract the pull of the gastrocnemius. With the foot held up in dorsiflexion and with the knee extended, the position for a heel-toe gait has been established. The gastrocnemius will have sufficient length and will not "pop" the knee back into hyperextension.

It is of little value to acquire this ankle stability for 30 minutes of treatment and then permit the patient to assume his old positions and habits. He must not reapply his braces and ambulate in his typical gait pattern. Nor should he return to his wheelchair where he will sit with weight on the balls of the feet. Randolph began working in the 1960s on a shoe that would free the forefoot from weightbearing and have the weight carried on the heel. The shoe began as an outrigger, which was U-shaped and allowed the foot to drop down between the two prongs. This was very heavy and awkward for the children to use for walking. Ultimately, with the assistance of physical therapists, physical therapy students, and orthotists, the present design of the platform shoe was achieved. Several examples of the shoes are seen in Fig. 5-10. The Howard A. Rusk Rehabilitation Center, Prosthetic and Orthotic Department, University of Missouri, Columbia, Mo., produced the professional looking, cosmetically acceptable shoe used in the following fabrication plans. Dr. Christopher (1974) and Frances Corley of Les Passes Center

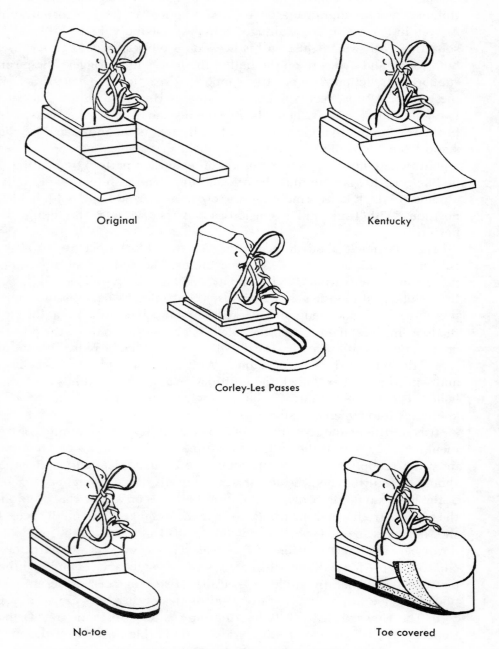

Original

Kentucky

Corley-Les Passes

No-toe

Toe covered

Fig. 5-10. Examples of Randolph platform shoes.

for Children in Memphis, Tenn., have used the concept of the platform shoe with adaptation for several years. It should be clearly understood that the toe bar on the shoe used by Les Passes is to prevent the strong clawing of the long toe flexor muscles. The clawing action of the flexor muscles prevents the long toe extensors from working in lateral dorsiflexion.

The description for measuring and constructing the Randolph platform shoe (pp. 130-131) should be self-explanatory. The value of the platform shoe is merely to carry over the good treatment of the inverted position to the squat stance position. If the shoes are needed for extended periods of time, the treatment sequence should be carefully evaluated. A good foot position with strong longitudinal arch is a prerequisite to the squat stance position. The longer a child is permitted to stand on a foot with a poor arch or with clawing long toe flexor muscles or on the positive supporting total extension pattern, the more ingrained the abnormal pattern becomes and the more difficult it is to correct. For that reason early attention to the action of the intrinsic muscles of the foot and the anterior and posterior tibialis muscles is important. There are very few congenitally flat feet or feet in equinovalgus or equinovarus that will not respond to vibration of the necessary muscles and platform shoes. A 27-minute sound-slide series explaining the neurophysiological basis of the platform shoes can be rented from the American Academy for Cerebral Palsy and Developmental Medicine, Suite 1030, 1255 New Hampshire Ave., N.W., Washington, D.C. 20036. The program number is 8(349 AAOS).

Step twelve in function is weight shifting, and this should occur in the entire range, from squat to erect stance. Weight shifting is heavy work movement because the foot is the fixed distal segment. Normal children will squat and play for extended periods of time, reaching and shifting in the activity. The weight shift should be in the same bilateral, unilateral, and contralateral directions seen in step nine.

When the child acquires weight shifting in the diagonal direction, he is ready to move on to step thirteen, which is a skill activity. Again the tonic lumbar reflex is critical to rotation of the pelvis and normal gait. We observed earlier that the pickup phase is a reciprocal innervation pattern. As weight is taken on the foot, there must be cocontraction at the ankle for stability. When the weight is shifted forward over the fixed foot in pushoff, the movement is in the heavy work category. Thus skill is a combination of the first three stages as they are needed in the activity.

Step fourteen in function is composed of all the activities of daily living that each person must accomplish to function efficiently. Each of these activities should be broken down into reciprocal innervation, coinnervation, and heavy work movement components. When the deficits are corrected, the sub-

Randolph platform shoes

1. Trace an outline of the child's foot.
2. Make the footplate out of plywood (¼ to ½ inch thick) the same size as the foot drawing (*A*).
3. Attach a thin layer of cork to the bottom surface of the footplate.
4. With the child in the standing position, place a block of wood under the heel (*B*). The key to the *appropriate height* of the block will depend on the security with which the heel is held. If the child's heel is not securely held on the block, the forefoot will drop excessively. The ball of the foot or the toes must *not* touch the floor.
5. Cut off the top and sole of a child's old high-top shoe back to the heel (*C*). It is essential that a high-top shoe be used so that the child's heel will be secure. In addition, it is essential to use a *small* size shoe so that the shoe will fit the heel snugly.

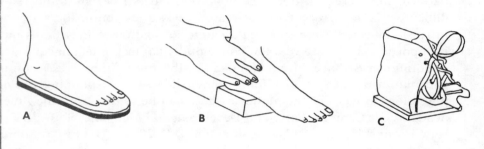

©Randolph, Tempfel, and Orton, 1975.

sequent skilled activity will automatically improve. Remember, skill is the ability of the muscles to run subcortically—one interferes cortically only to initiate, correct, or change patterns.

Each step in the developmental sequence is preparatory for the next step, and each has tremendous side benefits to which we may be completely oblivious. Each patient, regardless of diagnosis, should progress through the developmental sequence of vital and skeletal function. The treatment progression should follow a typical sequence of sucking and tonic labyrinthine inverted position, followed by the cocontraction patterns. There is a danger of falling into a set pattern of treatment for every patient, without assessing the subtle differences, needs, and reactions of each individual each time a treatment is given. There is no "cookbook recipe" for Rood's approach just as there cannot be for any other neurophysiological approach. The success of the treatment is directly related to the therapist's powers of observation and

6. Attach the cut off shoe to the block; then attach the block to the platform (*D*).
7. If a more finished look or greater warmth is desired, remove only the sole of the shoe, leaving the top intact (*E*).
   NOTE: Shoes must fit the child properly.
8. To produce a closed-shoe effect, sew a piece of leather the width of the block plus footplate to the shoe. Fasten Velcro (hook tape) around the edge of the footplate and Velcro (loop tape) around the edge of the piece of leather sewn to the shoe (*F*).
9. When the foot position is to be observed, open the Velcro and turn toe of shoe inside out.

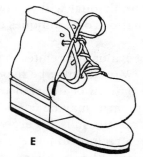

ability to adjust techniques to the immediate situation. The effectiveness of the Rood approach is directly related to the constant agreement of the four developmental sequences implemented on the foundation of Concepts 1, 2, and 4. For example, the correct muscle group in the correct part of the body must be performing the appropriate kind of work in the desired step of vital or skeletal function.

EVALUATION

The Rood evaluation may be divided into three sections. The first section is concerned with the age factor. It is important to consider the age of the individual as well as the age of the disorder. The age of the individual is important as it relates to an infant or a young child with trauma to the immature nervous system or to an adult with trauma to a mature nervous system. It is generally believed that trauma to an immature system may be more impairing because the normal developmental sequence has not been experienced. The mature system has experienced normal activity and should respond more rapidly.

The age of the disease has a similar connotation. If the disability has persisted for only a matter of days or weeks, it should respond more quickly than if it has persisted for years.

There is, however, a fallacy in both of these assumptions. Occasionally the older cerebral palsied child will respond to treatment more rapidly and dramatically than a similarly involved young child. Also, there are occasions when the stroke patient whose condition is of several years duration will respond more readily than one whose condition is of only a few months duration. These situations merely reemphasize the uniqueness of the individual and the receptiveness of the nervous system to change. It is impossible to predict how an individual will respond until he has been provided with a variety of combinations of techniques directed toward the most basic developmental deficit.

The second section of evaluation relates to the amount of muscle tone and the pattern of that tone. Muscles may be hypotonic or hypertonic. The tone may be in a reciprocal pattern of imbalance or a cocontraction pattern of balance. A typical spastic arm may be considered as hypertonic in a reciprocal pattern when the spastic muscles are viewed. The same arm may be considered hypotonic in a reciprocal pattern when the focus is on the weak, nonfunctioning antagonist to the spastic muscles.

A hypertonic state in a cocontraction pattern would be the rigid extremity in which there is excessive tone in both sets of opposing muscles. On the other hand the hypotonic state in a cocontraction pattern would be the typical flaccid extremity or one in which there is a balanced weakness.

The third component of muscle tone is the condition of hyperkinesia or excessive movement. This condition may be seen at rest, as in the "pill rolling" of parkinsonism, or whenever voluntary effort is initiated, as in the athetoid patient.

A decided advantage in looking at patients from this vantage point is that each body part may be considered separately. A decided disadvantage of conventional diagnosis and labels is the tendency for professionals to have a preconceived idea of what symptoms the individual will have and to overlook some very obvious aspects of function and treatment.

Another advantage of evaluating muscle tone is the direction it provides for treatment. In any situation of hypertonicity, the primary objective will be to decrease or inhibit the excessive tone. When the excessive tone is decreased, the antagonist muscle, which appeared hypotonic, may be capable of contracting simply because it has been freed from prolonged inhibition. This idea will be explored more completely in Concept 7.

The third section of evaluation is the four stages of function. Fig. 5-9 may be used as an evaluation form as well as for progress notes. The evaluator should observe the patient's performance through the complete vital and skeletal sequence to observe how each step is executed. Treatment is begun at the step in which difficulty is first observed. The typical problem areas will include tonic labyrinthine inverted position and the cocontraction patterns.

Since the inverted position uses the vestibular mechanism, it is our conviction that normal integration of this system is essential. It has been our experience that a deficit in the position portion of the mechanism frequently indicates a deficit in the motion portion and vice versa. Therefore the Ayres Postrotary Nystagmus Test is a desirable part of every patient evaluation. It is also our conviction that vestibular stimulation, both motion and position, is indispensable in any intervention program.

MEDIA
General principles

The primary rule to remember is that any medium may be facilitory or inhibitory depending on four parameters. These parameters were presented in Concept 2 but will be repeated here as they relate specifically to the Rood approach. The parameters include:
1. Where the medium is applied. Is the medium presented to the skin, to the muscle belly, or over a tendon?
2. How the medium is applied. Is the application fast brief, fast repetitive, maintained, or slow rhythmical?
3. What the medium is. Is the medium ice, touch, vibration, or vestibular stimulation?
4. The pattern in which the medium is applied. What stage of function is being used, for instance, inverted, prone on elbows, or squat stance?

Area. Whenever exteroceptors are to be stimulated, the media must be applied according to dermatome (Fig. 5-11). According to Eldred and Hagbarth (1954) when the dermatome over a muscle belly is at the same segmental level as the motor innervation, the muscle can be facilitated through the skin. Therefore brushing and icing, which are exteroceptive stimuli, must be done according to dermatome. Fortunately, many extensor muscles have appropriate dermatomes over their muscle bellies. The innervation of each muscle and related dermatome must be determined before stimulation is administered.

The skin area served by the posterior primary rami of the back is a specific skin area for the sympathetic nervous system. Since ice is routinely interpreted as a potentially dangerous stimulus, care should be used when applying it to this area.

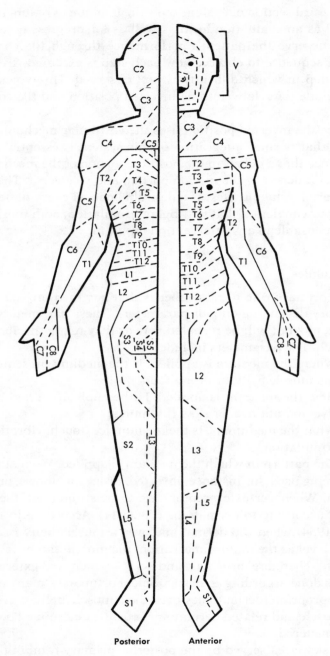

Fig. 5-11. Anterior and posterior dermatome chart.

The outer ring of the trigeminal nerve, which lies over the forehead, appears to be a potentially dangerous area. The central processes of the neurons of this nerve terminate extensively in the reticular inhibitory formation of the brain stem. Caution should be exercised whenever stimulating the skin in this area.

The use of exteroceptors should be judiciously controlled. These receptors after-discharge and recruit, so their effects may be long lasting and extremely potent in their alerting and orienting responses. Skin stimulation may not be the innocuous procedure that many people believe. This fact undoubtedly contributed to Rood's shift to proprioceptor stimulation in the late 1960s.

Rate. The rate of stimulation relates to the four rules of sensory input and motor output as discussed in Concept 2. The fast, brief stimulus is not a good treatment procedure because of the muscular rebound and reticular formation effects. It will, however, verify an anatomically intact reflex arc.

The fast, repetitive stimulus is an excellent way to provide C fiber nonspecific sensory input to the reticular activating formation. It is also a means of providing facilitory semicircular canal stimulation. The greatest asset of the fast repetitive stimulus is the production of a maintained contraction.

A maintained stimulus will produce a maintained contraction. Gravity is the most frequently overlooked and the least understood source of maintained stimulation. Contact of the supporting surface has been related to the body righting reflexes for many years. Only recently has there seemed to be application of this form of stimulation in a more specific fashion to specific muscles or patterns.

Slow, rhythmical, repetitive stimuli of low intensity and frequency deactivate mind and body by producing a trophotropic response.

Duration of stimulation. Duration of stimulation is directly related to the type of receptor being stimulated. When a phasic receptor is stimulated it adapts rapidly; so the duration of stimulation is brief. A tonic receptor is slow adapting; so the duration can be extended for longer periods.

Proprioceptors as a group do not recruit adjacent neurons in the area or after-discharge (continue to fire). Consequently when stimulation stops, the effect stops in the nervous system within a matter of seconds.

Exteroceptors as a group both after-discharge and recruit. Electrical activity can therefore be built up in reverberating circuits for extended periods of time. Clinically it can be demonstrated that the longer the duration of stimulation, the longer the period of reverberating activity. As the stimulation is continued for periods of days or weeks, the length of reverberating activity will extend from minutes to several hours. This is another reason to judiciously control exteroceptor stimulation to prevent development of inappropriate patterns.

Type of stimulus. Any sensation may be used as a source of stimulation. The reader should refer to Concept 2 for the discussion of special senses as well as the important distinction of specific and nonspecific sensory input. Every stimulus should be evaluated as to its ergotropic or trophotropic impact.

SPECIFIC MEDIA

The following 12 types of media are used in various combinations in treatment:

1. Light moving touch is used to elicit the parasympathetic or sympathetic response. The most convenient tool is a cotton Q-tip. At least 30 seconds should elapse between strokes to avoid primary afferent depolarization (PAD). (PAD will be presented in detail in Concept 7.)

2. Vestibular stimulation includes swinging, rocking, rolling, bouncing, tilting, and spinning. (Refer to pictures in Concept 3.) If these motions are performed rapidly, they are facilitory, but if performed slowly, they are inhibitory. Because of the habituation capacity of the vestibular mechanism, *acceleration* and *deceleration* must be emphasized. Continuous motion has questionable benefits. The dividing line between effective facilitation and inhibition will vary with each person and each treatment session.

We must appreciate the fact that vestibular stimulation is a potent type of stimulus that can be either dangerous or very advantageous. The presence of seizure activity is *not* a contraindication. This type of stimulation should never be imposed on the objecting child unless his objection is a manipulative behavior. Whenever possible, the child should be actively involved in providing his own stimulation. Extreme care should be exercised to recognize every undesirable reaction produced by vestibular stimulation, such as increased extensor muscle tone in the legs or asymmetrical patterns resulting from spinning. Complete data should be recorded on the type of stimulation used and the exact results obtained.

It is important for professionals as well as parents to understand that there are three directions of angular stimulation: the forward-backward direction as in somersaulting, the side-to-side direction as in log rolling, and spinning as on a pivot. There are also three directions of linear stimulation: swinging forward and backward, swinging side to side, and going up and down, as on an elevator or trampoline. Undoubtedly one of the most valuable sources of vestibular stimulation is a loving parent "rough-housing" the child. The standard spring horse also combines many directions of vestibular stimulation.

3. The inverted position is used as discussed in Concept 4. There is no limit to the ways in which this can be accomplished. If the child is small he can be held over one's arms, suspended by the pelvis in play, or laid across

the lap. If the individual is too large for these methods, a bolster, wedge, barrel, ball, or tilt table may be used. The most satisfactory method for extended periods of time or for use in the classroom is the tonic labyrinthine inverted board. The plans for measuring and constructing the board are at the end of Concept 4.

4. Ice can be used in many ways, but the appropriate method should be strictly followed. Icing may be labeled "A" or "C," which refers to the type of nerve fiber stimulated. "A" icing is applied in three quick swipes, blotting the water between each swipe. This gives a quick motor response. This is used primarily along the angle of the ribs on the abdomen to provide a reciprocal pattern between the diaphragm and the abdominal muscles.

"C" icing is rubbed on a superficial muscle belly with pressure and must be stopped before a painful stimulus is felt. Ruch and colleagues (1965) stated that if the skin temperature is dropped 10°, three fourths of all the C fibers in the area will be activated. Prior to 1970 this technique was used extensively in an attempt to activate the fusimotor system of hyposensitive muscle spindles to produce a ready steady state so the stretch reflexes could be used. This, of course, has been replaced successfully by the inverted position, which is more exact in its function and easier to manipulate. "C" icing remains an excellent technique for individual isolated muscles that need some additional assistance in a pattern.

Ice is excellent in the sucking pattern to facilitate lip and tongue activity. It is advisable to make the "popsicle" from plain water, avoiding sugar or flavoring, which stimulates salivation. Some infants and children may not like the ice because it is too threatening to them. It can be interpreted as potentially dangerous and trigger a sympathetic fight-or-flight reaction. This is usually the case in patients whose spasticity is said to increase when ice is used. Whenever this occurs more parasympathetic stimuli should be provided.

5. Brushing was one of the earliest mediums established by Rood. In the beginning brushing was done by hand with brushes of various kinds and having various strengths of bristles. It had to be done very rapidly and was labeled "A" brushing because it produced a quick motor response. The reader is referred to Concept 2 to review the size of nerve fibers and the four rules of sensory input if there is difficulty relating to this terminology. About 1964 the battery-operated brush was introduced, which moved more rapidly and was labeled "C" brushing. Again Ruch and associates (1965) stated that a fast repetitive stimulus would change the long, positive after-potential of the C fibers into a long negative after-potential. A long, negative after-potential makes the neuron fire easier after it has been fired once. Again the reason for "C" brushing was to stimulate fusimotor activity. This has been replaced

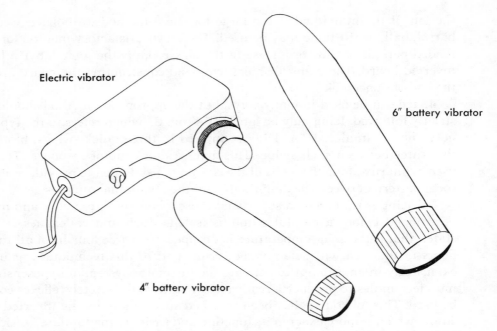

Electric vibrator

6″ battery vibrator

4″ battery vibrator

Fig. 5-12. Different types of vibrators. The electric one is essential for adults. The 4-inch one is excellent for babies or around the mouth for sucking.

by the inverted position. Like icing, brushing is still very acceptable for isolated muscles. It is not advisable to stimulate children under 6 years by brushing or icing simply because they are phasic by nature, and this seems to limit the phasic activity (Rood, 1970).

6. Vibration is used for two distinct purposes (Fig. 5-12). The first purpose is to desensitize the hypersensitive skin that inhibits the muscle activity directly beneath the skin. This is especially useful around the lips to release the orbicularis oris from the inhibition of the hypersensitive skin and to allow the lips to protrude for sucking. According to Sato and Ozeki (1966), if the pacinian corpuscle is driven by vibration, it will block all other sensation coming in from that area of skin. It seems that any frequency above 60 Hz or cps works very effectively for this purpose.

The second purpose of vibration is to use the tonic vibratory reflex, which stimulates the muscle spindle directly and activates a low-energy tonic muscle contraction. However, the frequency of this vibration must be close to 100 Hz to be effective on adults. Many of the electric vibrators do not exceed 60 Hz. On small children a lower frequency is effective in producing the tonic contraction; the battery-operated facial vibrator is adequate.

To clarify any confusion that might be present, the vibration did not replace the brushing and icing. Without good fusimotor activity to the muscle spindle, the vibration cannot produce a tonic contraction. The brushing and icing were *replaced* by the tonic labyrinthine inverted position, which affects the fusimotor neurons directly.

Do not vibrate a relaxed muscle. A better response is obtained when the muscle is contracting, is on stretch, or is facilitated in the tonic labyrinthine inverted position. Some research indicates that the vibration is more effective over the muscle belly, while other research indicates that the response is better over the tendon. The response to vibration will be increased as the many factors are added together. For this reason the patient is routinely placed in the inverted position and given an activity to perform that requires total extension during the vibration of midline extensor muscles. Hagbarth (1973) is an excellent reference on recent research related to vibration.

7. Pressure may be mechanical or manual. Mechanical pressure may include such things as buttons, bumpers, pads, cones, toys, or an orthokinetic cuff as described by Blashy and Fuchs (1959). Any of these devices may be facilitory or inhibitory at any time in any position. Manual pressure is facilitory when applied to muscle bellies in a stretch-pressure or friction type massage. Manual pressure applied crosswise on the tendon is inhibitory and is an excellent way to release spasticity and allow full range of motion without "stretching." This is a simple procedure and merely involves supporting the part, rubbing lightly across the tendon, increasing the pressure until the muscle relaxes, and then taking the part into the released range. The critical point is that this method changes the synaptic environment and the balance of inhibitory and facilitory impulses in the desired direction. Many limitations of motion that have been labeled contractures can be disproved in this fashion.

8. Body weight is inhibitory to all the muscles not being stretched by gravity. For this reason the erect posture, both sitting and standing, is devastating to individuals with poor trunk cocontraction. Remember to be cautious with the individual in the prone on elbows position. More than body weight is facilitory to cocontraction and should be used at every opportunity.

9. Resistance is related to the amount of work demanded of the muscles. There are many ways of grading the resistance with weights or with elastic material such as dental dam or surgical tubing.

10. Position relates to the tone from the various tonic reflexes. These reflexes may be used to produce a desired pattern as long as it is understood that the more the pattern is used, the more secure the synapses become, and the more difficult it may be to integrate those reflexes. It is important to realize that the only thing that makes a reflex undesirable or pathological is whether the reflex dominates motor behavior after it should have been inte-

grated. These reflexes do not disappear; they are merely incorporated into the individual's everyday activities.

11. Neutral warmth is an excellent tool for generalized relaxation and for shifting the autonomic resting base toward the trophotropic end of the continuum. Either the entire body or an extremity may be wrapped in a cotton blanket for about 3 to 5 minutes. As explained in Concept 2, the parasympathetic stimuli must be watched carefully to prevent the individual's switching over to a sympathetic reaction if the stimulation is excessive or prolonged. All forms of water and heat applications can be used in this homeostatic range.

12. Repetition is perhaps the most essential of all the media. The patient must practice the pattern. A goal-directed activity or toy will occupy the attention of the individual while the body produces the necessary movement patterns. The more meaningful the activity, the more likely the movement will be repeated and the more automatic it will become. According to Ayres (1975) the best integrator of sensory input is an adaptive behavioral response to a change in one's environment.

TREATMENT
Treatment progression

Each patient is evaluated with the skeletal and vital functions developmental sequence. The entire sequence should be used to determine the areas of deficiency and difficulty. Routinely the problem areas are sucking, midline trunk extension, and cocontraction patterns. Treatment may move back and forth between these three areas.

Ideally the following objectives should be included in every treatment program:

1. Provide appropriate ergotropic-trophotrophic balance for optimal performance of specific treatment activity.
2. Provide facilitation for and opportunity to participate in prolonged, resistive sucking activities (Fig. 5-13).
3. Provide appropriate activation and facilitation in the inverted position (Figs. 5-14 and 5-15).
4. Provide necessary facilitation and inhibition for the cocontraction patterns of neck, trunk, hip, and ankle (Figs. 5-16 to 5-18).

The specific goals for each patient should be developed according to his unique muscle strengths and weaknesses in patterns. It is our strong conviction that when the discrepancies and deficiencies of the inverted and cocontraction patterns are ameliorated, the patient will automatically move into heavy work movement and skill activities. It is also our firm conviction that having the patient attempt to cortically correct elements of a skill activity is fruitless. If the cerebellum and basal ganglions are the highest level of integration of motor activity (Evarts 1973), the missing elements of a pattern are more easily and rapidly provided at a lower level of automatic movement.

If the developmental sequence is studied carefully, it is possible to discover in which pattern each muscle is functioning initially and whether it is performing light or heavy work. It has been our experience that a muscle can be made to function in that initial pattern more easily and more rapidly than at a more advanced level. As an example, the anterior tibialis is seen to work initially in light work, dorsiflexion, and inversion in a total flexion pat-

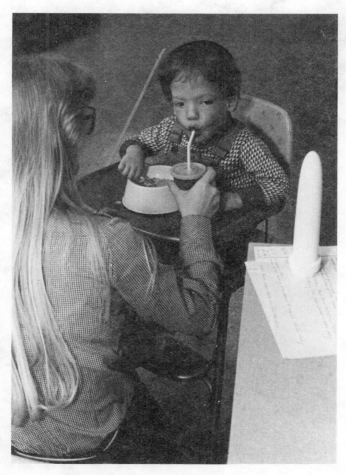

Fig. 5-13. Child sucking through a straw.

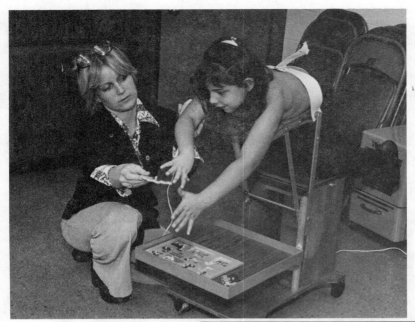

Fig. 5-14. Playing in the inverted position.

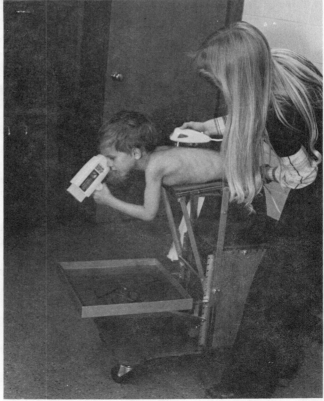

Fig. 5-15. Vibration is added to the inverted play activity.

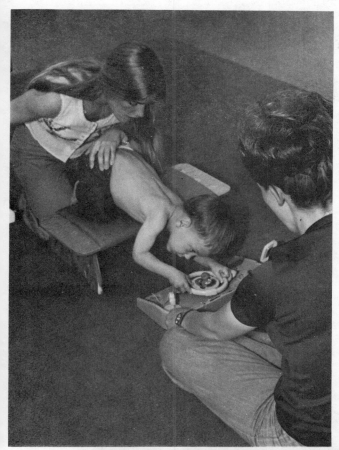

Fig. 5-16. Child in folded up all fours position showing the trunk and hip cocontraction.

Fig. 5-17. When cocontraction is present, the child will automatically shift his weight forward into the regular all fours position and begin to rock.

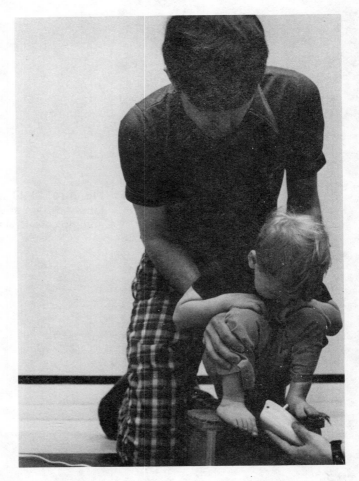

Fig. 5-18. Child in squat-stance activity to acquire ankle stability.

tern. It is then brought into a cocontraction pattern of ankle stability by the stretch of the soleus. Finally, the anterior tibialis works in a heavy work movement as the leg is pulled forward over a fixed foot in the erect weight-bearing pattern. When these three functions of the anterior tibialis are provided in sequence, the muscle will be seen to operate appropriately in every phase of gait.

Everted foot pattern

There is one situation in which a flexion pattern is employed prior to the sucking and inverted patterns. This situation occurs when the patient demonstrates dorsiflexion with eversion in a total flexion pattern. Many cerebral palsied children will demonstrate this pattern on either one or both feet. The

Fig. 5-19. Tendon pressure over toe extensor tendons given for inhibition while vibration is given to facilitate the anterior tibialis.

pattern is produced by the extensor digitorum longus and peroneus tertius overcontracting and inhibiting the anterior tibialis. Individuals so affected will also show poor posterior tibialis function, with essentially no longitudinal arch. A young child should not be permitted or encouraged to stand on the foot in this position. It has been our experience that an intervention program *prior* to weight bearing can correct this muscle imbalance rapidly. In older children it may be necessary to take them off their feet for a period of 2 to 3 months while this pattern is corrected.

The sequence is relatively simple in design, but in the beginning it may be difficult to obtain the desired results. The individual is placed in the backlying position with the leg in flexion. Tendon pressure is exerted on the long

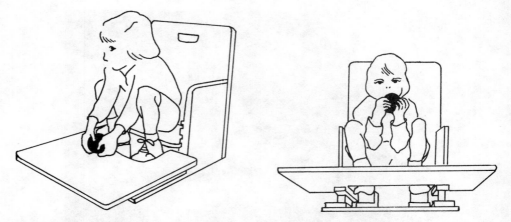

Fig. 5-20. A special table was designed by C. C. Shih to assist squat-stance activities in the platform shoes. The height of both the seat and the table are adjustable.

toe extensor muscle where it crosses the ankle joint. While tendon pressure is provided, the anterior tibialis muscle belly and tendon are vibrated. Some game or activity that requires a total flexion pattern of the legs should be used. Resistance to the total flexion pattern can be provided in combination with the tendon pressure. As the dorsiflexion with inversion improves, the leg is taken into more extension until isolated voluntary motion is possible without any facilitation or inhibition (Fig. 5-19).

As soon as the inversion action is fairly well established, the cocontraction pattern of squat stance may be started (Fig. 5-20). Routinely in these individuals additional vibration to the tendon of the posterior tibialis will be needed to assure a good medial longitudinal arch in the weight-bearing pattern. Again it has been our experience that when Randolph platform shoes are employed to carry over the good squat stance cocontraction pattern, the equinovalgus position can be corrected in a large number of patients in 3 to 9 months without surgery.

Sucking

As discussed in the developmental sequence, dividing function into four stages, there are three primary and four secondary sources of interference in the sucking pattern. In treatment it is important to attack the interferences in the appropriate order. The balance of the ergotropic and trophotropic system must be dealt with first to assure parasympathetic domination. If extensor tone is excessive and prevents flexion, the side-lying position may be the position of choice. It will be difficult to close the lips around the straw if the mandible is retracted. Many times the four secondary interferences play a

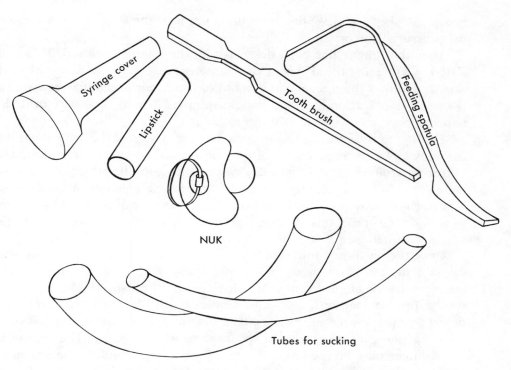

Fig. 5-21. Equipment used to facilitate sucking.

critical part in the success of the program and should not be ignored or neglected.

The three primary interferences may be found in any combination and any degree of domination. As treatment is administered, the dominance may shift from one to the other.

The hyperactive tongue is treated first. "Tongue walking," as it is called, is a rather difficult technique to perfect, especially with a very active tongue or a very hyperactive gag reflex. The procedure is to start at the tip of the tongue in the midline and exert firm pressure with a tongue depressor or a feeding spatula (Fig. 5-21) in small steps moving slowly back on the tongue. If and when the back of the tongue is reached, a constant pressure is exerted in hopes of triggering an automatic swallow. If a swallow is not elicited, the procedure is repeated. The number of times this procedure must be repeated varies from as few as five to as many as 30 or more in one session. The procedure may need to be repeated for several days before a swallow is initiated. Any time a swallow is triggered, the instrument must be withdrawn quickly to allow mouth closure and a normal swallow. If the gag reflex is produced, the "walking" has been done too fast, the steps are too large, or the pressure is incorrect.

After the tongue has been desensitized, the mouth is closed. This is assisted by vibrating the skin over the masseter muscle, which desensitizes the skin and allows the masseter muscle to contract. Since the masseter muscle is one of mastication and has muscle spindles, it may also be vibrated in hopes of producing a tonic vibrator reflex.

The key to the sucking sequence is the contraction of the orbicularis oris. In many cases the contraction of the muscle will spontaneously occur after vibration around the mouth to desensitize the skin. The orbicularis oris is a facial muscle and evidently does not have muscle spindles. A small 4-inch vibrator is excellent for its desensitization. A number of children have begun to suck on the end of this small vibrator within a few minutes after initiation of the treatment sequence.

Once the pattern is initiated, the critical factor in maintaining the sucking is firm contact or pressure above the upper lip. For this reason, NUK pacifiers are excellent for practice since the hard plastic shield fits well up on the lip. Sucking of bottles and nipples should be observed carefully to determine if the pressure is adequate. Plastic shields similar to that of the NUK pacifier may be placed on straws to provide pressure. The edge of the index finger may be used as substitute pressure or contact. The amount of pressure is varied to discover the ideal amount for each individual in each situation.

Ideally, a good sucking pattern should be developed before the infant begins to get teeth. When the teeth erupt, a stimulus is provided for biting and chewing. However, if an older child drools or does not suck well or both, a sucking program is definitely indicated at any age. A resistive sucking program will cause a secondary improvement in respiration pattern and midline trunk stability. Straw drinking through plastic tubing is better for the older child and is possible if sufficient inhibition and facilitation is provided to the primary and secondary interferences. Muller (1972), in her oral facilitation program, has many excellent suggestions that can be incorporated readily into these procedures.

Dynamic sling

The dynamic sling is a critical factor in early intervention treatment of the patient with a cerebral vascular accident. The sling on pp. 150-151 is a culmination of many individuals' contributions. It is neurophysiologically designed to provide appropriate inhibition and facilitation. The sling must be made to fit the individual patient and constantly adjusted to changes in muscle tone. When made and adjusted properly this sling will aid in:

1. Decreased edema in the hand in the early period because of position.

2. Decreased muscle tone (spasticity) in the finger and wrist flexor muscles from the hard tendon pressure of the cone and the rolled edge of the Orthoplast shell.
3. Increased muscle tone of the finger and wrist extensor muscles from the active field of the orthokinetic forearm splint.
4. Decreased muscle tone of the biceps muscle by positioning of the sling to eliminate gravitational pull.
5. Increased muscle tone of the triceps muscle from released spasticity of the biceps.
6. Marked decrease in painful and subluxated shoulder joints. The distal grasp on the cone or the elbow extension will be seen to reposition the humerus into the glenoid cavity.

Management

Any program of therapy is doomed to meager returns when administered 30 to 60 minutes a day even at a frequency of 5 days a week. Every program must be designed to be repeated frequently during the day and preferably 7 days a week. Adaptive equipment is of paramount importance in extending the effectiveness of treatment throughout the day. Family involvement is equally important for effectiveness of the program. It is our firm conviction that all family members must be trained to provide positive, constructive sensory input to the patient in everyday care and play.

As therapists, many of us have erred for years by providing home programs that were physically impossible for families to schedule. Instead we should be training the families to feed, dress, carry, and play with their children in the best neurophysiological manner possible. In this way they can provide the activation, facilitation, and inhibition needed in every situation throughout the day. The normal family activities can become a part of the "incorporated treatment" or "structured environment."

It is a simple task to teach a mother to do tendon pressure to release tight adductor muscles when changing diapers. It is also a simple task to teach a 9-year-old sister not to stand the baby on his feet and continuously stimulate the positive supporting reaction. Many medical personnel need to take a hard look at what they "think" families can understand and do. When properly trained, that same 9-year-old sister can become a strong positive remedial and preventive force in the life of a 1-year-old, severely involved spastic quadriplegic. But first the medical personnel must believe that anything is possible and operate on that premise. There is plenty of time to be "realistic" after every conceivable possibility and combination of techniques have been used diligently to reach the basic problems of autonomic nervous system balance, vestibular integration, and midline stability.

As discussed in the section on media repetitive goal-directed activity is

Dynamic sling

A. Cone for the hand
   1. Use any cone from commercial thread.
   2. Pass a loop of elastic through the center of the cone and over its surface. The fingers will slide under the elastic and the elastic will prevent the cone from falling out of the hand as the fingers release (A).
      NOTE: The cone is free. It is not attached to the sling.
B. Forearm orthokinetic segment
   1. Make the forearm segment out of Orthoplast or a similar material.
   2. The *inactive* shell (field) should cover the entire ventral surface of the forearm from the bend of the elbow medially and the olecranon process laterally to the flexed wrist (A).
   3. The open top of the shell should correspond to the muscle belly area of the wrist and finger extensors.
   4. At the wrist the edge of the shell is rolled down so that it applies pressure to the tendons of the wrist and finger flexors as the hand hangs down (B).
   5. Make the *active* field from elastic and attach one end to the medial side of the shell. Pass the elastic *diagonally* across the entire muscle belly area and fasten to the lateral side of the shell with Velcro (B).
      NOTE: Elastic should be just snug, *not* restrictive!
C. Sling harness
   1. Sew two pieces of 2-inch webbing together in a V shape (C). This V-shaped webbing should fit securely over the shoulder (D).
   2. Sew one end of a piece of 1-inch webbing to the front of the harness. Attach the free end of this webbing to the harness with Velcro, so that an adjustable loop is formed (E).
   3. Sew a loop of 1-inch webbing to the posterior part of the 2-inch shoulder webbing. Pass a piece of elastic tubing (or other elastic material) through the loop and attach both ends of the tubing to the medial side of the Orthoplast shell close to the elbow (F).
      NOTE: The length of the elastic tubing plus the length of the 2-inch posterior shoulder webbing and the loop should correspond to the length of the humerus.
   4. Attach a piece of 1-inch webbing to the medial and lateral upright tabs on the distal end of the Orthoplast shell. The lateral end should be fastened with Velcro to facilitate application and removal of the shell (G).

Illustrated by: S. Orton
Adopted from: Good Samaritan Hospital, O.T. Dept., Cincinnati; Randolph, 1975.

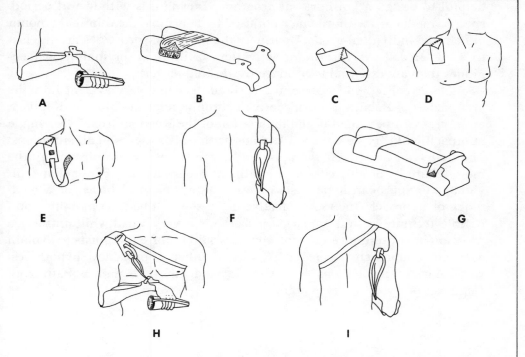

5. Attach a piece of elastic tubing to the webbing connecting the tabs of the Orthoplast shell (*H*).

   NOTE: Attach the elastic tubing so as to achieve the preferred position of forearm pronation.

6. Pass the 1-inch webbing on the anterior part of the harness (*E*) through a loop made at the end of the elastic tubing and fasten the Velcro attachment to the front of the harness (*H*).

   NOTE: Adjust the loop to the appropriate length—the biceps muscle must be protected from gravitational stretch.

7. To complete the sling harness and to prevent it from falling off the shoulder, sew a piece of 1-inch webbing to the posterior shoulder webbing. Bring it across the back, under the opposite arm (*I*), and across the chest to attach with Velcro to the anterior part of the shoulder harness (*H*).

very important for practicing the desired pattern. The therapist must constantly be on guard to stop the "busywork" of treatment and allow the patient to use the pattern as needed in a variety of activities. Frequently, it is helpful to design a "withdrawal program." During this withdrawal period, specific media are withdrawn or not used to determine the minimal amount of help the individual needs. Routinely the inhibitory processes are the last to be deleted. Never use more activation, facilitation, or inhibition techniques than are essential to produce the desired pattern.

As later concepts are presented it should become very evident how the approaches of Bobath, proprioceptive neuromuscular facilitation, Kephart, and Ayres can be added to the foundation of the Rood approach. No single approach will ever be the complete answer for all patients in all situations. The better an individual therapist understands basic neurophysiology the more secure he or she will be in treatment programs. The better that individual therapist can hypothesize the neurophysiological basis for a technique or approach, the more effective he or she will be in combining compatible techniques and approaches. Perhaps a very worthwhile in-service program or continuing education course would require therapists to explain a specific approach according to several other approaches' hypotheses, vocabularies, and theories. For example, what fun to explain Bobath from Kephart's or Ayres' vantage point.

KEY WORDS

abdominal muscles
activation
antagonist muscle
arrhythmical
body schema
cephalocaudal direction
cervical curve
coinnervation
DeLorme boot
dematomes
desensitize
distal segment
dorsiflexion
equinovalgus
equinovarus
expiration
extrafusal muscle fiber
facilitation
fusimotor activity
gamma
gastrocnemius
Golgi tendon organ
heavy work muscle fibers
hyperactive tongue
hypersensitive skin

hypertonic
hypotonic
inhibition
inspiration
inverted position
kinesthetic figure-ground
Landau reflex
light work muscle fibers
lumbar curve
maintained stretch
maximum range
midline neck muscles
midline trunk muscles
Moro reflex
motor end-plate
multiarthrodial muscle
muscle spindle
N-K table
nuclear bag
nuclear chain
NUK pacifiers
orbicularis oris
parasympathetic "toward"
   response
patellar tendons

phonation
"pill rolling"
platform shoe
primary afferent
   depolarization (PAD)
primitive postural reflexes
rhomboid muscles
scapular stability
skeletal function
spasticity
squat stance
stabilizers
submaximal range
sympathetic "away from"
   response
thoracic extension
tonic labyrinthine inverted
   response
tonic lumbar reflex
tonic muscles
trapezius
vibration

Kinesthetic figure-ground

genesis of perceptual-motor development

Concept
Background
  Tonic reflexes
    Tonic neck reflex
    Tonic lumbar reflex
    Tonic labyrinthine reflex
  Pacinian corpuscle
  Pain

Joint receptors
  Type I
  Type II
  Type III
  Type IV
Practical application
  Kinesthetic figure-ground
  Temporal growth
    Kephart
    Piaget

Approaches and techniques
  Neurodevelopmental
    treatment (Bobath)
  Proprioceptive
    neuromuscular
    facilitation
    (Knott and Voss)
  Passive range of motion
  Patterning (Doman-
    Delacato)

KEPHART

SPATIAL DIMENSION   TEMPORAL DIMENSION

PERCEPTUAL
PERCEPTUAL-MOTOR
MOTOR GENERALIZATIONS
MOTOR-PERCEPTUAL
KINESTHETIC FIG.GR'ND.

PIAGET   **AYRES**

INTUITIVE THINKING STAGE
PRE-CONCEPTUAL-THOUGHT
INVENTION OF NEW MEANS
COORDINATION OF TERTIARY CIRCULAR REACTIONS
SECONDARY SCHEMA
PRIMARY CIRCULAR
SECONDARY CIRCULAR
INNATE
AUTOMATIC
REFLEXIVE
A.N.S.
FUSIMOTOR
TACTILE
VESTIBULAR
birth
PROPRIOCEPTION
BODY SCHEMATA
PRAXIA
HEMISPHERE SPECIALIZATION
VISUAL SPATIAL
AUDITORY LANGUAGE
RECIPROCAL INNERVATION
CO-INNERVATION
HEAVY WORK
LIGHT WORK A.D.L. SPEECH SKILL
1 to 2 yrs.
3 to 5 yrs.
7 yrs.

ROOD

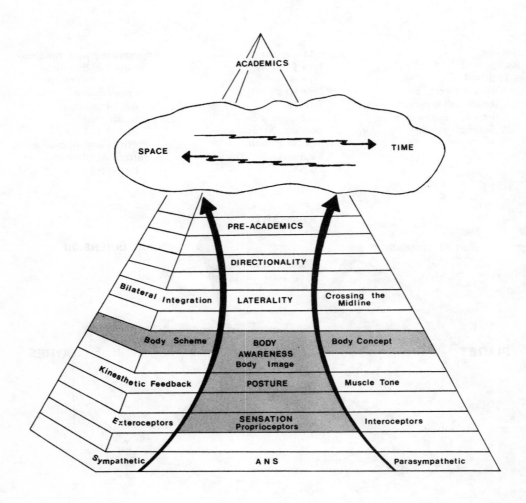

Concept The integration of all the proprioceptors is essential to kinesthetic feedback, with the joint receptors vitally involved in conscious awareness of kinesthetic figure-ground.

On the **tree** the proprioceptor roots that have not been discussed in previous concepts are the tonic reflexes, pacinian corpuscles, pain, and joint receptors. This sensory input will be discussed in the background and the integration of all the proprioceptors presented in the practical application.

On the **cross-section,** the sensory input is related to the central core and the 2-year-old area. The practical application will include the overlapping of the neurophysiological approaches of Piaget, Kephart, Bobath (neurodevelopmental treatment), Knott and Voss (proprioceptive neuromuscular facilitation), and Doman-Delacato (patterning).

In this concept the steps of the **pyramid** include the autonomic nervous system (ANS), sensation, posture and laterality, and body awareness.

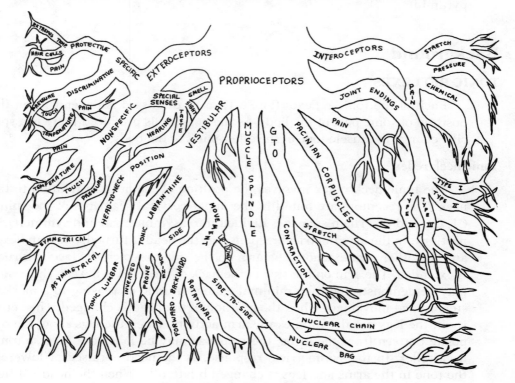

Fig. 6-1. Entire root system.

According to Frostig and Horne (1974) body awareness is made up of body schema, body image, and body concept. Body schema is the internal unconscious postural model of the body. This model is based on the tactile and proprioceptive input arising from the body as it interacts with the environment. Body image is what the individual feels about his body. The individual acquires attitudes, affects, and social perceptions about his body from social interactions with family and other people. Body concept is a completely learned process because it includes the names of body parts and their function.

Laterality is the internal awareness of the two sides of the body. It is the awareness that the two sides of the body work together and in opposition. This is an internal awareness. There are no directional labels attached to the movements, such as to the right, above, behind, or to the left.

As we progress up the pyramid we see that problems in the autonomic nervous system may lead to problems in sensation, which may contribute to problems in posture, body awareness, and laterality. The integration of all the proprioceptors is vital to the normal progression upward in the pyramid.

Background

TONIC REFLEXES

Each of the tonic reflexes (Fig. 6-1) to be discussed is dependent on the position of some part of the body. As the position is produced there is a specific change in muscle tone of the other parts of the body.

Tonic neck reflex

The tonic neck reflex involves the position of the head in relation to the neck. The receptors are found in the upper cervical segments of the spine, C1, C2, and C3. The response is divided into asymmetrical and symmetrical portions. In the asymmetrical response, as the head is turned, one arm flexes and the other arm extends. The arm on the side to which the face is turned is extended. The arm on the side of the back of the head is flexed. This reflex may be demonstrated by a minimal change in tone increasing to a marked stereotyped movement when the position of the head is changed. The activity in the legs usually mimics the arm activity. When the legs show the opposite pattern from the arms, the response may be labeled a reverse tonic neck reflex. In the symmetrical response, as the head is raised or lowered, the tone in the arms and legs is changed bilaterally. When the head is lifted or extended, both arms extend and both legs flex. When the head is lowered or flexed both arms flex and both legs extend. This reflex is most troublesome when it dominates the all fours position. As the child lifts his head, the arms extend but the legs flex and he sits on the heels. If his head drops, the arms immediately collapse and the legs extend sharply.

Tonic lumbar reflex

The tonic lumbar reflex involves the relationship of the upper part of the body to the pelvis and the corresponding distribution of tone in the extremities. The receptors for this reflex are found in the lumbar segments and divide the response into symmetrical and asymmetrical. As the trunk is dorsiflexed (pelvis has anterior tilt), there is extension of all four extremities. As the trunk is ventroflexed (pelvis has posterior tilt), there is flexion of all four extremities. The asymmetrical response actually consists of two types of stimulation—one of tilt and one of rotation. If deviation or tilt of the body is to the left and the trunk approaches the left hip, the left arm will flex and the left leg extend, with extension of the right arm and flexion of right leg. If the tilt or deviation is to the right hip, the reverse pattern will be seen. The right arm will flex and the right leg extend with left arm extended and the left leg flexed. In rotation of the trunk the same arm and leg pattern will be demonstrated. Rotation to the left means the ventral surface rotates toward the left hip, the left arm will flex, and the left leg will extend, with extension of the right arm and flexion of the right leg. Rotation of the ventral surface toward the right will reverse the pattern, giving flexion of the right arm and extension of the right leg, with extension of the left arm and flexion of the right leg. This is the normal pattern in gait. Without a well-integrated tonic lumbar reflex, an individual will have a very poor gait pattern with a pelvis that is not separated functionally from the trunk. Brunnstrom (1970) has long emphasized the importance of the lumbar reflex in her treatment of hemiplegic adults.

Tonic labyrinthine reflex

The tonic labyrinthine reflexes are associated with the position of the head as it relates to gravity. In the research done by Magnus and deKleijn, as reported by Tokizane (1951), maximum extensor tone was seen with the body in the supine position and with the mouth cleft at a 45-degree angle above the horizontal plane, and minimum extensor tone was seen with the body in the prone position and with the mouth cleft at a 45-degree angle below the horizontal plane. Unfortunately many therapists have attached the body positions of supine, prone, and side lying to this reflex instead of referring to the head position. It may be helpful to consider the labyrinthine effect as relating to maximum or minimum extensor tone. In the supine position the head is back or extended and extensor tone is maximal. When the body is prone, the head is brought forward, and extensor tone is minimal.

This decrease in extensor tone may be so marked that the individual becomes flexed, and it is impossible to place him or her prone unless the head position is altered. As the head is tilted to the side there is an increase in extensor tone on the side where the ear is approaching the shoulder, as in the side-lying position. There is decreased extensor tone on the opposite, or top, side of the body, which may result in a flexion pattern. The final component of the tonic labyrinthine response is seen in the inverted position, which was presented in detail in Concept 4.

PACINIAN CORPUSCLE

The pacinian corpuscle is the one receptor that has been proved consistently by research to serve the sensation of pressure. Wherever the corpuscle is found, the sensation of pressure is identified, and conversely wherever the sensation of pressure is found, pacinian or pacinian-like corpuscles can be identified. These receptors, as proprioceptors, are scattered throughout fascia and around muscle attachments and joints.

PAIN

Proprioceptive pain can be localized in muscle, tendons, and joints. This sensation is typically served by free nerve endings.

JOINT RECEPTORS

The joint receptors (Fig. 6-1) are the last group of proprioceptors to be discussed. The article by Wyke (1972), "Articular Neurology—a Review," is an excellent source of information. The importance of each receptor is related to the function of articular sensation and reflex influence on muscular activity.

Type I

Type I receptors are found in clusters of three to six in the superficial layers of the fibrous capsule. The clusters are more numerous in the areas that undergo more stress in normal joint movement. These receptors are found more frequently in the proximal joints of the extremities and in the cervical segments of the spine. Physiologically they have a low threshold, and are slow adapting. A certain percentage are active in every position of the joint, even when the joint is immobile. The rate of discharge is altered in the following three situations:

1. Any time the joint is moved actively or passively
2. Any time the tension in the muscles around the joints changes, either through isotonic (moving) or isometric (holding) contraction
3. Any time there is a change in the pressure gradient of the joint

Functionally type I receptors are both static and dynamic mechanoreceptors, involved in postural and kinesthetic perception. According to Wyke (1972), postural and kinesthetic perception is the conscious awareness of static joint positions and the direction, amplitude, and velocity of joint motion.

The reflex activity of this receptor influences muscle tone related to posture and gait and maintains muscle tone for prolonged periods of time in a specific position. The activity is mutually coordinated between antagonistic muscle groups, facilitating some and inhibiting others. The reflex is bilateral in effect and influences the activity of the same joint.

Type II

Type II receptors are elongated cones with a thick multilaminated capsule. They are found in the deeper layers of the fibrous capsule in clusters of two to four. These receptors are found more frequently in the distal joints of the extremities. Physiologically they have a low threshold, are fast adapting, and are entirely inactive in immobile joints. They fire briefly, less than ½ to 1 second at the onset of joint motion, when there is a sudden change in stress at the joint. Functionally these receptors are dynamic mechanoreceptors that signal acceleration or deceleration of joint movement, either actively or passively performed.

Type III

Type III receptors are identical in structure to the Golgi tendon organs. They are found in all the extrinsic and intrinsic ligaments of joints except the longitudinal and interspinous ligaments of the spine. Physiologically they have a high threshold, are slow adapting, are completely inactive in the immobile joint, and fire only at the extreme ranges of motion. They fire whenever there is considerable stress placed on the ligaments, either actively or passively, or when there is marked longitudinal traction. Functionally these receptors do not operate during normal physiological ranges of motion. They are active only during marked stress and reflexly produce profound inhibition of certain muscles crossing the joint and moderate facilitation of other muscles.

Type IV

Type IV receptors are noncorpuscular in structure and appear as latticelike plexuses or as free nerve endings. The latticelike plexuses are seen in the capsule and fat pads and the free nerve endings in the ligaments. Physiologically they have a high threshold, are nonadapting, and are inactive under normal circumstances. They fire whenever the tissue is subjected to marked mechanical tension or deformation or chemical irritation as a result of inflammatory exudates from damaged or necrotic tissue. Functionally these receptors serve articular pain sensation and are very active in the reflex spasm and splinting around injured joints.

Practical application

This concept concludes the presentation of the many facets of sensory input. In general, exteroceptors provide information about the external environment and interoceptors provide information about the internal environment of the individual. This information is relatively ineffective without the integration of the proprioceptors providing an adaptive behavior response. The adaptive behavioral response is dependent on kinesthetic feedback and kinesthetic figure-ground.

KINESTHETIC FIGURE-GROUND

Prior to the development of complex kinesthetic figure-ground, the infant must recognize the difference between movement and nonmovement. This is fostered by the waves or sweeps of movement passing over the body in a reflex fashion. These patterns are reciprocally innervated, with movements in one direction and a return to the starting position. During the periods of inactivity the muscle tone is minimal, affording the infant the experience of nonmovement.

Vestibuloproprioceptive input determines muscle tone. As the muscle tone in the extensor muscles develops it can be used to achieve cocontraction. The midline stability from cocontraction provides a stable base from which the extremities can move. This internal awareness of the difference between the muscle tone of the stable trunk (ground) and the changing tone of the extremities (figure), including the neck, is kinesthetic figure-ground.

The complex kinesthetic figure-ground is a result of the process of differentiation. Differentiation is the sorting out or separation of body parts from each other in a cephalocaudal and proximodistal direction.

Conjugate movement of the eyes initiates the differentiation process by separating the eye movement from the head movement. Normal eye movement is dependent on neck stability. Neck stability is essential to control the fluctuating tone from vestibular input. Once the neck is stable, it must then be differentiated from the trunk to afford free independent head orientation. As the differentiation progresses, the arms and legs are separated from the trunk as a unit. Subsequently each joint of the extremity will be isolated in a proximal to distal direction. The highest level or last step in differentiation is the separation of the thumb from the palm of the hand. Each step of differentiation is followed by a recombining of the elements into generalized movement patterns. These differentiation and generalization processes will be expanded in Concepts 7 and 8.

It is our opinion that the joint receptors are critical in this differentiation process. They are the receptors responsible for the conscious awareness of that internal "roadmap." Our definition of motor planning (praxia) is the automatic ability to initiate, direct, and stop the components of a skilled activity. Apraxia is the inability to initiate, direct, and stop the components of a skilled activity. As elaborated in Concept 5, a skilled activity such as creeping encompasses reciprocal innervation, coinnervation, and heavy work movement, as needed.

According to Kephart (1971) and Chaney (1978) the kinesthetic figure-ground is the first figure-ground relationship to develop. Once the child has a stable point of reference, he relates what is seen and heard back to his own body. Chaney refers to a visual-motor match and an auditory-motor match, which are processes of confirming with the body what is seen or heard. After the child makes the match to the body he is able to progress to a visual-auditory or auditory-visual match without the constant kinesthetic confirmation. Without the matching of visual to motor and auditory to motor, he is forced to live in two separate worlds, one motor and one perceptual.

TEMPORAL GROWTH

When we consider temporal growth of the individual we can relate to either the early stages of development of Kephart or those of Piaget as seen in the cross-section on p. 155. Kephart's stages deal specifically with sensory input and development of body information in the motor system. He is concerned with the development of kinesthesia and kinesthetic figure-ground. Piaget acknowledges the dominance of motor activity but focuses more on mental development. Piaget's influence can be recognized in much of Kephart's writings.

As an attempt is made to bring medical and educational professionals together in an interdisciplinary management, it is helpful to have authorities such as Piaget and Kephart reinforcing and complementing each other. It will probably be easier for most medical professionals to relate to the language and concepts of Kephart and then transfer to Piaget to complete their gestalt. The reverse process will probably be easier for most educational professionals, especially those teachers with limited backgrounds in anatomy, physiology, and medical terminology. We have believed for a long time that if *The Slow Learner in the Classroom* (Kephart, 1971) had been titled differently, the concepts and information it contains would have been used by many more medical professionals.

Kephart

The first stage of development according to Kephart (1971), Strauss and Kephart (1955), and Chaney and Kephart (1968) is the innate automatic or motor stage. This is the stage of reflexology that is the matrix of human development. These reflexes are the prewired circuits that provide protective survival responses to touch, position, and movement stimuli. During this period there are two types of movements possible. The first movements are stereotyped survival reflexes and result in minimal interaction with the environment. The second kind of movements are generalized waves of activity that begin at the head and traverse the body.

The second stage of development is the motor-perceptual stage. During this stage the child must modify and expand his reflex activity in order to interact in a meaningful way with his environment. There are three processes the child can use to accomplish this expansion. The first is that of chaining, wherein one reflex response is attached to another. The motor response of the first reflex becomes the stimulus for the second response. For example, in sucking, when the orbicularis oris muscle contracts, it stretches the buccinator, which initiates the stretch reflex to initiate contraction of the buccinator. This in turn stretches the superior pharyngeal constrictor muscle, causing it to contract.

The second process of expansion is integrating or tying reflexes together. One stimulus produces two or more reflex responses. An example of this is light touch at the corner of the mouth producing head turning and searching for the nipple together with arm bending and the hand coming to the mouth.

The third process is conditioning. An example is the Pavlovian dog, which salivated whenever a bell was rung. The modification and expansion of reflex activity is illustrated very clearly in the development of righting and equilibrium reactions presented by Bobath (1965).

As a result of these three processes of expansion, the child begins sorting out the parts of the body, one from another. This is differentiation because it results in isolated movements. As stated earlier, differentiation proceeds in a cephalocaudal, proximal to distal direction.

After the child has sorted out, separated, or differentiated the body parts into isolated movements, he begins to recombine them into schema. As he sorts out the movements and recombines them, he attends to the sensation of movement or the kinesthesia. As the child attends to the kinesthesia, kinesthetic figure-ground is developed. As the kinesthetic figure-ground becomes established, the newly developed schema become automatic. The body can operate without constant attention. The child can shift attention to what is seen and heard. However, he relates what is seen and heard back to the body for confirmation. This is the visual-motor match and the auditory-motor match, which move him into the perceptual-motor stage. The perceptual-motor stage will be presented in Concept 8.

Piaget

The stages of development according to Piaget are seen on the cross-section. The first six stages are designated sensorimotor and extend from birth to 2 years of age (Beard, 1969; Boyle, 1969; Phillips, 1969; Singer and Revenson, 1978).

The first month is considered the random reflex action stage. During this time the infant is dominated by primitive reflexes. The sensory stimulus produces a stereotyped motor response that becomes the initial body schema. "Schema" in this context means patterns of behavior.

The primary circular reactions stage exists from 1 to 4 months of age. "Circular" because the completion of the pattern is the stimulus for its repetition. "Primary" because the reactions are a part of the infant's innate behavior directed toward his own body. The infant is beginning to integrate primitive reflexes and develop a more elaborate body schema. He is beginning voluntary actions that come toward the body, especially the mouth. These first two stages are characterized by patterned sensory input, which establishes elementary reflex patterns or schema.

From 4 to 8 months of age the secondary circular reactions develop. "Secondary" because reactions are directed to surrounding objects. The infant's voluntary actions are now object oriented and he develops more elaborate schema. These patterns of behavior are repetitive and self-reinforcing. This is demonstrated by the manner in which an infant manipulates toys and babbles. During this stage, object permanence begins. This is demonstrated by the child searching for an object that has disappeared. Prior to this time, if an object was out of sight, it was out of mind; the object did not exist unless it was seen. Related to object permanence is the development of the dimensions of space and time, which will be presented in detail in Concept 8.

The fourth stage is coordination of secondary schemata and extends from age 8 to 12 months. Secondary schemata are intentionally separated or combined into means and ends. The individual is beginning to develop a simple organization of time because he foresees coming events and demonstrates anticipation. He recognizes an object by reproducing the action he used in the previous period, which represents a primitive "symbolic meaning." This is the beginning of rituals. The ritual correlates the visual feedback with the kinesthetic and tactile feedback. The sound he associates with the ritual forms the link between the visual image of the object and the tactile-kinesthetic image of the movement.

From 12 to 18 months of age the child is in the tertiary circular reaction stage. "Tertiary" because the child varies his actions to make new movements. The child deliberately manipulates the environment to see what will happen. This is the time when socially manipulative behavior begins. He becomes more interested in his own movements and participates in trial-and-error experimentation. He is very curious, exploring every facet of the objects in his environment. He repeatedly experiments with the relationship of objects to himself. His rituals become much more elaborate and are established as games.

The sixth stage extends from 18 months to 2 years of age and is designated invention of new means. The child has an image of the world around him and of his place in it. His manipulations have become internalized. He is beginning to have insights, to pretend, and to "make believe" by imitating animals and inanimate objects. This is the beginning of the symbolic process. At this point the child is capable of relating cause and effect as well as the reverse or the effect of a cause. This is possible because of the expansion of the space and time dimensions. The child is not locked into these two dimensions.

In summary let us relate the impaired individual to this temporal growth pattern. The individual of any age or diagnosis with the following problems may be placed developmentally in the first month of life:

1. Dominated by protective responses around the face and mouth
2. Inadequate sucking-swallowing patterns
3. Restless, irritable, with sleeping problems
4. Elimination difficulties such as constipation

The individual demonstrating the following difficulties is developmentally in the period from 1 to 4 months:

1. Dominated by primitive reflexes such as the Moro, flexor withdrawal, tonic neck, tonic labyrinthine, or associated reactions
2. In the prone position is unable to lift head and support on forearms or hands
3. Lack of conjugate eye movements that are separated from head movements
4. Lacks differentiation of head and arms, which is demonstrated by the inability to visually attend to manipulation of objects in the midline

The individuals with the following problems could be considered developmentally between 4 and 8 months:

1. Lacks the Landau reflex or the tonic prone extension of the entire body
2. Because of lack of extension, has not developed stability in the all fours position
3. Because of lack of midline stability is not differentiating body parts or developing kinesthetic figure-ground

4. Because of excessive tone, is not differentiating body parts or developing kinesthetic figure-ground.

The preoperational phase extends from 2 years of age to 7 years of age. During this time the child begins to take an interest in the people and things around him. This is, however, a very egocentered phase; so everything is in relation to his point of view. As the understanding of relationships and points of view improve, the child is less egocentric. This egocentrism is an intermediate step between the autism of the sensorimotor phase and full intelligent understanding (Boyle, 1969). To make this progression, the child must participate in play, imitation, and the use of language. This phase is divided into a preconceptual stage from 2 to 4 years of age and an intuitive thinking stage from 4 to 7 years.

The child in the preconceptual stage demonstrates an activity called transduction. This is a tendency of the child to link together adjacent events on the basis of individual similarities. A red circle may be linked to a red triangle by color, the red circle to a blue circle by shape, and the blue circle to a blue triangle by color. To the child the *four* things are alike. This child cannot form concepts because he is tied too closely to the perceptions. He can not yet form abstractions or generalizations. The development of concepts has to evolve from the development of mental imagery in which the signifier (for example, a gesture or word) is different from the real thing but does represent it. This is the actual basis of language use, of drawing and interpreting pictures, and of extending play into symbolic play or constructional games.

The child's play is not just preparation for adult activities. It is the process of developing the ability to think. Play begins as imitation. There is a definite sequence of imitation that evolves from purely reflex behavior to complex imitations of models. Accommodation is the simple copying of an act without an understanding of the movements. Assimilation is the child's use of a symbol such as a doll in his own game of waving bye-bye. Toward the end of the second year the child begins symbolic play. In this play the child uses something other than the original object to symbolize the object and perform certain behaviors of the original object, such as using a block of wood as a car in appropriate travel activity.

Ritualistic play in the sensorimotor stage becomes *practice* or a form of *mastery*. In this kind of play the child repeats the activity for the sheer pleasure of sensation—feeling, touching, moving, smelling, tasting, and even listening. What an impact this has on children who are prevented from playing because of abnormal muscle tone or because of illness or surgery. They do not experience and know the full enjoyment of all sensations. What a strong plea for early prevention rather than remediation months and years too late!

From age 2 through 5 years the major play is symbolic. A swing becomes a rocket; a box, a car; and a stick, a horse for the child in make-believe. The child can separate what is real and what is fantasy by this symbolic play.

Parallel play is seen frequently in preschoolers involved in their individual symbolic play side by side. They only interact in a superficial, fleeting way.

Compensatory play may be used by a child in order to dissociate an unpleasant act. For example, if a child is punished, he may punish a doll in the same way.

Games with rules do not begin to appear until 4 to 7 years of age and actually belong to the age of concrete operations, 7 to 11 years. There are some very simple games that are passed down from generation to generation such as "Mother May I," "Hide and Seek," or "Rotten Egg." Some ball-handling practice games may evolve into games with simple rules. Games with rules become the adult's world of play. The adult's fantasies become his symbolic games. The child who can continue his "play attitude" into adulthood is usually an imaginative, creative adult.

Before leaving play we should consider the purposes and benefits of children's play. Unfortunately, many people do not appreciate the critical importance of play to children or the need to provide specific kinds of play experience. Play is a valuable aspect of the child's growth in all cognitive, emotional, social, spiritual, and physical areas. The more early intervention programs that are initiated, the more critical the concept of children's play becomes.

Singer and Revenson (1978) present nine benefits of play. The first benefit of play is that through it the infant learns about his world or *sharpens his senses*. He must experience the world with all his senses and confirm from one sense to another if intersensory integration is going to occur. This intersensory integration is discussed in Concept 7. Each time a child masters some aspect of manipulation of the world around him, he feels more competent and effective, which builds his self-esteem. Unfortunately there is nothing like success to build self-esteem.

The second benefit of play is the development of *vocabulary*. A child must acquire the words needed to express the actions of play, such as pitch, field, guard; the objects used in play, such as bat, mitt, racket; and the rules of the game.

The third benefit of play is *concentration*. As the child continues in the play, regardless of the level, he is forced to attend, persist, and concentrate. The more enjoyable the game and the more skillful the child, the longer the periods of concentration.

A fourth benefit of play is to develop the child's *flexibility or imagination*.

Children should learn to be adaptive and to use whatever is available to substitute for what they need. This creative ability, which seems so lacking in many adults, may reflect a lack of experience in childhood.

The creation of an atmosphere of *harmony and cooperation* is perhaps one of the most vital benefits of play. Children learn respect, tolerance, sharing, rules, and structure in their play. The older they grow, the more advanced their social and emotional development and the more they should be able to cooperate with less adult supervision. The less physical ability the child possesses, the less effective he is going to be in the group and, frequently, the more disruptive he becomes, or he becomes an observer, always on the sidelines.

The sixth benefit of play is to *delay gratification*. If a child has to wait for his make-believe supper or for his turn at bat, he is learning patience, tolerance, and respect for other people's rights and feelings.

The seventh benefit of play is *assuming different roles*. This allows the child to practice society on a miniscale. The child experiences how people act and what their responsibilities are, for example, the mailman must put the letters in the mailbox.

Empathy, as the eighth benefit, develops out of role playing. The child begins to understand the feelings, desires, and frustrations of his pretend people.

The ninth benefit of play is the *expansion of the imagination and creativity*. Symbolic play, more than any other type of play, enables the child to experiment with sounds and movements; to pretend, he masters his environment, he distinguishes between reality and fantasy, and he works out alternate plans for problem-solving.

Some of the play discussed extends into the intuitive thinking stage. This stage extends from 4 to 7 years of age. The child begins to be able to give reasons for his beliefs and actions. When he does this he begins to form concepts at a low level. Children in this stage cannot make internal or mental comparisons; the comparisons have to be built up one at a time in physical action. In the absence of this mental representation, they are still bound by their perceptions of segments instead of totals. Since they are perceiving only one segment at a time, they cannot hold in their minds more than one relation at a time. The internalization of different views does not occur until operational thinking begins in the next stage. Children aged 4 to 7 by necessity are still very egocentric.

Related to the perceiving of segments is the lack of direction in children's thinking. The child cannot yet imagine an ordered sequence of events. He must move from step to step in each situation. In a later repetition of the situation the steps may be different because many of the perceptions will be different. With this lack of ordered sequence it is impossible for these children to reverse their thinking or to interrupt at some point and, after the interruption, continue. The child must return to the starting point.

The child can solve simple problems of space, time, and numbers but is unable to form even the simplest relations. Since the child cannot see the simple relations he is also unable to compare two relations. For instance, it is very confusing to be a brother to a sister. It is also very confusing for the child to relate between a whole and its parts.

At this stage a child is aware of rules and believes them to be absolute. Since the rules are absolute, to change them is frequently interpreted as "cheating." Moral judgments are tied to these absolute rules and are therefore judged by the consequences of the action instead of by the intent. For instance, lying would be all right if the child did not get punished.

APPROACHES AND TECHNIQUES

Since this concept involves the integration of all of the proprioceptors, it is only fitting that other neurophysiological approaches be explored. Some of their contributions will be presented.

Neurodevelopmental treatment (Bobath)

It would seem appropriate to credit the Bobaths with making the greatest impact on the therapist's comprehension of reflex activity and normalizing muscle tone. If we return to their earlier writings we find some very convincing concepts.

> In the child with cerebral palsy the proprioceptive system can mediate only the sensations of an abnormal muscle tone and of abnormal postures and movements. It can therefore only serve to lay down abnormal patterns of posture and movements. The child will experience only the sensations of undue weight of his limbs and the excessive effort required for intended movement. All he knows are a few abnormal postures and some abnormal movement patterns. With these sensory experiences he cannot be expected to develop normal movement patterns or a normal concept of his body.
>
> For this reason, cerebral palsy should be considered a sensorimotor disorder rather than only a motor defect. Treatment should aim at changing this state by influencing and redirecting the motor output from the sensory side, using all means of sensory stimulation—proprioceptive, visual, auditory, and tactile.
>
> Normal sensorimotor patterns can only be laid down on the basis of a normally functioning proprioceptive system. The first step in treatment is therefore to normalize muscle tone. . . .*

---

*From Bobath, K.: Cerebral Palsy Bull., vol. 1, no. 8, 1959.

In the same article are found some very essential facts concerning early motor development:

1. In the first 2 months of life the normal infant demonstrates a dominance of flexor tone.
2. The extremities are held close to the body, while the head moves freely but is poorly coordinated.
3. The distribution of muscle tone is symmetrical.
4. Head control develops rapidly, and by 3 to 4 weeks after birth the infant is lifting the head in the prone position and beginning to hold it when moved.
5. Normally extensor tone begins to develop during the second month. It progresses distally until at 6 months the infant is capable of bridging or arching on his shoulders and heels, which voluntarily exercises neck and trunk extensors.
6. The influence of tonic reflexes can be seen up to age 4 to 6 months in the normal infant.
7. In the normal child, tonic reflex activity is never enough to *interfere* with the child's movement.

Perhaps it is being redundant to again emphasize the importance of a neurophysiologically integrated approach to management. We are very intent, however, on continuing to impress on the reader that no one approach has all the answers. How very important it is to return to Concepts 1 and 5 and use Ayres's and Rood's techniques of vestibular stimulation and manipulation of muscle tone as an adjunct to the "handling" of Bobath. Righting and equilibrium reaction are essential components of developmental management. Rotation about the body axis is a vital key in normalizing muscle tone and in differentiation. How much better responses can be obtained by combining, in appropriate sequence, all of our available techniques. After 20 years it would seem that we should all be striving diligently to combine all of our techniques and approaches for the benefit of the patient. Perhaps at no other point in recent history have we had more knowledge, more techniques, and more potential for achieving the impossible. The only limitation is our own human doubts, inadequacies, and failure to believe and act with conviction.

Proprioceptive neuromuscular facilitation (Knott and Voss)

It has been our experience that physical therapists do not routinely use the proprioceptive neuromuscular facilitation approach for its motor-perceptual value. The manner in which the extremity is held provides tactile stimulus on the proper skin surface to encourage the correct direction of movement. There are few other approaches that provide the propriocep-tive stimulation to the kinesthetic feedback necessary for developing kine-sthetic figure-ground. The quick stretch stimulus fires the muscle spindle. The maximal resistance is automatically a maintained stimulus for a maintained contraction. The isometric contraction provides time for the muscle spindles in the holding muscle to adjust to the shorter length at the same time that the muscle spindles are relaxing in the lengthening muscle.

Each time an extremity pattern is performed it is in a spiral diagonal pattern that crosses the midline of the body (Knott and Voss, 1960). As the timing for emphasis is used with the movement patterns, differentiation is required to bring the body parts into their proper sequence. Combining arm patterns promotes bilateral integration of the two sides of the body. If arm and leg patterns are used together, there is integration of the superior and the inferior parts of the body unilaterally or diagonally.

All of the resistive movement in the all fours position in creeping, in standing, and in walking contributes to body awareness and laterality. Com-bining arm and leg patterns in the all fours position contributes to this de-velopment of laterality in a different position.

If the patient is encouraged to watch the extremity as it moves, eye-hand or eye-foot coordination is emphasized. All of these activities contribute to the normal progression upward in the pyramid of learning.

Passive range of motion

Passive range of motion has been a rehabilitation procedure for many years. It has, however, too frequently been administered neurophysiologi-cally incorrectly. Whenever spasticity is present, passive range of motion merely provides a stretch to muscle spindles that are already hypersensitive, as discussed in Concept 5. Attempting to maintain range of motion at the expense of increasing spasticity is fruitless. When tendon pressure, as pre-sented in Concept 5, is used to inhibit the spastic muscle, passive range of motion is appropriate for joint receptor stimulation. If, as Wyke (1972) indi-cates, the joint receptors are critical in the conscious awareness of kines-thetic and postural perception, a reappraisal of the value of passive range of motion is indicated.

Let us consider the hemiplegic patient with sensory loss, poor propri-oceptive responses, or unilateral disregard. Perhaps this patient needs a con-siderable amount of joint receptor stimulation to make him aware of those extremities.

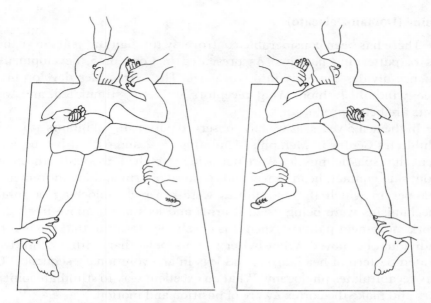

Fig. 6-2. The child is patterned in a homolateral pattern for 5 minutes at a time four times a day. In the homolateral patterning the arm and leg on the side that the face is turned to are flexed, while the extremities on the other side are extended.

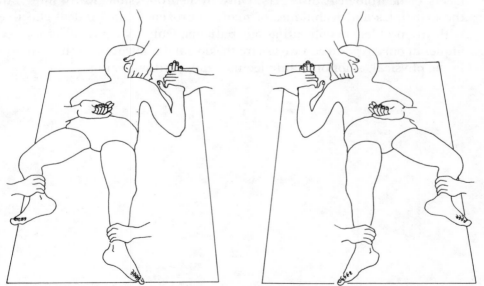

Fig. 6-3. Cross patterning is used when the child begins to creep. The arm on the face side is flexed and the opposite leg flexed. The arm on the side the face is turned away from is extended and the opposite leg is extended.

Patterning (Doman-Delacato)

There has been considerable controversy through the years over the merits of patterning patients. As presented in Concept 5, developmental sequence divides the body into two parts. The extremities develop first in a free, windmill fashion. What receptors are being stimulated, and what effects are being produced?

In the last 5 years, as we have observed patterning of infants at Les Passes Children's Center in Memphis, Tenn. (Figs. 6-2 and 6-3), it has become evident that spastic muscles were not being stretched. Evidently through position, skin contact, head movement, pattern of arm and leg movements, and manner in which the extremities were grasped, unlocking or inhibitory mechanisms were being used. If arms and legs are to move freely in light work movement patterns, then it is absolutely essential that the nonmoving individual be moved. What better way to move than with a primitive integrated pattern of head, arms, and legs in an evolutionary sequence! Ontogeny recapitulates phylogeny! What an excellent way to stimulate joint receptors and make the cortex aware of position and motion.

The impression that we would like to leave with the reader is one of unity. No single approach or technique is capable of correcting all of the many facets of neurological disorders. Only by neurophysiologically integrating the principles and techniques of many approaches can we deal effectively with the problems confronting our patients. Only by using all of the techniques at our disposal can we assure the optimal realization of the individual in the physical, emotional, intellectual, and spiritual realms.

KEY WORDS

abnormal movements
abnormal postures
conjugate movement of eyes
differentiation process
distal joints
fibrous capsule
figure-ground
  auditory
  kinesthetic
  visual

mechanoreceptor
ontogeny recapitulates
  phylogeny
passive range of motion
patterning
pelvic tilt
proprioceptive neuromuscular
  facilitation

static joint position
symmetrical response
tonic receptors
unlocking mechanisms

Synaptic activity

attention-hyperactivity-behavior

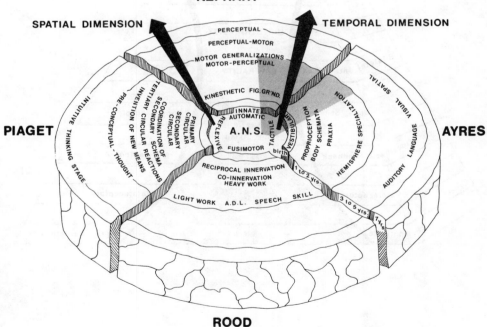

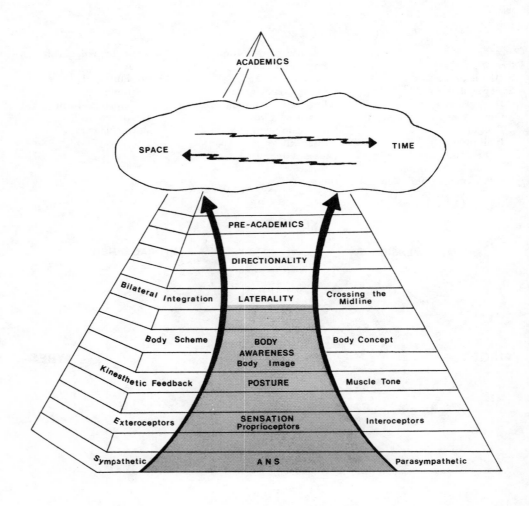

Concept   Facilitation or inhibition of synaptic transmission determines neuronal activity. Primary afferent depolarization (PAD) appears to be a sensory-filtering mechanism that focuses attention by eliminating irrelevant, trivial input. Convergent neurons provide a mechanism at the brain stem level for intersensory integration.

On the **tree,** PAD is symbolized as a triangle lying across the primary branches. This illustrates how all sensory input may be subjected to inhibition at the sensory neuron level. The convergent neurons are represented by the word integration connecting the vestibular, haptic, and tactile branches.

On the **cross-section,** synaptic activity extends from the central core out to the periphery. All activity is determined by facilitation and inhibition at synapses. Higher and higher levels of behavior are made possible by more complex patterns of synaptic activity.

The same situation is seen on the **pyramid,** on which synaptic activity is involved in every step and every activity. The filtering out of trivial sensory input and convergence of varied input become more critical as higher functions are approached.

Background

SYNAPTIC PROPERTIES

Synapses possess certain characteristic properties. Synapses allow the action potential or impulse to go in only one direction. They are classified as being unidirectional. This assures a forward progression of input to output in the central nervous system (CNS).

Synapses do not have to transmit faithfully what is presented to them. The synapse becomes the first level of integration. The integration may involve amplification of the input through the repetitive firing of a synapse or may involve diminution, delay, or complete stoppage of the impulse.

Synapses are susceptible to various conditions such as asphyxia and ischemia and to medications. Much of our information concerning CNS function has been learned from the reactions of specific synapses to different drugs. The activity in some synapses will be increased by certain drugs and decreased or completely interrupted by other drugs.

There is a synaptic delay of activity. The delay is fairly uniform for specific types of neurons. Because the speed of conduction can be calculated for the neurons, it is possible for researchers to determine how many neurons

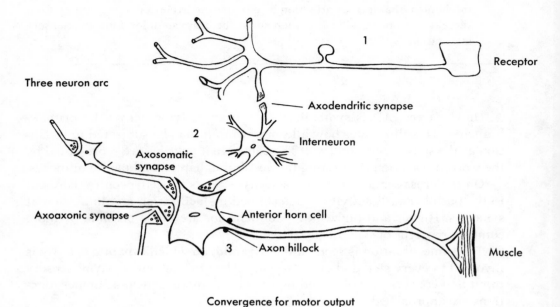

Fig. 7-1. Synaptic structure of a disynaptic reflex arc showing divergence and convergence.

are present in a circuit. The synaptic delay varies in magnitude from 0.3 to 1.0 msec.

Fig. 7-1 illustrates a typical disynaptic neuron chain. This chain consists of a sensory neuron, an association neuron or interneuron, a motor neuron, and two synapses.

SYNAPTIC ACTIVITY
Divergence

As was seen in Fig. 7-1, the sensory neuron enters the CNS and branches, forming many terminals. It is estimated that one neuron may form many hundreds or even thousands of synapses. This process is referred to as divergence. This divergence makes afferent information accessible simultaneously to many areas of the CNS such as the spinal cord, cerebellum, brain stem, and cortex. Contrary to immediate impression, divergence does not decrease the strength of the impulse. Regardless of how many terminals the sensory neuron has, the impulse has the same potential at every ending. The character of the synapse determines what happens in the second neuron.

The motor neurons demonstrate a similar type of divergence or branching as they enter the muscle to innervate individual muscle fibers. This ratio may vary from one axon to 15 muscle fibers in the external eye muscles of man to one axon to 1900 muscle fibers found in some of the muscles of the extremities in man.

Convergence

Convergence is the opposite of divergence and occurs at the interneurons and motor neurons. Fig. 7-1 shows many synapses occurring on the dendritic spikes as well as on the cell bodies of the neuron. These synapses are called axodendritic and axosomatic, respectively.

The threshold of the neuron must be reached at the site of the axon hillock in order to depolarize the neuron and initiate the action potential. The initiation of the action potential depends on the algebraic sum of all the facilitory and inhibitory influences occurring at any given time. The time factor is in the magnitude of a fraction of a millisecond. This process is very similar to the generator potential reaching the threshold of the sensory neuron and initiating the action potential in the sensory neuron, as presented in Concept 2. As the excitatory and inhibitory processes are discussed, the properties of the generator potential will be related to these excitatory and inhibitory potentials.

Excitation

It is believed that the electrical manifestation of any facilitation is the excitatory postsynaptic potential (EPSP). If sufficient EPSPs are produced, the neuron is depolarized, and an action potential is propagated. The EPSP possesses the same properties as the generator potential. It is stationary, is confined to the area of the dendrites and soma, and is conducted in the area with decrement. The amplitude is graded through a wide range because it can be summed and because it lacks refractory periods.

The time course of the EPSP is significant when compared to the two inhibitory processes that will be presented later. The EPSP begins about 0.5 msec after the primary afferent volley reaches the spinal cord. It reaches its peak in 1.0 to 1.5 msec and declines in 4 to 12 msec.

An understanding of this simplified concept of synaptic excitation is necessary to appreciate what is occurring in the clinical process of facilitation. A stimulus is applied to the receptor, which produces a generator potential. If the generator potential reaches the threshold of the sensory neuron, an action potential is initiated. When the action potential reaches the end of the central terminal it is confronted with a synapse.

The action potential causes the release of a transmitter substance that diffuses across the potential space or synaptic cleft to react with the receptor sites on the postsynaptic membrane. This reaction at the receptor site changes the permeability of the membrane to all ions, and ultimately an EPSP is produced. If the amplitude of the EPSP is sufficient, the threshold of the neuron is reached, and an action potential is initiated along the axon. If a motoneuron is receiving the EPSP, the impulse will be sent to the muscle. If an interneuron is receiving the EPSP, the impulse is sent along the neuronal circuit to the next interneuron or a motoneuron.

Inhibition

Direct inhibition. The opposite action of the EPSP is an inhibitory post-synaptic potential (IPSP). The same sequence of generator potential, action potential, and release of transmitter substance as outlined for the EPSP occurs here, but the end result is one of inhibition instead of facilitation. The time course of the IPSP is slower. It begins 1.25 to 1.5 msec after the afferent volley reaches the spinal cord, reaches a peak in 1.5 to 2.0 msec, but then declines in 3 msec, which is faster than the decline of the EPSP.

It would seem logical to hypothesize that inhibition would be more difficult to produce than excitation or facilitation simply from the time factor standpoint alone. As described in the definition of the Rood approach, of the three processes—activation, facilitation, and inhibition—inhibition is the most critical. If the proper inhibition is in the proper place at the proper time, much less activation or facilitation may be needed. We all need to be aware of the fact that a large percentage of our skilled activity is the result of inhibiting the unwanted action and allowing the desired pattern to operate.

The chemical process or ionic mechanism for the IPSP is more complicated than for the EPSP. The IPSP equilibrium potential is situated at -80 mV, which is approximately half way between the equilibrium potential for $K+$, at -90 mV, and for $Cl-$, at -70 mV. Because of the combined interaction of $K+$ and $Cl-$, the IPSP may operate in either a hyperpolarizing direction from -70 mV to -80 mV or a depolarizing direction from -90 mV to -80 mV. The crucial factor in producing the IPSP is the apparent fixation of the resting potential at the -80 mV, which makes it more difficult to fire the neuron.

This fixation of the membrane potential becomes tremendously important to the therapist dealing with patients who have spasticity. Consider the patient with a spastic biceps brachii. The spasticity is an active contraction, and through reciprocal innervation, IPSPs are produced on the triceps brachii motoneurons, stabilizing their resting potentials at -80 mV instead of the usual -70 mV. It would therefore appear that the technique of choice would be to inhibit the spastic contraction of the biceps, which would automatically and actively remove IPSPs from the triceps motoneurons. Berta Bobath demonstrated as early as the 1950s that if spasticity of one set of muscles is decreased, the inactive antagonist may spontaneously contract. The physiological explanation for this technique must be the active removal of IPSPs from the inactive antagonists. Instead of continuing to stimulate the muscle spindles in the spastic flexor, adductor, internal rotator, and two-joint extensor muscles, why not operate through the synaptic activity and manipulate the IPSPs?

As indicated earlier, the initiation of the action potential in the motoneuron is dependent on the algebraic sum of all the excitation (EPSPs) and inhibition (IPSPs) at any given time. Since the IPSPs stabilize or fixate the membrane at −80 mV, an actively inhibited neuron is more difficult to depolarize than one at the normal resting potential. An excellent, concise book, *Fundamentals of Neurophysiology*, edited by Robert F. Schmidt (1975), presents this material more completely for the interested reader.

Indirect inhibition. Until recent years most researchers believed that all inhibition was either of the direct IPSP variety or an indirect inhibition. Indirect inhibition is actually a result of the previous firing of the neuron. This inhibition corresponds to the refractory periods and the after potentials of the action potential, which were discussed in Concept 2.

Presynaptic inhibition. According to Schmidt (1971) the modern history of presynaptic inhibition began in 1957 when Frank and Fuortes described a depression of EPSPs that occurred without any postsynaptic potential changes. Unfortunately that pioneering work was never published in detail.

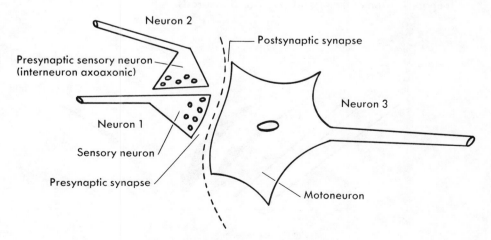

Fig. 7-2. Presynaptic inhibition.

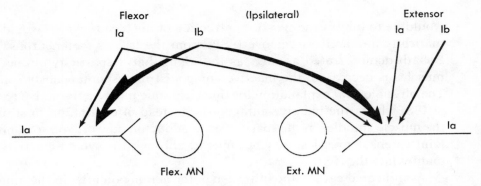

Fig. 7-3. PAD for Ia fibers. Fibers at the top produce ipsilateral depolarization of flexor and extensor Ia fibers to motor neurons at the bottom.

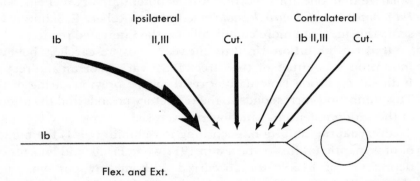

Fig. 7-4. PAD for Ib fibers. Fibers at the top produce ipsilateral and contralateral depolarization of flexor and extensor Ib neurons.

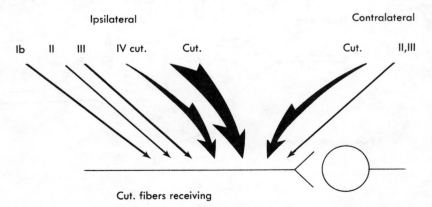

Fig. 7-5. PAD for cutaneous afferent fibers. Fibers at the top produce ipsilateral and contralateral depolarization of cutaneous fibers. Cut indicates myelinated fibers and IV cut indicates unmyelinated fibers.

Eccles, Eccles, and Magni in 1960 and 1961 confirmed the earlier work and instituted Frank and Fuorte's original term "presynaptic inhibition" to designate the phenomenon. The Schmidt article has an outstanding review of the literature up to 1971.

In presynaptic inhibition there is no change in the postsynaptic membrane. The inhibitory process results in a reduction in the amount of transmitter substance released, at the excitatory synaptic terminal. We are dealing with a third type of synapse—axoaxonic. Fig. 7-2 shows the axosomatic synapse of neuron 1 on neuron 3. It also shows the axoaxonic presynaptic synapse of neuron 2 on neuron 1. The sequence of events in presynaptic inhibition is quite unique. The sensory impulse enters the CNS on neuron 1, reaches the synapse, and releases the transmitter substance, which diffuses across the cleft to react with the receptor sites, and an EPSP is produced on neuron 3. If presynaptic inhibition is initiated, the action potential of neuron 2 releases only a portion of the transmitter substance of neuron 1, which is not sufficient to produce an EPSP. Subsequently, when another action potential on neuron 1 reaches the synapse, there is not sufficient transmitter substance left to produce an EPSP on neuron 3. Consequently the effectiveness of the second action potential of neuron 1 is reduced in the amount that the membrane has been depolarized by the action of neuron 2 and the transmitter substance wasted. A presynaptic inhibition of neuron 1 activity has been produced.

Neuron 2 is a multipolar interneuron that receives many converging impulses. It may be in the pathway of another central terminal of neuron 1, which means that the initial incoming action potential is capable of setting up its own PAD activity or intrasensory inhibition, for example, cutaneous input inhibiting cutaneous input. Neuron 2 may be in the pathway of a completely different type of sensory input, which produces an intersensory inhibition, for example, Ib input inhibiting Ia input.

At the spinal cord level there are three systems of intrasensory and intersensory PAD activity. Fig. 7-3 illustrates the source of PAD for Ia fibers from the muscle spindles of both flexor and extensor muscles. The thickness of the arrows gives an estimate of the strength of the various pathways. Evidently not all types of group I muscle afferents are equally potent in producing PADs on flexor or extensor Ia fibers (Schmidt, 1971). Fig. 7-4 illustrates the source of PAD for Ib fiber from the Golgi tendon organs of both flexor and extensor muscles. The thickness of the arrow again represents an estimate of the strength of the pathways. The contralateral sources are much weaker than the ipsilateral source (Schmidt, 1971). Fig. 7-5 illustrates the source of PAD induced in cutaneous afferent fibers. The cutaneous afferent fibers produce a very extensive PAD on themselves both ipsilaterally and contralaterally.

As was seen in Fig. 7-3, Ib fibers are involved in producing an intersensory PAD on Ia fibers. Group II fibers, which are low-threshold myelinated afferents, and group III fibers, which are high-threshold myelinated afferents, produce intersensory PAD on the Ib fibers. The group IV cutaneous fibers, which are unmyelinated C fibers, appear to induce only an ipsilateral PAD in cutaneous afferent fibers.

Eccles (1964) indicates that presynaptic inhibition provides a mechanism for suppressing sensory input before it can exert a synaptic action. The cutaneous afferent system of PAD is a powerful force in suppressing trivial input and clearing the system for urgent action. In Eccles' terms, PAD is the first stage in "perceptual attention."

Schmidt (1971) indicates that a system of PAD similar to the spinal cord system exists at the gracilis and cuneate nuclei for those sensory neurons ascending in the posterior columns of the spinal cord. There is undoubtedly both an intrasensory and intersensory PAD system present. This system focuses perceptual attention at the brain stem level as it does at spinal cord levels.

Schmidt (1971) discusses descending suprasegmental inputs to spinal cord PADs. Generally it appears that Ia fibers do not receive a PAD (are not depolarized) from cortical areas. However, the medial longitudinal fasciculus appears to carry input from the brain stem and cerebellum to Ia fibers of flexor muscles. The Ib fibers receive input from the sensorimotor cortex. The effect from sensory area I was predominately contralateral, while the effect from sensory area II was bilateral. The effects seem to be carried by both pyramidal and extraspinal pathways. Several areas of the brain stem and cerebellum provide PADs to the Ib fibers by way of the same medial longitudinal fasciculus as the Ia fibers. It has been found generally that those supraspinal structures that produce PADs on Ib fibers will also produce PADs on cutaneous afferent fibers.

In summary, it must be kept in mind that much of the research concerning PAD has been performed on cats. There is always the question of to what extent animal research can be transferred to man. It would certainly seem permissible to assume, since these systems exist in cats, that at least similar systems exist in man. The magnitude of implications for anyone dealing with sensory stimulation of individuals is staggering. The questions that begin to come to mind are fascinating. Is there a developmental sequence to the production of PAD? If so, what kinds of stimulation and activities influence the sequence? If the PAD does "focus attention," is it possible that some of the short attention span and distractibility problems in children are really a result of too few PADs? Is it possible that the autistic child has too many sensory stimuli filtered out? More specifically, as we use stretch, pressure, and all types of tactile stimulation, are we aware that PADs are being produced? If the trivia is being sorted out, surely we must put tremendous emphasis on having the individual actively engaged in the goal-directed activity we are stimulating. Ayres (1972) emphasizes that the adaptive behavioral response is the best integrator of intersensory input. Perhaps that is because PADs are not functioning to stop the information.

INTERSENSORY INTEGRATION
Prenatal period

At this point it is necessary to turn our attention to intersensory integration. As Sherrington (1951) so amply expressed it: The naive would expect evolution in its course to have supplied us with more various sense organs for ampler perception of the world. . . . The policy has rather been to bring by the nervous system the so-called "five" into closer touch with one another. . . . Not new senses but better liason between old senses. . . .

As one ascends the evolutionary series from the simplest life form to man, unimodal sensory control of behavior is replaced by multimodal and intersensory control mechanisms. In lower animals one may demonstrate gustatory stimuli modulating and modifying visually determined responses where tactile stimuli were unable to influence the response (Birch and Lefford, 1963).

Instead of beginning our investigation of intersensory integration at birth we would like to explore the prenatal period. Hooker (1952) and Humphrey (1969) have contributed heavily to our knowledge and appreciation of prenatal behavior. They have repeatedly emphasized that the sequence in which an activity develops during fetal life is repeated during early postnatal development.

According to Hooker there is a definite spread of skin sensitivity to tactile stimuli prenatally. At 7½ weeks after conception only the area around the lips and the alae of the nose are sensitive. By 8 through 9½ weeks this area has increased to include the chin and the lateral parts of nose and mouth. The sensitive area extends upward to include the eyelids by 11 weeks. By 11½ weeks all the fetuses studied (131) were sensitive over the entire face, and the sensation was spreading downward over the chest. The sides of the head by the ears are sensitive by 14 to 15 weeks. The back and top of the head remain insensitive until after birth.

The palms of the hands are sensitive between 10 to 11 weeks. The soles of the feet become sensitive shortly after the upper extremities, and their sensitivity is complete by 12 weeks. As in the upper extremities, the lower legs and thighs become sensitive shortly after the soles.

Proprioceptive responses to stretch were obtained from arm muscles by 9½ weeks. The response from leg muscles appeared a few days later.

The first movement elicited by Hooker (1952) to light touch (tactile) stimuli was contralateral neck flexion identified as an avoidance reaction at 7½ weeks. This response advances to include neck, trunk, and pelvic motion, with a backward motion of the arms at 8½ weeks. From 8½ to 9½ weeks, when the entire pattern is vigorous, the mouth opens, and the tongue moves to the floor of the mouth. Ipsilateral patterns are fewer in number and appear later than contralateral ones. By 11 weeks the contralateral flexion is replaced by neck and trunk extension, which are also avoidance in type. Not until 12½ weeks is neck flexion toward the stimulus seen, and it is combined with swallowing at 14 weeks.

By 13½ to 14 weeks many of the specific reflexes of the neonatal period have appeared. Those reflexes that are present involve the trunk, extremities, head, and face. They are not complete but lay the framework for reflexes of postnatal life.

A sequence can be seen in the function of the hand. The first response to palmar stimulation is seen at 10½ weeks and consists of incomplete closure of the fingers with no activity of the thumb. All four fingers act as a unit combined frequently with wrist flexion and forearm flexion and pronation. The thumb begins to participate by 12 to 12½ weeks by moving across the palm. At 13 weeks the index finger participates less than the other three fingers. Maintained closure is present at 15½ weeks. Grasp is present but weak at 18½ weeks. By 27 weeks, grasp is nearly sufficient to support the weight of the fetus. A very similar sequence is seen postnatally in the development of prehension, which includes finger closure and then grasp.

It is well to keep in mind, from a study of prenatal activity, that the neural tube closes first at the midcervical level and progresses in both directions. The cervical motor neurons mature and function earlier; so the reflexes controlling head movements are the first to appear. Further, as descending fiber tracts develop, their connections will be made first in the cervical area; so voluntary control will follow the same pattern.

The oxygen requirement of reflexes is another important factor in activity. Postnatally those reflexes that are oldest require less oxygen. More recent centers and reflexes require more oxygen and so are damaged sooner (Humphreys, 1969). It would seem advisable to establish these early reflex patterns first in order to build on them and provide an appropriate sequence of development.

In contrast to Humphrey's belief is a unique idea of Snapp's (1979). He believes, in cases of anoxia, that the higher centers stop functioning first, are put at rest, and so are protected. The primitive systems continue to function and try to save the organism. Consequently, with intense anoxia, it is actually the primitive systems that are destroyed. They are then not available for automatic activity when it is requested by the higher centers. The individual is left with a commander (the cortex) but no army (the primitive pattern) to do the work.

Snapp is challenging us with the importance of assuring the normal sequence of prenatal activity before attempting to elicit postnatal sequences. Life does not begin at birth. Everything happens on a time line. He believes that all of our abilities are genetically coded and available to us in the appropriate environment.

Reticular core

Bergstrom (1969) has shown by gross electrical activity and response to electrical stimulation that the first part of the fetal brain to function is the whole reticular core. The maturation develops from this reticular core to the periphery. He has shown that this central core contains randomly connected elements that display "tonic" characteristics in the input-output relations of information. The higher developed structures are arranged in a parallel fashion on the periphery and display a more "phasic" characteristic in input-output relations of information with a more exact time-space relation. As reflexes are studied, a definite change is seen from tonic to phasic. This change appears to be correlated with the appearance of inhibitory mechanisms.

Ayres (1972) indicates that this reticular core has been considered the master control mechanism in the CNS. In lower animals this system provided sufficient organization for the animal to interact with his environment at least in a primitive way. In order for this to happen, sensory input from many sources had to be fed into the system. Whenever input is derived from many sources there is usually convergence of that input and subsequent integration. Whenever a neural structure receives input from many sources, it is apt to have a widespread influence over other neural structures.

One of the major roles of the ascending reticular activating system is a general alerting of the cortex and improved attention. This tends to increase the discriminatory power of the individual and prepare him to deal more effectively with the stimulus. The reader is reminded of the nonspecific C fiber aspect of Concept 2 and the importance of these fibers in arousal.

Since this reticular formation is a core or hub of the nervous system, receiving information from all areas and influencing all structures, it has an extensive integrative role. It organizes sensory information through facilitation, inhibition, augmentation, and synthesis. The world is not perceived through one sense but through all the senses, on the basis of vestibular orientation of the body image in space.

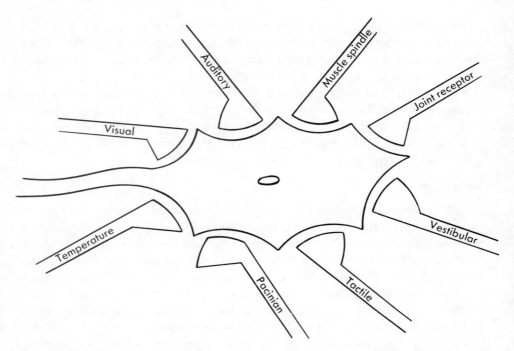

Fig. 7-6. Convergent neuron with a variety of sensory input. Each neuron has a specific combination of input that is required for firing.

Convergent neurons

Convergent, or polysensory, neurons are found at brain stem levels in the reticular formation. These neurons respond to stimuli from several different sensory sources (Fig. 7-6). The most common sources of stimuli are skin, joints, muscles, and the vestibular mechanism. It seems functionally that the vestibular mechanism is the most critical source in the firing of the neuron (Ayres, 1976). We believe that this convergence of sensory information on a foundation of vestibular input is critical to the establishment of intersensory integration in the body's orientation to the force of gravity. Without this orientation to the force of gravity, the entire neurological development will be altered.

Developmental sequence

In recent years Ayres (1976) has emphasized the importance of a developmental sequence of intersensory integration and influence. It has been shown that during the prenatal period tactile stimuli produce avoidance reactions and then toward reactions and that proprioceptive reflexes are present. There is considerable evidence that the vestibular mechanism is formed early prenatally and that at birth the pathways for coordinating vestibular-eye-neck reactions are myelinated. de Quiros (1976) has emphasized that vestibular responses are elicitable within hours after birth.

Chaney (1979) has indicated in her model of the body (Concept 8) that the child must develop and attend to kinesthesia. He then matches the sensations of tactile to kinesthetic, visual to kinesthetic, and auditory to kinesthetic. It is a two-way street; the match goes backward from the sensation of kinesthetic to tactile to visual to auditory.

In discussing Piaget in Concept 6 we stressed the importance of the sound associated with the object that a child is manipulating. It is the sound that links the visual with the tactile-kinesthetic movement of the child. We must learn to use our senses together to confirm one impression in one sense with the impression from another sense.

Birch and Lefford (1963) studied the equivalent relationship of visual, haptic, and kinesthetic sense in geometric form recognition. The term "haptic" referred to active manipulation of the test object. Kinesthetic sense was obtained by passive arm movement related to the test object. The objects were judged to be identical or nonidentical. The intersensory combinations included visual-haptic, visual-kinesthetic, and haptic-kinesthetic. They found that at as early as 5 years of age some subjects made no errors in visual-haptic judgment. In the visual-kinesthetic and haptic-kinesthetic areas some subjects made as little as one error at 5 years. The errors in all combinations decreased with age, substantiating the theory that development of intersensory function improves with age. They found that visual-haptic discriminative judgment of both identical and nonidentical forms developed earliest and was highly effective by 5 years. This level of efficiency, using the kinesthetic modality, was not obtained until 7 years of age. By age 11 years there were minimum errors in all conditions of the experiment. In summary, by extrapolation they suggested that visual-haptic equivalence has its most rapid growth in the third and fourth years after birth. Visual-kinesthetic equivalence has the greatest growth during the sixth through the eighth year. This age difference may explain the discrepancy between the accuracy of perceptual recognition of shapes and gross inaccuracy in their reproduction.

To further emphasize the importance of intersensory integration it is helpful to consider what influence brain damage has on function. Belmont and colleagues (1965) demonstrated, in a study of hemiplegias, that changes in both intrasensory and intersensory organization occurred. Intersensory integrative function was more vulnerable and demonstrated more damage than intrasensory organization.

Birch and Belmont (1964) showed that brain-injured adults were inferior to normal adults in their ability to use somesthetic information in judging a visual vertical task. The task was to adjust a luminous rod to true upright position in a fully darkened room. The brain-injured (hemiplegic) adults were also defective in their ability to analyze complex visual patterns. It appears from this study that less complex and earlier developed intrasensory integration, such as visual-visual, is left intact, while intersensory integration, such as visual-somesthetic, is seriously affected.

Moving on to higher levels of intersensory integration Birch and Belmont (1965) found that auditory-visual equivalence was most rapid in the early school years and reached an asymptote by fifth grade. This development of integrative organization is essential in learning to read since visually presented and spatially distributed stimuli must be treated as equivalent to auditorily presented and temporally distributed stimuli. This space-time relationship will be presented in detail in Concept 8. A closer look at this growth reveals that the most rapid period occurs between kindergarten and second grade, with performance reaching the 80% level. There is a slow and steady growth until fifth grade. This rapid period of auditory-visual integration corresponds to that found for visual-haptic, visual-kinesthetic, and haptic-kinesthetic integration. It is evident that many significant changes are occurring during this period that are important in determining whether the child is ready for the formal educational experience. This readiness level will be explored in detail in Concept 9.

Practical application

In this practical application we would like to present a brief historical sketch of the identification of learning disabled children. Our reasons are threefold:

1. To make the reader acutely aware that in the 1930s and 1940s characteristics used to identify adults with problems were used to identify children and that they are still applicable today.
2. To alert the reader to the unifying nature of the early classical writings as a framework for the voluminous present-day research.
3. To emphasize the importance of a holistic management of individuals from birth to death in the physical, emotional, intellectual, and spiritual areas.

HISTORICAL REVIEW OF LEARNING DISABILITIES

Learning disability as an entity emerged with the publication of the now classical *Psychopathology and Education of the Brain-injured Child*, by Strauss and Lehtinen (1947). Their concept evolved from two sources: (1) the philosophy and methods of education of mentally handicapped children and (2) clinical research on brain-injured adults.

Itard, Seguin, and Guggenbuehl were nineteenth century educators who laid the foundations for advances in education of the mentally handicapped. Perhaps Sequin contributed the most to special education by directing specific training to the impaired senses to provide correct information to the brain, thus laying the foundation for many of the present-day sensory training techniques.

Head and Goldstein (1976) worked with young adult soldiers who received head injuries during World War I. With intensive study, definite qualitative differences were established between these "traumatic dements" and individuals affected with the already well-known senile dementia.

A logical question arose: Were the disturbances that were present in brain-injured adults also present in children? This question led to a second question: Was there a difference between the amentia or dementia of brain-injured children and the amentia of genetic origin? Did the brain-injured child show the same characteristics as the genetically mentally defective child, or did the patterns of the child resemble more closely the psychopathological patterns of the "traumatic demented" adult?

Strauss and Lehtinen (1947) defined a brain-injured child as one who prenatally, natally, or postnatally sustained an injury or infection of the brain. Such a child may demonstrate disturbances in perception, thinking, or emotional behavior as a result of the organic impairment. These children may be diagnosed on the bases of mental retardation, history of brain injury, minor neurological symptoms, and conspicuous organic behavior.

The adult characteristics identified in children by Strauss and Lehtinen include*:

1. Emotional lability or the "catastrophic reaction" of Goldstein
2. Perceptual disturbances that "in children differ little from the perceptual disturbances in adults"
3. Distractibility "which is better understood and interpreted in adults and includes two aspects":
   a. Undue fixation of attention upon irrelevant external stimuli
   b. Fluctuation or instability of figure-ground
4. Hyperactivity
5. Perseveration

Strauss and Kephart (1955) emphasized that brain injury to a child is further complicated because the organism is not fully developed. It is impor-

---

* From Strauss, A. and Lehtinen, L. E.: Psychopathology and education of the brain-injured child, Vol. 1, New York 1947, Grune & Stratton, Inc.

tant to realize that the adult is never static but is constantly changing and developing. This is true in the adult but even more true and to a greater degree in the child. We must consider the effects of the injury, but even more important is the effect on the development in process and the impact on the individual of the deviation in development. Is there any better or more forceful argument for early intervention than a management aimed at promoting and assuring as normal a developmental process as possible?

Gearheart (1973), in presenting the environmental control systems of educating learning disabled children, indicates that Cruickshank's approach is an extension and expansion of Strauss and Lehtinen's original ideas.

Cruickshank and associates (1961) outline his teaching methods for brain-injured and hyperactive children. They also include data from his 2-year demonstration–pilot study. In the book they list six psychological characteristics of brain-injured children: distractibility, motor disinhibition, disassociation, disturbance of figure-ground relationships, perseveration, and absence of well-developed self-concept and body image. They indicate that these could be consolidated into three by making the second, third, and fourth items all part of distractibility, which would make perseveration the second factor and absence of self-concept and body image the third factor.

Perhaps one of the most useful books for parents and teachers is Cruickshank's *The Brain-Injured Child in Home, School and Community* (1967). In this book he points out the basic problem of labeling the child by indicating that there are more than 40 terms in the literature. Some of these are:

Minimal brain-injured child

Brain-damaged child

Hyperactive child

Perceptually handicapped child

Child with developmental imbalance

Child with minimal brain dysfunction

Child with dyslexia

Different professions, as well as the same professions in different parts of the country, use different terms. The child presents the same problems and requires the same attention regardless of what label is used.

Cruickshank (1967) explains the characteristics in a very easy, readable fashion.

1. *Hyperactivity or distractability*
   a. Sensory hyperactive children are unable to refrain from responding to a sensory stimulus. Any stimulus sight, sound, smell, tactile or movement may serve to distract him as well as internal stimuli such as hunger, gas, or a need to void.
   b. Motor hyperactivity is often referred to as motor disinhibition. Mo-

tor disinhibition is the inability of the child to refrain from reacting to stimuli with a motor response. Consequently, everything within sight is pushed, pulled, poked, twisted, pounded, etc. This behavior is frequently called hyperkinetic.

c. Because of the sensory and motor hyperactivity these children frequently respond to an unexpected situation with a "catastrophic reaction". In this reaction the total body seems to react in an uncontrolled fashion. These responses in time lead to a very confused, unsure, immature, or aggressive behavior.

2. *Disassociation*

Disassociation is the inability to see the parts of a thing as a whole or a gestalt. These individuals see the trees but never the forest. They see the components of a letter but never the letter.

3. *Figure-ground relationship*

Figure-ground disturbances are characterized by the confusion of what is figure and what is ground, by the reversal of figure and ground, or by the inability to separate the figure from the ground.

4. *Perseveration*

Perseveration may be defined as the inability of the individual to shift from one mental activity to another. Here it appears to be the prolonged after-effect of a stimulus on subsequent activities. Perseveration may be evident in speech, laughter, or motor acts.

5. *Self-concept and body image*

Out of a good and positive body-image comes a good and positive body concept. From the body-concept comes the strong ego forces to cope with our society. For the brain-injured child this may not be possible simply because of the previous psychological characteristics. Disassociation interferes with his perception of himself. Figure-ground reversals may confuse him about his body and environment. Hyperactivity may prevent him from receiving lasting sensations about his body or from performing motor acts in the appropriate way. Consequently their body-images may become very distorted and their self-concept very negative.

In Volume I of *Psychopathology and Education of the Brain-Injured Child* (Strauss and Lehtinen, 1947) the clinical syndrome of the brain-injured, mentally defective child was presented. In Volume II (Strauss and Kephart, 1955) the concept had to be enlarged to include the clinical syndrome of the brain-injured child who is not mentally defective. When the child is tested he reveals a "normal I.Q. but he functions in a 'defective' manner."

Johnson and Myklebust (1967) designated children with adequate motor ability, average to high intelligence, adequate hearing and vision, and adequate emotional adjustment but with a deficiency in learning as having psychoneurological learning disabilities. The term "psychoneurological" indicates that the disorder is in behavior and that the cause is neurological. In discussing the characteristics of distractibility, perseveration, and disinhibition, they believe it is more advantageous for diagnosis and remedial training to consider the characteristics as a breakdown in *attention* instead of disturbance of perception.

This idea fits well into our concept of synaptic activity, of PAD focusing attention, and of convergent neurons integrating intersensory information. As indicated in Concept 6, in the motor-perceptual stage the child first attends to kinesthesia, or the sensation of movement. He must identify the difference between movement and nonmovement. As the child does this he develops internal awareness of his body. He must have appropriate sensory information integrated at the brain stem level to assure an automatic postural mechanism as a foundation for his movement. The critical nature of a well-functioning vestibular system in this postural mechanism has been repeatedly emphasized. If the child is unable to control his body he will, in fact, be unable to control his behavior. His behavior will demonstrate the characteristics of distractibility, perseveration, and disinhibition.

With the preceding as a foundation, we believe that Kephart's approach of behavior control through movement control, which is presented later, is valuable. The approach may be adapted to the management of physically disabled children as well as the overly manipulative child.

It is our belief that the major contributions of this procedure are structure and physical activity. As the activity is performed the child must attend to one extremity, initiating, maintaining, and terminating the action. The satisfaction or reward is the sensory feedback of performing the action with its influence on body image, plus the successful completion of the task promotes good positive self-concept.

CAUSES OF UNDESIRABLE BEHAVIOR

According to Chaney and Miles (1974), appropriate behavior and motor control as well as undesirable behavior are learned. From the moment a child is born he is receiving positive or negative reinforcements. He is receiving reinforcement for acceptable behavior as well as unacceptable behavior. It is rather alarming how frequently adults are unaware that they are actually reinforcing the behavior they do not want more than the behavior they do.

There are basically three causes of undesirable behavior. The first is immaturity. Everyone expects and accepts a young child who fusses and cries if he is kept waiting too long for food or confined when he wants to be free.

This is not acceptable from an older child, but the behavior may be present and is the result of the same problem of immaturity. Older children are more adept at avoiding situations with which they cannot cope. They may even attempt to change the rules or regulations to benefit their immaturity. Society is demanding more of them than they are willing or capable of producing. This will be discussed further in Concept 9 as it relates to grade placement, chronological age, and behavioral age.

The second cause of undesirable behavior is difficulty with movement control. This is a complex problem because there may be an isolated problem or a combination of several problems. Many children lack adequate kinesthetic feedback. We have seen how, because of this lack of kinesthetic feedback and hypotonicity, the child may have to depend on visual control of his body. On the other hand the child may lack differentiation. He may use only large segments of his body, which do not have fine control, for many of his activities. He may also be very tense because of the lack of differentiation; so hypertonicity interferes with control. Finally the child may lack automatic movements. These automatic movements include balance adjustments such as shifting from sitting to standing or standing to walking. The other area of automatic movements is the ability to initiate, maintain, and stop movements. If a child cannot initiate movement, he will not start his tasks and will "dawdle," requiring considerable prodding. The child who cannot maintain his movements is the child who seems to become fatigued or to lose interest before the task is finished. The child who cannot terminate movements will constantly be crashing into people and things and be accused of hurting because he squeezes too hard and will frequently damage objects.

The third cause of undesirable behavior is the inability to integrate data. This appears to be a processing problem. The cortex may be attempting to perform deficient lower level functions. There may not be hemisphere specialization, so the brain is undecided as to how to deal with the data. These problems may be aggravated by presenting material too rapidly or without adequate sequential breakdown.

HALOS OF BEHAVIOR

The concept of a halo of behavior can be found in *Steps to Achievement for the Slow Learner* by Ebersole, Kephart, and Ebersole (1968). If one assumes that there is damage to the brain at birth, the damage and the halo are essentially the same size. As the infant matures, the ring of behavior becomes larger than the actual damage. The more the infant or young child is allowed to structure and manipulate the environment, the larger the halo becomes (Fig. 7-7). Even a 1-year-old child may be seen to manipulate all the adults in his environment so that they are adhering to his structure (rigid behavior)

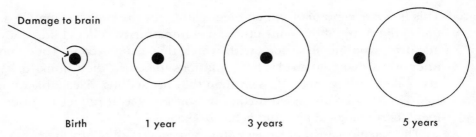

Fig. 7-7. The halo of behavior around the original brain damage gets larger as the child gets older if he is allowed to structure his own environment.

instead of his adapting to their structure. Normal children learn to conform to expected behaviors very early, but the hyperactive child does not learn to adapt. The parents become harassed, and the level of conflict between all family members becomes so great that it is easier to give in than to fight the child's behavior. This is understandable but extremely unfortunate because it disrupts the normal family-child relationships. Perhaps the relationship that suffers the earliest and most acutely is the mother-child relationship. A constant war develops wherein the child may rarely receive any positive rewarding interaction from the mother and the mother rarely receives any satisfactory fulfillment from the child. Early intervention by professionals may be the best deterrent to this breakdown, but how many mothers have been told by professionals, "He is just very active and will outgrow the problem"? It is unfortunate that those professionals do not experience a 24-hour day with the child in order for them to appreciate the magnitude of the problem.

There are essentially six avenues of management open to these families. The first avenue is either denial of the problem or avoidance of the problem; both are equally destructive to the family unit. The second avenue is placing the child on medication to make him more manageable. The third avenue is the use of behavior modification techniques using primary and secondary reinforcers. A fourth avenue is the approach of Cruickshank and colleagues (1961) and Cruickshank (1967) in which the environment is structured. The fifth approach is that of controlling diet. Smith (1976) is concerned with the total diet and the possibilities of allergies, while Feingold (1975) emphasizes the impact of artificial coloring and flavoring. A sixth approach is behavior control through movement control as originated by Kephart. This approach was designed to break through the halos of behavior (Fig. 7-8). A major difficulty with this avenue is that Kephart never published the entire procedure. Segments of the philosophy and technique may be found in Chaney

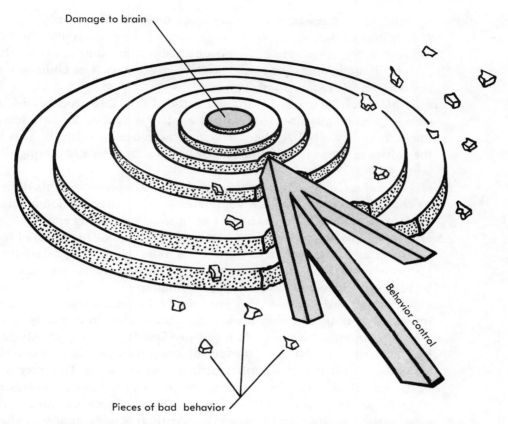

Damage to brain

Behavior control

Pieces of bad behavior

Fig. 7-8. Behavior control is used to break through the halos of behavior.

and Kephart (1968), Ebersole, Kephart, and Ebersole (1968), and Chaney and Miles (1974).

In 1969 Heiniger received instruction in this approach from Kephart and his staff (Kephart, 1969). As she used the techniques in the ensuing years (Chaney and Miles, personal communication, 1969, 1970, 1972) she was repeatedly frustrated by the lack of published material available to parents and professionals. To combat this continued frustration, we have chosen to present this approach in considerable detail in the subsequent sections.

LEVELS OF BREAKDOWN OF BEHAVIOR

From Heiniger's experience with hyperactive children, she has identified eight levels of breakdown of behavior. Each child progresses through a definite sequence in the breakdown of his behavior. Each child is also unique in the amount of time spent on any specific level of his behavioral breakdown.

Both the sequence and the time may vary in each session of control.

Level 1: Initially cooperative. At the beginning of the activity the child is interested and cooperative. This cooperation is not unusual since the activity is new, interesting, and loosely structured. The child is unpressured and anxious to please.

Level 2: Minimal attention. At this point the child's attention begins to wander, and he attempts to change the activity. He may act silly, leave the activity, or verbalize about unrelated activities or subjects. This is the initial attempt to manipulate the environment by distracting the adult.

Level 3: Verbal resistance. During this level the child verbalized his desire to change activities by such comments as "I'm tired of doing this," "This is baby stuff," "It's too hard, I want to do something else."

Level 4: Verbal avoidance. By this time the child is anxious to get out of the situation and is determined to leave the room. He will verbalize that he has to go to the bathroom, he has to get a drink, he has a headache, he is sick, or he has to tell his mother something.

Level 5: Physical resistance. At this level the verbalization becomes more intense and is threatening toward the adult. The child makes comments such as "I hate you," "I'll tell my Daddy on you," or "My big brother will beat you up." The verbalization may change to physical resistance of hitting, kicking, screaming, and swearing. The intensity of the verbalization and strength of the physical resistance continues to increase. There are additional manipulative tactics initiated such as vomiting, wetting, and holding the breath. It is important to realize that the child has used all the acceptable means of manipulation, but because they have not worked to stop the activity, he is desperate and will try anything.

Level 6: Protective physical resistance (animal-like). The intensity and strength of the behavior at this level is unbelievable. It seems that the child is fighting for his very life as he attempts to get the adult to let him out of the activity. This is the very height of his sympathetic fight reaction.

Level 7: Shattered behavior. At this time the adult has broken through the halo and shattered the behavior. There may be a brief period when everything stops. The adult must not allow this to persist for more than a very few minutes. The adult may have to use excitatory stimuli to reestablish contact with the child. Following this "shutdown period" the child will do the activity with no resistance and according to the adult's structure. This can be very frightening for the adult and potentially dangerous period since the child seems to be completely at the mercy of the adult. Levels 6 and 7 may be extremely stressful for the adult and must be managed with discretion and maturity.

Level 8: Positive behavior. During this last level, the adult discusses with the child the reasons the child acted as he did. The adult then tells the child that he, the adult, understands why the child acted as he did. The adult reassures the child that now both will work together to overcome the difficulty the child is experiencing. The adult promises to help the child to do the things he does not seem able to do alone. The discussion is most effective when the adult holds the child close, with considerable body contact, and provides parasympathetic stimuli.

These eight levels are typical of the child who projects a sympathetic fight reaction. The time involved to work through the eight levels varies with each child. For example, one child may go from level 1 to level 5 or 6 in a matter of minutes. Another child may take as much as 1 hour to go from level 1 to level 5 or 6. A child may take only a few minutes to go from level 5 to 6 on through level 7 and into level 8. Another child may take as much as an hour or more to go from level 5 or 6 through to level 8. There will be some children who will never reach level 5 before they adhere to the adult's structure and to the activity. Each treatment session, whether at home or in the clinic, is an isolated situation and will produce a different picture. Do not anticipate a set reaction from the child, rather deal with what is presented.

The child who projects a sympathetic emotional withdrawal or flight reaction is much more difficult to manage because there is no overt reaction. For the adult this may be a much more frustrating experience and require even more control of his or her own reactions. The adult must maintain contact with the child by using the voice in a stimulating way. Methods need to be found that will assist these children, who are in sympathetic emotional flight, to lash out instead of retreating. If the child does not lash out in some manner, it is very difficult to deal with the behavior. We believe these children are more susceptible to serious personality problems than those who react with a fight reaction. There seems to be a decided advantage in venting intense emotions. Emotional outbursts are frequently very revealing as to the child's fears, experiences, or deep personal feelings.

RESTRUCTURING THE ENVIRONMENT

If this treatment approach is to be used with a child, complete parental cooperation is essential. Both parents must understand the procedure and appreciate the potential problems. The parents must be totally appraised of the possible reactions of the child. If the behavior at home is obnoxious at the beginning of treatment, it will intensify tenfold during the first 2 to 3 weeks of treatment. However, this is one of the primary advantages of this method. The behavior worsens for 2 to 3 weeks and then begins to show decided improvement. It is not unusual during the third or fourth week for outsiders to observe and comment on the change in the child's behavior.

The regimen includes a treatment at least once a day, six days a week. A time should be scheduled that ensures at least 1 hour without interruptions. The parent has two alternatives. The first alternative is to work through the behavior until the desired performance is achieved, regardless of how long it takes. The second alternative is for the *adult* to terminate the session with the understanding that both parties will return to the activity and complete it later in the day. In the second case it is essential that the same activity be initiated at the same point it was terminated. It is important that one adult be in command of the situation and that there be no discussion in front of the child. If Mother terminated the session, then Mother initiates the completion. If Father is doing an activity, it should not be the same one that Mother had to terminate earlier.

Kephart and Chaney (1963) indicate that in each situation of working with a child there are three levels of endeavor. The level of tolerance is when the child has learned to perform the activity easily. At this point he should be allowed to use the activity as play time experimentation. The level of challenge occurs when the child needs a little help to perform the task. The adult challenges him by setting the stage and insisting that the task be performed now. The level of frustration occurs when the child cannot perform the activity even with help. This latter situation should be avoided. However, should the situation develop, the adult should not abandon the task completely; rather it should be subdivided in such a way that the child can succeed with some element of the activity.

A general discussion of the principles of restructuring the environment may be found in books by Chaney and Kephart (1968), Ebersole, Kephart, and Ebersole (1968), and Chaney and Miles (1974).

We believe that there are four essential considerations related to each treatment session. The first consideration is to ensure enough time and enough structure to work through the eight levels of behavior. In the unusual situation, in which treatment has to be interrupted by the adult, it must be emphasized that both parties will finish the activity at a later time. The critical issue is that the child knows the adult is interrupting the treatment session and that the child has not managed to manipulate the situation.

The second item to consider is choosing an activity that the adult knows the child can physically accomplish and that the adult can physically control. An example is sitting on the floor putting blocks in a container. The adult must remain orientated to the activity or task and not become emotionally "trapped" by the child's behavior.

The third consideration is perhaps the most critical to the success of the treatment session because it involves verbalization by the adult. The instructions must be given slowly, clearly, and simply with no more conversation than absolutely necessary. For example, "Take your arm up," "Bring your arm down," "If you don't do it, I'll have to do it for you." The voice must remain calm, evenly pitched, and commanding but not threatening. Equally important to success is the method of giving the command. The adult must wait for the response but not wait too long. He or she should anticipate the child's movement and correct or guide it the instant it is not as desired.

The fourth consideration is the attitude and behavior of the adult. The attitude toward the child must be objective and sensitive, but firm. It is important for the adult to be aware of his or her own reactions and how they are affecting the child's behavior. Where the adult is operating on the ergotropic-trophotropic continuum is critical to the success of the session.

SPECIFIC MANAGEMENT

It has been our experience in treating children with behavioral problems that two different methods are effective. Both methods encompass the concepts of behavior control through movement control. The first method affords the adult the opportunity to observe the breakdown of behavior in a simply structured situation. We designate this method "activity control." The second method is directed to controlling a very specific isolated movement; so it is designated "movement control."

Activity control

The choice of the activity is critical to the success of the endeavor. The child must be physically capable of performing the task at a level that meets the adult's expectations. The adult must be able to physically control the child completely (Fig. 7-9) in order to ensure that the activity will be done exactly to the adult's expectations.

Before the performance of the activity is initiated the structure must be established. The child should be taken to the bathroom and given a drink of water to avoid the use of these items in manipulating the situations. The geographical boundaries should be established, that is, "Do not get off the mat," "You may play with only the things on the mat."

The child is allowed to position himself as long as he performs adequately. The instant the behavior begins to breakdown, the adult must physically position the child in such a manner that the performance of the activity is completely controlled. Usually the best controlling position is one with the adult sitting crosslegged against the wall with the child in his lap. As levels 5 and 6 in the breakdown of behavior are reached, even this position may become difficult to maintain.

At the beginning of the activity, the instructions to the child must be clear and concise. Commands and verbalization must be kept to a minimum. The adult must not become trapped in lengthy explanations or conversations. Keep the commands to the child to the point, that is, "Put the blocks in the box." If the adult wants the blocks put in the box quietly one at a time, then this should be indicated. The adult should give the command and wait. If there is no performance, the command should be repeated. Following the second command with no performance the adult makes the statement "I will have to do it for you" and takes the child's hand and does the activity once. The command is repeated, and the child is given the opportunity to perform. If no performance is forthcoming, repeat the statement "I will have to do it for you—this is your work and you must do it." The entire sequence of commands and waiting for performance is repeated over and over as the levels of breakdown progress.

With experience, the many methods of manipulation used at the various levels of breakdown of behavior will become obvious to the adult. As the adult's skill in anticipating the method of manipulation develops, the situa-

Fig. 7-9. The adult must be able to completely control every facet of the child's activity.

tion is controlled more easily. However, the adult must constantly be on guard because the child may begin to use more subtle methods of manipulation, which are more difficult to recognize.

The ultimate goal of this activity control is to work through the halo of behavior. The child will receive his own positive feedback from succeeding at the activity within the adult's structure. He will also receive positive reinforcement from the adult as the situation is discussed during level 8.

The apparent rigidity of this method becomes an obstacle for many people during their initial exposure because of their own emotional reaction. With repeated experience the flexibility of the structure becomes more evident, as does the behavior of the child. The critical issue becomes is the child in control through manipulative behavior or is the adult in control through structuring?

Movement control

In this method the child is positioned on his stomach on a mat on the floor. The head is turned to one side, the arms are relaxed at the sides of the body, and the legs are straight with a comfortable distance between the feet.

Before the activity is begun the child's outer clothing should be removed

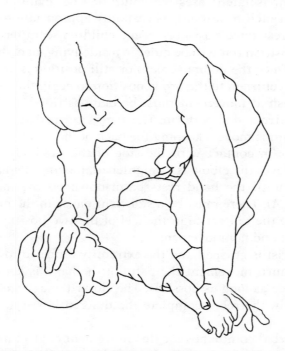

Fig. 7-10. The adult is controlling completely the child's movements.

leaving only the diaper, panties, or shorts. An older child is more comfortable in a swimming suit. The shoes are removed for the adult's protection.

In the beginning the child should experience the difference between movement and nonmovement. This is accomplished by instructing the child to lie still and allow the adult to lift arms and legs individually and drop them gently to the mat. Many children will find it very difficult to remain perfectly still and quiet.

If the behavior begins to breakdown at this early stage, the child can be positioned by the adult in such a way that only one extremity at a time is free to move (Fig. 7-10). This is accomplished by bending the child's knees in order that the adult may kneel astride them. One arm can be tucked between the adult's knee and the body of the child. The adult can use one arm to keep the buttocks down and the head turned to the desired side. This position completely controls the child's head, body, legs, and one arm while leaving the adult one free hand to direct and guide the movement of the free arm of the child. This total physical control of the child's body requires the optimal use of the adult's entire body. As a result of the tremendous strength of the child during levels 5 and 6 this physical control may be extremely difficult with a large child.

In a few isolated cases the child may be unable to adjust to this face-lying, restricted position. It is certainly appropriate to experiment with alternative restricted positions. Some children seem terrified when placed in a prone position but will be quiet in a side-lying, back-lying, or totally flexed position. Once the nonmovement or still position is accomplished the child should be returned to the prone position to begin the movements.

The desired movement must be demonstrated several times before the child is instructed to perform. The arm is grasped at the wrist with the palm up. The arm is moved, keeping the back of the hand on the mat surface with the thumb in contact with the side of the the body. As the hand reaches shoulder level the elbow is straightened, moving the hand along the side of the head until the hand rests palm down on the mat with fingers open (Fig. 7-11, A). There must be a sufficient pause in the motion for the child to appreciate the difference in the feel of the two positions and the feel of the movement and nonmovement.

The wrist is grasped and the extremity returned to the starting position. On the return movement the palm of the hand is kept in contact with the mat surface as long as possible. The closer the extremity is kept to the side of the body, the more complete the differentiation at shoulder, elbow, and wrist.

The verbal commands for this movement control method are "Take your arm up," as the arm is extended overhead, and "Bring your arm down," as the arm is returned to the side of the body. The same sequence of commands is followed as was used for the activity control. The command is given, and the adult waits. If no performance is initiated, the command is given a second time, and the adult waits. Following the second command and no performance, the adult makes the statement "I will have to move it for you" and takes the arm through the motion once. The command "Bring your arm down" is given, and the child allowed an opportunity to perform. If no performance is initiated, the statement, "I will have to do it for you—this is your work and you must do it," is made by the adult and the action carried out. This sequence of commands and waiting for performance is repeated over and over as the levels of breakdown progress.

As stated in the general principles of management, the use of the voice is very important. The continuous repetition of the same command serves a dual purpose. The first purpose is to restrict the amount of verbalization. The second purpose is to provide a slow rhythmical repetitive voice stimulus to both the child and the adult. This is especially helpful for the adult who needs assistance to remain emotionally detached from the situation and in a parasympathetic state.

One advantage of this method is that the adult can shift the movement from one arm to the other. The activity can also be shifted to the legs when the complete physical control of the body is no longer needed.

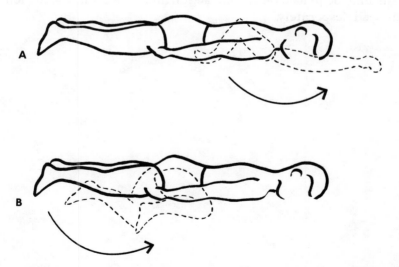

Fig. 7-11. A, In movement control the arm is moved from the side of the body to the above the head position and returned. **B,** In movement control the leg is moved from the extended position to the frog position and returned.

If the leg patterns are to be used they must be demonstrated several times prior to the initiation of motion by the child (Fig. 7-11, *B*). The extremity is grasped at the ankle and the medial surface of the knee is moved along the surface of the mat, with the sole of the foot in contact with the medial surface of the opposite leg. There must be a pause between the motions. The return motion is controlled by keeping the sole of the foot in contact with the medial surface of the opposite leg. The verbal commands for this pattern are "Take your leg up," as the hip and the knee are bent, and "Take your leg down," as the leg is returned to the starting position.

When the child is instructed to perform the movement, he may demonstrate difficulty initiating it, carrying it through the range, or terminating it. These difficulties may be manifestations of the breakdown of behavior. Frequently, however, these difficulties are the direct results of faulty kinesthetic feedback and body schema.

We believe the value of this method of treatment lies in the following: The behavior control through movement control forces the child to control his body, thus controlling his behavior. The adult is able to control the movement and break through the halos of behavior. The adult is able to guide and direct the movements to assure proper sensation. Kinesthetic feedback and differentiation are essential for conscious awareness of kinesthetic figure-ground. It has been our experience that these children are hypotonic and sorely lacking in midline stability. Once the behavior is controlled, the emphasis may be placed on cocontraction and differentiation, which these children need desperately.

KEY WORDS

action potential
adaptive behavioral response
afferent
amplification
ascending reticular activating
  system
asphyxia
association or interneuron
axosomatic synapse
body image
"catastrophic reaction"
convergent neurons
cutaneous afferent fibers
depolarization
direct inhibition
disassocation
distractability
disynaptic neuron chain

divergence
emotional lability
excitatory postsynaptic
  potential (EPSP)
facilitation
figure-ground disturbances
focus attention
generator potential
halo of behavior
haptic
hyperactivity
indirect inhibition
inhibition
inhibitory postsynaptic
  potential (IPSP)
intersensory inhibition
intersensory integration
intrasensory integration

ischemia
milliseconds
motor disinhibition
multipolar interneuron
periphery
permeability of the
  membrane
perseveration
polysensory neurons
postsynaptic membrane
presynaptic inhibition
propagated
reticular core
self-concept
senile dementia
synaptic transmission
threshold of the neuron
"traumatic dements"

Space-time structure

stability against gravity

Concept
Background
  Models of development
    Model of the body
    Model of the environment
    Model of the universe
  Dimensions of space
    Vertical dimension
    Horizontal dimension
    Transverse dimension

Dimension of time
  Rhythm
  Pace
  Sequence
Practical application
  Motor generalizations
    Posture and maintenance
      of balance
    Locomotion
    Contact
    Receipt and propulsion

Purdue perceptual-motor
  survey
  Categories
    Balance and posture
    Body image and
      differentiation
    Perceptual-motor match
    Ocular pursuit
    Form perception
  Aspects
    Laterality
    Perceptual-motor match
    Directionality

211

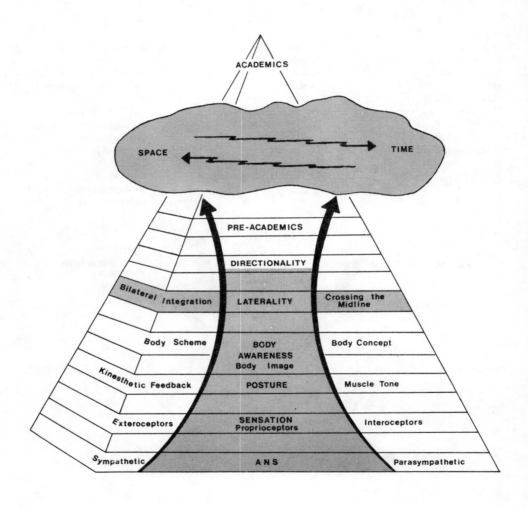

Concept   The first step in developing a space-time structure is dealing with the effects of *gravity.* The individual must first establish the space-time structure in relationship to his own body and how it responds to the force of gravity. When this structure is established he can then deal effectively with space and time in his environment.

On the **tree,** this concept is placed just above the word integration and encompasses all of the branches. The components of space and time are inherent in the function indicated by each of the branches. All sensory input must have a consistent space-time structure in order to be integrated and translated into a specific motor output, be it language, nonverbal communication, or perceptual-motor skills.

The space-time structure develops from the very center of the **cross-section** to the periphery. The structure begins at the core, with body reactions to the force of gravity, and progresses outward. When the child deals effectively with gravity, he can begin to deal with objects in his environment. As he deals effectively with concrete objects, he can begin to deal with symbols and abstract concepts.

On the **pyramid** this concept begins at the very base and progresses upward through each step to reach academics. In the lower steps the lack of a space-time structure may not be as obvious; however, the incoordination of the awkward child is directly related to space and time. The recognition of letters in their proper position and in a left-to-right progression is also directly related to space and time.

Background

It is our belief that Chaney (1974 to 1977), with her models of development, and Kephart (1971), with his dimensions of space and time provide useful tools for organizing an approach to deal with the very complicated process of space and time perception.

MODELS OF DEVELOPMENT
Model of the body

Chaney (1974 to 1979) presents three models in the development of the child. Fig. 8-1 is our elaboration of Chaney's models. The first model is of the body, which is made up of the reflexes present at birth and the development of body schema. This model extends from birth to approximately 2 years of age. The model includes the innate automatic and the motor perceptual

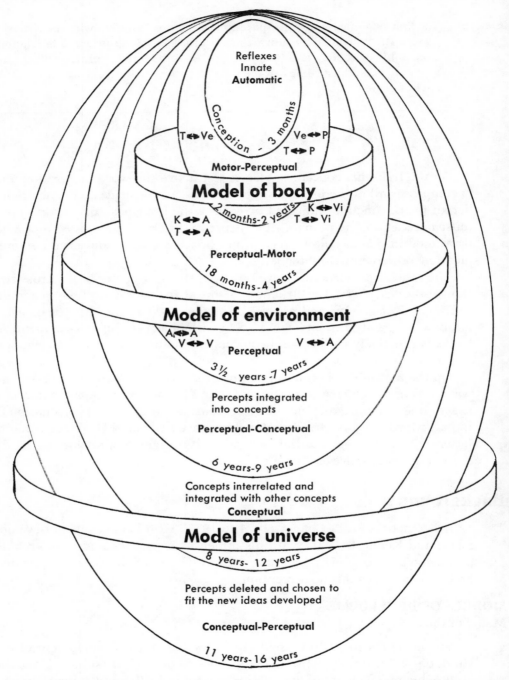

Fig. 8-1. The three models of development. *T*, Tactile; *Ve*, vestibular; and *P*, proprioceptive. Tactile, vestibular, and proprioceptive combine to form kinesthesia (*K*). Vi, Visual; A, auditory.

stages and part of the perceptual-motor stage of Kephart, as discussed in detail in Concept 6. The model of the body is dependent on an internal awareness. The three areas of touch, position, and movement must be matched to each other to produce this awareness. The terms tactile, vestibular, and proprioceptive may also be used for the three areas. The matches are tactile-vestibular, vestibular-tactile (T↔Ve), tactile propioceptive, proprioceptive tactile, (T↔P) and vestibular-proprioceptive, proprioceptive-vestibular (Ve↔P). When the child accomplishes all of these matches his "aha" phenomenon is kinesthesia (Fig. 8-1, *K*). Without kinesthesia the infant, child, or adult is dominated by his primitive, protective responses.

We believe that the reason Snapp (personal communication, 1979) does not find children with vestibular disturbances is because his treatment is developmentally low enough to deal only with the touch and movement matches. The child is in reduced light to limit visual stimuli and flat on the floor so he is not orienting his head to the force of gravity. When the child has matched the tactile stimuli to all of the flexion-extension, adduction-abduction, internal-external rotation movements, he has the ability to move upward into the third dimension, which requires the orientation of the head to the force of gravity. The matches of tactile-vestibular, vestibular-tactile and proprioceptive-vestibular, vestibular-proprioceptive are acquired rapidly. Undoubtedly, as we move developmentally lower in our treatment management, improvement will occur more spontaneously.

As the child attends to the kinesthesia, he develops kinesthetic figure-ground. As the kinesthetic figure-ground becomes established, the schema becomes automatic. As the schema becomes automatic, the space-time structure relating his body to gravity is established. He has now developed a postural model and can plan his motor activity. He has developed normal postural reflex mechanisms, which are demonstrated by the presence of righting and equilibrium reactions. It does not matter whether one uses the terminology of Kephart, Ayres, or Bobath; the issue is how the body relates to the force of gravity and interacts with objects in the environment. This ability is dependent on a well-integrated vestibular system (Concept 3), which assists extensors to develop (Concept 4) in order to provide cocontraction (Concept 5), which is essential to the orientation of the body to the force of gravity.

Model of the environment

The second of Chaney's models is of the concrete environment, which is expanded from the model of the body. This model overlaps with the first model and extends from approximately 18 months to 6 years of age. During this time the child manipulates and relates to concrete objects in his environment. The child is matching visual and auditory stimuli to his well-established kinesthesia and tactile stimuli. He is now able to match kinesthesia with auditory stimuli (K↔A), kinesthesia with visual stimuli (K↔Vi), tactile with auditory stimuli (T↔A), and tactile with visual stimuli (T↔Vi). If these matches are not made, then he lives in two separate worlds—one of perception and one of movement. Only after the visual stimuli have been matched to the kinesthesia and the auditory stimuli have been matched to the kinesthesia can the appropriate visual-auditory and auditory-visual (Vi↔A) matches be made. At this point what he sees, hears, and feels is equated. This enables him to deal with elements or percepts. He compares, associates, and integrates his percepts. As he combines his percepts he is beginning to form a concept. An example of this is the concept of a square. He must combine the four lines and the angles they make into the basic shape of a square. This process requires the ability to hold each isolated element as he combines the other elements into a total concept. This model corresponds to Kephart's perceptual-motor and perceptual stages. The child is discovering what things are, how they work, how they come apart, and how they go together. He is dealing with the elements of the object and developing relationships or percepts. He is building a foundation of percepts related to size, shape, weight, color, and position. He then recombines the percepts into associations that can be transferred from one situation to another.

Model of the universe

The third model is of the universe. The child is beginning to combine percepts into concepts. The concepts can be broken down into percepts or elements and the percepts reorganized into new concepts. The child moves from needing to manipulate the concrete objects to being able to intellectually manipulate the percepts. This model extends from approximately 6 years of age into adulthood. As he uses his previously established models of the body and concrete environment the child builds a more elaborate model of the universe. He can take a concept and project it outward in a divergent manner to predict its broad aspects. He can reverse the process and, by taking a broad concept, he can focus inward in a convergent manner and predict the minute aspects of that concept.

Our concern is the number of children entering kindergarten with poor kinesthesia. It is not difficult to predict what is happening to their models of body, concrete environment, and universe.

DIMENSIONS OF SPACE

Euclid's spatial system is the most frequently used system for organizing space. There are three dimensions of space (Fig. 8-2) which include the vertical, horizontal or lateral, and transverse, or fore and aft, as described by Kephart (1971).

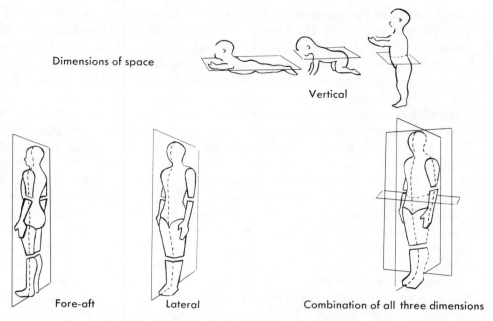

Fig. 8-2. The three dimensions of space.

Vertical dimension

Gravity pulls everything toward the center of the earth. The vertical dimension divides the infant's world into an up motion, or position, against the force of gravity and a down motion, or position, with the force of gravity. As seen in the developmental sequence dividing the body into two parts (Concept 5), the first thing the infant does is lift his head against gravity when he is in the face-lying position. He is dealing with gravity in the vertical dimension. He learns to let the muscles relax slowly against the force of gravity or he mashes his nose. This is an internal awareness of position and motion. This dimension will ultimately give the child the external labels of top and bottom and above and below.

Horizontal dimension

Horizontal dimension begins at the center of the body or midline and progresses laterally in both directions. This dimension is dependent on the force of gravity. The horizontal dimension divides the infant's world into two sides—from midline to the left and from midline to the right.

The horizontal dimension is the foundation for the concept of laterality. A definition of laterality is the internal awareness of the two sides of the body and how they work together or in opposition. Difficulty in laterality is demonstrated by one of three behaviors. *Confusion* exists when there is no dominant hand. The right hand does activities on the right side of the body and the left hand does activities on the left side of the body. *Symmetry* exists if both hands participate when one hand would be sufficient or when one hand mirrors the activity of the other hand. *Asymmetry* exists when crossing the midline is avoided by doing all of an activity with one side of the body. The ultimate development in this dimension is the establishment of the left-right gradient within the body as a measuring device for objects approaching from one direction, crossing the midline, and continuing to the other side.

According to Gesell (1940) man is duplex, with two arms, two legs, two eyes, two ears, and two hemispheres of the brain. The pairs must be interwoven and made to work together. He refers to a reciprocal interweaving of the two sides of the body as a foundation for functional asymmetry. He indicates that man attacks and retreats from situations on a diagonal, which necessitates a dominate hand, eye, foot, and ear. It is our strong belief that many children with lack of dominance, problems in laterality, and problems in crossing the midlines are not well integrated bilaterally. These same children frequently lack trunk stability because they demonstrate weak midline extensor muscles and poorly integrated vestibular systems.

Transverse dimension

This dimension also begins at the center or midline of the body and progresses in a forward and backward direction, in relationship to the force of gravity. This dimension divides the infant's world into front and back. The transverse dimension is the foundation for depth perception. The eyes play a dominant role in this dimension. For this reason any stimulus approaching from the back, out of sight, will be interpreted as potentially more dangerous than one approaching from the sides or front.

Once the isolated dimensions have been established they are combined into a spatial system in which the three dimensions intersect at a common point. For the body this point is referred to as the center of gravity. For objects the three dimensions must come together at a point to stabilize the object in space. If one or more of the dimensions are unstable the object will seem to vary in its position. Each object must be stable before it can be brought into relationship with another object. The most critical element in this perception is the realization by the child that his environment is *stable* and that it is either his body or the object that is moving.

DIMENSION OF TIME

Kephart (1971) considers time as a fourth dimension of space. The point of origin of the temporal dimension is simultaneity—events that have a zero temporal interval between them. The zero point on the temporal scale is simultaneity just as the zero point of space was the center of gravity. Simultaneity is first experienced motorically with the cocontraction of neck and trunk muscles. In Concept 5 it was seen that a strong extensor would drive a flexor to contract in a balanced simultaneous cocontraction. As the trunk is stabilized the two arms or two legs may move simultaneously or sequentially. For events to be considered simultaneous they must truly happen exactly together. Otherwise the temporal dimension will be unstable just as the spatial dimensions were unstable when the child's concept of the center of gravity was not clear. As the contrast between simultaneous movements and sequential movements becomes clear and sharp, this knowledge can be abstracted. It is the abstraction that forms the base for a temporal dimension. Consequently the importance of the stability of the neck and trunk cannot be overemphasized as the foundation for the development of a space-time structure. Lacking the temporal dimension derived from his body, the individual may find it very difficult to distinguish visual and auditory events that occur together or in sequence.

Rhythm

The first component of the time dimension is *rhythm*. Rhythm is difficult to define, but lack of rhythm is easy to observe. Fluency or smoothness is an essential component of rhythm. Rhythm is to the time scale what inches are to the space scale. Rhythm can be identified in all areas of behavior. The most basic rhythms are those vegetative functions of respiration, circulation, and digestion. We are probably more cognizant of the lack of rhythm in gross and fine motor activity. However, in auditory and visual perception one must hear and see a repetitive pattern or rhythm to discriminate. Without a constant repetitive pattern or rhythm only the bits and pieces are identified. Lack of fluency is evident in speech problems existing in the severely aphasic patient, the stutterer, the mild dysarthric patient, or the individual who speaks in a monotone. Lack of rhythm in higher visual expressive language occurs in the individual who, when reading aloud, reads isolated words instead of the entire sentence.

Pace

The second component of the time dimension is *pace*. Pace is defined as the alteration in the size of the temporal unit. A fast pace has small temporal units, whereas a slow pace has large temporal units. The rhythm maintains the consistency between units regardless of the pace. Many children have difficulty varying their pace in activities. For instance, the hypotonic child cannot speed up and the hyperactive child cannot slow down. Both types of children will exhibit problems in rhythm.

Sequence

The third component of the time dimension is *sequence*. When rhythm has produced a temporal scale of consistent units, the final problem is the organizing of events into a sequence. The importance of sequence has long been recognized. The dependency of sequence on the existence of a temporal scale may not be as readily or widely recognized. Sequencing cannot be taught until simultaneity is established. This again points up the critical nature of the vestibular system's feeding of the fusimotor system to provide extensor muscle function necessary to promote cocontraction of midline muscles as an origin for the temporal scale. From this stable origin, rhythm can develop as equal temporal intervals in the dimensions of space. Feldenkrais (1949) states, "Phasic movements are normally not attempted until after considerable tonic postural apprenticeship. The correction of the kinesthetic sense and control should be well on the way before phasic movements are taught, so that properly integrated responses to gravitation are spontaneously elicited."

• • •

We would like to digress briefly to emphasize the proper integration of treatment approaches. Certainly Ayres' emphasis on vestibular stimulation to normalize function is essential before using Rood's approach. Minimal benefits will be derived from the inverted position to build strong extensor muscles to promote cocontraction, and simultaneity is essential before using Bobath's equilibrium techniques. Ayres has emphasized the value of adaptive behavioral response to a change in environment as being the best integrator of sensory input. When the foundations are laid, Bobath's techniques for stimulating equilibrium reactions are ideal. When equilibrium is automatic, the rhythm and sequence of movements of Kephart, Chaney, and Miles are appropriate.

Before we leave the dimensions of space and time, the translation from one to the other must be discussed. The individual must in fact make the temporal dimension a fourth dimension of space. He must be able to move freely from one dimension to the other without losing meaning. The space and time structure has to be so correlated that elements have the same meaning in either dimension. Unless he can translate back and forth from one to the other there is constant confusion. For example, as a child looks at a picture many elements are organized in all three axes of space but simultaneously in time. He must attend to elements one at a time in sequence on a temporal series but not lose the relationship of the intial context of the whole. Otherwise, he sees only the trees as elements and never the forest.

Consider language from this perspective. Both speech and language are extended in time. Any instant of speech is an isolated sound. The speech aspect is derived from the relationship of sounds on the temporal dimension. Language is derived from the ability to expand on both the space and time dimension at the same time. As a child listens he hears isolated sounds that he must organize on the temporal dimension and ultimately integrate into a mental image (visualization) of the space dimension.

Practical application

The end result of the motor-perceptual stage of development is the motor generalizations of Kephart (1960, 1971). These generalizations include posture and maintenance of balance, locomotion, contact, and receipt and propulsion.

MOTOR GENERALIZATIONS
Posture and maintenance of balance

As discussed earlier, when the three dimensions of space and the dimension of time are established within the body, the individual will demonstrate a flexible posture. As the process of integration progresses, midline stability is established, and the individual will demonstrate the ability to maintain balance in a myriad of positions.

Locomotion

Locomotion is moving through space. Locomotion is initiated by the movement of the head followed by movement of the body in such patterns as rolling, crawling with the abdomen in contact with the surface, scooting in the sitting position, creeping on hands and knees, walking, running, jumping, hopping, and skipping. This wide variety of movement patterns allows the child to explore and interact with his environment. The level of the locomotion pattern is not the critical factor, but rather the opportunity to explore and interact with the environment. This demands that an individual, child or adult, be provided the opportunity to participate in locomotion at his level in order to actively interact with his environment instead of being a passive observer. The elementary physical education program provides the unique contribution of presenting to the child a tremendous variety of movement opportunities and explorations, all of which will enhance body schema, body image, and body concept.

Contact

Contact includes reaching, grasping, and releasing. This allows the child to manipulate and explore objects in relationship to his body. He must have differentiated the shoulder, elbow, wrist, fingers, and thumb in order to accomplish these motor generalizations. As discussed in Concept 2 the tactile defensive individual is thwarted in this motor generalization because of his attentional deficit, lack of differentiation, and lack of movement control.

Receipt and propulsion

Receipt and propulsion refer to the individual's ability to relate to moving objects. Receipt is the ability to interact with objects coming toward the body by deflecting them or catching them. Propulsion is the ability to give motion to an object by pushing, pulling, kicking, throwing, or hitting.

The individual must establish distance and speed as related to himself and to the object, first with his body stationary and ultimately with both his body and the object moving. When problems are evidenced in this area, attention should be directed to earlier motor generalizations, especially posture and maintenance of balance.

When Kephart's space-time structure is considered as a totality, the high level of integration is evident. The end product is the result of the developmental acquisition of each minute facet!

One of the most common examples of this space-time structure integration may be seen in baseball teams of 6- to 8-year-old children. The player with good integration will demonstrate excellent propulsion in his batting as he relates to the moving ball. He demonstrates excellent receipt as he moves under a fly ball. Also, as he positions his body in front of a ground ball, he is demonstrating receipt. This star player is the result of a symphony of motor generalizations that are automatically at his disposal and contribute to his continuous success and peer approval.

On the same team are the players who demonstrate lack of integration. The lack of integration in propulsion will be evidenced in batting by the following behaviors: swinging too soon, too late, too high, or too low; looking away from the ball; and not watching the ball from the pitcher to the bat. Lack of integration in receipt will be evidenced by protective reactions of avoidance and remaining stationary and reaching for the ball instead of moving the body into relationship with the ball. These problems of lack of integration of the space-time structure frequently stem from inadequate motor generalization of posture and maintenance of balance plus deficits in ocular control. Posture and balance problems may be evidenced by hypotonicity, fatigue posture, hypermobile joints, lack of endurance, and general incoordination.

How often is the child's inability to hold the bat in the air, keep his elbow up, stand with his feet apart, and swing the bat with reasonable force related to his lack of strength? How often is the child's inability to get all the pieces, such as stance, grasp, bat position, and swing, together related to his lack of kinesthetic feedback and kinesthetic figure-ground? How often is the child's inability to cross the midline and integrate the two sides of the body as well as the top and bottom of the body related to his lack of midline cocontraction or stability and the integration of the primitive reflexes?

It would undoubtedly be very revealing to evaluate these children with Ayres Postrotary Nystagmus Test, Rood's inverted position, and the balance and posture items of Kephart's Purdue Perceptual-Motor Survey. It would undoubtedly be startling to see how many of these same players were plagued with learning disorders. Is it any wonder that these children suffer from negative self-concept, demonstrate a defeatist attitude in almost every area of endeavor, and develop emotional problems?

How many of these children demonstrate the fatigue introverted posture? What is cause, and what is effect? Where are the physical development programs from infancy that emphasize good vestibular stimulation, strong extensors, and good neck and trunk stability as prerequisites to optimal realization of physical, emotional, intellectual, and spiritual potential.

PURDUE PERCEPTUAL-MOTOR SURVEY

In normal development the child progresses from motor performances through perceptual-motor matching to the development of form perception and a space-time structure. This development typically occurs during the preschool years. When the child reaches age 6 or 7 this early development should be available for academic use. In many children the process is broken down, interrupted, or delayed. Many of the breakdowns reveal themselves in the early elementary grades in learning difficulties and low academic achievement. The Purdue Perceptual-Motor Survey identifies the areas in which the child is deficient in performance. For this reason it is important for the practitioner to have a thorough understanding of Kephart's stages of development before administering the survey. Frequently attention is directed to the isolated item instead of what the performance is revealing about development or the breakdown of development.

The following presentation of the Purdue Perceptual-Motor Survey is intended to broaden the reader's understanding and appreciation of the survey. It is not intended to replace the manual (Roach and Kephart, 1966) in administering the survey.

The purpose of the Purdue Perceptual-Motor Survey is to assess the individual's behavior in a series of tasks. It is a survey of basic motor skills that lay the foundation for preacademic skills; it is not a pass-fail test. What is important is the way the individual deals with the task and the underlying explanation of why he performs the way he does. It is also important to be aware of the interfering factors that prevent him from performing in the expected way.

A major criticism of this survey is that it is loosely structured; this is, in fact, what makes it such a valuable tool. We are concerned with how and why the individual solves the problems presented to him as he does. If he is unable to perform, additional instructions and structure are provided. For example, the child is instructed, "Walk forward on the balance beam." If he questions, "How do you want me to do it?" then the response is "Do it the way you think it should be done." If the child continues to have difficulty, the examiner tells him to "step up on the board and put one foot in front of the other and walk down to the other end." All of these instructions provide him with more structure. If at this point he is unable to perform, the examiner demonstrates how to execute the activity. The final step in structuring the situation is to hold the child's hands, assist him to step up on the board, and if necessary physically move one foot at a time while he walks the beam. Consequently in each activity there are four levels; the first is unstructured verbal instructions, and the last level is physically helping the child to perform the task. The scoring system provided was standardized for first-through fourth-grade children. The value is not in the numbered scores but in the observations of what is happening.

Categories

The survey is made up of 11 subtests grouped into five categories of performance. The categories are balance and posture, body image and differentiation, perceptual-motor match, ocular pursuit, and form perception.

Balance and posture. The first category of balance and posture includes the subtests of walking board and jumping. The walking board test is performed forward, backward, and sideways; jumping is with both feet, one foot, then skipping, and finally hopping in place with even and uneven alternating rhythms. These activities may demonstrate problems in flexibility. The problems may range from rigid, tied-together, stereotyped patterns to hypotonicity and excessive ranges of movement. The child may attempt to avoid balance by changing the speed or altering the manner of performance. There may be asymmetry in the two sides of the body. The absence of rhythm should be obvious.

Body image and differentiation. The second category of performance is body image and differentiation. This category includes the subtests of identification of body parts, imitation of movements, obstacle course, Kraus-Weber, and angels-in-the-snow. In the identification of body parts the examiner asks the child to touch his head, eyes, knees, toes, elbows, etc. It is important that he uses both hands to touch paired parts and that he knows where the parts are without looking or feeling for them. In touching the elbows he must cross the midline of his body. In the imitation of movements, the movement is first unilateral, becomes bilateral, and ends as contralateral. The sequence is very important and must be memorized by the examiner to assure close observation of the child's performance. The obstacle course involves going under, over, and between objects. This demonstrates the relationship of the body to the available space. The Kraus-Weber evaluates the strength of upper trunk extension and lower trunk extension as two separate tasks. Angels-in-the-snow movements are executed unilaterally (one extremity), bilaterally (both arms or both legs), homolaterally (arm and leg on one side of the body), and contralaterally (opposite arm and leg).

These activities exhibit problems in kinesthetic feedback as demonstrated by the child feeling for the body parts, hesitations, overestimations of movement, overflow into other body parts, and the need for visual attention to what the body parts are doing. These activities also exhibit problems in differentiation or "sorting out" the body parts. The problem most frequently overlooked is separation of the top from the bottom of the body as required in the Kraus-Weber test.

At this time it would seem appropriate to focus on one of the problems involved in integrating our thinking. If we view the Kraus-Weber test from Kephart's vantage point, we are concerned with back extensor muscle strength but equally with the differentiation or sorting out of the top from the bottom of the body. If we view this activity from Ayres' viewpoint, we are encouraged because the child can extend against gravity and against the flexion facilitated from the tonic labyrinthine reflex of the prone position. Her interpretation would undoubtedly be that the tonic labyrinthine reflex is integrated because it no longer dominates the muscle tone. If we view the same activity from Rood's vantage point we would emphasize the extension facilitated from the tonic labyrinthine inverted reflex because the head has gone from the erect position to the horizontal position or 90 degrees of the arc of motion. In fact, do they not each have a piece of the puzzle? We must consider all of the possible influences and explanations in hopes of ultimately arriving at **truth**!

The child's inability to maintain an activity for a period of time is also demonstrated in the differentiation tasks. This is beautifully illustrated if he is asked to simply continue doing any of the activities instead of stopping with one performance as indicated in the manual.

Before leaving this performance area it is important to emphasize that problems in body image and differentiation can be anticipated by certain behaviors related to the walking board and jumping. An example would be rigid posture that is not differentiated. Also the problems of balance and posture will be carried over to body image and differentiation. An example would be postural leaning while executing the imitations of movement or loss of balance in the obstacle course.

Perceptual-motor match. The third category of performance is perceptual-motor match and includes the subtests of chalkboard and rhythmical writing. The child is asked to draw a single circle on the chalkboard right in front of his body. He is then asked to use two pieces of chalk and draw two circles at the same time. For the lateral lines, the examiner places two Xs about 24 to 30 inches apart at shoulder height. The child should not watch the Xs being placed on the board. The child is then told to draw a line from one X to the other X. For vertical lines the examiner places two Xs toward the top of the chalkboard so the child must extend his arms over his head. Again he should not watch the Xs being placed. He is told to take a piece of chalk in each hand and draw two straight lines from the Xs to the bottom of the board. The rhythmical writing should not be scored on children under 8 years of age, but it can be observed on younger children, affording insight into their orientation, flow of movement, and visual-motor translation. The motifs start with a series of simple square-topped drawings and progress to complex combinations of cursive letters such as *pb*'s.

Midline problems are demonstrated by:

1. The single circle being placed to the side
2. Double circles that are flat at the midline
3. A multitude of difficulties with the lateral line such as turning the body, changing hands at midline, or walking along the board
4. Vertical lines that bow either in or out

Problems with direction are typically seen in the lateral line when the orientation is not left to right. They are also seen in rhythmical writing where the motifs are upside down or drawn in a right-to-left direction.

Problems in differentiation can be seen in the circles as well as in the motifs. There is typically an increased tension in the fingers and wrists, and the entire body is used in the drawing.

Ocular pursuit. The fourth category of performance is ocular pursuit and includes the subtests of horizontal and vertical tracking of both eyes and each eye individually and convergence. When testing tracking, the examiner should hold the object about 20 inches from the child at eye level and move it in an arc from one side to the other, up and down, diagonally, and in a circle. Convergence is tested by starting with the object at arms length, approaching the nose, and returning to arms length. With the object about 6 to 8 inches from the child, the child is told to look at you and then at the pencil and back to you.

A striking problem demonstrated in this activity is the inability of the eyes to cross either the horizontal (side-to-side) or vertical (up-and-down) midline. Some children will exhibit a strong fixation at the midline and are forced to move the head instead of the eyes, the most basic problem in differentiation. Most children will function better when both eyes are being tested than when using each eye individually.

An equally prevalent problem is the inability of the eyes to converge on the moving object. The eyes must work simultaneously to hold a single image as the object approaches the nose. Many children will shift from using one eye to using the other or will suppress one eye completely instead of converging the two eyes. Snapp (1979) indicates that children cannot converge with movement within arms length before the age of 8 years. Consequently requiring fine eye-hand skills within arms length before 8 years is forcing the child to use only one eye. The use of only one eye will limit perception to two dimensions or a flat surface. Both eyes are required for depth perception or three-dimensional perception.

Form perception. The fifth category of performance is form perception as seen in the subtest of visual achievement forms. The visual achievement forms are the circle, cross, square, triangle, divided rectangle, vertical diamond, and horizontal diamond. Attention should be directed toward the starting point, the direction, the flow of movement, stopping and starting, and the size of the forms as they are reproduced. Also the organization of the forms on the paper should be from left to right and from top to bottom.

The reproduction of these achievement forms is closely related to kindergarten readiness skills. These forms will demonstrate problems in left-to-right and top-to-bottom progression. As the examiner becomes skillful in observation, problems in all performance areas may become evident. For example, problems in balance and posture will be seen in the sitting position and problems in body image and differentiation will be seen in orientation to the paper and the manner in which the pencil is used. Problems in perceptual-motor match and ocular pursuit will be seen in the way in which the hand and eye work together to reproduce the forms.

• • •

The element frequently overlooked in using this survey is the very critical factor of sequencing. Sequencing is essentially the coordination of muscle groups in posture and movement. Sequencing or lack of sequencing is evidenced in each of the performance areas. The inability of the child to maintain alternating hopping is the best example of a problem in sequencing in the balance and posture area. Any kinesthetic feedback problem is also a problem in sequencing and may be very obvious in imitations of movement and angels-in-the-snow. If the child is instructed to continue making double circles, problems with sequencing will show up in the desynchronization of the two hands and eventual stopping of one hand. In ocular pursuit, sequencing is the two eyes working smoothly together as they follow the object. Starting, changing direction, and stopping the movement when reproducing the visual achievement forms are also related to sequencing. Perhaps the highest level of sequencing is the way in which the eye and hand work together as the geometric forms are drawn. This factor of sequencing will be further elaborated in Concept 9.

In looking totally at the Purdue Perceptual-Motor Survey one may consider three steps in processing the information. First the information from the actual performance of each of the 22 test items is considered. Second the test items may be considered under the five categories of balance and posture, body image and differentiation, perceptual-motor match, ocular pursuits, and form perception as presented in the previous section. During this process it is important to recognize how problems in each area may be demonstrated in each of the test items. The more adept the evaluator is in this processing, the more meaningful and useful the tool will become.

Aspects

The third step in processing the Purdue Perceptual-Motor Survey information is relating the test items to three aspects. The aspects include laterality, perceptual-motor match, and directionality.

Laterality. By our definition, laterality is the internal awareness of the two sides of the body and how they work together and in opposition. This internal awareness necessitates a good body awareness made up of body concept, body image, and body schema. Body schema is an internal postural model of the body. Posture is dependent on muscle tone and the kinesthetic feedback. Kinesthetic feedback is sensation, and the interpretation of sensation is controlled by the autonomic nervous system. In Concept 2 the effect of the autonomic nervous system on exteroceptor sensory input was presented. It is important to realize in this sequence that the autonomic nervous system also influences kinesthetic feedback. When the body is in a totally sympathetic withdrawal pattern, the kinesthetic feedback will be from flexors, adductors, and internal rotators. If the extremities are constantly withdrawn to avoid stimuli, the flexors, adductors, and internal rotators will have increased muscle tone and increased kinesthetic feedback. With this imbalance in sensation it will be extremely difficult for the individual to develop adequate laterality.

As the internal awareness of the body develops, the difference between the sides of the body will become apparent to the individual. From many motor experiences the child learns the difference between activities on the right side of the body and the same activities on the left side of the body. He develops a right-left gradient as he determines how far things are to the extreme right, through the zero point of the force of gravity (midline), and out to the extreme left. The right-left gradient within the body will become the basis for his concepts of the dimension of space (vertical, horizontal, and transverse) (Roach and Kephart, 1966). We believe that it is extremely important that the labels right and left be reserved for directionality. Many clinicians begin using the labels long before the laterality process is finalized. In this process of developing a right-left gradient the child will also be differentiating extremities from the body, the sides of the body from each other, the top from the bottom of the body, and the segments of the extremity. It should be evident that problems in laterality are not isolated academic ones but are rather the result of a complex series of deficiencies.

As the evaluator considers the individual test items of the Purdue Perceptual-Motor Survey, it becomes evident that laterality is an integral part of each activity. The coordination and flexibility of balance is impossible without adequate laterality. Deficits in laterality are most evident by the rigidity of the body, compensatory movements, and the domination of visual control.

Perceptual-motor match. The information from the individual test items should also be related to the aspect of perceptual-motor match. In the previous aspect of laterality the individual is learning from the inside of his body to the outside. He is building up information in his motor system from sensory input arising from his vestibular mechanism and from the proprioceptors found in muscles and tendons (Ball, 1971). With this initial body of information in the motor system the infant is now ready to begin the development of his perceptual system. Roach and Kephart (1966) remind us that initial perceptual information is without form, shape, direction, figure-ground relationship, or spatial orientation. It is only through experimentation in comparing new perceptual information with existing motor information that the two bodies of information come to mean the same thing. As explained earlier, without this perceptual-motor match, the individual lives in two separate worlds, one motor and one perceptual.

There are many children who are disadvantaged because the appropriate channel for input may be defective or absent. For example, the auditory input may be inadequate or distorted to the extent that vision is forced to compensate. If a child is dependent on seeing information in order that his perceptual and motor worlds agree, he is going to have tremendous difficulty functioning in a predominately auditory environment. There are thousands of people who experience difficulty "getting" material presented in the classroom by way of a lecture. Those same people can read a book on a very difficult subject and comprehend the material immediately because they can use their eyes. The person who must write a word as it is spelled to him in order to identify the word is demonstrating his inability to use the auditory channel as efficiently as the visual channel.

The critical issue is that in the beginning each channel must be related back to kinesthesia to remove the distortions and to develop constancy. At this point each channel may be integrated with every other channel because the data are equivalent and intersensory integration is possible.

It is important to move one step further to consider hemisphere specialization. The child who has not developed his motor system to the point of dominance is not developing hemisphere specialization (de Quiros, 1976).

The child is being forced to use high-level function to attempt to control a defective motor system. This defective motor system is not providing a consistent model as a basis for eliminating the distortions in the other channels. It must be extremely confusing to not know if the distortion and lack of constancy is in the body information of the motor system or in the visual, auditory, tactile, smell, or taste information.

We believe that the importance of the perceptual-motor match is an integral part of Ayres' theory of sensory integrative dysfunction. The individual must develop not only the match between two different sensations or perceptual models but the intersensory integration of sensation from several different sources. Ayres has continuously emphasized the point that the best integrator of sensory input is an adaptive behavioral response.

Our apparent obsession is to emphasize that each person with a theory of intervention has a piece of the total puzzle. It seems imperative to put all of these pieces together into a meaningful program of management. The frustration to us is the apparent trend toward moving higher and higher into remediation of cognition when, in fact, it seems so obvious that the need is to go lower in body function. One reason behind our increasing numbers of learning disabilities may be the impact of our environment on the most basic prenatal and neonatal movement patterns (Snapps, 1979). It is our opinion that the earlier academic demands are placed on children, the more likely is the possibility of deficits in kinesthesia and distortions in perceptual-motor match.

According to the Purdue survey, chalkboard activities are in the section on perceptual-motor match. These activities involve matching a visual perception to a high-level skilled motor act. A much lower perceptual-motor match is the imitation of movements. The imitations are performed in an erect posture, which makes them more difficult than the angels-in-the-snow. The angels should be one of the easiest of all the activities and can be changed from a visual-motor activity to a tactile-motor activity by having the child close his eyes and the examiner touch with pressure the body parts to be moved. In the angels-in-the-snow it is also possible to evaluate the perceptual-motor match of the lower extremities as well as the combination of an upper and a lower extremity.

Directionality. The third aspect in processing the information from the Purdue Survey is directionality, which is closely related to the first aspect of laterality. According to Radler and Kephart (1960), physical coordination is, in fact, essentially the combination of these two aspects. Laterality is the map of one's internal space. Directionality is the map of one's external space. Space has direction (up and down, side to side, before and behind) only in relation to the person who is looking at it. Direction exists only as it is related to the body as part of motor patterns.

Laterality is the basis for the individual's spatial concepts. Unless a right-left gradient has been established in reference to the line of gravity through the body, there is no basis for directionality. The individual must progress through his perceptual-motor matches to firmly establish the constancy of the perceptual and motor worlds. When the perception of laterality is projected externally, it becomes directionality. Directionality is a learned process. The process must develop from the body outward to objects before it can develop between objects. For example, an object must be to the right of the body and a second object to the left of the body before the first object can be to the right of the second object.

A left-right progression must develop very early in the process of directionality to make possible the establishment of a fixed starting point. This left-right orientation is going to be delayed if the child is having difficulty crossing the midline of his body because of problems in laterality. The process of shifting from a right-left gradient in laterality to a left-right orientation in directionality is paramount. Without this shift from laterality to directionality the child appears lost in his spatial concepts. Any midline problem should immediately alert the examiner to this crucial transition.

• • •

We believe that the real value of this third way of processing information is its simplicity. Instead of being ensnared in 22 test items or five categories, all function is related to three aspects:

1. Is the body information accurate and does the body function superbly?
2. Does the perceptual world match the motor world?
3. Can the perceptual-motor world be projected into the external environment and function automatically?

In summary the first step in developing a space-time structure is dealing with the effects of gravity. Gravity through the vestibular system affects every function of the body. Gravity through the vestibular system is critical to the development of a healthy personality. Gravity as it relates to the space-time structure is primal in the acquisition of academics and cognitive skills. We have again come full circle to accentuate the urgency of not separating mind, body, and spirit. The human organism functions as a total unit with indivisible sensory-intellectual-emotional-somatic reactions.

KEY WORDS

body schema	flexibility	propulsion
contact	gravity	receipt
convergence	kinesthetic feedback	rhythm
differentiation of body parts	kinesthetic figure-ground	simultaneity
Euclid's spatial system	laterality	temporal dimension
fixation at midline	perceptual-motor match	

Readiness

spontaneous development of personality

Concept
Background
  Personality development
    Autonomic nervous system
      influence
    Exteroceptor sensory input
      influence
    Vestibular mechanism
      influence
  Montessori—absorbent mind
  Strauss—confident child
  Dobson—discipline

Practical application
  Ames—behavioral age
  Therapists screening format
  Testing environment
  Vestibular integration
  Extensor muscle tone
  Cocontraction

Body awareness
Sequence (timing)
Fine motor organization
Early prevention of school
  failure
Integrated motor activities
  scale

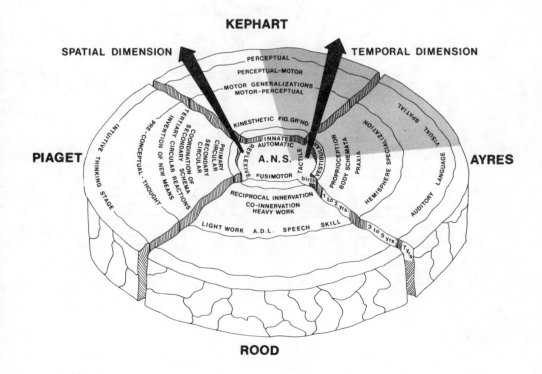

KEPHART

SPATIAL DIMENSION   TEMPORAL DIMENSION

PIAGET   **AYRES**

ROOD

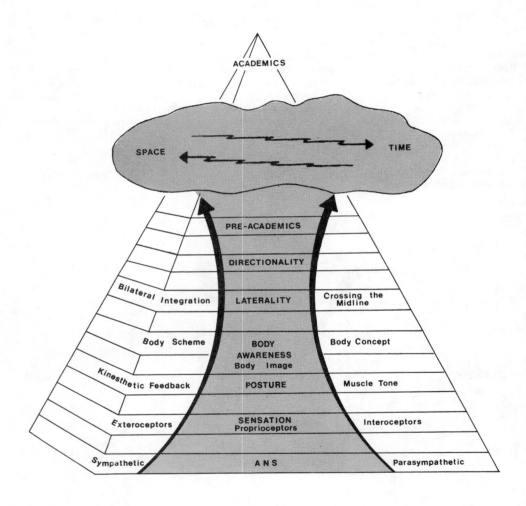

Concept   Basic motor skills lay the foundation for preacademic readiness. Assessment of
these skills and remediation of deficits should ensure a more successful educational experience. The aim of education should be the spontaneous development of the physical, emotional, intellectual, and spiritual personality.

To us personality encompasses all learning in the physical, intellectual,
emotional, and spiritual domains. Spontaneous development occurs when
interfering factors are at a minimum.

On the **tree** this concept encompasses the entire model. We have dealt
with the autonomic nervous system, all of the sensory input, the integration
of the input and motor output, and interpersonal relationships. Each individual is ready for certain learning experiences in certain sequences on a
specific time line. Education does not begin with entrance into kindergarten.
It begins prenatally with an environment rich in stimuli (wetness, warmth,
darkness, touch, and pressure) and all joint movements within the limitations of the uterine cavity. Birth is merely a change in environment and
stimuli that will use the movement patterns learned prenatally.

The **cross-section** shows the temporal growth from the prenatal period to
7 years of age. Again this concept encompasses the entire model.

The **pyramid** perhaps better than any model illustrates how academics,
at the peak, are built on a broad base of all the activities that came before.
Learning and education begin prenatally and should progress throughout
our lives.

Background

As we approach this last concept it may be wise to survey the intent and
purpose of this book. As was stated in the preface, our firm conviction is that,
for an individual to reach the optimal level of physical, emotional, intellectual, and spiritual development, there must be an interdisciplinary, neurophysiologically integrated approach to management. We have repeatedly
emphasized that the mind, body, and spirit must not be separated. Concept
by concept we have built a structure for dealing with the four areas of development. The major reference to mind has been its function in cognitive or
academic areas. At this point the concept of mind as it relates to personality
must be considered.

PERSONALITY DEVELOPMENT
Autonomic nervous system influence

We are of the opinion that the development of personality begins in Concept 1. As we consider the continuum from ergotropic to trophotropic reactions, there is merit in considering related personalities. One might hypothesize that there exists an ergotropic-type personality at one extreme and a trophotropic-type personality at the other extreme. There will be many varieties and mixtures of personalities between the two extremes.

The ergotropic personality could be characterized as the person who is operating close to the stress threshold with frequent outbursts of sympathetic fight-or-flight reactions. This individual would demonstrate many of the sympathetic physical characteristics of excessive muscle tone, fast heart rate and increased blood pressure, and frequent intestinal upsets with poor ingestion, digestion, and elimination. This individual would probably be very active, alert, and involved in many activities—an organizer, a driver, and a go-getter—but would not be noted for patience, tolerance, or compassion.

The trophotropic personality could be characterized as the person who operates in a very relaxed way, unhurried or unruffled in the most stressful situations. He would demonstrate many of the parasympathetic or vegetative physical characteristics of low muscle tone, relative inactivity, and good ingestion, digestion, and elimination. This individual would probably be the peaceable, passive, nonaggressive observer.

In consideration of the growth and development of personality the realm of manipulation exists just as it did in Concept 1. It is conceivable that the irritable infant demonstrating frequent episodes of colic is at risk for developing an ergotropic personality. If there is a genetic history of "explosive tempers," the infant may also be at risk for developing an ergotropic personality. This will be especially true as he becomes mobile and inquisitive, requiring frequent correction. The environment by necessity will need to be structured to allow freedom but with definite limitations. Parasympathetic stimuli may need to be used to assist this child to alter his behavior. As the child ages he should be taught physical methods of altering his position on the ergotropic-trophotropic continuum. It is relatively unproductive to excuse or blame ergotropic behavior on great grandfather's temper.

At the other extreme, the placcid, "too good" infant may be at risk for developing a trophotropic personality. He may need frequent sympathetic stimuli to activate his muscles, to increase tone, and to assure investigation of his environment instead of passive observation.

It is our belief that the highest level of maturity is the achievement of the correct balance of ergotropic and trophotropic reactions in each situation.

There are some situations that require trophotropic management; however, there are other situations in which an ergotropic management is definitely appropriate.

Exteroceptor sensory input influence

Concept 2 should also be related to a discussion of personality. As presented previously, the correct combination of information by way of C neurons and A neurons is essential for normal sensation. Without the appropriate foundation of nonspecific generalized tactile stimulation the protective function will not be inhibited to allow discrimination to develop. The overactive protective system results in everything being interpreted as potentially dangerous, which triggers the ergotropic response. Considerable parasympathetic stimuli are needed to deactivate the sympathetic system and move the individual below the stress threshold.

There are numerous animal studies that show the effects of petting on heart rate and blood pressure. Some of the early studies of monkeys illustrated the important effect of contact with the mother monkey on later emotional development. The medical journals as well as newspapers and magazines are full of articles about touching, the importance of contact, loving, and skin hunger.

Davis (1978) made some very good points in her article "Skin Hunger, An American Disease." She emphasized the infant's need for comforting touch long before he can produce or understand any words. Each of us has the memory of comfort and security from touching and being touched. Unfortunately, as we grow up, touching takes on certain rules and hidden meanings. Our society has loaded touching with sexual overtones. People are dying everyday—starved for some form of physical contact. Touching is a two-way process that is equally beneficial to the toucher and the touchee. Maybe instead of the bumper sticker "Have you hugged your kid today?" we need one that says "Have you hugged someone today?"

Buscaglia (1972, 1977) in his books and lectures has made us aware of the need to learn to love and to learn how to express that love openly. How do we give of ourselves to each other? Do we care? When did we say to someone that he had done a good job? Do we understand peoples' needs? Do we look at each other and listen to each other? Are we aware of the continual wonder of life? Do you know how your spouse or a friend has changed in the last 6 months? All of these things are related to personality and interpersonal relationships. All are intimately interrelated with autonomic nervous system function and tactile stimulation.

There is voluminous material available on the psychosomatic approach and how the mind influences the body. Especially interesting is how stress and emotional disturbances can produce disorders of the skin. Montagu (1971) presents the opposite approach of how the skin as a tactile organ affects the mind. He asks the question, what influence do various kinds of cutaneous experiences, especially in early life, have on development? What kind of skin stimulation is necessary for healthy physical and behavioral development? Equally important is the determination of the effects of a lack of particular kinds of skin stimulation.

Animal studies show that licking is essential in keeping the gastrointestinal, genitourinary, respiratory, circulatory, digestive, reproductive, nervous, and endocrine systems adequately stimulated. From these animal studies Montagu (1971) postuates that in humans tactile stimulation is fundamental to the development of healthy emotional relationships. Since tactile stimulation and love are so closely connected, one learns to love by being loved, not by instruction.

Space and time do not permit detailed coverage of the many enlightening aspects of Montague's book; therefore the reader is strongly urged to place it high on the priority list of subsequent reading. Equally important for its implications to early handling is Ribble's *Rights of Infants* (1943).

Vestibular mechanism influence

A third aspect of personality development is the influence of gravity and the role of the vestibular system. Since gravity is the only constant force, our relationship or orientation to that force is the most basic. Without the appropriate orientation to gravity, all development will be disrupted.

As presented earlier, the vestibular system is responsible for providing the sensory stimuli to the fusimotor system of extensor muscles. The infant must develop tonic midline extensor muscles against the force of gravity. In Concept 5 the process of using the strong extensor muscle to drive the flexor muscle into cocontraction was presented. Midline neck and trunk stability is the essence of orientation in space against the force of gravity. The vestibular system influences and undergirds every sensory system and every human function. How very critical is de Quiros' (1976) finding that there are many individuals born with deficits in their vestibuloproprioceptive mechanism! How urgent vestibular intervention is to every area of development!

In a book by Feldenkrais (1949) we found some very enlightening references to the vestibular system.

1. Orientation in space is essential to any living organism.
2. All perception and sensation take place on a background of muscular activity that is strictly shaped by gravity.
3. No sensation is possible without some motor background.

4. The vestibular system influences the autonomic nervous system.
5. Disorders in the vestibular apparatus distort other sensory information.
6. We cannot perceive unless we are aware of the attitude and orientation of the body.
7. We cannot appreciate any sensory experience, emotion, or feeling without presenting to ourselves our relation to the vertical.
8. In general there is no isolated sensory experience. There is a tendency to test each new sensory experience by the other senses.
9. The vestibular system coordinates the sensory motor impressions into a coherent picture with the image and orientation of our body in space.

Feldenkrais explains that the very first experience of anxiety is a result of stimulation of the vestibular nerve by loss of support. The stimulation of the nerve diffuses through the brain stem and produces a halting of breath. The halt is a sudden disturbance in the diaphragmatic and cardiac regions and is sensed as anxiety. Very loud noises excite the cochlear branch of the vestibulocochlear (eighth cranial) nerve sufficiently to diffuse and excite the vestibular nerve, producing the same halt in breath.

Feldenkrais emphasized the importance of sensory-intellectual-emotional-somatic reactions that are indivisible. Consequently the emotional as well as vegetative and somatic planes must be reached before there is total personality adjustment. Chronic anxiety inhibits antigravity muscles, leading to posture with decreased extensor muscle tone. It can be demonstrated that people with emotional trouble have difficulty performing full extension (Feldenkrais, 1949).

The fear and anxiety caused by stimulation of the vestibular nerve are actually abated by general flexor contraction, particularly of the abdominal region. The flexor response lowers the head, crouches the body, bends the knees, and brings the limbs in front and near the body to protect the soft parts. This posture gives the best possible protection and produces a feeling of safety, quiets the pulse, and restores normal breathing.

This pattern of flexor contraction is reinstated every time the person reverts to passive protection in stressful situations. Thus an introverted posture is produced, which in fact inhibits extensor muscles. Extroverts, on the other hand, have an erect posture with strong extensor muscles, which provide equal opportunity for all acts and muscular combinations.

This raises a very critical question—what is happening to the personality of the individual constantly maintained in the flexed position? Also what is being initiated by encouraging the total flexion pattern in certain treatment approaches. Does it not seem more emotionally and physiologically sound to use the vestibular system to assist the extensor muscles to orient against the force of gravity?

King (1974) has been instrumental in linking Schilder's studies in the 1930s with Ayres' sensory integrative approach in the treatment of schizophrenia. Schilder noted that schizophrenics were markedly hyposensitive to vestibular stimulation as measured by postrotational nystagmus. Ayres has set forth the critical role of vestibular and tactile input in organizing and integrating sensory stimuli. King indicates that it seems plausible that abnormal vestibular reactions may reflect defective brain stem processing, which may be the cause of perceptual inconstancy in the schizophrenic population. The tendency of autistic and schizophrenic children to whirl, rock, and shake their heads may be an attempt to obtain needed vestibular stimulation, just as the same self-stimulatory techniques in the mentally retarded may show a need for vestibular stimulation to normalize all perception.

Schilder (1964) states that "in every action, the individual must start with an orientation toward his own body and the bodies of others. Every action is based on the body image." The body is in a state of equilibrium before an action takes place and returns to this equilibrium at the completion of the action. We never deal with a mere change in space and time, therefore we cannot be separated from our perception of space and time which are so influenced by the force of gravity and dependent on vestibular integration.

The reader should understand that we believe personality is rooted in everything in an individual's environment and experience. Muscle tone and early movements lay the foundation for one's feelings about oneself. If one's body does not perform as it should, negative feelings about the self will begin, and the seeds of personality problems will be planted. Self-esteem may suffer to the point that the individual questions his very value and purpose in life.

It may seem to some readers that we have continued to neglect the spiritual aspects of development. Other readers may question vigorously the appropriateness of this aspect in a neurophysiology book. It is not our purpose to preach, to dictate, or to judge. It is our purpose to affirm the importance of a spiritual foundation and dependency by acknowledging the source of our strength, convictions, and destinies.

In each area of development we need to be aware of the importance of early childhood education. In this concept we would like to clarify this progression and identify the responsibility for that education.

MONTESSORI—ABSORBENT MIND

Many people will question whether a method devised over 70 years ago is of value today. We have frequently brought the readers' attention to the importance of the "old literature." With the present-day emphasis on abstract concepts being introduced earlier and earlier in the academic process, it may be very helpful to look carefully at Montessori and her methods.

According to Hainstock (1978), Maria Montessori was the first woman to receive her doctorate in medicine from the University of Rome in 1896. She brought her scientific methods into the classroom, considering it a laboratory for observing children and testing and retesting ideas and aids to their growth. She had studied the work of such men as Rousseau, Pestalozzi, and Froebel. Froebel started the first kindergarten in 1837 as a "place where children could grow like flowers through their *play.*"

Montessori started her work with retarded children with whom she had opportunity to use Itard's and Sequin's sensory teaching materials and to modify them to her own use. She was so successful with retarded children that she began to question the caliber of "normal" education, just as Sequin had before her, as many have since, and as each of us should today.

We have taken from Hainstock (1978) a method of identifying sources of information for the Montessori material as they are quoted.

1965	*Dr. Montessori's Own Handbook*	H
1967	*The Absorbent Mind*	AM
1966	*The Secret of Childhood*	S
1964	*The Montessori Method*	MM
1978	Hainstock's *The Essential Montessori*	Ha

Montessori (1964, 1965, 1966, 1967) has some very important things to say to us.

1. Children are human beings to whom respect is due. (H, 133)
2. Without knowing it, we ignore the creation of man, and trample on the treasure which God himself placed in every child. (AM, 239)
3. We are unaware of the spiritual germs, the creative nebulae that the child hides in himself when he enters our world to renew mankind. (AM, 240)
4. It is the child who makes the man and no man exists who was not made by the child who he once was. (AM, 15-16)
5. The first thing to be done is to discover the true nature of a child and then assist him in his normal development. (S, 166-167)
6. Education is not something a teacher does but is a natural process which develops spontaneously in the human being. (AM, 8)
7. All education of little children must be governed by the principle of helping the natural psychic and physical development of the child. (MM, 216)

The Montessori method was scientifically designed to develop the whole personality of the child at his own natural rate of progress and thus free his potential for self-development within a prepared environment. The ultimate goal was to create in the child independence, self-discipline, concentration, motivation, and sensitivity to things around him. Again Montessori has some critical things to say to us.

1. The years from birth to six are most formative and are too often wasted by not realizing the child's true potential. (Ha, 33)
2. Early sensorial activities lay the foundation for later intellectual activities. (Ha, 36)
3. The hands are the instruments of man's intelligence. (AM, 27)
4. The first essential for a child's development is concentration. It lays the whole basis for his character and social behavior. . . . The child who concentrates is immensely happy. For the time being his spirit is like a hermit, a new consciousness has been born in him, that of his own individuality. The spiritual process is evident, he has detached himself from the world in order to attain the power to unite himself with it. (AM, 216, 272, 273)
5. A child possesses an active psychic life even when he cannot manifest it, and must secretly perfect this inner life over a long period of time. (S, 14)
6. It is the spirit of the child that can determine the course of human progress (S, 9) and reveal the plan that is natural to man. (S, 23-24)

If the prenatal period, according to Montessori, is for the formation of the body, the period from birth to 3 years for formation of the mind, and the period from 3 to 6 years for formation of character and society, then a knowledge of sensitive periods is important. Montessori felt that children possess sensitivity to things at different times in their lives. A particular sensitivity is like turning a bright light on some object but not on others, making that object the whole of the child's world. It is important to realize that the sensitivity is transient and limited to acquiring a specific trait. Once the trait is acquired, the sensitivity disappears. It is the sensitivity that brings the child into contact with his world and passes him from conquest to conquest in a constant rhythm filled with the joy and happiness of exploration. Table 7 shows Montessori's sensitivity periods from birth to 6 years.

Hainstock (1978) has adapted some of the Montessori classroom activities for early use in the home. The practical life and early sensorial activities begin at 2½ years of age. The reading and writing activities and the arithmetic exercises begin at 3 years.

Packard (1972) indicates that one of Montessori's fundamentals was defining education as self-development in a prepared environment. Instead of courses or subjects she spoke of four ways humans deal with reality, producing four main areas of educational work. These are

1. Sensorial activity, or the strategies for observation
2. Practical life activity, or the strategies for work
3. Language, or the strategies of communication
4. Mathematical reasoning, or the strategies of thinking in quantitative relationships and symbols

Table 7. Sensitive periods*

Birth-3 years	Absorbent mind
	Sensory experiences
1½-3 years	Language development
1½-4 years	Coordination and muscle development
	Interest in small objects
2-4 years	Refinement of movement
	Concern with truth and reality
	Aware of order sequence in time and space
2½-6 years	Sensory refinement
3-6 years	Susceptibility to adult influence
3½-4½ years	Writing
4-4½ years	Tactile sense
4½-5½ years	Reading

*From Hainstock, E.G.: The essential Montessori, New York, 1978, The New American Library, Inc.

The child from birth to 3 years is characterized by his "absorbent mind." He absorbs impressions through all his senses like a sponge absorbs water. The opportunities in the environment determine his nourishment. He refines his senses through exercises of attention, comparison, and judgment. Is this not the same intersensory integration that was discussed in Concept 7?

As the child approaches 3 years he is developing a sense of order in time and space. The traditional sensorial materials isolate fundamental qualities that may be perceived through the senses, such as color, form, temperature, texture, weight, scent, or taste. These qualities are present in pairs to match, collections to sort, and series for grading. All activities necessitate manipulation, which provides opportunities for the child to coordinate his movements and integrate his sensations. By the nature of the activity the child corrects his own errors.

Through all of this, one must realize that a child's sensitive period lasts until he is almost 5 years old. This allows him to assimilate images from his environment through his many senses and to bring them into play with each other. The rather frightening aspect is that once the child has passed the age of a certain need it is never possible to obtain it fully; a specific development has missed its proper time.

Finally we need to draw from Montessori her convictions about independence and obedience. The acquisition of independence at each stage of development is one of the most important parts of the educational process. To constantly serve a child is to limit his independence. The child who is not taught to do, does not know how to do. By not teaching the child how to do things and how to be independent, we suffocate his useful, spontaneous activities.

All children possess an innate desire to please. Before the child is 3 he cannot obey unless the order corresponds with his own vital urge (AM, 258). Montessori indicates three levels of obedience: in the first the child can obey but does not always, in the second he can always obey because he has the control, and in the third he can absorb another's wishes and express them in his own behavior.

This area of independence and obedience brings our thinking to the rather delicate subject of discipline and parental responsibility. Perhaps in no other area has so much been written on philosophies and techniques, conflicts and agreements.

STRAUSS—CONFIDENT CHILD

Raising children is a serious responsibility. Is it not ironic that for practically every job some kind of special training or license is required except for the job of being a parent? Where does the responsibility start? Is each child valued just because he **is**? Have we as parents acknowledged that "each child is a gracious gift, from God, a lovely legacy from the Lord entrusted to our care to be loved, cherished, provided for and properly molded"*

Why does it take so long to nurture a child? Animals seem to survive as a matter of instinct. Life for humans involves intellectual and emotional character, moral and esthetic values, and volitional choices. All of these things have to be taught and developed if the individual is to have a useful and satisfying life.

What are we to use for our model? For those individuals with a faith in God, He is the model parent. There are many scriptures that compare God's parenthood to ours. Without that faith, successfully rearing a child seems like a superhuman task. Christian counselors have discovered that a person's image of God is often patterned after his image of his own parents. If this is true, the child's entire spiritual life may be at stake.

Ephesians 6:4 sums up God's method of rearing children—*discipline* and *instruction*. In this context discipline involves setting goals, teaching them, and patiently but persistently guiding children toward those goals. Strauss has outlined some very excellent goals for children regardless of what kind of home they are in. These goals are to teach them:

1. Prompt and cheerful obedience and respect for authority. They should develop a willing submission and respect for duly constituted authority.
2. Self-discipline. A happy life is a controlled life; particularly in the

---

*From Strauss, R.L.: Confident children and how they grow, Wheaton, Ill., 1975, Tyndale House Publishers.

areas of eating, sleeping, sex, care of the body, use of time and money, and desire for material things.

3. To accept responsibility for happily and efficiently accomplishing their tasks, caring for their belongings, and taking responsibility for the consequences of their own actions.

4. The basic character traits of honesty, diligence, truthfulness, righteousness, unselfishness, kindness, courtesy, consideration, friendliness, generosity, justice, patience, and gratitude.

The word "instruction" literally means "to place in the mind." Internalizing the goals and related standards as well as each family's religious beliefs, if any, is the process of making them an integral part of each child's life. These beliefs must be planted deeply in the very soul of the child so that they are a vital part of his being, belonging to him not to his parents. All of the parents' rules and structure are only temporary. They prepare the child for freedom—the satisfying freedom of living in harmony with his Maker. The whole process is a beautiful spiritual plan. During our childhood we have rules that regulate our behavior while we are taught biblical standards. As the child develops an inner discipline and control, more outward restrictions are decreased, and independence is increased. The ultimate goal is the self-disciplined, God-directed adult who is free to move through life seeking and fulfilling the unique plan for his life, acknowledging the source of his strength and destiny. How sad it is that so many people remain in a spiritual kindergarten, never experiencing the freedom and joy of God's love.

DOBSON—DISCIPLINE

Returning to Strauss' first goal of prompt obedience and respect for authority, Dobson (1970, 1974) has excellent practical suggestions for parents and teachers. He recommends a simple principle.

> When you are defiantly challenged, win decisively. When the child asks, "Who's in charge?" tell him. When he mutters, "Who loves me?" Take him in your arms and surround him with affection. Treat him with respect and dignity, and expect the same from him.*

Our society has gone through a period of permissiveness that did not work and that many people believe was downright disastrous. As adults it is time we realized that children thrive in a consistent structure of genuine love undergirded by reasonable discipline. Discipline does not mean just punishment. Discipline is a way to help children learn self-discipline and

---

*From Dobson, J.: Dare to discipline, Wheaton, Ill., 1970, Tyndale House Publishers.

responsible behavior. It is through this self-discipline and responsible behavior that we nurture the entire personality as expressed in this concept.

Dobson (1970) believes that discipline properly applied works! He indicates that through it tender affection is made possible by *mutual* respect. It bridges the generation gap. It allows God to be introduced to our children. It permits a teacher to do the kind of job in the classroom he or she is supposed to do. Discipline in the classroom is not very different from discipline at home. Discipline must be reinstated at home (the first obligation) but also reestablished at school. There must be a mutual respect and cooperation between the school and home if there is to be consistent discipline.

Perhaps everyone working with children needs to acknowledge that each child has a desire for evil and a desire for good and that each child was designed by God the way He wanted him for the plan that He has for that life. However, He gave each of us a free will to choose between the two sides of our nature—the good or the evil. A child has to be taught and trained to choose good because evil is always so desirable and tempting (La Haye, 1977). Who would choose evil if it were not so attractive and appealing? How many times is choosing good less attractive, less fun, and more difficult?

Dobson (1974) states that we should declare all-out war on the destructive value system of our society—a stupid, insane system that evaluates human worth on the basis of physical beauty and intelligence. What has happened to such virtues as honesty, integrity, courage, humor, patience, and craftsmanship? How can we help to build strong egos and indomitable spirits in children?

Dobson (1974) outlines ten strategies to establish and contribute to self-esteem from infancy onward.

1. Examine the values in your own home. You cannot build esteem in a child if your own feelings are in the way. How do you see the child? More importantly, how does he think you "see" him? Be careful of self-doubt and guilt.

2. Reserve adolescence for adolescents. Keep activities appropriate for the age! There are things to be done at 5 years of age and things to be done at 10 years and other things at 15 years. A 5-year-old child has no need or business being involved in 15-year-old activities.

3. Teach your child a "no-knock" policy. Do not allow self-criticism and downgrading. Everyone has unique strengths and attributes.

4. Help your child to compensate. Help him to face problems and profit from frustrations. Help him find ways to counterbalance his weaknesses by capitalizing on his strengths. Inferiority can either crush and paralyze a person, or it can provide tremendous emotional energy for success and achievement.

5. Help your child compete. We have to live in the world and play the social games, but we must have a foundation of the *true* values in life: kindness, love of mankind, integrity, etc. Our children must have this inner strength and stability, especially during adolescence. Recent studies show that suicide may be the third most common cause of death for students 19 years old and younger.

6. Discipline without damaging self-esteem. Rules and boundaries must be established. When those rules are broken, punish. "If willful defiance is involved, no other form of discipline is as effective as spanking." Do not spank for mistakes or accidents. After spanking make sure the child knows you love him. Spanking should be completed by 8 or 9 years. The big difference is between breaking the "spirit" of the child, which is fragile and brittle, resting on self-esteem, and breaking the "will," which is made of steel. We need to shape the will while leaving the spirit intact.

7. Keep a close eye on the classroom. It is important to understand that academic failure is a symptom of a more specific cause. There is a difference between the underachiever who is not working and the slow learner who is unable. This entire book is dedicated to helping people to identify what the problems are and to develop a strategy for dealing with them.

8. Avoid overprotection and dependency. It is difficult to avoid an over-dependent relationship, but "turning loose" has to start early, even at 3 or 4 years of age when the child is allowed out in the neighborhood. The best preparation for adulthood is training for responsibility during childhood. Start early to develop independence and responsible freedom.

9. Prepare for adolescence. Again, this preparation begins early, not when the child is 12 or 13. Help the child to realize that trials are only temporary and that everyone has to pass through the same situations. Perhaps at no time is self-esteem more threatened or inferiorities more obvious.

10. Message to discouraged adults. All of the problems of inferiority in children and need for self-esteem are just as real in adulthood. Perhaps the best prescription for each of us is "a healthy dose of self-esteem and personal worth (taken three times a day)."

Practical application

There seem to be several groups of children presenting themselves to the school system. The first group are those children who possess all of the basic motor skills and who, in every aspect, are ready to come to school and learn. Ames (1966) in a 3-year study of kindergarten, first-grade, and second-grade children found that only about one third of the children were fully ready for the work of the grade in which chronological age had placed them.

A second group of children, readily identified, are those with some type of physical disability. These children may or may not have related learning difficulties.

A third group of children includes those who were "high-risk infants." As a result of ever-improving medical care, more of these children are enrolling in school systems. Also, because of Public Law 94-142, school systems are required to provide for these individuals at an earlier age. Because of these children's stormy beginnings in life, many possess subtle physical impairments. All of these factors contribute to the importance of appropriate intervention programs. There is grave danger of programs for birth to 3 years emphasizing language or behavior modification or both at the expense of the development of basic motor skills and normal motor development. For many of these children the consequences of this kind of program may be disastrous. This type of program forces children to compensate for problems and frequently results in emotional and behavioral disturbances, instead of providing for remediation of their problems at an early age.

There is equal danger in the early intervention program that emphasizes only the prevention or remediation of the physical problems without attending to the emotional, behavioral, and language implications. There are numerous children from these physically oriented programs who have achieved their normal motor skills, who do not demonstrate hyperactive reflexes, and who appear to be operating in a normal fashion. However, when they are confronted with the demands of school, they demonstrate difficulties in perceptual areas and social interactions. As a result of the tension and frustration in these perceptual and social areas, these children may revert to more primitive physical patterns. These patterns may include walking on the toes, carrying the arm in a spastic position, or demonstrating the asymmetrical tonic neck reflex. It is therefore evident that any early intervention program must be a combined interprofessional endeavor.

The fourth group of children consists of supposedly "normal" children. These children come to kindergarten with grossly physically inadequate bodies. They exhibit poor muscle tone with resultant "fatigue" postures of flat feet, protruding abdomens, rounded shoulders, sunken chests, dangling arms, and forward-positioned heads. They lack the endurance and coordination necessary to participate in play activities and consequently become passive, sideline spectators.

We believe these are the children identified by Knickerbocker (1980) as possessing pseudo–learning disorders that deviate from the classical form. The importance of the term "pseudo–learning disorders" lies in the presumption that preventive measures can be taken. This group of children can be benefited from the holistic approach because much of the programming can be conducted by educators in the preschool and elementary grades rather than by medical professionals.

Knickerbocker hypothesizes that there are four factors operating in our society that are creating an impact on childhood development. She believes that two of these are closely related. Society is increasingly mobile and mothers are taking infants outside the home environment more often during their first 6 months. Related to this mobility is the use of some form of plastic infant seat. During the first 6 months of life the rate of neurological development is faster than at any other period. It is imperative that the infant not be restricted by environmental factors in his fulfillment of the designed pattern and timetable of this normal neurological development. It seems reasonable that the earlier an environmental influence makes an impact on the infant, the more pronounced the resulting learning disorder will be. Snapp (1979) has also emphasized the impact of carpeted floors on this early development. The carpet prevents the infant from moving freely as he would on a slick floor. Snapp also laments the practice of using the infant seat to facilitate visual stimulation, which dominates behavior before the body senses have been appropriately developed.

Knickerbocker's (1980) reference to the value of holding the infant, which provides touch-pressure information, that activates the tactile-kinesthetic receptors, correlates nicely with Liedloff's (1977) concepts of the importance of "in arms time." In arms time is needed by all human beings. The feeling of an infant in arms is that of "rightness or essential goodness." Think for a moment what an impact this lack of "rightness" will have psychologically on the pseudo–learning disordered child!

Knickerbocker (1980) indicates that the third factor influencing childhood development is kindergarten and the fourth factor is television. When kindergartens were publicly funded, they became curriculum-directed, creating the expectation that **all** children should master tasks that many are not developmentally mature enough to acquire. When the emphasis is on gross motor experiences and constructive play, children have a better chance of becoming neurologically mature enough to master reading and writing skills when they are introduced in first grade.

The passive, almost addictive, quality of television watching can have a destructive effect on learning according to Knickerbocker. The main reason is that it robs children of available time and motivation with which to participate in active exploratory activities.

Recently, many programs for socially and culturally underprivileged children have been initiated. A great deal of money is allocated to these programs, but ironically, little concern or effort is expended on programs for the grossly physically inadequate child. It is our belief that masses of middle- and upper-class suburban children are equally underprivileged because of their inadequate bodies and resultant motor skill deficits. If these children are to have a successful school experience, a physical remediation program prior to and during the kindergarten year needs to be instituted. Once the cycle of frustration and failure has been established, remediation becomes much more difficult. It is inexcusable to label these children immature or incoordinated or clumsy and expect them to outgrow the problem with no intervention. What happened to the ancient concept that "an ounce of prevention is worth a pound of cure"? Merely repeating kindergarten is not going to improve muscle tone or body awareness. On the other hand, repeating kindergarten may in fact precipitate emotional or behavioral problems, especially if nothing is done about the underlying physical problems.

This concept states that basic motor skills lay the foundation for preacademic readiness. Careful prekindergarten screening is essential therefore to identify the potential problem learners. The ideal situation is to identify the strengths and weaknesses of all children and to tailor specific teaching methods to the strengths and weaknesses of the whole group as well as to individuals within the group. This procedure should minimize learning disorders. The kindergarten teacher occupies a key position in the child's successful orientation to the school environment. Ames (1966) indicates that the dropout problem begins long before the child actually stops going to school. She quotes a New England principal: "The drop-out problem starts right down there in kindergarten and first grade with children whose parents start them in school before they are ready." * She also quotes a West Virginia educator: "We are all too ready in our schools, to force children to respond to learning stimuli before their neuromuscular systems are capable of making correct responses." *

AMES—BEHAVIORAL AGE

Ames (1966) indicates that "no child sets out in life to be a failure, a retardee, a drop-out, or a juvenile delinquent. He learns to be one." * He actually learns to be each of these things by being forced to adjust to learning stimuli that he is incapable of adjusting to.

There is much to be said about the way in which children are deemed ready for school. Unfortunately in most states the only criterion is chrono-

*From Ames, 1966.

logical age. Many people are aware of the differences in development and readiness between girls and boys. Perhaps one of the most simple ways to decrease the number of boys with learning disorders would be to keep them out of the school setting for an extra year.

Ames presents a strong case for determining whether the child is of the appropriate behavioral level to attend school. She quotes many letters from parents who found that their children were in grade levels above their ability to achieve. Being immature is not something "bad"; it just means the child is not yet ready to achieve at a higher level. It is quite interesting that such a simple thing as whether a child has lost his teeth according to the expected time schedule correlates with his behavioral maturity. In a group of 80 children Ames found that, of the children who were ahead of schedule in teething, 60% were in the top academic group and only 4% were in academic trouble. Of the group that was behind schedule in teething only 6% were in the top academic group and 54% either repeated or should have repeated kindergarten.

If a child is having difficulty at school, his behavior at home may be the first indication. Whenever there is a marked change in behavior or attitude about school, parents should be alerted to the possibility of over placement. Certainly it is permissible to allow a child to repeat kindergarten or first or second grade. In fact, it is desirable to repeat at this early stage before too much failure has been experienced. Beware of the untrue cliches that are so very often used as arguments against repeating a grade: First, there is the statement "he is not quite ready but will catch up." There is no way a child is going to catch up when behaviorally he is not going to develop more than a year in 1 year's time. Second, there is the statement, "he could do better if he would try." No child is going to try to fail. Finally, there is the statement "age doesn't matter, it's the intelligence that counts." Again, it doesn't matter what the IQ is; a child cannot interact at a higher level than he is physiologically and behaviorally ready for.

If the child has managed to "get by" even into junior high, parents should have the courage and conviction to let him repeat. In the end most children will profit emotionally, socially, and academically by the additional year of development.

THERAPIST'S SCREENING FORMAT

For those medically oriented individuals who might find themselves in need of a kindergarten screening instrument, we would like to propose a possible format. We believe that the concepts presented in this book could be used as a base. For example, any instrument must deal first with the interactions of the child and the examining environment. This environment includes the individual administering the assessment as well as the room and the elements related to the tasks. All of the information presented in Concepts 1 and 2 is relevant to this testing situation.

Testing environment

Concept 1. *The body's adaptive processes to external or internal stressors may be altered by manipulation of the ergotropic-trophotropic elements.*

Concept 2. *Normal sensation is dependent on parasympathetic nervous system domination and the appropriate combination of specific and nonspecific sensory input.*

When establishing rapport with the child, the examiner's attention must be directed toward that rapport and toward the resting base of the child's autonomic nervous system. The child is undoubtedly going to be apprehensive about the situation and may demonstrate sympathetic nervous system characteristics. Many parasympathetic-type stimuli such as slow stroking with voice and manner, contact by holding the child's hand, and presenting an appealing, nonthreatening task may be used to decrease his hesitancy and assure a parasympathetic discriminative situation.

Early detection of the tactile defensive child is essential to avoid further activation of his sympathetic nervous system, which would distort the assessment results. The essence of rapport is finding the optimum point of operation on the continuum from ergotropic to trophotropic reactions for the individual in the present testing situation. From our experience we conclude that there is a fine line between appropriate sympathetic nervous system activity, somatic muscle activation, and the necessary cortical desynchronization needed to deal effectively with a testing situation and too much activity, which triggers a total fight-or-flight reaction.

• • •

The basic motor skills that we believe are essential to preacademic readiness for kindergarten include vestibular integration, extensor muscle tone, cocontraction, body awareness, sequencing (timing), and fine motor organization.

Vestibular integration

Concept 3. *Vestibular sensory input is related either to motion or position of the head in relationship to the force of gravity. The integration of the motion portion of the vestibular mechanism may be demonstrated by dizziness or nystagmus or both after stimulation.*

As discussed in detail in Concept 3, the Ayres Postrotary Nystagmus Test can be used to evaluate the integration of the vestibular mechanism. The vestibular system should be integrated and functioning at birth. It has been our experience that this test can direct attention to the very beginning of either physical problems or readiness problems.

As a result of our evaluations, we have identified three problem areas. First, children who score below 6-seconds duration, and especially those with zero nystagmus, are potential problem learners because of their related hypotonicity. Second, children who score above 30-seconds duration are potential problem learners because they also demonstrate hypotonicity. They often demonstrate an aversion to motion. Third, children who demonstrate abnormal patterns such as small excursions, vertical patterns, asymmetrical eye patterns, or intermittent patterns should be observed carefully throughout the assessment for subtle problem areas.

Extensor muscle tone

Concept 4. *The position portion of the vestibular mechanism may be used in treatment by placing the individual in the inverted position. This position produces three sequential responses: (1) decreased blood pressure from carotid sinus stimulation, (2) decreased generalized muscle tone from fusimotor inhibition, and (3) increased fusimotor activity to key extensor muscles from the vestibular system. The third response lays the foundation for cocontraction.*

As discussed in Concept 4, the muscle tone of neck and midline trunk extensors and the other deep one-joint extensor muscles is essential to cocontraction. Extensor muscle tone can be evaluated in a variety of ways. Kephart uses the Kraus-Weber test. Ayres uses the tonic labyrinthine reflex in the prone position. Rood uses the inverted position.

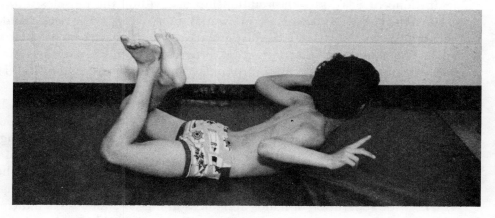

Fig. 9-1. Child demonstrates typical problems in prone extension. The knees bend and the arms drift out to the sides.

Prone extension is probably the simplest procedure to use in evaluating maintained extensor muscle tone. This total extension pattern should be maintained for at least 5 seconds. Children with poor tone will tend to bend the knees, bring the arms out to the sides instead of up by the head, or relax the top or bottom of the body (Fig. 9-1). This simple task may identify differences in the two sides of the body, differences in the top and bottom of the body, and overflow into abnormal patterns as well as decreased muscle tone.

Cocontraction

Concept 5. *Strong one-joint extensor muscles can be developed in the inverted position. These extensor muscles are placed on stretch in their physiological maximally lengthened range to use their muscle spindles' second classical function, which facilitates the flexor muscles in a cocontraction pattern. The cocontraction should override the inhibition from the low-threshold Golgi tendon organs and provide the foundation for kinesthetic figure-ground.*

A well-integrated vestibular mechanism can be used in the inverted position to develop good extensor muscle strength. The muscle can then be put on stretch in its maximally lengthened range to drive the flexors in cocontraction. Since the second classical function of the muscle spindle has survived since the late 1850s, it would seem plausible today to accept Rood's technique of achieving cocontraction. We may in the near future have to change the identity of the portion of the muscle spindle responsible for that reaction from the secondary ending to some other portion. However, the clinical significance of stability and posture being a direct result of deep one-joint extensor strength should not be ignored.

In Concept 5 we saw the relationship of dividing the muscles into two groups, the body into two parts, and work into two limits. The neck and deep back muscles must shorten against gravity so that they can be used for stability. This stability, or cocontraction, progresses from head to tail. The sequence can be seen in the infant from neck stability to trunk stability to hip stability to ankle stability.

The easiest method for evaluating scapular stability is placing the child in the all fours position. Fig. 9-2 shows the marked elevation of the scapulae from the trunk with associated droop of the head and locked elbows. Fig. 9-3 illustrates a similar elevation plus a marked degree of abduction of the scapulae laterally around the chest wall. In the all fours position, as the head is elevated, the additional instability of the trunk and pelvis appears (Fig. 9-4). The wide separation of hands and knees in Figs. 9-2 and 9-3 is indicative of the lack of cocontraction in neck, scapulae, trunk, and hips.

The erect posture is neurophysiologically a poor position. In this position

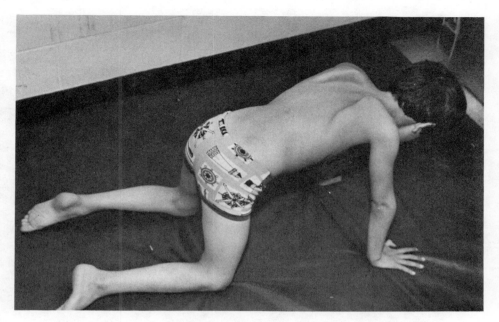

Fig. 9-2. Scapular instability with elevation away from the trunk.

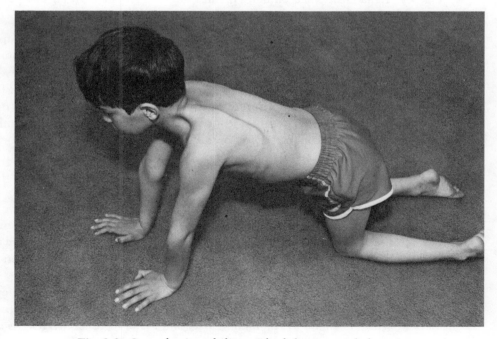

Fig. 9-3. Scapular instability with abduction and elevation.

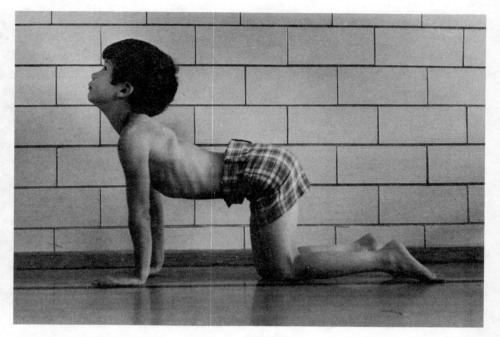

Fig. 9-4. Head position accentuates the instability of scapulae, trunk, and pelvis.

the force of gravity is not acting on extensor muscles and the mechanism for cocontraction is not available. Many children will appear reasonably straight when viewed from the front (Fig. 9-5); however, when they are viewed from the side, the typical fatigue posture becomes very evident (Fig. 9-6). The feet are widely separated, knees are locked back, abdomen is relaxed and protruded, producing a lumbar lordosis, chest is flat and sunken, shoulders are cupped forward, scapulae are abducted or winged, thoracic spine is rounded, and head is projected forward. Any time these characteristics are seen, one should be alerted to decreased muscle tone and poor cocontraction.

Body awareness

Concept 6. *The integration of all the proprioceptors is essential to kinesthetic feedback, with the joint receptors vitally involved in conscious awareness of kinesthetic figure-ground.*

Concept 7. *Facilitation and inhibition of synaptic transmission determines neuronal activity. Primary afferent depolarization (PAD) appears to be a sensory-filtering mechanism that focuses attention by eliminating irrelevant, trivial input. Convergent neurons provide a mechanism at the brain stem level for intersensory integration.*

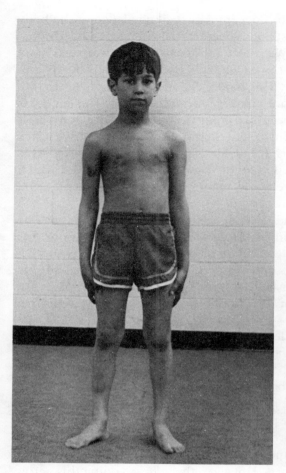

Fig. 9-5. Erect posture viewed from the front.

Fig. 9-6. Typical fatigue posture viewed from the side.

Body awareness as discussed in Concept 6 is the knowledge of the body and is composed of three elements: body schema, body image, and body concept (Frostig and Horne, 1973). We prefer the term "body awareness" and include under it all aspects of the three elements. Body schema is the unconscious postural model of the body. This model changes from moment to moment as voluntary responses are anticipated within the brain. This model is based on the tactile and proprioceptive input arising from the body as it interacts with the environment. The interaction begins with primitive reflex patterns and develops through righting and equilibrium responses. This model provides the individual with a stable frame of reference from which he can automatically initiate movements, maintain or alter movements, and stop movements when necessary.

Body image is what the individual imagines or feels about his body. The image is built on sensations from his body. However, a large part of this image is a result of how his parents and other people relate to him and his body. The child acquires attitudes, affects, and social perceptions about his body from these social interactions with others. The body and body parts are conceived as good or bad, clean or dirty, and pretty or ugly from these same interactions.

Body concept is a completely learned process because it includes names and number of body parts and their functions. It is through body concept that all the labels are established.

In prekindergarten screening, body awareness could be assessed by using the following three activities. The first activity is having the child touch the body parts as they are named. The parts are arranged according to difficulty; so they should be presented in order, that is, nose, toes, ears, knees, back, elbows, ankles, shoulders, hips, and wrists. By age 6 all but a few children should be able to identify these parts. However, the value in doing this activity is observing the use of the two sides of the body. The cause of any asymmetry must be determined. If the child must feel for the part, he lacks appropriate kinesthetic feedback.

The second activity is having the child draw a picture of himself. The picture will indicate how he sees himself or actually what his body image is. A good picture will include a head, eyes, nose, mouth, hair or hat, body, and arms and legs coming from the body. Some pictures may have hands and feet. The size of the head and the length of the arms and legs should be in proportion to the size of the body.

The third assessment activity of body awareness involves touching one part of the body to another. This activity requires not only knowledge of body parts but also a plan of action to integrate the two parts. The activities used could be hands between the knees, place heel to heel, place both hands to the same side of the body, place fingertips to fingertips (one finger at a time), and place right hand to right knee. This activity is a valuable tool in determining how the child solves the problem. Any deficit in body schema will become extremely obvious because of inability to plan motor activities.

Sequencing (timing)

Concept 8. The first step in developing a space-time structure is dealing with the effects of gravity. The individual must first establish the space-time structure in relationship to his own body and how it responds to the force of gravity. When this structure is established he can then deal effectively with space and time in his environment.

Sequence or timing was discussed in Concept 8 as a part of the dimension of time. It is important to realize that timing is inherent in each of the concepts. The rhythm and sequence of autonomic nervous system function should be obvious. The timing in all types of sensory stimulation is related to the rate of stimulation as well as the sequence of stimulation and reaction. Kinesthetic feedback is the key to correcting faulty timing in the execution of activities.

Timing is perhaps the most essential part of any screening procedure. It is vital in establishing and maintaining rapport. When do you praise, comfort, assist, or tighten or loosen the structure? When do you touch, not touch, change the emphasis, or stop the activity?

The timing element of the child's performance is frequently the most neglected but most critical observation. Does the child initiate movements immediately on command? Does he maintain the movements over time or does he stop after the first two or three repetitions. Does he continue the activity several times after he is told to stop? Even more specifically, what is the relationship of different parts of the body? Does the activity of trunk and extremities progress smoothly and correctly? Is one side of the body ahead or behind the other side? Does the child begin to move arms or legs before his trunk is stable? Within the extremity sequence is he able to motor plan in proper order, such as shoulder then elbow then wrist and finally fingers? Does his hand open or close out of time to the position of his arm?

There are many many ways of checking this timing in both gross and fine motor activities. Just observing the child as he moves and plays will provide tremendous insight. Some of the most frequently used activities are balancing on one foot, skipping, imitation of positions, buttoning, lacing, or copying geometric designs.

Fine motor organization

It is our belief that the highest level of timing is seen in fine motor organization and that it is perhaps the best indicator of preacademic readiness. A prerequisite of fine motor organization is differentiation of wrists and fingers. The level of differentiation may be determined by the skill evidenced in the child's coloring ability. The higher the level of differentiation, the better the child will stay within the lines of the picture and the smoother and more uniform will be the shading. The child who lacks differentiation will demonstrate problems in grasping the crayon, large gross movements of the entire arm, failure to stabilize the paper with the opposite hand, and heavy irregular scribble lines.

Fine motor organization involves paper and pencil activities with a left-to-right and top-to-bottom plan of action. When this plan of action is evidenced, the child has organized himself and his environment and has a system for dealing with unfamiliar situations. This fine motor organization may be assessed by having the child produce geometric forms or symbols from verbal directions or models. According to Roach and Kephart (1966), the child may show lack of organization if the various shapes are of different sizes and are scattered all over the paper with no organization. The most primitive organization would be circular, with a shape in the middle and all others going around the central figure. The next highest level of organization is in the top-to-bottom direction. The highest level of organization consists of shapes all the same size arranged in a left-to-right and top-to-bottom direction. Care should be taken not to structure or direct the child in his organization.

EARLY PREVENTION OF SCHOOL FAILURE

In 1976 Heiniger became a consultant to the Title III ESEA Early Prevention of School Failure Project, Peotone, Ill. Her primary responsibility was to revise the Motor Activity Scale that they were using in their screening process. In the years 1976 and 1977 Heiniger evaluated 265 children with her revised Motor Activity Scale. The original format and results of the screening remain with the Peotone Project. The scale was again revised in 1979 and is now identified as Title IV ESEA, Part C.

Heiniger's second consultation responsibility to the Peotone Project was in-service education of staff and teachers in participating school systems. There was a tremendous need for teachers to learn why and how to incorporate motor activities of a lower functioning or coordination level into the classroom.

O'Quinn has some very pertinent why's for developing physical skills in the book *Developmental Gymnastics*.

Physical skill is the most important commodity in the world of children. For a young child, physical movement is the source of discovery, the vehicle of expression, and the method of survival. For children, movement is an extremely satisfying experience . . . and provides them with feelings of discovery, freedom and a sense of being alive. It is a great mistake, however, to assume that because of their natural interest in physical play children will develop all the skills they need without the guidance, thought, or planning of adults.*

O'Quinn goes on to say that preschool children are motivated by the pleasure of movements themselves. Between kindergarten and second grade, social factors of criticism or praise determine to a large extent whether children participate or avoid performing. A highly skilled child sets a standard that is out of reach for many children. Consequently the children do not perform and are left lacking in skills they could easily learn if appropriate progression was provided.

As stated earlier in this concept, there are many, many children entering school with physically inadequate bodies. We agree wholeheartedly with O'Quinn that

> If we are to raise the level of human development across our nation, we must begin with an orderly well-thought-out plan of physical development. The development of body control and physical skills in our children is too important to be extracurricular. Our elementary and pre-elementary schools should include the development of physical skills as an integral part of the established educational environment.*

The development of our children's bodies is too important to neglect or leave undirected until they get to school. Parents must become as involved and concerned with physical development as they are with speech or reading or spiritual values. Snapp (1979) indicates that the physical environment of many homes is limiting infant development. Many homes are completely carpeted; so the infant is never placed on a large slick surface to crawl on the abdomen and really learn about his body. Many infants are kept in infant seats where they can "see around" or in play pens to protect them. Snapp repeatedly emphasized the danger of too much visual stimuli before the infant is aware of his body and quite skillful in its manipulation.

Perhaps one of the simplest ways of correcting many problems in early development is to capitalize on parent-child play. A charming book, *T.S.K.H. (Tickle, Snuggle, Kiss and Hug)* by May (1977) has delightful ways to interact with a child. Many of the activities are broken down into simple progressions to assure success and develop self-confidence. It seems that one of the frequently overlooked objectives in activities is to just enjoy the feeling of our bodies working and to do things because they are **fun**. May acknowledges the influence of Bonnie Prudden and her book *How to Keep Your Child Fit from Birth to Six* (1964). This book includes activities to use with the infant.

---

*O'Quinn, G., Jr.: Developmental gymnastics, Austin, 1978, University of Texas Press.

Another book for infants is *Baby Exercise* by Lévy. A quick word of caution on using any book as a format or as a list of activities. Be very sure that as a practitioner you understand the neurophysiological basis and explanation for what you are doing.

INTEGRATED MOTOR ACTIVITIES SCALE

As Heiniger worked in the school system with prekindergarden screening, it became evident that an instrument incorporating the concepts of this book was needed. She believed it should be an instrument that teachers could be taught to administer, score, interpret, and implement in their classroom activities.

From the screening of the children for the Peotone Project four things became evident. First, body awareness did not correlate with overall performance. There was a significantly large group of children who scored well even though they could not locate all body parts. The same was true with the low performers. They might know the body parts but scored low on the other items. This section is valuable as an observation section and is useful in developing rapport. Second, observation of ocular control was necessary. Frequently children are seen with heads tilted to one side, or lying on the paper while doing fine motor activities. Knowledge of ocular control of the two eyes as well as each eye would be valuable in evaluating whether the deficits were in eye control, hand control, or the coordination of eye and hand. Third, the fine motor activity area needed to be expanded. It is essential to observe individual finger movements to evaluate the degree of differentiation that has developed. It is further necessary to evaluate children's ability to coordinate hands and eyes in an activity that involves handling tools in a controlled manner. Fourth, there was a need to develop an area of auditory-visual discrimination and sequencing that could be combined with a motor activity. Many children demonstrate lack of listening skills. They frequently begin activities before directions are completed and demonstrate altered states of attentiveness. With an auditory-visual discrimination section, the most efficient learning channel can be identified as well as the least efficient channel.

In 1978 and 1979 Heiniger screened over 600 children ages 4 through 6 years with her Integrated Motor Activity Scale (IMAS). The test performance summary of 391 children is found in Appendix A.

The IMAS is divided into four observation sections and three scored sections. The four observation sections include eye control, dominance, body awareness, and general. Eye control includes binocular horizontal and vertical pursuits, monocular horizontal and vertical pursuits, and convergence. The dominance activities determine eye, hand, and foot preference. Body awareness checks a total of 12 body parts. The general observations include posture–muscle tone and behavior patterns.

The scored sections include auditory-visual-motor tasks, eye-hand coordination items, and gross motor activities. Auditory-visual-motor tasks consist of ten series of clap-tap actions (Fig. 9-7). The eye-hand coordination items include three wrist and finger differentiation motions (Fig. 9-8), one coloring task (Fig. 9-9), and three mazes (Fig. 9-10). The gross motor activities include balancing on one foot, hopping on each foot within a 1-foot square (Fig. 9-11), skipping at least 10 feet, and tossing and catching a yarn ball. When the child tosses the ball up in the air and catches it himself he must remain in the 1-foot square.

The IMAS is based on the premise that basic motor skills lay the foundation and provide the building blocks needed for the perceptual-motor skills of the classroom. This screening instrument determines the level to which motor activities have been integrated into the child's behavior. It pinpoints the child's methods of problem solving as well as the factors that are interfering or preventing him from completing tasks satisfactorily.

Perhaps one of the strongest points of the IMAS is its simple design. It does not require a lot of expensive equipment. It can be completed in ap-

Fig. 9-7. Clap-tap actions.

Fig. 9-8. Series of wrist and finger motions. **A**, Wrist motion. **B**, Snapping the fingers. **C**, Copying finger model of examiner.

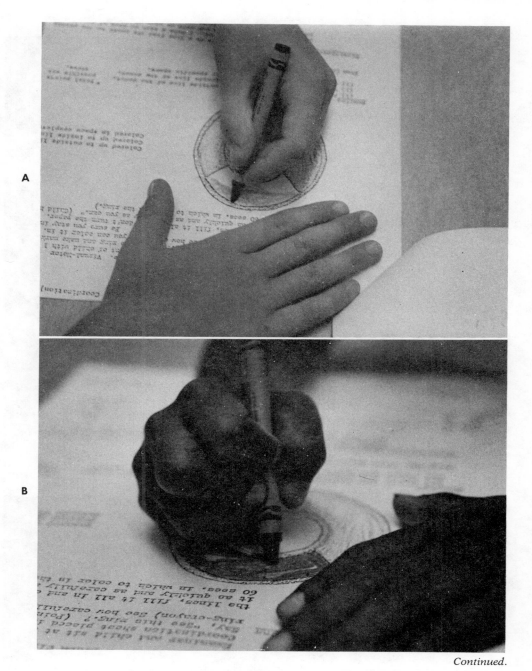

Continued.

Fig. 9-9. Coloring task. **A** represents proper grasp and pressure. **B**, **C**, and **D** show abnormal grasp of crayon.

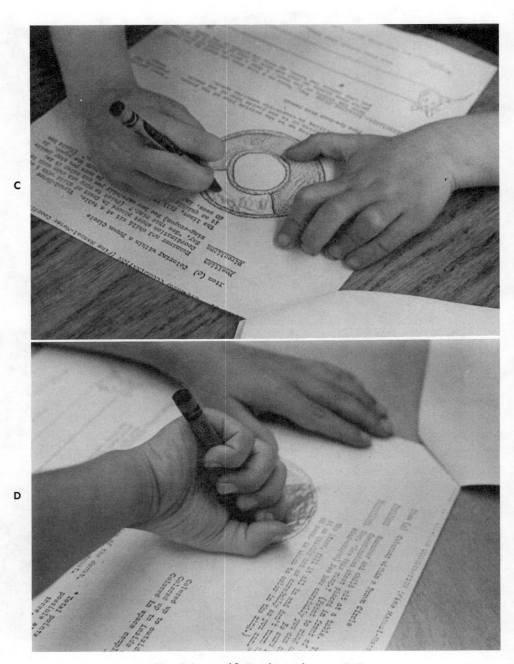

Fig. 9-9, cont'd. For legend see p. 265.

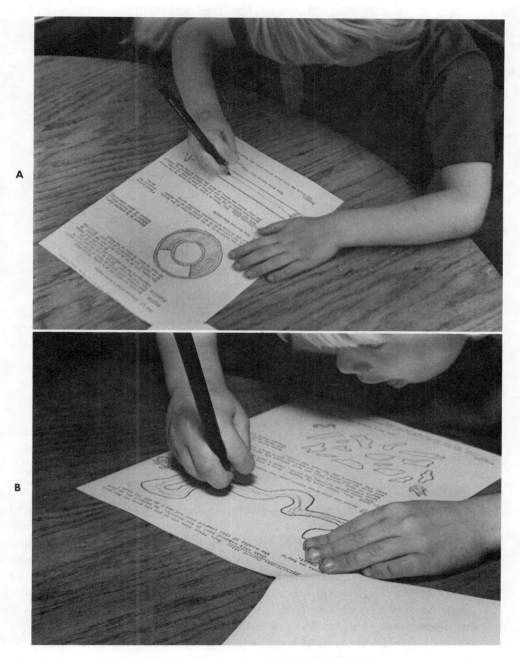

Fig. 9-10. A, Easiest maze. **B**, More difficult mazes.

Fig. 9-11. Balancing on one foot.

proximately 20 minutes in a relatively small area. The observations can be noted while the child is doing the activity. There is no elaborate scoring to be completed or profile to be compiled. Individuals can be taught to administer, score, and interpret the IMAS in from 1 to 4 hours. As they administer the instrument their skill in observation will improve rapidly. There is no need for extensive background in theory because all of the neurophysiology is an integral part of the hierarchy of test items. The essence of each of the eight concepts of this book is related to the IMAS.

In design the IMAS is comparable to the Purdue Perceptual-Motor Survey. The items of the IMAS are scored and used to identify the age-equivalent performance level of the individual. The observations indicate what is interfering with the child's ability to perform the specific task. Since the tasks are arranged in a hierarchy, it is possible to identify the most basic problem in performance. By identifying these basic interferences the teacher is able to plan intervention activities that will correct the problem instead of drilling the child on the task that is incorrectly performed.

For example, in the task of coloring the donut, many problems may be identified. The grasp of the crayon will identify finger differentiation. The movements of the fingers and wrist will indicate lack of differentiation. The pressure of the crayon on the paper as it relates to the shading (dark, light, or not solid) indicates the kinesthetic feedback and coordination of the extremity. The tilt of the head is indicative of monocular vision or eye preference. The direction of the coloring strokes will identify only finger motion (vertical), wrist or arm motion (horizontal), or coordinated finger and wrist motion will give combined strokes of equal shading. Orientation of the paper with the head or the body will be indicative of midline problems.

Failure to follow directions may indicate either visual or auditory distractibility.

This kind of analysis is built into the observation of each of the items in each of the three scored sections. In this way the IMAS is a useful tool for the teacher to provide classroom remediation of basic, low-level deficiencies in development. An occupational or physical therapist could use this scale to explain in a very orderly, professional manner what basic motor skills are absent or deficient.

Preliminary norms have been developed from data obtained from the first 391 children screened. The initial results, based on professional judgments and statistical data, suggest that the IMAS is a powerful tool for identifying children with potential learning problems.

The reliability of this instrument will be influenced by the instruction the teachers receive in administering the test. As with many screening devices, the real value lies in the observation of the items rather than the actual score obtained by the child. As the teacher's sensitivity to the execution of the test items increases, his or her ability to translate the problems into a remediation program will be enhanced.

It is desirable to administer this screening in the spring before the children enter kindergarten in the fall. Any child with low scores can then be given a complete diagnostic case workup and can be referred to a remediation program in the summer. Those children in the remediation program who have not acquired the necessary skills by fall should definitely be considered not ready and allowed an extra year of growth as suggested by Ames (1966).

Heiniger is conducting a longitudinal study of three groups of children from the original kindergarten screening through the fourth grade. The data from the longitudinal study should confirm that the children identified by the screening as potential problem learners did require special services. It should also show if certain kinds of problems at the time of screening required specific kinds of remediation or services.

Three parts of the IMAS have been placed in Appendix A. The test booklet is the complete screening instrument. The test manual includes the purpose, theory and rationale, background, description of the individual items in the three observation sections and the three scored sections, and assessing profile levels. The technical report includes all of the statistical data on the first 391 children.

As we have developed this Tree of Learning, our primary conviction has become the absolute necessity of not separating body and mind. All learning must involve the interaction of the body and mind at every level of development. There must be no interruption between therapy and education. The medical professionals must relate their therapies to the classroom situation. The classroom teacher must understand and appreciate the neurophysiological foundation of learning. There will always be the exceptional child, who in kindergarten reads at a first-grade level. However, the physical use of this child's body is grossly inadequate and his social interactions are decidedly lacking and immature. There will also be the exceptional child who is a superb athlete but who demonstrates difficulty in reading and writing.

We believe that a large area of involvement is being neglected by many occupational and physical therapists in the school system. This is an awareness program for the teachers. The therapists must assist the classroom teacher to recognize deficits in muscle tone, posture, body awareness, and laterality. The IMAS can be used to assist the teacher in recognizing the deficits in first- and second-grade children. She must then be assisted in a systematic process of correcting the maximum number of problems in the minimum space and time in an enjoyable, rewarding fashion for the children. In no way is this to be misconstrued as therapy but rather seen as a system of low-level basic activities that will meet the needs of all the children to enhance their physical potentials. By enhancing all children's physical potentials we can avoid the pitfall of becoming merely remedial educators.

Do we intend to develop individuals to their fullest optimum potential? Shall we be concerned with their quality of life? Then we must attend to their physical, emotional, intellectual and spiritual growth from the most basic neurophysiological aspects to the highest cognitive function. What a fantastic challenge we have received. What an incredible body, mind, and spirit has been created for our use! How will we meet this challenge? How will we fulfill the obligations that each of us has received from his God?

Glossary*

abducens nerve Cranial nerve number six (VI), innervating the lateral rectus muscle, which abducts the eyeball or moves it away from the midline. *(3)*

acceleration The increase of motion. *(3)*

  linear Straight line motion.

  angular Motion at an angle such as rotation or rolling.

action potential The electrical current that is moved along a neuron, also known as the nerve impulse. It is initiated by the generator potential. *(2)*

activation Used when referring to Rood's initiation of the muscle tone in the nuclear bag and nuclear chain fibers, which is necessary for stretch reflexes to occur. *(5)*

adversive reaction A protective survival reaction produced when the sympathetic nervous system is dominating behavior. *(2)*

afferent Neurons carrying information to a nucleus. *(1)*

after-potentials The condition of a neuron after the refractory period, resulting from stimulation.

  negative A period when the neuron is more easily excited than before it was stimulated.

  positive A period when the neuron is more difficult to excite than before it was stimulated. *(2)*

ampullar crest Receptor organ in the three semicircular canals. *(3)*

anterior hypothalamus The portion of the hypothalamus that regulates parasympathetic nervous system activity. *(1)*

asphyxia Condition resulting from the lack of oxygen. *(7)*

autonomic nervous system The portion of the nervous system responsible for involuntary automatic activity. It is divided into two parts.

  parasympathetic Concerned with vegetative

functions and maintenance of the body such as eating, digestion, elimination, and temperature control.

  sympathetic Concerned with protective survival fight-or-flight reactions. *(1)*

beaded network Same as a hediform plexus, which is one of the ways to explain the way C size neurons end as free nerve ends in the superficial skin. *(2)*

body awareness A term usually related to the writings of Frostig in which she incorporates:

  body concept Entirely conscious, consisting of all the names of the body parts and what they do. *(7)*

  body image Partially conscious and partially unconscious, resulting from sensation and others' emotional reactions toward the individual's body.

  body schema Unconscious postural model of the body.

body schema A term frequently reserved for the unconscious postural model of the body, usually related to Piaget's writings. *(5)*

brain stem The central nervous system lying between the spinal cord and the thalamus, including the medulla oblongata, pons, and midbrain. *(2)*

caloric test A test that produces nystagmus when warm or cold water is introduced into the external auditory canal. *(3)*

carotid sinus Sensory receptor found in the internal carotid artery that regulates blood pressure. *(4)*

caudal Toward the tail end of an organism. *(3)*

chain ganglia A series of ganglia lying on each side of the spinal column, containing the cell bodies of postganglionic neurons of the sympathetic nervous system. *(1)*

ciliary muscles Muscle of the lens of the eye that changes the focus of the light waves on the retina. *(1)*

cingulate gyrus Found on the medial aspect of the cerebral hemisphere superior to the corpus callosum. It is part of the limbic lobe or

---

*The number following each definition indicates the concept in which the term was *first* used.

"visceral brain" involved in all essential activities of self-preservation and reproduction.

cocontraction pattern Condition of stability produced when strong one-joint extensor muscles are placed on stretch in their maximal physiologically lengthened range and used to facilitate flexors in a balanced contraction. *(2)*

coinnervation Neurophysiological process when both agonist and antagonist are receiving facilitation to produce a balanced contraction of stability as opposed to movement. *(5)*

conducted with decrement As a potential moves, the size or amplitude decreases. *(2)*

conjugant movement The coordinated movement of both eyes together in any desired direction. *(6)*

convergence The coming together of many different impulses to one place. This occurs typically at the motor neuron and is the opposite of divergence. *(2)*

convergent neurons A special kind of neuron that in order to be stimulated must receive a specific combination of sensory stimuli, the usual combination being muscle, joint, tendon, and labyrinthine. *(7)*

cortical desynchronization Used extensively by Gellhorn relating to an alert cortex and currently referred to as alpha activity. *(1)*

cortical synchronization Used extensively by Gellhorn related to a inactive cortex as in sleep and currently referred to as beta activity. *(1)*

cupula The projection of sensory hair cells into the fluid in the endolymphatic space of the canal. As the fluid is moved it distorts the hair cells of the cupula and initiates the nerve impulse.

deceleration The decreasing of motion.
    linear Straight line motion.
    angular Motion at an angle such as rotation or rolling. *(3)*

depolarization Chemical process that occurs in a neuron when an action potential is conducted. *(2)*

dermatomes Portion of the skin that is embryologically associated with each segmental block of the body. Nerve, muscle, skin, and bone each develop from the segmental block of tissue and are always functionally related. *(5)*

detrusor muscle Circular muscle of the bladder that contracts to empty the bladder of urine in the micturition reflex. *(4)*

developmental apraxia Inability to motor plan. Usually associated with the writings of Ayres. *(2)*

diencephalon Structure just superior to the midbrain. It contains the epithalamus, thalamus, which is the major integration center between lower centers and the cerebral cortex, hypothalamus, which is the highest integration center for the autonomic nervous system, and the subthalamus. *(1)*

differentiation Process of sorting out the parts of the body one at a time, until each is isolated and controlled, in order to recombine the parts in a higher level skill. *(6)*

dilated pupil A pupil that has been opened by a sympathetic nervous system reaction or as a result of diminished light. *(1)*

directionality External projection of laterality. *(8)*

disassociation Seeing only pieces of a picture instead of the entire thing; seeing four lines of a square instead of a unit. *(7)*

distractability A condition experienced by an individual with a short attention span, which results in his flitting from thing to thing never settling for more than seconds or minutes on one activity. *(2)*

disynaptic neuron chain Means there are two synapses in the reflex pathway, which requires one association neuron between the sensory and motor neurons. *(7)*

divergence The dispensing or spreading of information, as when a sensory neuron enters the central nervous system and branches many hundred times to form synapses. *(2)*

dorsiflexion Upward movement of the foot at the ankle as if one was standing on one's heels. *(2)*

efferent Neuron carrying information away from a nucleus. *(1)*

emotional lability Sweeps of emotion from sad to happy or happy to sad with very little warning. *(2)*

epicritic Used at one time to denote a highly developed discriminative nervous system. *(2)*

EPSP Excitatory postsynaptic potential; the electrical manifestation of facilitation. *(7)*

ergotropic The combination of sympathetic nervous system activity, somatic muscle activation, and cortical desynchronization (alpha rhythm). Ergo means work. *(1)*

exteroceptors Those receptors that provide information about the external environment. *(2)*
    nonspecific Providing generalized noncritical

information that is carried on small, size C, slow-conducting neurons.

specific Providing very critical vital information that is carried on larger size A, fast-conducting neurons.

extraocular muscles Muscles responsible for the movement of the eye ball; include the medial and lateral rectus, superior and inferior rectus, and superior and inferior oblique. *(3)*

facilitation Central nervous system activity that makes it possible to initiate an action potential on a neuron. *(2)*

foot position Abnormal position of the foot when weight is on the toes; called equinus. *(5)*

equinovalgus Means the foot is toe down with the outside of the foot raised so that the longitudinal arch is flat.

equinovarus Means the foot is toe down with the inside of the foot raised so that the longitudinal arch is exaggerated.

fusimotor system Motor neurons from the spinal cord to the contractile portions of the muscle spindle. *(1)*

gamma Previously used to denote the motor supply to the muscle spindle, usually referred to as the fusimotor at present. *(5)*

ganglion Group of cell bodies outside the central nervous system. *(1)*

gelatinous substance Column of cells running the entire length of the spinal cord at the periphery of the dorsal gray horn. Also known as lamina II. *(2)*

generator potential Electrical current originating in the receptor that initiates the nerve impulse or action potential. *(2)*

gestational age Age of an individual during the prenatal period, figured from the time of fertilization. *(1)*

Golgi tendon organ Sensory receptor of the tendons involved with feedback of muscle tension. High-threshold ones are protective in function, low-threshold ones function throughout the entire range of muscle contraction from twitch to tetany. *(5)*

habituation Ability of a system such as the vestibular to become accustomed to a stimulus so that it no longer responds. *(3)*

halo of behavior Rings of undesirable behavior that are built up from the time of birth if the infant is not structured properly. The manipulative behavior gets more rigid as the child gets older. *(7)*

haptic Applied to the combined sensation of movement and tactile stimuli. *(7)*

hippocampus Portion of the archiocortex that forms the floor of the temporal horn of the lateral ventricle. *(1)*

homeostasis A state of balance or equilibrium, used to denote vegetative function of parasympathetic nervous system. *(1)*

hyperactive gag reflex The gag reflex is a normal protective survival reflex to prevent the ingestion of harmful substances. When the tongue is hypersensitive, the gag reflex may be hyperactive, which interferes with normal sucking-swallowing behavior. *(5)*

hyperactivity Usually thought of as excessive motor activity, a result of distractability and perseveration. *(2)*

hypertonic More than the normal amount of muscle tone. *(5)*

inhibition Central nervous system function that prevents a neuron from being fired. *(2)*

innate reflexes Those prewired reflexes with which an infant is born. *(2)*

interneurons Also known as association or internuncial neurons. They are the neurons lying between sensory neurons and motor neurons. *(3)*

interoceptors Receptors that provide information about the individuals internal environment, such as oxygen level, blood pressure, pain, and pressure of peristalsis. *(4)*

intersensory integration Combining of different sensory input into a functional unit. For instance, what is seen is matched to what is heard and what is felt, and all three are the same. *(7)*

intrasensory integration Combining of the same kind of sensory input into a functional unit. *(7)*

inverted position Any time the body is taken from the erect position of 180 degrees to the completely upside-down position of 0 degrees. *(5)*

IPSP Inhibitory postsynaptic potential; the electrical manifestation of inhibition. *(7)*

ischemia Condition resulting from the lack of adequate blood supply. *(7)*

kinesthetic feedback Sensory information returning to the central nervous system from the proprioceptors, which are stimulated during muscle contraction or joint movement. *(2)*

kinesthetic figure-ground Found in most of Kephart's writings. It is perhaps the first figure-ground relationship to develop; the holding tone of the trunk is the ground and the moving tone of the extremities is the figure. *(5)*

labyrinth Receptor of the vestibular mechanism; includes three semicircular canals, arranged for the three planes of motion, the saccule, responsible for position and linear motion from side to side and forward and backward, and the utricle responsible for position and motion up and down and forward and backward. *(3)*

lamina Areas in the central gray matter having functional differences. *(3)*

Landau reflex A normal reflex appearing around 6 to 9 months of age that is a tonic maintained contraction of midline deep back extensor muscles. *(5)*

lateral horn Lateral projection of gray matter found in the thoracic and lumbar segments of the spinal cord in which the preganglionic cell bodies of the sympathetic nervous system are found. *(1)*

laterality Internal awareness of the two sides of the body and how they work together and in opposition. *(8)*

limbic system Frequently called the "visceral brain" because it is involved in all self-preservation activities. It is influenced by all sensory systems. The main outlet is the hypothalamus to the brain stem and spinal cord (largely by way of the autonomic nervous system) and to the pituitary gland (endocrine system). *(2)*

low energy system Functioning of the body that requires the least amount of energy to perform the activity. Commonly applied to automatic, reflex, subcortical activity. *(2)*

maintained stretch Any stretch or resistance that is maintained for a period of time as opposed to a brief stretch. *(5)*

mechanoreceptors Those sensory receptors that are stimulated by a mechanical deformation such as touch or pressure, as opposed to a chemoreceptor that is stimulated by such things as oxygen level. *(6)*

medial lemniscus Large pathway carrying information from the gracilus and cuneate nuclei to the thalamus. Primary pathway for tactile and proprioceptive information. *(1)*

medial longitudinal fasiculus (MLF) Fiber pathway connecting the vestibular system with the eye muscles and descending to the neck muscles. It is the first fiber tract to myelinate and is functioning at birth. *(3)*

medulla oblongata The portion of the central nervous system between the spinal cord and the midbrain. It is an area of transition from spinal cord to higher nervous systems. *(1)*

membrane Outermost covering of a cell.

  postsynaptic membrane Membrane on the opposite side of the synapse. *(7)*

  presynaptic membrane Membrane prior to the synapase.

monosynaptic Refers to a reflex arc with only one synapse between the sensory and motor neurons. *(3)*

Moro reflex Primitive survival reflex involving the phasic contraction of superficial back extensor muscles. Initiated by stimuli of sound and loss of body support. This reflex is integrated as the Landau reflex dominates prone behavior. *(5)*

motor disinhibition Inability to stop motor activity. Child is constantly pulling, pushing, fingering, poking, and bending. *(7)*

motor end-plate Point at which the motor neuron makes contact with muscle fibers.

multiarthrodial muscle Any muscle that passes over more than one joint, such as the hip and knee. It may cross several joints as the wrist and fingers. Also referred to as a two-joint muscle. *(5)*

multipolar neuron Neuron that has many many dendrites or processes. *(7)*

muscle fibers

  extrafusal fibers Parts that do the actual work.

  intrafusal fibers Muscle spindles. Although they have contractile properties they contribute no force to the work ability of the muscle. They are the sensory receptors for muscle length. *(5)*

muscle range Each muscle has a neurophysiological range through which it can contract or be stretched.

  maximal range Longest neurophysiological range to which the muscle can be stretched without damage, usually the last 20 degrees.

  submaximal range From the shortest contracted range of the muscle to the point where maximal range begins. *(5)*

muscle spindle The sensory receptor of the muscle involved with feedback of muscle length. The component fibers include nuclear bags and nuclear chains with elaborate sensory and motor innervations. *(5)*

muscles

  phasic Muscles that produce quick, rapid,

single or repetitive movements. Frequently referred to as light work muscles.

tonic Muscles that produce a maintained contraction, affording posture or stability or long-sustained action. Frequently referred to as heavy work muscles. *(5)*

myelinated neurons Those neurons that have a myelin sheath around them that serves as insulation. *(2)*

neonatal period Usually the first month after birth. *(1)*

neuron Structural unit of the nervous system including the cell bodies and all processes. *(2)*

neutral warmth Conservation of body temperature so that it is maintained in a homeostatic range. *(2)*

nonadapting receptors Those slow-adapting receptors that appear to not adapt no matter how long the stimulus is continued. *(2)*

nonpropagated Indicates that a potential is stationary or nonmoving; nonconducted. *(2)*

nonspecific Frequently associated with a portion of the nervous system or sensation. It is frequently used synonymously with the function of small, C size neurons. *(2)*

nucleus A group of cell bodies inside the central nervous system. *(1)*

nystagmus Normal horizontal eye motion produced by rotating the body, placing water of different temperatures into the external auditory canal, or moving a pattern rapidly in front of the eyes. *(3)*

ontogenetic development Sequential development of the individual. *(3)*

orbicularis oris Facial muscle that circles the mouth. When it contracts the lips are protruded and puckered as in kissing or sucking. *(5)*

pacinian corpuscle Sensory receptor found in the exteroceptors, interoceptors, and proprioceptors that always serves the sensation of pressure. *(4)*

patterning Usually applied to a technique of Temple-Faye and Doman-Delecato in which the arms and legs are moved in a specific sequence with the turning of the head. Either the arm and leg on the same side are flexed and the others extended in a homolateral pattern or the opposite arm and leg are flexed in a cross pattern. *(6)*

pelvic tilt Moving the pelvis in a forward or backward direction. If the back is flattened, the pelvis is posteriorly tilted; if the lumbar

curve is increased, the pelvis is anteriorly tilted. *(6)*

perceptual motor match Ability to take in a sensory stimulus and match it to the appropriate motor response. *(8)*

perioral area Skin area around the mouth, which when stimulated tactilly will produce movement patterns. *(1)*

perseveration Inability to shift from one activity to another. *(7)*

phasic receptors Also called fast-adapting receptors because they respond for only a brief time to a sustained stimulus. *(2)*

phonation Step in the developmental sequence of speech when the individual is beginning to make all kinds of sounds. *(5)*

phylogenetic development Development of the phylum or species. *(3)*

pituitary Master gland of the endocrine system. The endocrine system is made up of glands, which deposit their hormones directly into the blood stream. *(1)*

plantar flexion Downward movement of the foot at the ankle as if one was standing on one's toes. *(2)*

posterior hypothalamus Portion of the hypothalamus that regulates sympathetic nervous system activity. *(1)*

postganglionic neuron Neuron of the autonomic nervous system whose cell body is in a ganglion and whose processes extend to the effector organ, such as the salivary glands, heart muscle, or muscle of the intestinal tract. *(1)*

preganglionic neuron Neuron of the autonomic nervous system whose cell body is in the central nervous system and whose process extends to ganglions outside the central nervous system. *(1)*

premature Any infant born before 43-weeks gestational age or with a birth weight of less than 5 lb. *(1)*

primary afferent depolarization (PAD) Neurophysiological process occurring on the presynaptic side of the synapse rendering an action potential less effective. Also referred to as presynaptic inhibition. *(5)*

proprioceptors Those receptors found in muscles, tendons, and joints. *(2)*

protective reaction The physiological and emotional reaction expressed in physical fight, physical flight, or emotional flight (withdrawal). These reactions are produced by the domination of the sympathetic nervous system. *(1)*

protopathic Used at one time to denote a protective primitive survival nervous system. *(2)*

rebound reaction Compensatory reaction as a result of an original reaction. The system is seeking a state of equilibrium. Similar to the swinging of a pendulum. *(1)*

receptors Specialized organs that respond to specific stimuli and initiate an action potential on the neuron.

    nonadapting Protective receptors that continue to fire indefinitely.

    phasic Fire briefly then adapt.

    tonic Adapt slowly so they continue to provide information for long periods of time.

reciprocal pattern Movement produced when one group of muscles is facilitated and the antagonist muscles are inhibited. *(2)*

repolarization Chemical process required to prepare the neuron to conduct a second impulse after it has been depolarized by the first impulse. *(2)*

reticular facilitatory area Found in the lateral brain stem; gives rise to the ascending system, which is involved with the level of arousal or the sleep-wake pattern. *(1)*

reticular inhibitory area Found in the medial brain stem; gives rise to the descending system, which is associated with somatic and visceral motor activities. *(1)*

rostral Toward the head end of an organism. *(3)*

salivary glands Glands that produce saliva.

    parotid In front of the ear. *(1)*

    sublingual Under the tongue.

    submaxillary or **submandibular** Below the lower jaw.

scapular instability Results when the midline back extensors are not sufficiently developed to provide a tonic stable origin for the muscles attaching the scapulae to the trunk. The scapulae appear to float on the back, move excessively about on the rib cage, literally stand on edge, or protrude from the back. *(5)*

self-propagated Indicates that the potential moves itself along the neuron once it is initiated. *(2)*

somatic muscle Muscles of the body (trunk) and extremities that are embryologically derived from somites as opposed to smooth muscle of the gastrointestinal tract. *(1)*

somatic sensation That sensation derived from the receptors associated with the somatic muscles. *(2)*

special senses Those senses served by cranial nerves, including smell, sight, hearing, and taste. *(2)*

specific Frequently associated with a portion of the nervous system or sensation. It is frequently used synonymously with the function of large, A size neurons. *(2)*

sphincter muscle of iris Muscle that opens and closes the pupil of the eye, allowing more or less light into the retina. *(1)*

squat-stance-squat Important step in Rood's skeletal developmental sequence in which the individual goes from a squat position to erect and back down to squat. This is the key position to develop ankle stability and assure a heel-toe gait pattern. *(5)*

startle reflex Primitive protective reflex. *(3)*

stress threshold Point at which a protective, avoidance, fight-or-flight sympathetic nervous system reaction is initiated. *(1)*

synapse Potential space between two neurons through which a nerve impulse must pass. There are three kinds of synapses.

    axoaxonic Between the axon of one neuron and the axon of the second; this synapse is actually a presynaptic synapse. *(7)*

    axodendritic Between the axon of one neuron and the dendrites of the second neuron.

    axosomatic Between the axon of one neuron and the cell body of the second.

synaptic transmission Chemical process that is initiated by an action potential and is responsible for initiating an electrical current on the other side of the synapse.

tactile defensive Condition in which all tactile stimuli is interpreted as potentially dangerous, producing a sympathetic fight-or-flight reaction. *(2)*

temporal growth Growth of an individual from fertilization until death. Measured in weeks, months, and years. *(1)*

threshold Condition of the neuron in which a generator potential will initiate an action potential. *(2)*

tonic lumbar reflex Tonic reflex involved with the distribution of muscle tone in the extremities as determined by the relationship of the pelvis to the trunk. The reflex may be divided into symmetrical and asymmetrical. In the symmetrical, when the pelvis is tipped posteriorly, all four extremities are flexed; when the pelvis is tipped anteriorly, all four extremities are extended. In the asymmetrical, when the pelvis is raised or rotated on one side, the free leg is flexed, the opposite arm is flexed, the support leg is extended, and the opposite arm is extended. This is the normal arm and leg pattern seen in walking. *(5)*

tonic receptors Receptors that respond as long as the stimulus is maintained. Also called slow adapting. *(2)*

transducer Device that changes a physical stimulus into an electrical current, such as a sensory receptor. *(2)*

trochlear nerve Cranial nerve number four (IV) innervating the superior oblique eye muscle, which pulls around a spool to turn the eyeball down and inward toward the nose. *(3)*

trophotropic Combination of parasympathetic nervous system activity, somatic muscle deactivation, and cortical synchronization (beta rhythm). Tropho means vegetative. *(1)*

unlocking mechanisms A selection of tech-niques used to reduce the spasticity in extremities, usually related to some type of rotation. *(6)*

vasoconstriction Closing of the blood vessels in the skin produced by the sympathetic nervous system. *(1)*

vasodilation Opening of the blood vessels in the skin produced by decreasing the sympathetic effect. *(1)*

vestibular mechanism The receptor mechanism in the labyrinth involved with posture and equilibrium. Frequently referred to as the vestibular apparatus. *(3)*

visual figure-ground The ability to distinguish the critical vital parts of a picture from the ground or background. For instance, being able to attend to the letters on a page and not be distracted by the coloring or blemishes in the paper. *(6)*

References

CONCEPT 1

Atkins, R. C.: Dr. Atkins diet revolution, New York, 1973, Bantam Books, Inc.

Cooper, J. T., and Hagan, P.: Dr. Cooper's fabulous fructose diet, New York, 1979, M. Evans & Co., Inc.

Currier, W. D.: Foreword. In Davis, A.: Let's eat right to keep fit, New York, 1954, Harcourt Brace Jovanovich, Inc.

Davis, A.: Let's cook it right, New York, 1970, The New American Library.

Davis, A.: Let's eat right to keep fit, New York, 1970, Harcourt Brace Jovanovich, Inc.

Davis, A.: Let's get well, New York, 1965, New American Library.

Davis, A.: Let's have healthy children, New York, 1972, New American Library.

Donsback, K.: Minerals, Huntington Beach, Calif., 1977a, International Institute of Natural Health Sciences, Inc.

Donsback, K.: Vitamins, Huntington Beach, Calif., 1977b, International Institute of Natural Health Sciences, Inc.

Evarts, E. V.: Brain mechanisms in movement, Sci. Am. **229:**96-103, July 1973.

Fredericks, C.: New & complete nutrition handbook, Canoga Park, Calif., 1976a, Major Books.

Fredericks, C.: Psycho-nutrition, New York, 1976b, Grosset & Dunlap, Inc.

French, J. D.: Reticular formation, Sci. Am. **196:**54-60, May 1957.

Gellhorn, E.: Principles of autonomic-somatic integration, Minneapolis, 1967, University of Minnesota Press.

Hofmann, L., editor: The great American nutrition hassle, Palo Alto, Calif., 1978, Mayfield Publishing Co.

Hooker, D.: Pre-natal origin of behavior, Lawrence, Kan., 1952, University of Kansas Press.

Jacobson, E.: You must relax, New York, 1978, McGraw-Hill Book Co.

Jacobson, M.: Our diets have changed but not for the best. In Hofmann, L., editor: The great American nutrition hassle, Palo Alto, Calif., 1978, Mayfield Publishing Co.

Koizumi, K., and Brooks, C.: The integration of automonic system reactions: a discussion of autonomic reflexes, their control and their association with somatic reactions, Ergeb. Physiol. **67:**1-68, 1972.

Leboyer, F.: Birth without violence, New York, 1975, Alfred A. Knopf, Inc.

Pelletier, K. R.: Mind as healer, mind as slayer, New York, 1977, Dell Publishing Co., Inc.

Pfeiffer, C.: Nutrition as preventive medicine. In Hofmann, L., editor: The great American nutrition hassle, Palo Alto, Calif., 1978, Mayfield Publishing Co.

Reuben, D.: The save your life diet, New York, 1975, Ballantine Books, Inc.

Reuben, D.: Everything you always wanted to know about nutrition, New York, 1979, Avon Books,

Ribble, M.A.: The rights of infants, New York, 1943, Columbia University Press.

Rood, M.: Class notes, 1957, 1958, 1960, 1970, 1974, 1975.

Selye, H.: Stress without distress, Philadelphia, 1974, J. B. Lippincott Co.

Selye, H.: The stress of life, revised edition, New York, 1976, McGraw-Hill Book Co.

CONCEPT 2

Ayres, A.J.: Sensory integration and learning disorders, Los Angeles, 1972, Western Psychological Services.

Ayres, A.J.: Class notes, 1976.

Buscaglia, L.: Love, Thorofare, N.J., 1972, Charles B. Black, Inc.

Cheal, M.: Social olfaction: a review of the ontogeny of olfactory influences on vertebrate behavior, Behav. Biol. **15:**1-25, 1974.

Davis, F.: Skin hunger: an American disease, Woman's Day, p. 48, Sept. 1978.

Elkind, D.: Growing up too fast, Psychol. Today, pp. 38-46, Feb. 1979.

Erlanger, J., Gasser, H. S., and Bishop, G. H.: Am. J. Physiol. **70:**624, 1970.

Farber, S. D.: Olfaction in health and disease, Am. J. Occup. Ther. **32**(3):155-160, 1978.

Ganong, W.: Review of medical physiology, Los

Altos, Calif., 1969, Lange Medical Publications.

Haagen-Smit, A. J.: Smell and taste, Sc. Am. **186:**28-32, 1952.

Head, H.: Studies in neurology, Vol II, Oxford, 1920, Oxford University Press.

Huss, A. J.: Touch with care, or a caring touch? Am. J. Occup. Ther. **31**(1):11-18, 1977.

Iggo, A.: A single unit analysis of cutaneous receptor with C afferent fibers, CIBA Foundation study group no. 1, Pain and Itch, Boston, 1959, Little Brown & Co.

Kennell, J. H., Trause, M. A., and Klaus, M. H.: Evidence for a sensitive period in the human mother, Parent-Infant Interaction, Ciba Foundation Symposium 33, Amsterdam, 1975, Elsevier.

Kephart, N. C.: Class notes, 1969.

Kephart, N. C.: The slow-learner in the classroom, ed. 2, Columbus, Ohio, 1971, Charles E. Merrill Publishing Co.

Klaus, M. H., Trause, M. A., and Kennell, J. H.: Does human maternal behavior after delivery show a characteristic pattern? Parent-Infant Interaction, Ciba Foundation Symposium 33, Amsterdam, 1975, Elsevier.

Leboyer, F.: Loving hands, New York, 1976, Alfred A. Knopf, Inc.

Lynch, J.: The broken heart: the medican consequences of loneliness, New York, 1977, Basic Books, Inc.

Melzack, R. and Wall, P.: On the nature of cutaneous sensory mechanisms, Brain **85:**331-356, 1962.

Melzack, R., and Wall, P. D.: Pain mechanisms: a new theory, Science **150:**971-979, 1965.

Montagu, A.: Touching: the human significance of the skin, New York, 1971, Harper & Row, Publishers, Inc.

Mountcastle, V. editor: Medical physiology, Vol. 1, ed. 14, St. Louis, 1979, The C. V. Mosby Co.

Poggio, G. F., and Mountcastle, V. B.: A study of the functional contributions of the lemniscal and spinothalmic systems to somatic sensibility, Bull. Johns Hopkins Hosp. **106:**266-316, 1960.

Rood, M.: Class notes, 1970.

Ruch, T., and others: Neurophysiology, ed. 2, Philadelphia, 1965, W. B. Saunders Co.

Schmidt, R. F.: Presynaptic inhibition in the vertebrate central nervous system, Ergeb. Physiol. **63:**20-101, 1971.

Schmidt, R. F., editor: Fundamentals of neurophysiology, New York, 1975, Springer-Verlag, New York, Inc.

Schneider, R. A.: Newer insights into the role modification of olfaction in man through clinical studies, Ann. N.Y. Acad. Sci. **237:**217-223, 1974.

Selye, H.: Stress without distress, Philadelphia, 1974, J. B. Lippincott Co.

Snapp, E.: Class notes, 1979, Pflugerville, Texas.

Steiner, J. E.: Innate discriminative human facial expressions to taste and smell stimulation, Ann. N.Y. Acad. Sci. **237:**229-233, 1974.

CONCEPT 3

Ayres, J. A.: Sensory Integration and learning disorders, Los Angeles, 1972, Western Psychological Services.

Ayres, J. A.: Southern California postrotary nystagmus test, Los Angeles, 1975, Western Psychological Services.

Ayres, J. A.: Class notes, 1976, Chicago.

de Quiros, J. B.: Diagnosis of vestibular disorders in the learning disabled, J. Learn. Disabilities **9**(1):39-47, 1976.

de Reuck, A. V. S., and Knight, J., editors: Myotatic, kinesthetic and vestibular mechanisms, New York, 1967, American Elsevier Publishers, Inc.

Eviatar, L., Eviatar, A., and Naray, I.: Maturation of neurovestibular responses in infants, Dev. Med. Child Neurol. **16:**435-446, 1974.

Gainer, W. L., and others, editors: Santa Clara inventory of developmental tasks, California State Department of Education, Santa Clara, Calif., 1974, Richard L. Zweig Associates, Inc.

Lawrence, M. M., and Feind, C. R.: Vestibular responses to rotation in newborn infant, Pediatrics **12:**300-305, 1953.

Matthews, E.: Effects of age on the vestibular system (Unpublished), Morgantown, W.Va., 1978, Physical Therapy Department, University of West Virginia.

Matthews, P. B. C.: Mammaliam muscle receptors and their central actions, Baltimore, 1972, The Williams & Wilkins Co.

Mountcastle, V., editor: Medical physiology, Vol. 1, ed. 14, St. Louis, 1979, The C. V. Mosby Co.

Nauton, R. F., editor: The vestibular system, New York, 1975, Academic Press, Inc.

Pomeiano, O., and Brodal, A.: Spino-vestibular fibers in the cat: an experimental study, J. Comp. Neurol. **108:**353-382, 1957.

Sage, G. H.: Introduction to motor behavior: a

neuropsychological approach, Reading, Mass., 1971, Addison-Wesley Publishing Co., Inc.

Schilder, P.: Mind: perception and thought in their constructive aspects, New York, 1942, Columbia University Press.

Walberg, F. The physiology of the vestibular nuclei and their connections with the eighth nerve and the cerebellum. In Nauton, R. F., editor: The vestibular system, New York, 1975, Academic Press, Inc.

Westfall, M.: Comparison of postrotory nystagmus between young adults and children (Unpublished), Morgantown, W.Va., 1977, Physical Therapy Department, University of West Virginia.

Wilson, V.: The physiology of the vestibular nuclei. In Nauton, R. F., editor: The vestibular system, New York, 1975, Academic Press, Inc.

CONCEPT 4

Doman, R., and others: Children with severe brain injuries: neurological organization in terms of mobility, J.A.M.A. **174:**257-262, 1960.

Gellhorn, E.: Principles of autonomic-somatic integration, Minneapolis, 1967, University of Minnesota Press.

Rood, M.: Class notes, 1970, Newington, Conn.

Stilwell, J.: Tonic labyrinthine inverted table and its use in sensory integrative therapy, 1977, Unpublished paper.

Tokizane, T., Murao, M., Ogato, T., and Kodo, T.: Electromyographic studies on tonic neck, lumbar, and labyrinthine reflexes in normal persons, Jpn. J. Physiol. **2:**130-146, 1951.

CONCEPT 5

Ayres, J. A.: Class notes, 1975.

Barker, D.: The innervation of mammalian skeletal muscle. In de Reuck, A. V. S., and Knight, J., editors: Myotatic, kinesthetic and vestibular mechanisms, New York, 1967, American Elsevier Publishers, Inc.

Bessou, P., and Laporte, Y.: Responses from primary and secondary endings of the same neuromuscular spindle of the tenuissimus muscle of the cat. In Barker, D., editor: Symposium on muscle receptors, Hong Kong, 1962, Hong Kong University Press.

Blashy, M. R., and Fuchs, R. L.: Orthokinetics: a new receptor facilitation method, Am. J. Occup. Ther. **13:**226-234, 1959.

Bobath, K. and Bobath, B.: Abnormal postural reflex activity caused by brain lesions, London, 1965, William Heinemann Medical Books Ltd.

Christopher, R. P.: Recent advances in mechanical aids in the management of children with brain damage, South. Med. J. **67:**399-405, 1974.

Crutchfield, C., and Barnes, M. L.: The neurophysiological basis for patient treatment, Vol. 1, Muscle spindle, Morgantown, W.Va., 1973, Stokesville Publishing Co.

DeGail, P., Lance, J. W., and Neilson, P. D.: Differential effects on tonic and phasic reflex mechanisms produced by vibration of muscles in man, J. Neurol. Neurosurg. Psychiatry **29:**1, 1966.

Eldred, E., and Hagbarth, K. E.: Facilitation and inhibition of gamma efferen by stimulation of certain skin areas, J. Neurophysiol. **17:**59, 1954.

Evarts E. V.: Brain mechanisms in movement, Sci. Am. **229:**96-103, July 1973.

Hagbarth, K. E.: The effects of muscle vibration in normal man and in patients with motor disorders. In Desmedt, J. E., editor: New developments in electromyography and clinical neurophysiology, Vol. 3, Basel, 1973, S. Karger AG.

Hooker, D.: Pre-natal origin of behavior, Lawrence, Kan., 1952, University of Kansas Press.

Houk, J.: Feedback control of muscle: a synthisic of the peripheral control. In Mountcastle, V. B., editor: Medical physiology, ed. 13, St. Louis, 1974, The C. V. Mosby Co.

Lance, J.: A physiological approach to clinical neurology, Sevenoaks, Kent, 1970, Butterworth & Co.

Lance, J. W., DeGail, P., and Neilsen, P. D.: Tonic and phasic spinal cord mechanisms in man, J. Neurol. Neurosurg. Psychiatry, **29:**535, 1966.

Matthews, P. B. C.: Muscle spindles and their motor control, Physiol. Rev. **44:**219, 1964.

Matthews, P. F. C.: Evidence that the secondary as well as the primary endings of the muscle spindles may be responsible for the tonic stretch reflex of the decerebrate cat, J. Physiol. **204:**365-395, 1969.

Matthews, P. F. C.: Mammalian muscle receptors and their control actions, Baltimore, 1972, The Williams & Wilkins Co.

McMinn, R. M. H., and Vrbova, G.: Motoneurone activity as a cause of degeneration in the soleus muscle of the rabbit, Q. J. Exp. Physiol. **52:**411-415, 1967.

Moore, J. C.: The Golgi tendon organ and the muscle spindle, Am. J. Occup. Ther. **28:**415, 1974.

Muller, H. H.: Facilitating feeding and prespeech, In Pearson, P. H., editor: Physical therapy services in developmental disabilities, Springfield, Ill., 1972, Charles C Thomas Publisher.

Rood, M.: Class notes, 1957, 1958, 1960, 1970, 1974, 1975.

Ruch, T., and others: Neurophysiology, ed. 2, Philadelphia, 1965. W. B. Saunders Co.

Sato, M., and Ozeki, M.: Initiation of impulses by mechanosensory nerve terminals. In deReuch, A. V. S., editor: Touch, heat and pain. Boston, 1966, Little, Brown & Co.

Stockmeyer, S. A.: An interpretation of Rood to the treatment of neuromuscular dysfunction, Am. J. Phys. Med. **46:**900-961, 1967.

Ward, J., and Fisk, G.: The difference in response of the quadriceps and the biceps brachii muscles to isometric and isotonic exercise, Arch. Phys. Med. Rehabil. **45:**614-620, 1964.

CONCEPT 6

Beard, R.: An outline of Piaget's developmental psychology, New York, 1969, Basic Books, Inc., Publishers.

Bobath, B.: Abnormal postural reflex activity caused by brain lesions, London, 1965, William Heinemann Medical Books Ltd.

Bobath, K.: The neurophysiology of cerebral palsy and its importance in treatment and diagnosis, Cerebral Palsy Bull., vol. 1, no. 8, 1959.

Boyle, D. G.: A student's guide to Piaget, Elmsford, N.Y., 1969, Pergamon Press, Inc.

Brunnstrom, S.: Movement therapy in hemiplegia: a neurophysiological approach, New York, 1970, Harper & Row, Publishers, Inc.

Chaney, C. M.: Class notes, 1978.

Chaney, C. M., and Kephart, N. C.: Motoric aids to perceptual training, Columbus, Ohio, 1968, Charles E. Merrill Publishing Co.

Frostig, M., and Horne, D.: Teacher's guide: the Frostig program for the development of visual perception, revised edition, Chicago, 1974, Follett Educational Corp.

Kephart, N. C.: The slow learner in the classroom, ed. 2, Columbus, Ohio, 1971, Charles E. Merrill Publishing Co.

Knott, M., and Voss, D.: Proprioceptive neuromuscular facilitation and techniques, ed. 2, New York, 1968, Harper & Row.

Phillips, J. L., Jr.: The origins of intellect: Piaget's theory, San Francisco, 1969, W. H. Freeman & Co., Publishers.

Singer, D. G. and Revenson, T. A.: A Piaget primer: how a child thinks, New York, 1978, The New American Library, Inc.

Strauss, A., and Kephart, N. C.: Psychopathology and education of the brain-injured child, Vol. 2, New York, 1955, Grune & Stratton, Inc.

Tokizane, T., Murao, M., and Kendo, T.: Electromyographic studies on tonic neck, lumbar, and labyrinthine reflexes in normal persons, Jpn. J. Physiol. **2:**130, 1951.

Wyke, B.: Articular neurology—a review, Physiotherapy **23:**94, 1972.

CONCEPT 7

Ayres, J. A.: Sensory integration and learning disorders, Los Angeles, 1972, Western Psychological Services.

Ayres, J. A.: Class notes, 1976, Chicago.

Belmont I., Birch, H. G., and Karp, E.: The disordering of intersensory and intrasensory integration by brain damage, J. Nerv. Ment. Dis. **141**(4):410-418, 1965.

Bergstrom, R. M.: Electrical parameters of the brain during ontogeny. In Robinson, R. J., editor: Brain and early behavior, New York, 1969, Academic Press, Inc.

Birch, H. G., and Belmont, L.: Perceptual analysis and sensory integration in brain-damaged persons, J. Genet. Psychol. **105:**173-179, 1964.

Birch, H. G., and Belmont, L.: Auditory-visual integration, intellegence, and reading ability in school children, Percept. Mot. Skills **20:**295-305, 1965.

Birch, H. G., and Lefford, A.: Intersensory development in children, Monographs of the Society for Research in Child Development, Serial No. 89, 1963.

Chaney, C. M.: Class notes, 1974, 1975, 1976, 1977, 1978, 1979, Danville, Ill.

Chaney, C. M., and Kephart, N. C.: Motoric aids to perceptual training, Columbus, Ohio, 1968, Charles E. Merrill Publishing Co.

Chaney, C. M., and Miles, N.: Personal communication, 1969 to present.

Chaney, C. M., and Miles, N.: Remediating learning problems: a developmental curriculum, Columbus, Ohio, 1974, Charles E. Merrill Publishing Co.

Cruickshank, W. M.: The brain-injured child in home, school, and community, Syracuse, 1967, Syracuse University Press.

Cruickshank, W. M., Bentzen, F. H., Ratzenbury, F. H., and Tannhauser, M. T.: A teaching method for brain-injured and hyperactive children, Syracuse, 1961, Syracuse University Press.

de Quiros, J. B.: Diagnosis of vestibular disorders in the learning disabled, J. Learning Disabilities, **9**(1):39-47, 1976.

Ebersole, M. L., Kephart, N. C., and Ebersole, J.: Steps to achievement for the slow learner, Columbus, Ohio, 1968, Charles E. Merrill Publishing Co.

Eccles, J. C.: Presynaptic inhibition in the spinal cord, Prog. Brain Res. **12**:65-91, 1964.

Feingold, B. E.: Why your child is hyperactive, New York, 1975, Random House, Inc.

Gearheart, B. R.: Learning disabilities: educational strategies, St. Louis, 1973, The C. V. Mosby Co.

Hallahan, D. P., and Kauffman, J. M.: Introduction to learning disabilities: a psycho-behavioral approach, Englewood Cliffs, N.J., 1976, Prentice-Hall, Inc.

Hooker, D.: The prenatal origin of behavior, Lawrence, Kan., 1952, University of Kansas.

Humphrey, T.: Postnatal repetition of human prenatal activity sequences with some suggestions of their neuroanatomical bases. In Robinson, R. J., editor: Brain and early behavior, New York, 1969, Academic Press, Inc.

Johnson, D. J., and Myklebust, H. R.: Learning disabilities: educational principles and practices, New York, 1967, Grune & Stratten, Inc.

Kephart, N. C.: Class notes, 1969, Fort Collins, Colo.

Kephart, N. C. and Chaney, C. M.: Aids to motoric and perceptual training, Madison, 1963, Wisconsin Bureau For Handicapped Children.

Schmidt, R. F., editor: Fundamentals of neurophysiology, New York, 1975, Springer-Verlag, New York, Inc.

Schmidt, R. F.: Presynaptic inhibition in the vertebrate central nervous system, Ergeb. Physiol., vol. 63, 1971.

Sherrington, C.: Man on his nature, Cambridge, 1951, Cambridge University Press.

Smith, L. H.: Improving your child's behavior chemistry, Englewood Cliffs, 1976, Prentice-Hall, Inc.

Snapp, E.: Class notes, 1979, Pflugerville, Texas.

Strauss, A., and Lehtinen, L. E.: Psychopathology and education of the brain-injured child, Vol. 1, New York, 1947, Grune & Stratton, Inc.

Strauss, A., and Kephart, N. C.: Psychopathology and education of the brain-injured child, Vol. 2, New York, 1955, Grune & Stratton, Inc.

CONCEPT 8

Ball, T.: Itard, Seguin and Kephart, Columbus, Ohio, 1971, Charles E. Merrill Publishing Co.

Buscaglia, L.: Love, New York, 1972, Charles B. Slack, Inc.

Buscaglia, L.: Lecture notes, 1977, Knoxville, Tenn.

Chaney, C. M.: Class notes 1974, 1975, 1976, 1977, 1978, 1979, Danville, Ill.

Davis, F.: Skin hunger: an American disease, Womans Day, Sept. 1978.

de Quiros, J. B.: Diagnosis of vestibular disorders in the learning disabled, J. Learning Disabilities **9**(1):39-47, 1976.

Feldenkrais, M.: Body and mature behavior, New York, 1949, International University Press.

Gesell, A., and others: The first five years of life, New York, 1940, Harper & Row, Publishers, Inc.

Kephart, N. C.: The slow learner in the classroom, Columbus, Ohio, 1960, Charles E. Merrill Publishing Co.

Kephart, N. C.: The slow learner in the classroom, ed. 2, Columbus, Ohio, 1971, Charles E. Merrill Publishing Co.

King, L. J.: A sensory-integrative approach to schizophrenia, Am. J. Occup. Ther. **28**(9):529-536, Oct. 1974.

Montagu, A.: Touching: the human significance of the skin, New York, 1971, Columbia University Press.

O'Quinn, G., Jr.: Developmental gymnastics, Austin, 1978, University of Texas Press.

Radler, D. H., and Kephart, N. C.: Success through play, New York, 1960, Harper & Row, Publishers, Inc.

Ribble, M. A.: The rights of infants, New York, 1943, Columbia University Press.

Roach, E., and Kephart, N. C.: Purdue perceptual-motor survey, Columbus, Ohio, 1966, Charles E. Merrill Publishing Co.

Schilder, P.: Contributions to developmental neuropsychiatry, New York, 1964, International Universities Press.

Snapp, E.: Class notes, 1979, Pflugerville, Texas.

CONCEPT 9

Ames, L.: Is your child in the wrong grade? New York, 1966, Harper & Row.

Dobson, J.: Dare to discipline, Wheaton, Ill., 1970 Tyndale House Publishers.

Dobson, J.: Hide or seek, Old Tappan, N.J., 1974, Fleming H. Revell Co.

Early Prevention of School Failure Project, Luceille Werner, Project Director, 114 North Second Street, Peotone, Illinois, 60468, 1976 Sponsored by Illinois Office of Education Title III ESEA; 1979 Sponsored by Illinois Office of Education Title IV ESEA, Replication National Diffusion Network.

Frostig, M., and Horne, D.: Frostig program for the development of visual perception, revised edition, Chicago, 1973, Follett Publishing Co.

Hainstock, E. G.: The essential Montessori, New York, 1978, The New American Library, Inc.

Knickerbocker, B.: Holistic approach to treatment of learning disorders, Thorofare, J., 1980, Charles B. Black, Inc.

La Haye, B.: How to develop your child's temperament, Irvine, Calif., 1977, Harvest House Publishers.

Liedloff, J.: The continuum concept, New York, 1975, Warner Books, Inc.

May, B.: TSKH (tickle, snuggle, kiss and hug), New York, 1977, Paulist Press.

Montessori, M.: The Montessori method, New York, 1964, Schocken Books, Inc.

Montessori, M.: Dr. Montessori's own handbook, New York, 1965, Schocken Books, Inc.

Montessori, M.: The secret of childhood, Notre Dame, Ind., 1966, Fides/Claretian.

Montessori, M.: The absorbent mind, New York, 1967. Dell Publishing Co., Inc.

O'Quinn, G., Jr.: Developmental gymnastics, Austin, 1978, University of Texas Press.

Packard, R. C.: The hidden hinge, Notre Dame, Ind., 1972, Fides Publishers, Inc.

Snapp, E.: Class notes, 1979, Pflugerville, Texas.

Strauss, R. L.: Confident children and how they grow, Wheaton, Ill., 1975, Tyndale House Publishers.

APPENDIX A

Integrated Motor Activities Scale

MARGOT C. HEINIGER and CHARLES W. LEWIS

Test manual (experimental form)

PURPOSES OF THE IMAS

The Integrated Motor Activities Scale (IMAS) was developed primarily to identify prekindergarten children who are likely to have potential learning difficulties. It was designed for use by teachers and paraprofessionals who may encounter children with minimal overt clues of learning deficiency. These children often go on to have academic problems. Results of this scale can provide diagnostic data in specific areas of weakness so that appropriate prevention or remediation can be undertaken promptly.

THEORY AND RATIONALE

The IMAS is based on the premise that basic motor functions lay the foundation and provide the building blocks for the development of complex perceptual-motor skills required for learning in school.

A child's early preschool years are spent learning neuromuscular control of his body. He must devote a great deal of time and energy to attending to his movements. He pays close attention to the internal awareness, or kinesthesia, associated with his movements. As this internal awareness develops, more and more actions become automatic. He can, for example, spend less energy on "how to" balance and devote more to applying that skill. A keenly developed internal awareness frees a child to direct his attention to exploring his external environment. His body is then an excellent reference point for these ventures.

The child who enters kindergarten should bring with him the automatic movement adjustments of balance and posture. He should *not* have to attend to his movements. He should be free to concentrate on the perceptual information within his immediate learning environment—school.

The IMAS assesses the level to which motor activities have been integrated into the behavior of the child. The critical element in this assessment is that the IMAS pinpoints the child's *methods* of problem solving and, con-comitantly, the interfering factors that prevent him from completing tasks satisfactorily.

BACKGROUND

The IMAS was developed as an outgrowth of activities of the Title III, ESEA, Early Prevention of School Failure Project.* The staff of that project developed an instrument entitled *Motor Activity Scale*† in 1971. The new in-strument (IMAS), although inspired by the original MAS, is unique. The IMAS is based on the neurobiological science orientation of Heiniger. The scale relies heavily on the current approaches of Ayres‡ and Kephart.§ Em-phasis is on the integration of auditory and visual input with kinesthetic-tactual feedback and motor responses.

The IMAS is presently in an experimental form. Eventually, a shorter scale should emerge that gives results as valid as this longer version. At pres-ent, the IMAS has been administered to 391 children 4 to 7 years of age, and preliminary norms have been developed. Initial results based on professional clinical judgments and statistical data suggest that the IMAS is a powerful tool for identifying children with potential learning problems.

GENERAL DESCRIPTION OF THE IMAS
Materials needed

Two yarn balls (approximately 1 oz each)
One standard size classroom wastebasket
One box No. 8 crayons
One primary pencil (no eraser)
One regular No. 2 pencil with eraser
Watch with second hand
Roll of masking tape
Test booklet
IMAS Child's Work Sheet
Performance guidelines

---

*Early Prevention of School Failure Project. Title IV, ESEA, Part C. Funded by the Illinois Office of Education. Lucille Werner, Project Director.
†Motor activity scale, Test Manual, Peotone, Ill., Early Prevention of School Failure Project, 1977, (mimeographed).
‡Ayres, A. J.: Sensory integration and learning disorders, Los Angeles, 1972, Western Psycho-logical Services.
§Kephart, N. C.: The slow learner in the classroom, ed. 2, Columbus, Ohio, 1971, Charles E. Merrill Publishing Co.

Administration time

The IMAS is primarily a performance rather than a timed test. Only three items are timed. Generally speaking, the IMAS requires approximately 16 minutes per child to administer and score.

Ages

The major target population for the IMAS is prekindergarten-age children. Generally, these children are 4½ to 5½ years of age. Even though the IMAS was designed primarily for this age group, items were selected to appeal to children 4 to 6½ years of age. Preliminary performance guidelines for interpreting scores have been developed for ages in 6-month intervals from 4 years to 6 years 11 months.

Test sections

The IMAS consists of observational items (not scored) and performance items (scored). These two sections are woven into the test administration so that recording is made easy and interpretation of performance is enhanced. Clinical experience indicates that scores *plus* anecdotal notations markedly improve the quality of diagnostic data that can be generated.

Observational sections. There are three general observational sections at the beginning of the testing session. The first set of observations is for the purpose of evaluating the child's eye control, lack of which is a frequent cause of learning problems.

A second set of observations consists of activities designed to assist the examiner to determine a child's hand, eye, and foot preference. Because established or mixed dominance may influence a child's performance on scored sections of the test, this attribute is identified early in the testing session.

A third series of observational activities is designed to assess the child's level of body awareness. These activities are intended to help establish rapport with the child, but they also have educational implications. By having the child locate specific body parts, he is required to sort out those parts and show development of body schema (awareness of the postural model of the body). Adequate development of body schema provides the child with a foundation for dealing with more complex perceptual-motor experiences.

Observation and notation of other significant behaviors are encouraged throughout the testing session. Checklists or more common problems accompany each of the scored sections.

At the end of the examination, a brief checklist of negative patterns of behavior is given. The examiner can indicate overall impressions that may have affected the child's performance adversely.

Scored sections. The IMAS consists of three scored sections. Each is designed to evaluate a particular type of motor activity awareness. The three sections are: (1) auditory-visual-motor, (2) eye-hand coordination, and (3) gross motor. The purposes of the activities within each section and their educational implications are presented below.

SPECIFIC DESCRIPTION OF SCORED SECTIONS
Section I: Auditory-visual-motor

Purposes. The activities in the auditory-visual-motor section are designed to evaluate the child's ability to discriminate and sequence auditory-visual stimuli. The child is required to differentiate between two sound-acts "tap and clap" and to recall their sequence. The sound-acts begin with two single patterns and progress to double patterns with varied rhythm. These activities require progressively more complex integration processes.

Educational implications. Three important educationally related activities are used in this section of the test.

1. Attention to auditory-visual stimuli and the ability to discriminate between sounds are necessary for understanding and developing oral language. Children need to be able to differentiate between speech sounds and background noise, to hear parts of words and draw correct inferences about the total context, and to discriminate among competing educational stimuli such as teacher comments and audiovisual materials.

2. Abilities to hold two or more stimuli, to consider their relationship, and to respond are the essential components of short-term memory. These skills are important in following verbal directions, learning rhymes and songs, repeating story sequences, and learning names and addresses.

3. Neuromuscular control is involved in the timing of muscle activities in this section. The ability to initiate, maintain, and terminate movement using the two sides of the body is important for gross and fine motor control in school activities requiring coordination and dexterity.

Section II: Eye-hand coordination

Purposes. Eye-hand coordination activities are designed to evaluate several aspects of fine manual motor coordination. Snapping fingers involves action between the thumb and middle finger while the wrist is held stationary.

The "rabbit wiggling his ears" task evaluates the ability to keep some fingers in contact with each other while moving others and to add wrist movement.

The "coloring within a donut" activities necessitate skill in controlling the fingers while holding an object. The ability to coordinate hand and eye is required to color within the restricted area.

"Fine eye-hand with pencil" activities are used to assess the ability to combine manual dexterity with coordination of hand and eyes.

Educational implications. The abilities to reach, grasp, and release are prerequisites to fine control in such activities as dressing and handwriting. Appropriate pencil grasp, pencil pressure, size of written symbols, and organization of written material on the page require high-level eye-hand coordination. Manipulation of tools, toys, and other learning objects becomes increasingly complex as the child progresses in school. Therefore the child must become increasingly adept in these skills.

Section III: Gross motor

Purposes. Activities in the gross motor section are designed to evaluate control of large muscle groups in the body. Items deal with static and dynamic balance, timing, endurance, and adjustment to moving objects.

Balancing on one foot with hands on head involves the ability to coordinate two sides of the body in a static balance activity. Stationary hopping on each foot adds the dimensions of endurance and sustained action. Skipping requires a high level of neuromuscular control, timing, and spatial movement.

Tossing and catching the yarn ball incorporates the highest level of neuromuscular control into tasks children comprehend. The activities assess the child's ability to maintain control of the body while at the same time dealing appropriately with the movement of objects in reference to the body.

Educational implications. Children must learn to deal automatically with tasks involving laterality, body image, and neuromuscular control so they can devote maximum energy to visual and auditory stimuli in the learning environment of the classroom. Inadequacies may be observed later in chronic fatigue posture, restlessness, right-left confusions, reversals in numbers, clumsiness, excessive leaning on elbows, and low-level endurance.

SCORING PROCEDURES

Although items in the observational sections are not scored, attention should be given to the careful recording of behaviors. Frequently these notations provide clues to identifying specific problems or treatment procedures.

Each of the three scored sections contains a maximum of 10 points. Points allocated to the various items of the scale are:

Section I: Auditory-visual-motor

Each correct response on the ten clap-tap sequence items earns 1 point.	10 points

Section II: Eye-hand coordination

1. Snapping fingers	2 points
2. Rabbit saying "Hello"	2 points
3. Coloring within donut	3 points
4. Straight alley	1 point
5. Maze	1 point
6. Curved alley	1 point

Section III: Gross motor

1. Balancing, each foot, hands on head	2 points
2. Stationary hopping on each foot	3 points
3. Skipping	2 points
4. Tossing yarn ball	1 point
5. Catching yarn ball	1 point
6. Tossing and catching	1 point

Scores for each section are transferred to the front of the test booklet. Section scores are combined to obtain the total.

ASSESSING PERFORMANCE LEVELS

Once the child's age and IMAS scores have been determined, the examiner may refer to the appropriate age table on the following pages to assess relative performance levels on the IMAS. Scores that fall into the category "Periodic Review Suggested" or "Provide Special Attention" merit greatest consideration.

For those who wish more precise indications of performance, technical data and summary statistics, including percentile ranks and stanines, follow the age tables.

Performance guidelines—ages 4 years through 4 years, 5 months

Performance levels		Raw scores			
		Section I	Section II	Section III	Total
Satisfactory	High	5	8 to 10	5 to 10	15 to 30
	Above average	4	5 to 7	4	11 to 14
	Average	3	4	3	9 to 10
Review progress periodically	Below average	1 to 2	2 to 3	1 to 2	4 to 8
Provide special attention	Low	0	0 to 1	0	0 to 4

Performance guidelines—ages 4 years, 6 months through 4 years, 11 months

| | | Raw scores | | | |
Performance levels		Section I	Section II	Section III	Total
Satisfactory	High	6 to 10	9 to 10	8 to 10	19 to 30
	Above average	4 to 5	7 to 8	5 to 7	15 to 18
	Average	3	6	4	12 to 14
Review progress periodically	Below average	2	3 to 5	1 to 3	8 to 11
Provide special attention	Low	0 to 1	0 to 2	0	0 to 7

Performance guidelines—ages 5 years through 5 years, 5 months

| | | Raw scores | | | |
Performance levels		Section I	Section II	Section III	Total
Satisfactory	High	8 to 10	10	9 to 10	24 to 30
	Above average	6 to 7	7 to 9	6 to 8	18 to 23
	Average	5	6	5	16 to 17
Review progress periodically	Below average	2 to 4	4 to 5	2 to 4	10 to 15
Provide special attention	Low	0 to 1	0 to 3	0 to 1	0 to 9

Performance guidelines—ages 5 years, 6 months through 5 years, 11 months

| | | Raw scores | | | |
Performance levels		Section I	Section II	Section III	Total
Satisfactory	High	9 to 10	10	10	27 to 30
	Above average	6 to 8	9	7 to 9	21 to 26
	Average	5	8	6	18 to 20
Review progress periodically	Below average	3 to 4	4 to 7	3 to 5	13 to 17
Provide special attention	Low	0 to 2	0 to 3	0 to 2	0 to 12

Performance guidelines—ages 6 years through 6 years, 5 months

| | | Raw scores | | | |
Performance levels		Section I	Section II	Section III	Total
Satisfactory	High	9 to 10	10	9 to 10	26 to 38
	Above average	7 to 8	9	7 to 8	22 to 25
	Average	6	8	6	20 to 21
Review progress periodically	Below average	4 to 5	6 to 7	4 to 5	15 to 19
Provide special attention	Low	0 to 3	0 to 5	0 to 3	0 to 14

Performance guidelines—ages 6 years, 6 months through 6 years, 11 months

		Raw scores			
Performance levels		Section I	Section II	Section III	Total
Satisfactory	High	9 to 10	10	—	28 to 30
	Above average	7 to 8	9	10	25 to 27
	Average	6	8	8 to 9	23 to 24
Review progress periodically	Below average	5	—	6 to 7	19 to 22
Provide special attention	Low	0 to 4	0 to 7	0 to 5	0 to 18

Technical report

TEST PERFORMANCE SUMMARY

The purpose of this report is to provide descriptive statistics and preliminary guidelines to aid in the interpretation of the IMAS, an assessment tool developed in conjunction with the Title III ESEA Early Prevention of School Failure Project.

The major target group of the test is preschool-age children. Because the usual age for pre-kindergarten assessment would be 4 years, 5 months through 5 years, 5 months, the majority of subjects (N = 159) were selected at this level. If assessments were conducted in the fall of the year, the potential for encountering children 5 years, 5 months to 5 years, 11 months of age is increased. Therefore a large group (N = 122) at this level was also tested. Professional experience suggested that even within this total group of 281 children, different criteria should be used for younger and older children to assess potential learning problems. Therefore data have been categorized according to 6-month intervals. Relatively smaller samples of other age groups were also tested to provide a broad range of age-related performance data. The number of pupils tested at each age level were

Age	Number
4 years through 4 years, 5 months	44
4 years, 6 months through 4 years, 11 months	53
5 years through 5 years, 5 months	106
5 years, 6 months through 5 years, 11 months	122
6 years through 6 years, 5 months	54
6 years, 6 months through 6 years, 11 months	12
TOTAL	391

Overall results

Table 1 (p. 294) contains the distribution of scores earned for each age group. Percentile ranks, stanines, mean, and standard deviation, as well as cutoff scores for the lower quarter, median, and upper quarter are also shown. Table 1 may be used as a preliminary norms' table for assessing performances on the IMAS. Inspection of Table 1 indicates a general tendency for scores to increase with age. The means and medians tend to advance approximately 3 points with each successive age category.

If one were to consider performances at the first and second stanines as low and potentially in need of special attention, the cutoff points indicated below emerge. The mean or expected score for each group is also presented. Performances between the two figures may suggest periodic review. Scores at or above the mean would generally be considered appropriate and acceptable for the age level indicated.

Age	Special attention score (at or below)	Mean score (rounded)
4 years through 4 years, 5 months	4	9
4 years, 6 months through 4 years, 11 months	7	13
5 years through 5 years, 5 months	9	16
5 years, 6 months through 5 years, 11 months	12	19
6 years through 6 years, 5 months	14	20
6 years, 6 months through 6 years, 11 months	18	23

Clinical judgments of those persons associated with the project anticipated that scores below 10 were of potential concern. The statistical results were very consistent with those clinical assessments, especially for the target population of five-year-old children.

Item analysis

In addition to summary statistics, item analyses were computed to determine the extent to which the various items of the IMAS discriminated between the highest and lowest scorers on the total instrument. Discrimination indexes for each item and for each age level are presented in Table 2 (p. 296).

Section I: Auditory-visual-motor. The discrimination indexes for the ten clap-tap sequence items appear to be age related. Items at the beginning of the auditory-visual-motor section discriminated best for the younger children while items at the end of the section differentiated better among the older pupils. Only items 1, 6, and 10 did not have any index above 0.50 for at least one age group.

Section II: Eye-hand coordination. Snapping fingers and wrist action seemed to result in the best discrimination indexes across age levels for the eye-hand section. Indexes in the 0.50 to 0.59 range were most common. Coloring a donut-shaped design (three items) produced indexes of 0.49 to 0.59 for the target population, 5-year-old children. Generally speaking, the three items of fine eye-hand coordination, requiring children to draw lines through mazes, were not good discriminators between high and low performers. However, they served to build rapport and motivate continued participation.

Section III: Gross motor. With the exception of tossing a ball into a basket, items in the gross motor section resulted in discrimination indexes between 0.30 and 0.91 for the 5-year-old group. Hopping and skipping items were especially good.

•   •   •

In general, it appears that the items were well selected from a discriminatory standpoint, especially for the 5-year-old group.

Performances of inner city children

Attempts were made to assess the extent of differences in scores between inner city children and others. At each age level, children of both groups were compared on the following scores:

Body awareness (a nonscored section)

Section I: Auditory-visual-motor

Section II: Eye-hand coordination

Section III: Gross motor

Total test score

Means, standard deviations, and t-values are presented in Table 3 (p. 297). At each age level the inner city children had significantly different body awareness scores from the other children. It should be noted that this section is *not* used in assessing a person's total score.

Only three other differences approached statistical significance, and all were on subsection scores. For ages 4 years through 4 years, 5 months, there was a difference between the two groups on Section I: auditory-visual-motor. At the 4 years, 6 months through 4 years, 11 months age level, scores were statistically different on Section III: gross motor. For the children 5 years through 5 years, 5 months, a difference occurred between the inner city and others on Section II: eye-hand coordination.

No *total* score differences between the inner city and other children occurred. In addition there were no consistent patterns of differences among the age group on the scored sections of the test. Therefore it appears that the IMAS serves equally well the inner city and other socioeconomic groups of children.

Table 1. IMAS summary statistics

Score	4 years to 4 years, 5 months			4 years, 6 months to 4 years, 11 months			5 years to 5 years, 5 months			5 years, 6 months to 5 years, 11 months			6 years to 6 years, 5 months			6 years, 6 months to 6 years, 11 months		
	f	Percentile	Stanine	f	Percentile	Stanine	f	Percentile	Stanine	f	Percentile	Stanine	f	Percentile	Stanine	f	Percentile	Stanine
30										1	99	9			9			9
29										1	99	9	2	99	9			8
28							3	99	9	3	98	9			9	1	99	8
27							2	97	9			8	4	96	8			7
26							1	95	8	6	95	7	1	88	8	3	91	6
25							2	94	8	11	90	7	1	87	7	1	66	6
24							4	92	8	7	81	7	4	85	7	3	58	5
23				1	99	9	5	88	7	7	76	7	5	77	6			5
22						9	4	83	7	5	70	6	3	68	6			4
21						9	6	80	7	10	66	6	7	62	5	2	33	4
20				3	98	8	8	74	6	9	58	5	2	50	5			3
19				3	92	8	2	66	6	9	50	5	5	46	4			3
18				2	86	7	6	65	6	9	43	5	7	37	4	1	16	2
17	1	99	9	1	83	7	4	59	5	9	36	4	4	24	4			2
16	3	97	8	5	81	6	7	55	5	3	28	4	2	16	3			1
15			8	6	71	6	9	49	4	9	26	3	1	12	3	1	8	1
14	2	90	7	6	60	5	9	40	4	7	18	3	1	11	2			
13	1	86	7	3	49	5	8	32	4	3	13	3	1	9	2			
12	4	84	6	4	43	5	7	24	3	3	10	2	2	7	1			

	1	2	3	4	5	6	7	8	9	10	11
		2	3								1

Frequency distribution (by raw-score row):

Score											
11	8	75	6	5	35	4	6	17	3	4	8	2
10	9	56	5	3	26	4	3	12	3	1	4	1
9	2	36	5	3	20	3			2	4	4	1
8	1	31	4	2	15	3	6	9	2			1
7	2	29	4	2	11	2	1	3	2	1	1	1
6	2	25	3	1	7	2	1	2	1			1
5	3	20	3			1			1			
4	3	13	2			1	2	1	1			
3			2	3	5	1						
2	2	6	1									
1	1	2	1									

	N = 44	N = 53	N = 106	N = 122	N = 54	N = 12
Total N	44	53	106	122	54	12
Mean	9.46	13.04	16.41	19.19	20.18	23.25
Standard deviation	3.86	4.48	5.52	5.03	4.40	3.72
Twenty-fifth percentile	6.50	10.25	12.56	15.33	17.57	22.0
Fiftieth percentile	10.17	13.58	15.64	19.39	20.50	24.17
Seventy-fifth percentile	11.50	15.85	20.58	23.29	23.20	25.83

Table 2. IMAS item analyses—discriminant indexes

Item	4 years to 4 years, 5 months	4 years, 6 months to 4 years, 11 months	5 years to 5 years, 5 months	5 years, 6 months to 5 years, 11 months	6 years to 6 years, 11 months
Section I: Auditory-visual-motor					
Clap-tap sequence					
1	0.42	0.14	0.07	0	0.07
2	0.59	0.28	0.31	0.12	0.27
3	0.42	0.21	0.52	0.52	0.14
4	0.51	0.49	0.31	0.39	0.48
5	0.51	0.49	0.49	0.61	0.62
6	0.17	0.14	0.35	0.46	0.21
7	0.17	0.14	0.45	0.55	0.62
8	0.08	0.14	0.56	0.64	0.69
9	0.25	0.21	0.38	0.58	0.69
10	0.08	0.14	0.35	0.39	0.48
Section II: Eye-hand coordination (fine manual-motor coordination)					
Snapping fingers	0.34	0.49	0.63	0.49	0.55
Rabbit eating lettuce					
Wiggle fingers	0.34	0.35	0.35	0.27	0.27
Wrist action	0.51	0.56	0.59	0.52	0.34
Coloring donut					
Color outside donut	0.34	0.56	0.35	0.30	0.27
Color inside donut	0.59	0.49	0.35	0.15	0.27
Color complete donut	0.42	0.56	0.49	0.18	0.21
Fine eye-hand with pencil					
Straight alley	0	−0.07	0	0.03	0
Curved alley	0.34	0.56	0.31	0.33	0.14
Fish	0.42	0.28	0.35	0.21	0
Section III: Gross motor (control of large muscle groups)					
Balancing on one foot					
Balance on right foot	0.34	0.49	0.35	0.30	0.27
Balance on left foot	0.42	0.70	0.31	0.49	0.34
Stationary hopping					
20 hops dominant foot	0	0.35	0.66	0.79	0.41
15 hops nondominant foot	0.08	0.28	0.77	0.91	0.34
Skipping	0.17	0.63	0.73	0.58	0.55
Toss yarn ball into basket	0.42	0.14	0.17	0.09	
Catching yarn ball	0.42	0.07	0.63	0.43	0.34
Toss and catch ball	0.34	0.35	0.70	0.49	0.34

Table 3. Comparisons of scores for inner city (IC) and other children

Age	Variable*	Mean		Standard deviation		t Value
		IC	Other	IC	Other	
4 years through 4 years, 5 months	1	5.62	8.40	1.84	2.06	-4.719§
	2	1.92	3.30	1.38	2.08	-2.638†
Culturally deprived N=24	3	4.38	4.60	2.16	2.06	-0.351
Other N=20	4	2.79	2.05	1.88	1.50	1.420
	5	9.04	9.95	3.95	3.90	-0.764
4 years, 6 months through 4 years, 11 months	1	6.79	8.89	2.17	2.18	-3.371‡
	2	3.00	3.95	1.44	2.22	-1.885
Culturally deprived N=34	3	5.85	5.58	2.36	2.39	0.403
Other N=19	4	4.91	2.21	2.34	1.69	4.423§
	5	13.73	11.79	4.32	4.74	1.519
5 years through 5 years, 5 months	1	7.69	9.49	1.83	1.87	-4.277§
	2	4.19	4.86	1.96	2.55	-1.224
Culturally deprived N=26	3	5.58	6.91	2.52	2.31	-2.504†
Other N=80	4	5.81	4.98	2.53	2.68	1.394
	5	15.54	16.69	4.92	5.734	-0.917
5 years, 6 months through 5 years, 11 months	1	8.42	9.99	2.06	1.86	-3.329‡
	2	5.16	5.42	1.98	2.41	-0.443
Culturally deprived N=19	3	7.16	7.76	2.54	1.88	-1.206
Other N=103	4	6.95	5.87	2.59	2.60	1.655
	5	19.26	19.17	5.34	5.02	0.070
6 years through 6 years, 5 months	1	8.53	10.05	2.33	1.56	-2.783‡
	2	5.53	5.79	2.45	1.87	-0.422
Culturally deprived N=15	3	7.87	8.10	1.85	2.02	-0.393
Other N=39	4	7.07	6.21	2.25	1.88	1.427
	5	20.47	20.08	4.97	4.29	0.286

†P<.05
‡P<.01
§P<.001

*Variable 1—Body awareness
Variable 2—Section I: Auditory-visual-motor
Variable 3—Section II: Eye-hand coordination
Variable 4—Section III: Gross motor
Variable 5—Total test

Table 4. IMAS Summary statistics for subsections*

Score	Section I: Auditory-visual-motor			Section II: Eye-hand coordination			Section III: Gross motor			Score
	f	Percentile	Stanine	f	Percentile	Stanine	f	Percentile	Stanine	
10			9			9			9	10
9			9	1	99	9			9	9
8			9	1	97	8			9	8
7	1	99	9	8	95	7	7	99	9	7
6	1	97	9	5	77	6	1	97	9	6
5	3	95	8	7	65	6	3	95	8	5
4	10	88	7	5	50	5	7	88	7	4
3	6	65	5	8	38	4	10	72	6	3
2	9	52	4	6	20	3	6	50	4	2
1	7	31	3	3	6	2	10	36	3	1
0	7	15	2			1	6	13	2	0
Total N		44			44			44		
Mean		2.54			4.48			2.45		
Standard deviation		1.83			2.07			1.72		
Twenty-fifth percentile		1.07			2.75			1.00		
Fiftieth percentile		2.39			4.50			2.50		
Seventy-fifth percentile		3.90			6.30			3.64		

*Ages 4 years through 4 years, 5 months.

Table 5. IMAS summary statistics for subsections*

Score	Section I: Auditory-visual-motor			Section II: Eye-hand coordination			Section III: Gross motor			Score
	f	Percentile	Stanine	f	Percentile	Stanine	f	Percentile	Stanine	
10			9	2	99	9	2	99	9	10
9	1	99	9	6	96	8	2	96	9	9
8	2	98	9	4	84	7			8	8
7	3	94	8	9	77	6	4	92	7	7
6	5	88	7	11	60	5	3	84	7	6
5	11	79	6	5	39	4	8	79	6	5
4	14	58	5	5	30	3	12	64	5	4
3	10	32	3	3	20	3	6	41	4	3
2	5	13	2	8	15	2	7	30	3	2
1	2	3	1			1	5	16	3	1
0							4	7	2	0
Total N	53			53			53			
Mean	3.34			5.75			3.94			
Standard deviation	1.78			2.33			2.46			
Twenty-fifth percentile	2.13			3.95			2.11			
Fiftieth percentile	3.18			6.00			3.88			
Seventy-fifth percentile	4.30			7.36			5.22			

*Ages 4 years, 6 months through 4 years, 11 months.

Table 6. IMAS summary statistics for subsections*

Score	Section I: Auditory-visual-motor			Section II: Eye-hand coordination			Section III: Gross motor			Score
	f	Percentile	Stanine	f	Percentile	Stanine	f	Percentile	Stanine	
10	2	99	9	17	99	8	7	99	9	10
9	3	98	9	7	83	7	8	93	8	9
8	13	95	8	19	77	6	9	85	7	8
7	12	83	7	9	59	5	9	77	6	7
6	8	71	6	21	50	5	14	68	6	6
5	14	64	5	13	31	4	13	55	5	5
4	17	50	4	10	18	3	14	43	4	4
3	14	34	4	3	9	2	13	30	3	3
2	13	21	3	5	6	1	11	17	3	2
1	9	9	2				6	7	2	1
0	1	1	1	2	1	1	2	1	1	0
Total N	106			106			106			
Mean	4.70			6.58			5.18			
Standard deviation	2.42			2.41			2.64			
Twenty-fifth percentile	2.75			5.00			3.08			
Fiftieth percentile	4.44			6.45			5.04			
Seventy-fifth percentile	6.79			8.37			7.22			

*Ages 5 years through 5 years, 5 months.

Table 7. IMAS summary statistics for subsections*

Score	Section I: Auditory-visual-motor			Section II: Eye-hand coordination			Section III: Gross motor			Score
	f	Percentile	Stanine	f	Percentile	Stanine	f	Percentile	Stanine	
10	4	99	9	20	99	7	8	99	8	10
9	7	96	8	30	83	6	16	93	7	9
8	17	90	7	25	59	5	19	80	7	8
7	18	77	6	20	38	4	19	64	6	7
6	9	62	6	12	22	3	9	49	5	6
5	17	54	5	3	12	2	15	41	4	5
4	17	40	4	5	9	1	15	29	3	4
3	22	27	3	5	5	1	8	17	3	3
2	8	9	2	1	1	1	6	10	2	2
1	2	2	1	1	1	1	3	5	1	1
0	1	1	1				4	3	1	0
Total N	122			122			122			
Mean	5.38			7.66			6.04			
Standard deviation	2.33			1.99			2.61			
Twenty-fifth percentile	3.39			6.67			4.13			
Fiftieth percentile	5.15			8.06			6.55			
Seventy-fifth percentile	7.36			9.15			8.16			

*Ages 5 years, 6 months through 5 years, 11 months.

Table 8. IMAS summary statistics for subsections*

Score	Section I: Auditory-visual-motor			Section II: Eye-hand coordination			Section III: Gross motor			Score
	f	Percentile	Stanine	f	Percentile	Stanine	f	Percentile	Stanine	
10	3	99	9	15	99	7	3	99	9	10
9	3	94	8	10	72	6	8	94	8	9
8	5	88	7	14	53	5	5	79	7	8
7	7	79	6	6	27	4	11	70	6	7
6	7	66	5	2	16	3	9	50	5	6
5	13	53	4	3	12	2	7	33	4	5
4	9	29	3	2	7	1	8	20	3	4
3	6	12	2	1	3	1	2	5	2	3
2	1	1	1	1	1	1	1	1	1	2
1			1			1			1	1
0			1						1	0
Total N	54			54			54			
Mean	5.72			8.04			6.44			
Standard deviation	2.00			1.94			1.99			
Twenty-fifth percentile	4.22			7.25			4.86			
Fiftieth percentile	5.35			8.36			6.50			
Seventy-fifth percentile	7.14			9.60			8.00			

*Ages 6 years through 6 years, 5 months.

Table 9. IMAS summary statistics for subsections*

Score	Section I: Auditory-visual-motor			Section II: Eye-hand coordination			Section III: Gross motor			Score
	f	Percentile	Stanine	f	Percentile	Stanine	f	Percentile	Stanine	
10			9	1	99	9	6	99	6	10
9	1	99	8	3	91	7	3	50	5	9
8	2	91	7	5	66	5	1	25	5	8
7	5	75	6	3	25	2			4	7
6	1	33	4			1	1	16	3	6
5	1	25	3			1			2	5
4	2	16	2			1			1	4
3			1			1			1	3
2			1				1	8	1	2
1			1						1	1
0			1						1	0
Total N	12			12			12			
Mean	6.58			8.17			8.50			
Standard deviation	1.50			0.90			2.40			
Twenty-fifth percentile	5.50			7.50			8.50			
Fiftieth percentile	6.90			8.10			9.50			
Seventy-fifth percentile	7.50			8.83			10.00			

*Ages 6 years, 6 months through 6 years, 11 months.

Test booklet

Name_____Date_____

Sex_____Date of birth_____Age_____Yrs_____Mos

School_____Examiner_____

Summary of observational sections

I. Eye control (areas to check)

☐ Binocular
☐ Monocular
☐ Convergence
☐ General

II. Dominance (circle)

Eye: R L M*
Hand: R L M
Foot: R L M

III. Body awareness (12 maximum)

IV. General (areas to check)

☐ Posture muscle tone
☐ Behavior patterns

Summary of scored sections

Section I: Auditory-visual-motor (10)	Section II: Eye-hand coordination (10)	Section III: Gross motor (10)	Total score (30)
☐	☐	☐	☐

General evaluation or recommendation

☐ Satisfactory
☐ Review progress
☐ Refer for diagnostic case study conference

Suggested follow-up conferences or referrals

☐ Parents
☐ Classroom teacher
☐ Speech therapist
☐ Physical therapist

☐ Special education teacher or coordinator
☐ Occupational therapist
☐ Physical education teacher
☐ Other (specify)

Comments:

*M means mixed dominance.

GENERAL DIRECTIONS

1. Prior to the testing session check the following supplies:
   a. Two yarn balls (approximately 1 oz each)
   b. One standard size classroom wastebasket
   c. One box No. 8 crayons
   d. One primary pencil (no eraser)
   e. One regular No. 2 pencil with eraser
   f. Watch with second hand
   g. Roll of masking tape
   h. IMAS Child's Work Sheet (p. 321)
   i. Performance guidelines
2. Construct a 1-foot square on the floor using the masking tape.
3. Prepare chairs on opposite sides of a table for child and examiner. Be sure chair and table are appropriate working height for the child.
4. Conduct the first three observational sections.
5. During the administration of the scored sections record observations in the space provided.
6. After the completion of the scored sections, record general observations in the space provided.
7. Transfer scores to the front cover and complete the required information.
8. Refer to the test manual for performance guidelines to assist in making recommendations.

FIRST OBSERVATIONAL SECTION: EYE CONTROL
Binocular pursuits

Directions. Seat the child opposite you. Use the eraser on the end of a pencil as the object to track. Hold the pencil at eye level so the distance from the eraser is approximately the length of the child's arm. Hold child's head steady.

Move the pencil slowly in a *horizontal* arc three times in a range of approximately 18 in to the right and left of center.

Say, "Watch the eraser wherever it goes. Move only your eyes."

Horizontal pursuits:

☐ Smooth movement   ☐ Unable to track
☐ Loss at midline   ☐ Loss at extreme range
☐ Eye rolls in   ☐ Eye rolls out

Move the pencil slowly in a *vertical* arc three times at a range of approximately 18 in above and below eye level.

Vertical pursuits:

☐ Smooth movement   ☐ Unable to track
☐ Loss at midline   ☐ Loss at extreme range
☐ Eye rolls in   ☐ Eye rolls out

Monocular pursuits

Directions. Examiner uses hand to cover child's *left* eye. Be sure child cannot see through or around fingers.

Say, "This time watch the eraser with just *one* eye. Do not move your head."

Move the pencil slowly in a *horizontal* arc three times in a range of approximately 18 in to the right and left of center.

Say, "Watch the eraser wherever it goes. Move only your eyes."

Move the pencil slowly in a *vertical* arc three times at a range of approximately 18 in above and below eye level.

Cover the child's *right* eye.

Repeat procedures for *horizontal* pursuit.

Repeat procedures for *vertical* pursuit.

Horizontal pursuits:

Right eye: ☐ Smooth   ☐ Loss (specify)
Left eye: ☐ Smooth   ☐ Loss (specify)
Comments:

Vertical pursuits:

Right eye: ☐ Smooth   ☐ Loss (specify)
Left eye: ☐ Smooth   ☐ Loss (specify)
Comments:

Convergence

Directions. Hold the pencil approximately 20 in from the child's head at eye level.

Say, "Watch the eraser wherever it goes."

Move the pencil slowly toward the child's nose. Stop approximately 4 in from the face. Hold in this position for two seconds.

Do the procedure three times.

On the third trial say, "Look at me. Now look back at the pencil."

☐ Smooth	☐ Slow	☐ Uneven/jerky
Eye remains	☐ Right	☐ Left
stationary:		
Eye rolls:	☐ Right in	☐ Right out
	☐ Left in	☐ Left out

General eye condition

Directions. Indicate any eye conditions observed that are not covered above.

☐ Frequent blinking	☐ Red	☐ Watering
Other:		

SECOND OBSERVATIONAL SECTION: DOMINANCE

Directions. Have the child stand in the masking tape square that was made prior to the testing session. Read each instruction to the child. Check the preferred eye, hand, or foot. Within each section dominance is R (all right), L (all left), or M (mixed right and left).

1. *Eye preference* **Right** **Left**

Make an O with your thumb and a finger and look ☐ ☐
    through it at my nose.
Look at me through this tube (rolled paper). ☐ ☐
Look through this hole (tear in paper). ☐ ☐
               Eye dominance (circle)   R   L   M

2. *Hand Preference*
Show me how you brush your teeth. ☐ ☐
Make me a circle in the air with your entire arm. ☐ ☐
Show me how you throw a ball. ☐ ☐
              Hand dominance (circle)   R   L   M

3. *Foot preference*
Show me how you kick a ball. ☐ ☐
Step on this yarn ball with one foot (place yarn ball ☐ ☐
    on floor directly in front).
Stamp your foot for me three times. ☐ ☐
              Foot dominance (circle)   R   L   M

THIRD OBSERVATIONAL SECTION: BODY AWARENESS

Directions. Position the child facing you. Say, "Touch your nose." Do not demonstrate. Continue in the same manner for each item below. Place a check for each correct identification.

1. Nose	☐	7. Wrists	☐
2. Ears	☐	8. Eyebrows	☐
3. Shoulders	☐	9. Index finger	☐
4. Elbows	☐	10. Middle finger	☐
5. Knees	☐	11. Chin	☐
6. Ankles	☐	12. Waist	☐

TOTAL BODY AWARENESS ☐

SECTION I: AUDITORY-VISUAL-MOTOR TEST

Directions. Demonstrate several taps (T) by tapping the table top with both hands. Say, "What am I doing?" If necessary, inform the child that you are tapping.

Demonstrate several claps (C). Say, "What am I doing?" If necessary, inform the child that you are clapping.

Say, "We are going to play a clapping-tapping game. I will do it first. Then you do it. Watch carefully, so I don't trick you."

Demonstrate clap, clap, tap (CCT). Have the child repeat the actions. Repeat until child understands the procedure.

Do each action below, and have the child repeat the action. A second trial may be given if the first is unsatisfactory. Be sure to use a delay or pause of 2 seconds where indicated by –.

Mark if incorrect.

Discontinue after three consecutive items are missed.

1. T C	☐ ☐	6. C T C C T	☐ ☐
2. T C T	☐ ☐	7. T C – C T	☐ ☐
3. C C T C	☐ ☐	8. C – T C T	☐ ☐
4. T T – C	☐ ☐	9. T T C – C	☐ ☐
5. C – C C	☐ ☐	10. C – T – T C	☐ ☐

Scoring. 1 point for each item correct within two trials.

TOTAL SCORE FOR SECTION I ☐

Check any behaviors observed:

☐ No recognizable pattern
☐ Perseveration
☐ Hesitation and delay in responding
☐ Unable to wait for completion of directions; impulsive
☐ Lack of integration of two arms. One hand leads other in tapping
☐ Additional kinesthetic feedback needed; loud clapping or tapping
☐ Reversals in pattern sequences

Comments:

SECTION II: EYE-HAND COORDINATION TEST
1. Snapping fingers

Directions. Say, "See if you can snap your fingers like this."
Demonstrate action of snapping with noise several times.
Child may use thumb and middle finger of either hand.

Scoring. 2 points for snapping fingers with snapping   _____
noise.

No partial credit is allowed.

Check any behaviors observed:
- ☐ No noise
- ☐ Picks nail
- ☐ Slow to plan action (even with repeated demonstration)
- ☐ Unable to attempt action (even with repeated demonstration)

Comments:

2. Rabbit saying "hello"

Directions. Say, "Place your elbow on the table. Now, put
your fingers like this."

Demonstrate by positioning first and second fingers to
make the letter "V" while thumb is over the bent ring and
little finger. Help the child if necessary.

Say, "This is a rabbit. Here are his two ears."

Demonstrate by wiggling or bending both "ear" fingers.
The primary movement is bending the fingers at the two upper joints. Repeat several times.

Say, "Make *your* rabbit wiggle his ears."

Scoring. 1 point for wiggling ears, bending primarily at   _____
the two upper joints.

Say, "Now, bend your wrist up and down, making your
rabbit say "Hello" like this."

Demonstrate bending hand at wrist several times.

Say, "Now, make *your* rabbit say, 'Hello.'"

Scoring. 1 point for bending wrist up and down. Give   _____
credit if there is definite wrist action. Movement at elbow is
acceptable.

Check any behaviors observed:
Finger action
    ☐ Unable to plan action of thumb to fingers
    ☐ Unable to maintain thumb position
    ☐ Unable to bend fingers at upper joints (only at base of fingers)
    ☐ Unable to repeat bending action of fingers
    ☐ Overflow movements; where?
Comments:

Wrist action
    ☐ Lacks isolated movement of wrist
    ☐ Unable to repeat action several times in succession
    ☐ Overflow movements; where?
Comments:

3. Coloring within a donut

    Directions. Fold the child's work sheet so that only the donut design is visible. Place the work sheet in front of the child.
    Say, "This is a donut."
    Point to the blank portion. Then mark an arc in the blank portion with a crayon. Give the child a crayon.
    Say, "See how carefully you can color the rest of it in. Go all the way to to this line (point to outer edge of ring). Go all the say down to this line (point to the inner edge of the ring). Be sure to stay inside the lines. Fill it all in and don't turn the paper. Do it as quickly as you can."
    Time limit. 60 sec.
    Scoring
        1 point for coloring flush with the outer edge of ring. _____
        1 point for coloring down to the inner edge of the ring. _____
        1 point for coloring the blank portion completely (no _____
            white spaces).

Check any behaviors observed:

Grasp of crayon
- ☐ Primitive
- ☐ Between index and middle fingers

Control of fingers and wrist
- ☐ Uses fingers only
- ☐ Frequent repositioning of crayon
- ☐ Light pressure
- ☐ Heavy pressure
- ☐ Makes only marks in area to color

Position of head
- ☐ Head tilted to right
- ☐ Head tilted to left
- ☐ Head close to or resting on table

Perceptual organization
- ☐ Colors in one direction only
  - Horizontal ☐   Vertical ☐
- ☐ Rotates paper
- ☐ Makes frequent adjustments of
  - body ☐   head ☐
- ☐ Fails to follow directions; colors entire donut
- ☐ Distracted by visual stimuli

Comments:

4. Straight alley

Directions. Fold the child's work sheet so that only the straight alley design is visible. Place the work sheet in front of the child.

Place two pencils (one primary and one regular No. 2) in front of the child. Have the child select one of the pencils.

Say, "Draw a line from the mouse to the cheese down the middle of the road."

Place a mark on the edge of the mouse, point down the road, and place a mark on the edge of the cheese as the instructions are given.

Say, "Be careful to stay inside the lines. Go down the middle of the road."

Scoring. 1 point for line drawn within path (may touch path's edge). _____

5. Maze

Directions. Fold the child's work sheet so only the fish-worm maze design is visible. Place the work sheet in front of the child.

Say, "This fish is hungry. Draw a line from the fish to the worm going between the rocks."

Make a mark on the nose of the fish, begin to draw a line between the first two rocks, then make a mark on the worm.

Say, "Be careful you don't touch the rocks. Take the shortest way between the rocks."

Scoring. 1 point for line from fish to worm. The line may touch edge of rocks but may not run through any. Any route between the rocks is acceptable. _____

6. Curved alley

Directions. Fold the child's work sheet so only the curved alley design is visible. Place it on table facing the child.

Say, "This time see if you can make the boy walk down this crooked road to his bicycle."

Place a mark on the boy, begin to draw a line into the road, then make a mark on the bicycle as the instructions are given.

Say, "Be careful to go down the middle of this crooked road with your pencil. Don't go off the road."

Scoring. 1 point for line drawn within path. Line may touch edge of path. _____

TOTAL SCORE FOR SECTION II

Observations of pencil and paper activities 4, 5, 6

Check any behaviors observed:

Grasp of pencil
- ☐ Primitive (palmar grasp)
- ☐ Between index and middle fingers
- ☐ Other

Pressure with pencil
- ☐ Hard
- ☐ Soft

Lack of control of wrist and fingers
- ☐ Uses only fingers
- ☐ Frequent repositioning of pencil
- ☐ Change of pencil angle at midline (should be pointing toward shoulder)
- ☐ Change of pencil angle throughout activity

Head position
- ☐ Head tilted to right
- ☐ Head tilted to left
- ☐ Head too close to paper
- ☐ Head resting on table

Body position
- ☐ Shifts body at midline
- ☐ Shifts body throughout activities
- ☐ Rotates paper

Perceptual organization
- ☐ Works from right to left
- ☐ Distracted by visual stimuli
- ☐ Fails to wait for completion of directions before beginning; impulsive
- ☐ Needs repeated instructions
- ☐ Needs encouragement

Comments:

SECTION III: GROSS MOTOR TEST
1. Balancing on each foot, hands on head

Directions. Have the child stand on the floor in the masking tape square that was made prior to the testing session.

Have the child face you. Instruct the child to put his hands on top of his head.

Say, "I want to see how long you can balance on one foot in this square. Now lift *this* leg up."

Touch the left leg of the child to show which leg to lift.

Say, "Be sure to keep your hands on top of your head while you balance. I will count slowly to ten."

Give a second trial *if* child does not succeed on first attempt. Child must remain standing inside the square for credit.

Repeat procedures above for other foot.

Record number of seconds balanced for each foot (10-sec maximum).

Right_____   Left_____

Scoring. 1 point for each foot. Balance must be held for 10 _____ seconds.

Check any behaviors observed:
☐ Unable to remain in square
☐ Unable to remain facing examiner (turns)
☐ Lacks kinesthetic feedback
   ☐ Wobbles
   ☐ Tense, wraps one leg around the other
   ☐ Sways
☐ Trunk leaning
☐ Unable to keep hands on top of head
Comments:

2. Stationary hopping on each foot

Directions. Have the child stand inside the taped square.
Say, "See how many times you can hop on this foot."
Tap your own *right* leg to show which foot to hop on.
Say, "Stay inside the box and stay facing me. Do not stop until I say time."
Observe hopping for 10 sec.
Give a second trial if the child does not seem to understand the procedure. Urge the child to continue even if he stops or interrupts his hopping. Observe his endurance.
Repeat procedures above for other foot.
Record number of hops *until* a stop or interruption within 10 sec time limit.

Right_____   Left_____   Total_____

Scoring. 1 point for 20 or more hops without stopping on _____
dominant foot within time limit.
1 point for 15 or more hops without stopping on nondom- _____
inant foot within time limit.
1 point for 50 or more hops total without stopping within _____
time limit.

Check any behaviors observed:
☐ Unable to remain in square
☐ Must turn as hopping
☐ Stops frequently
☐ Out of breath
☐ Unable to maintain hopping for 10 sec: Right ☐ Left ☐
Comments:

3. Skipping at least 10 ft

Directions. Say, "Do you know how to skip? See if you can skip to the wall and back."
Demonstrate if child cannot automatically initiate pattern.

Scoring. 2 points for maintenance of good skipping with   _____
reciprocal arm swing and leg pattern. No partial credit given.

Check any behaviors observed:
- ☐ Lacks flow, done in a stiff manner
- ☐ Gallops: ☐ Right foot held back   ☐ Left foot held back
- ☐ No pattern
- ☐ Unable to jump with both feet together
- ☐ Unable to hop: ☐ Right foot   ☐ Left foot

Comments:

4. Tossing a yarn ball underhand into a wastebasket

Directions. Have child stand in the taped square. Place wastebasket 6 ft in front of child.

Say, "See if you can toss the yarn ball into the basket like this."

Demonstrate tossing the yarn ball *underhanded* into the basket.

If necessary, give the child two attempts.

Scoring. 1 point if toss is successful within two trials.   _____

Check any behaviors observed:
- ☐ Lacks control in tossing at basket
  - ☐ Tosses upward
  - ☐ Tosses to side
- ☐ Unable to toss underhand; able to do overhand throw
- ☐ Unable to control toss to self; tosses too high, away from body

Comments:

5. Catching a yarn ball

Directions. Say, "This time I'm going to toss the ball to you. Catch it with your two hands in front of you and not with your body."

If necessary, give the child two attempts.

Scoring. 1 point if catch is successful within two trials. No credit for trapping the ball against the chest.   ____

6. Tossing and catching a yarn ball

Directions. Say, "This time I want you to toss the ball up in the air and catch it. Do not toss it too high. I will show you what I mean."

Demonstrate the procedure by stretching arms to the fully extended position above your head. Hold the ball in one hand.

Say, "I will toss my ball as high as my hands." Demonstrate.

Say, "Now, it's *your* turn. Stretch your arms as high as you can holding your ball. That is how high I want *you* to toss *your* ball. Now, see if you can toss the ball up and catch it yourself while you stand in the box."

Two trials may be given if necessary.

Scoring. 1 point for catching yarn ball with extended arms within the two trials. No credit for trapping the ball against the chest.

TOTAL SCORE FOR SECTION III

5-6. Catching and tossing and catching a yarn ball

Check any behaviors observed:
- ☐ Lacks control of hands and eyes (misses object)
- ☐ Lacks automatic movement of arms toward object (arms held in cupped position)
- ☐ Protective blinking of eyes as object approaches body
- ☐ Hands cover face in protective manner
- ☐ Unable to remain in tape square when tossing and catching

Comments:

GENERAL OBSERVATIONAL SECTION

1. Posture and muscle tone

Check any behaviors observed:

Fatigue postures
- ☐ Head held forward
- ☐ Head tilted
- ☐ Mouth open
- ☐ Dark circles under eyes
- ☐ Rounded shoulders, arms rotated inward, held close to body
- ☐ Bent hips, protruding abdomen, bottom out
- ☐ Knees held back in hyperextension
- ☐ "Knock-kneed" (knees together, feet apart)
- ☐ "Pigeon-toed" (feet point inward)
- ☐ "Flat-feet" (lacks longitudinal arch in foot)

Flexibility of body
- ☐ Tense, rigid, wraps one leg around the other
- ☐ Clumsy, floppy, stumbles and falls frequently
- ☐ Slow to initiate, hesitates to begin activities

Comments:

2. Patterns of behavior during testing

Check any behaviors observed:

- ☐ Distracted by visual stimuli
- ☐ Distracted by auditory stimuli
- ☐ Restless, wiggles, constantly moves in chair
    - ☐ Throughout testing
    - ☐ Only under stress when tasks become difficult
- ☐ Low motivation
- ☐ Loss of interest rapidly
- ☐ Giggles, laughs inappropriately
- ☐ Verbalizes excessively
    - ☐ Throughout testing
    - ☐ Says tasks are "too hard"
    - ☐ Says tasks are "too easy"
- ☐ Needs directions repeated more than twice
- ☐ Perseveration
- ☐ Impulsive

Comments:

IMAS CHILD'S WORK SHEET

Name_____ Date_____

II. 3. Coloring within a donut

II. 4. Straight alley

Continued.

IMAS CHILD's WORKSHEET—cont'd

II. 5. Maze

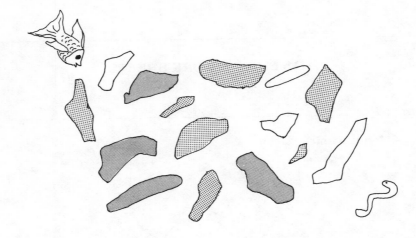

II. 6. Curved alley

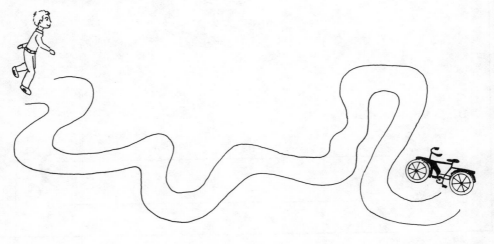

APPENDIX B

Case studies

Case study 1

This case study is presented with the primary purpose of showing that with appropriate early intervention the motor manifestation of cerebral palsy can be prevented or eliminated.

J. was a 5 lb, 11 oz nonidentical twin of 36- to 37-weeks gestation, born Jan. 29, 1976. His Apgar score was 6, with 1 off for tone and activity and 2 off for color, at 1 minute, and 9, with 1 off for tone, at 5 minutes. The newborn examination was consistent with a male of 36- to 37-week gestation. Neonatal difficulties included mild hyperbilirubinemia (less than 10 mg/100 ml) and low body temperature, requiring intermittent use of a warmer.

When J. was 2 months old, his mother noted that he had poor head control, continued difficulty in breast feeding, and occasional opisthotonus, with stiffness of arms and legs. His head circumference had gone from the third percentile to the fifth and was asymmetrical. The child was referred to a pediatric neurologist for evaluation.

The 4-month neurological evaluation showed that the head remained at the fifth percentile but symmetrical. The child's thumbs were inside fists, his arms were flexed at the elbows, and his legs scissored when he was suspended and showed little steppage or support reactions. The Moro reflex was moderately active. A strong grasp was demonstrated, but when the child was pulled to a sitting position there was marked head lag. Muscle stretch reflexes were 3+, and plantar stimulation produced withdrawal but without toe extension. The diagnosis was cerebral palsy, specific cause unknown. On May 11, 1976, at 4 months of age, he was referred to physical therapy by the pediatrician.

Physical therapy evaluation showed poor oral activity. The tongue was hypersensitive, producing a gagging-thrusting motion on contact. The lips did not purse to encircle the nipple. His mother was holding the breast in his mouth and at times working his mandible to assist him to feed in a period of 45 minutes.

In the prone position he could lift his head and support himself on his extended arms, but his head was tilted to the left. His left eye showed moderate internal strabismus. When he was held horizontally with support un-

323

der the abdomen, his head could be held in line with the trunk for only 5 to 10 seconds. There was excessive tone in his arms and legs. When placed in the sitting position, he demonstrated a strong extensor pattern, making it impossible to maintain the position.

Treatment taught to the mother included:

1. Tongue walking with finger to densensitize tongue and gentle rubbing of gums, cheeks, and roof of mouth
2. Vibration around mouth to desensitize skin over orbicularis oris and assist pursing of lips
3. Maintained contact on upper lip with finger to maintain sucking activity
4. Tummy kneading (Corley) to decrease excessive tone
5. Inverted position and vibration of midline back extensors from occiput to buttocks for 2 to 3 minutes each time the diaper was changed
6. Construction of a flexion seat (Corley) to be used for positioning in total flexion
7. A sequence of activities that altered position from flexion seat to prone to seat to supine at approximately 30 to 45 minute intervals.

By June 15, 1976, J. was showing complete extension of trunk when held under the abdomen; legs were almost in line with trunk and arms were at shoulder level and beginning to reach over head. The head remained slightly tilted to the left. When the child was suspended under the arms, the asymmetrical tonic neck reflex pattern was completely integrated. Both arms were flexed and hands came together in midline. The legs were flexed and extended alternately as he rubbed his feet together. The tongue was flattened nicely when he cried, and he was nursing in 15 to 20 minutes maximum.

By the middle of July a larger flexion chair had to be made to position him correctly. Within 10 minutes of his being seated in a properly fitting chair, the excessive extension was under control, and he was playing with his toes. (When children are in this type of program, their muscle tone and related problems can worsen or be corrected in a matter of hours or days.) J. was rolling both to the right and to the left from prone to supine and supine to prone. He was supporting himself with his arms and pivoting around in a circle. In this extended position he was able to bend his knees and rub his feet together freely.

By the middle of August J. was up on his hands and knees rocking. He showed some scapular instability on the right side. He was beginning to go from all fours position to sitting and back.

In September he was given the run of the house to explore in creeping. There was some internal rotation of his arms. In sitting he continued to show an infantile total C curve of the back.

The therapy during these months consisted primarily of directing the developmental activities—providing vibration to particular muscles that appeared lacking in specific patterns and tendon pressure inhibition to any muscles showing even slight tightness.

In November, at 10 months of age, he was reevaluated by the pediatric neurologist who noted that he showed "a great deal of progress!!" He was sitting, babbling, and transferring objects and was socially responsive. The muscle stretch reflexes were still "extremely brisk"; no clonus was noted. He demonstrated an infantile lumbar curve when sitting and tended to "slip" when suspended by the armpits.

In January he began to rotate around the body axis in sitting, and within a matter of days he developed a normal lumbar curve in sitting. He was pulling to standing and walking sideways (cruising) around furniture.

In February, at 13 months of age, he was walking independently very well. He could carry an object, patty-cake while walking, and change from erect to squat to erect position at will without holding on.

J. has shown very little difficulty in the early childhood years and is a very active boy. When he was 3 years old he was started in nursery school to provide more structure and an opportunity for social interaction in a restricted environment.

At 4 years, 5 months J. was screened with the IMAS to determine his prekindergarten readiness. On the binocular pursuits he continuously lost the target both horizontally and vertically, primarily at the midline. There was considerable head movement. On the monocular pursuits he was unable to follow horizontally without head movement. There was more difficulty with the right eye. Also the right eye was unable to follow the vertical pursuits. He was able to converge at near point but could not hold the position.

He showed strong right eye and right hand dominance but mixed foot dominance. Two of the activities were done with the left foot and one with the right foot.

He named all of the body parts appropriate for his age level. He missed all of the parts above his age level.

He received a score of one (1) on the auditory-visual-motor activities. He was impulsive, would not wait for the demonstration to be finished, perseverated one pattern, and was constantly distracted visually, requiring excessive auditory clues to watch and wait.

He received a score of three (3) on the eye-hand coordination activities. He was slow to motor plan, with difficulty in wrist and finger differentiation. In the coloring activity he tilted his head and was much too close to the paper. He was aware when he went outside the lines. He showed a tendency to go from right to left. Again, as in most activities, he was impulsive and would not wait for all the directions.

He received a score of one (1) on the gross motor activities. He was very tense in his balancing and demonstrated problems with kinesthetic feedback. He could not stay in the square nor could he maintain his balance for 10 seconds. He, of course, then could not hop without the one-legged balance. His skipping also had no pattern. In the ball activities he lacked good eye-hand coordination.

In summary, when the 4-year scores were used, he was below average in all the scored items. However, when the 4-year, 6-month scores were used he dropped to the low range on auditory-visual and total score. He was only 16 days from the 4-year, 6-month level, which puts him at the borderline; there is cause for concern. His eyes are definitely in trouble, which is undoubtedly contributing to his attending skill difficulty. He needs intervention **now** to assure his readiness for kindergarten.

In conclusion, we would like to emphasize the importance of follow-up and readiness screening. This is a beautiful, healthy, alert, normal-appearing child, but he is going to have difficulty in school unless his deficits are corrected. We must remember that we are concerned about the physical, emotional, intellectual, and spiritual growth of this child.

Case study 2

This case study is presented in depth to demonstrate several points. The first point is that the most valuable 2 years and 4 months of this child's life was essentially wasted. It was worse then wasted because inappropriate sensorimotor patterns were allowed and encouraged. Spasticity was increased by passive range of motion and inappropriate handling procedures. The second point is how progress can be repeatedly interrupted and hampered by additional medical complications, in this case, bladder infections, ear infections, and sore throats. The third point is to demonstrate the continuous altering of the program as dictated by progress or lack of progress. The fourth point is to illustrate that nutrition is an integral part of any intervention program.

M. was born on April 29, 1975, 2 months premature. She weighed 3 lb, 11 oz. During the first 10 months of life she did not sleep more than 2 hours at a time because of colic. In February 1976, at 11 months of age, she was evaluated by a pediatric neurologist. She was said to have slow reflexes and could be classified as cerebral palsied. No treatment was indicated, the neurologist saying, "Just take her home, love her, and move her arms and legs; when she begins to sit up, contact me, we may want to do some physical therapy."

In March 1976 she had eye surgery for internal strabismus of both eyes. After the surgery she was a changed child, sleeping more regularly and having less colic. She developed a virus infection, laryngitis, and an ear infection the day after she went home from the hospital, which lengthened her recovery time.

She was referred to a Cerebral Palsy Clinic for the baby class. The treatment program consisted of passive range of motion and cross-legged sitting. In May, at her first orthopedic evaluation, she was at the 5-month level. In January 1977 she was doing many 15- to 18-month-old activities.

On Aug. 24, 1977, at 2 years, 4 months of age, she was referred to Randolph for evaluation and treatment. The Ayres Postrotary Nystagmus Test was administered with the child held in position by her mother. She cried throughout the testing, which made it difficult to observe her eyeballs. However, the nystagmus appeared to be minimal in both excursion and duration. In the inverted position, suspended under the abdomen, she demonstrated only slight neck extension, severe kyphosis of thoracic spine, no lumbar curve, and approximately 45 degrees of hip flexion bilaterally. Neck cocontraction was minimal and not in line with the trunk. In the prone on elbows position the scapulae were widely abducted and unstable. In the folded up all fours position the entire back was rounded in a curved posture. In standing with maximum support at hips, she demonstrated the typical scissor position, with marked equinovalgus that was more pronounced on the right side. In all activities her right side was more involved than her left. The right eyelid drooped and right eye squinted and showed persistent internal strabismus of a moderate degree. The mandible was markedly retracted. Any attempt at language was a gross pattern of overflow with gusty expulsion of one or two words.

Randolph's impressions were:
1. Poorly integrated vestibular system
2. Hypotonic midline extensor muscles with essentially no trunk stability
3. Marked spasticity in flexor, adductor, and internal rotator muscles
4. Very poor oral position, sensation, and function, including tongue, lips, mandible, and breath control

Treatment program was:
1. Extensive vestibular stimulation play: rocking, rolling, bouncing, and swinging
2. Inverted position and vibration of entire midline extensors
3. Total flexion pattern of lower extremities with tendon pressure to inhibit lateral dorsiflexor muscles and vibration to activate the anterior tibial.

The mother was taught how to administer the treatment. Emphasis was placed on incorporating as much of the treatment into the daily activities as possible. She was encouraged to do the vibration for short periods 3 to 5 minutes at a time but many times a day. For instance, each time the diaper was changed, the child was laid across the lap and vibrated while she was undressed.

In September M. was fitted with a pair of Randolph platform shoes to attempt to break up the positive support pattern of the legs. She had a bladder infection, which seemed to increase spasticity and decrease functional ability.

All vestibular stimulation activities that involved straight legs were discontinued in October because of increased extensor thrust. She was placed in the all fours position on a hard surface for motion stimulation, and the tone began to reduce. She was also placed in a flexion seat (Corley box seat) to begin using back extension for cocontraction; also this afforded a better position for manipulative play. An inverted tonic labyrinthine board was made to afford another play position and make it easier for the mother to administer vibration to the back.

In December she had another incident of cold, diarrhea, and bladder infection, which resulted in a 1- to 2-month setback in muscle tone and function.

A reevaluation was done in January 1978. The midline trunk extension had improved markedly, the head was completely extended, the thoracic area was only slightly kyphotic, and the legs were in line with the trunk with slight abduction. The arms were straighter and the right hand was opening more completely and staying open momentarily.

Activities were started on the rocking vestibular board to encourage equilibrium in prone, tailor sitting, and all fours positions. Vibration of the lateral pterygoids and straw sucking was started to correct the retracted mandible.

The March evaluation showed remarkable progress. The Landau position was almost complete and was held for 1 minute. The arms lacked only about 30 degrees of being straight with the trunk. At this point she was 3 years old and had finally attained the 6- to 9-month level of midline back extension. There was essentially no overflow into feet and mouth during hand activities. The speech was remarkably improved, with breath control sustained for 6 to 7 words. Her vocabulary was extensive. Side sitting with feet to the right was possible was a straight back. She was able to lift her right arm to shoulder height and maintain it for a count of ten.

Snapp's deep bone pressure on hands and feet was started as well as his light stimulation in the dark.

Early in April 1978 she was showing some rather remarkable progress in eye function. The right one was no longer squinting. Her visual perception appeared more clear and accurate as evidenced by her verbalization of what she saw in the house. In mid April she developed a severe bladder infection for the third time in 9 months. Within 36 hours she had lost her good eye control, her inverted foot position, and her closed mouth position and was unable to say "Hi" to her grandmother over the phone. Her spasticity was incredibly strong, approaching the level of 3 to 4 months earlier.

She had a complete urinary tract work-up. Her bladder was able to hold 110 ml of urine. There was no indication of kidney damage. The urine, however, was backing up into the kidney. The x-ray films of the urinary tract showed no dislocation of the hips. Two weeks after clearing of the bladder infection, she was toilet trained, staying dry at night.

All previous treatment was terminated and emphasis placed on providing a trophotropic environment. Mother was instructed to return to: (1) inverted position with no vibration to obtain generalized relaxation, (2) tummy kneading (Corley) to decrease muscle tone, (3) all types of slow, rhythmical repetitive movements, and (4) tendon pressure on particularly limiting muscles. As the spasticity was decreased, the treatment was slowly reestablished.

M. did not regain her previous level of physical ability until early in June. She continued to show overflow in her speech. She did, however, make considerable social progress in the 2 months. She was much more responsive to strangers and interested in the unfamiliar. Her social explorations increased markedly, showing confidence and positive expectations.

On June 19 she was again ill with strep throat and a bladder infection. The urologist wanted to do a bladder pressure study and, if the nerves were badly damaged, to put her on medication to prevent urination. The mother would then catheterize her four times a day. His belief was that she would never be toilet trained. The parents refused the study as well as the projected management on the basis that M. was cooperating with toilet-training procedures. By the end of July she was making progress, muscle tone and overflow were at approximately the level they were in early April.

M. participated in the 6-week play group provided by the mothers of five of the children. Her social interactions continued to advance; M. showed real enjoyment of and interest in group activites and beginning level academic tasks.

The major accomplishment from September through December was the completed toilet training! She began to get into the kneeling position on her own. Pelvis position was not good; the right hip was flexed, and weight was carried on the the left knee with evidence of scoliosis.

In January 1979 she showed marked improvement. Her movements were much freer. Her platform shoes were removed for a trail period, The pelvis was assuming a much more normal position, with the scoliosis essentially corrected. M. started separating her knees voluntarily when supine with feet on floor. She started opposing the thumb to all finger tips on the left hand and had the idea on the right hand.

M. started attending nursery school two afternoons a week. Her attendance was frequently interrupted because of illness. On January 22, 1979, she attained the hands and knees position and rocked. On request she took four creeping steps alone.

In March M. received glasses; the vision in her right eye was terribly nearsighted. Deep bone pressure was started on the back, scapulae, and dorsal surface of the hands and arms. Within 2 or 3 days she was moving more freely, to the extent that for the first time she was belly crawling from room to room instead of asking or waiting to be carried.

At the end of April she had another bladder infection in spite of being on sulfisoxazole (Gantrisin). She had not had an infection for the 10 months she had been on this medication. She was hospitalized for a Pseudomonas infection. The x-ray studies showed no reflexing, which might indicate she had developed a neurogenic bladder. The mother began exploring the possibility that the infections were allergic responses.

In May M. was evaluated by an orthopedist for dislocation of hips. Surgery was suggested because of the adductor tone, which was present even during sleep. The parents preferred to try other methods first. A gluteus medius muscle facilitation belt was made to be worn even at night for a period of time.

M. was tested for academic readiness in August. She tested in the good to excellent levels in anything that did not require vision. Her auditory memory age was 9 to 10 years, and her language skills were 5 to 6 years. Her chronological age was 4 years, 3 months.

In August M. had another bladder infection, which did not clear for several weeks. The medical professionals were still not helpful in determining the cause of the repeated bladder infections. The concern was only to administer medication after the infection was present.

At this time M. had been in treatment with Randolph for 2 years. It was believed that a major change in program might be beneficial. The primary problem was still a high level of spasticity, which interfered with desired fine and gross motor activities. She was now able to get into the all fours position very quickly and was beginning to creep. The movement was very slow and restricted. Midline extension had continued to improve; the scoliosis was corrected and controlled. The lower trapezius was evident to the ninth thoracic level. She was doing a lot of sitting between her legs (W sitting), and her feet had returned to the everted position.

In conference with the parents in August, the decision was made to place

M. on Snapp's prenatal exercise program for a trial period. The treatment included:

1. Deep bone pressure with special attention to the consistency of sensorimotor response. It was found that there was a wide discrepancy in her awareness of pressure, especially on her back.
2. Prenatal light touch patterns for release of arms and legs.
3. Tuck (total flexion) pattern to auditory stimulus.
4. Total extension pattern to auditory stimulus.
5. Rest time in inner tube in the dark to reduce muscle tone.
6. Basic crawling pattern with emphasis on the movements of individual extremities on linoleum in oil.

In September the bladder distress recurred in the form of a Klebsiella infection, and she was placed on cephalex in monohydrate (Keflex).

By October M.'s movements were much freer, especially in the oil on linoleum. She was coming to the kneeling position and throwing herself forward into the oil and sliding 2 to 3 ft on the linoleum. Her Moro reflex was essentially controlled in the freedom and enjoyment of sliding in the oil. She was able to go from W sitting to legs out in front sitting independently by using her hands to bring one leg at a time around in front.

An airplane type creeper (Corley) was built to encourage a creeping pattern and increase floor mobility. Within a few days she had learned to come to a kneeling position on the creeper and begun knee walking.

A figure eight light cotton cord device was constructed by M.'s mother to provide constant inhibitor pressure to the pectoralis major tendons in an attempt to free arm motions. It worked remarkably well.

In December the otolaryngologist indicated that he believed M. should have tubes put in both ears since she had seven infections during the year. The ophthalmologist indicated that he did not think her vision would improve any more because of the damage to the eye. Without glasses the right eye had been 20/400 to 450. When started with glasses in March, the right eye was 20/250; in December it was 20/150. At the end of the month M. had another bladder infection.

After another bladder infection in January 1980 it became evident that M. needed nutritional evaluation. Her refined foods were limited; 15 to 20 oz of tap water were drunk daily. Vitamin C was supplemented and worked up over a period of weeks to 5000 mg of sodium ascorbate a day. Twenty-five milligrams three times a day of vitamin B complex were supplemented.

A nutritional work-up and professional analysis of her metabolic function was begun in March. Complete urinalysis, blood analysis, and hair analysis were done. She was taken off all supplements for a period of time before the tests were done.

The urinalysis showed bacterial deposits, indicating a tendency toward a septic kidney. There were deteriorated epithelial cells, indicating kidney degeneration. The presence of amorphous urate crystals indicated poor absorption of essential nutrients. Finally, there were white blood cells present, indicating a urinary system infection.

There were three significant blood test findings:

1. Elevated inorganic phosphorous, which indicated a tendency toward hypoparathyroidism or adrenal hormone deficiency or both
2. Elevated lactic dehydrogenase, which indicated either destruction of kidney, liver, heart, or skeletal muscle tissue or a problem in handling carbohydrates
3. Elevated serum glutamic oxaloacetic transaminase, which indicated either a breakdown of heart, liver, brain, kidney, pancreas, or skeletal muscle tissue or difficulty in handling amino acids

There were eight significant findings in the hair analysis:

1. Deficient potassium, which usually results from stress or refined carbohydrate consumption
2. Elevated zinc, which is associated with anemia and hormonal disorders
3. Deficient iron, which affects normal oxygen–carbon dioxide transportation plus decreases the production of hydrochloric acid by the stomach
4. Deficient chromium, which is associated with impaired growth, poor carbohydrate utilization, and inadequate lipid and protein metabolism
5. Deficient selenium needed to assist in all tissue healing
6. Elevated sodium-potassium ratio, which indicates inadequate transfer of nutrients into the cells
7. Elevated magnesium-postassium ratio, which indicates a tendency toward alkalinity and low levels of hydrochloric acid
8. Elevated zinc-copper ratio, which may be the best indicator of malabsorption

From the preceding findings major organs and tissues were rated as to function, with 1 being extremely deficient tissue function and 10 being superior function. The adrenals and kidneys were rated 2, the liver was rated 3, and the muscles and small intestine were rated 4.

The summary of the findings indicated kidney degeneration with systemic toxicity as evidenced by lowered resistence to infection and chronic fatigue. The secondary effect of poorly filtered blood was stress to the entire body but most drastically to the liver and adrenals. The adrenal irritation caused a tendency for allergic symptoms. The third major problem was poor general assimilation of important nutrients, which impaired virtually all body functions to some degree. There was evidence of some breakdown of muscle tissue, which had to be stopped immediately.

The recommendations included a low-stress diet, emphasizing fresh fruits, vegetables, and juices, with no refined carbohydrates, pork, processed meats, or soft drinks and with no more than three small servings of meat per week. M. was to drink a total of 34 oz a day of distilled water, 10 oz of which was to be lemon water (juice of one lemon in 1 qt of water).

The nutritional supplements included:

1. Vitamin ACP complex—one tablet three times a day
2. Cyrofood multiple vitamin and mineral—one tablet two times a day
3. Pantothenic acid to reduce allergic reactions—one tablet two times a day
4. Vitamin E complex—one tablet two times a day (includes selenium)
5. Potassium gluconate—one tablet a day (500 mg)
6. Renatropin to assist kidney function—one tablet two times a day
7. Manganese—5 mg. once a day
8. Pancreatic enzyme—one tablet at mealtime

The new diet and supplements were started on March 10, 1980. There was some difficulty in getting the 34 oz of water in each day. The first 10 days M. was very sluggish and grumpy and complained of headaches and stomach ache. She developed a cold.

The second through the fourth weeks were rather up and down. Some days she was very loose with minimal spasticity, others quite tight with increased spasticity. She continued to complain of headaches and had an upset stomach. She developed the 6-hour flu. Her joints exhibited considerable "popping" but were not painful. Toward the end of the fourth week the frequency of urination began to decrease.

The therapy had been reduced to a minimum during the time of dietary adjustment. Orthokinetic segments for the right forearm and both lower legs were made. She began riding her tricycle at school. She had become a qualified "motor mouth," talking, singing, or humming almost constantly. She had begun to do more activities on her own, such as balancing on her knees (5 seconds), coloring, and naming her pictures before drawing. She did not have a bladder infection from January to the end of May with only ½ teaspoon of sulfamethoxazole-trimethoprim (Septra) at bedtime. For the first time in her 5 years of life she was not seriously ill in the month of April. Her birthday party was a very successful social experience for everyone.

The follow-up nutritional report on May 12, 1980 indicated that:

1. M. had gained 5½ lb in 6 weeks.

2. Her coloring was much improved.

3. Her hypertonicity was much reduced.

Her pantothenic acid was reduced to one tablet a day, and her renatropin was discontinued.

M. had improved rather dramatically in 6 weeks. As her general health and nutrition continue to improve, her resistance to infections should increase. It is our conviction and hope that as the infections are controlled, our therapy can be much more effective. What improvement we accomplish from week to week can be built on instead of suffering repeated setbacks, which require weeks for regaining the previous level.

Index

Tables are indicated by t.